# Twentieth-Century American Poetry

# BLACKWELL GUIDES TO LITERATURE

*Series editor: Jonathan Wordsworth*

This new series offers the student thorough and lively introductions to literary periods, movements, and, in some instances, authors (Shakespeare) and genres (the novel), from Anglo-Saxon to the Postmodern. Each volume is written by a leading specialist to be invitingly accessible and informative. Chapters are devoted to the coverage of cultural context, the provision of brief but detailed biographical essays on the authors concerned, critical coverage of key works, and surveys of themes and topics, together with bibliographies of selected further reading. In the case of Shakespeare space otherwise afforded to authors will be devoted to documenting the theatre of the day. Students new to a period of study (for example, the English Renaissance, or the Romantic period) or to a period genre (the nineteenth-century novel, Victorian poetry) will discover all they need to know to orientate and ground themselves in their studies, in volumes that are as stimulating to read as they are convenient to use.

*Titles published to date include*

| | |
|---|---|
| The English Renaissance | *Andrew Hadfield* |
| Children's Literature | *Peter Hunt* |
| The Gothic | *David Punter and Glennis Byron* |
| Twentieth-Century American Poetry | *Christopher MacGowan* |

BLACKWELL GUIDES TO LITERATURE

# Twentieth-Century
# American Poetry

## CHRISTOPHER MACGOWAN

**Blackwell**
Publishing

BLACKWELL PUBLISHING
350 Main Street, Malden, MA 02148-5020, USA
108 Cowley Road, Oxford OX4 1JF, UK
550 Swanston Street, Carlton, Victoria 3053, Australia

First published 2004 by Blackwell Publishing Ltd
Reprinted 2004 (twice)

*Library of Congress Cataloging-in-Publication Data*

MacGowan, Christopher J. (Christopher John)
    Twentieth-century American poetry / Christopher MacGowan.
        p. cm. – (Blackwell guides to literature)
    Includes bibliographical references and index.
      ISBN 0-631-22025-9 (alk. paper) — ISBN 0-631-22026-7 (pbk. : alk. paper)
    1. American poetry — 20th century — History and criticism.  I. Title:
20th-century American poetry.  II. Title.  III. Series.

PS323.5.M25  2004
811'.509—dc21

                        2003012196

A catalogue record for this title is available from the British Library.

Set in 10½ / 13 pt Dante
by Graphicraft Typesetters Ltd, Hong Kong
Printed and bound in the United Kingdom
by MPG Books Ltd, Bodmin, Cornwall

For further information on
Blackwell Publishing, visit our website:
www.blackwellpublishing.com

# Contents

## Texts                                              167

# Acknowledgments

I would like to thank Andrew McNeillie for catching me at an MLA Convention book exhibit while I was hunting for a coffee stand and suggesting that I take on this project, and to Karen Wilson, Janet Moth, Emma Bennett, and the patient editorial and production staff at Blackwell for all their help. I have benefited greatly by suggestions from my colleagues at the College of William and Mary, Tom Heacox, Henry Hart, Hermine Pinson, and Nancy Schoenberger. Writers and teachers Sam Kashner and Lizbeth Keiley also provided helpful information. Christopher Bram, a William and Mary graduate who returned for a stint as Writer in Residence, generously reviewed and commented upon my proposed texts and writers. Burton Hatlen at the National Poetry Foundation kindly answered some questions. Glen MacLeod at the University of Connecticut solicited for me the helpful views of a number of contemporary poets, including Marilyn Nelson, Marilyn Hacker, and Margaret Gibson, and also shared his expertise on Wallace Stevens. Finally, I will always be grateful to the late Tony Tanner and to A. Walton Litz for being exemplary teachers, and for introducing me to the world of American literature and modern American poetry.

The author and publisher also wish to thank the following for permission to use copyright material. Excerpt from "Rock and Hawk," from *Selected Poetry of Robinson Jeffers* by Robinson Jeffers. Copyright © 1925, 1929 and renewed 1953, 1957 by Robinson Jeffers. Reprinted by permission of Random House, Inc.

Excerpt from "Since feeling is first," from *Complete Poems: 1904–1962* by E. E. Cummings, edited by George J. Firmage. Copyright © 1926, 1954, 1991 by the Trustees for the E. E. Cummings Trust. Copyright © 1985 by George James Firmage. Reprinted by permission of Liveright Publishing Corporation.

Excerpt from "Black Tambourine," from *Complete Poems of Hart Crane* by Hart Crane, edited by Marc Simon. Copyright © 1933, 1958, 1966 by Liveright

Publishing Corporation. Copyright © 1986 by Marc Simon. Reprinted by permission of Liveright Publishing Corporation.

"Thus Hides the Parts . . ." from *New Collected Poems* by George Oppen. Copyright © 2000 by Linda Oppen. Reprinted by permission of New Directions Publishing Corporation.

Excerpts from "Cuttings" and "Cuttings (later)," from *The Collected Poems of Theodore Roethke* by Theodore Roethke. Copyright © 1948 by Theodore Roethke. Reprinted by permission of Doubleday, a Division of Random House, Inc.

Excerpts from *The Dream Songs* #76, #145, #384 by John Berryman. Copyright © 1969 by John Berryman. Copyright renewed 1997 by Kate Donahue Berryman. Reprinted by permission of Farrar, Straus and Giroux, LLC.

Excerpt from "I know a Man" by Robert Creeley, from *Collected Poems of Robert Creeley, 1945–1975*. Copyright © 1983 The Regents of the University of California. Reprinted by permission.

Excerpt from "The Day Lady Died," from *Lunch Poems* by Frank O'Hara. Reprinted by permission of City Lights Books.

Excerpt from "For William Carlos Williams," from *What a Kingdom It Was* by Galway Kinnell. Copyright © 1960, renewed 1988 by Galway Kinnell. Reprinted by permission of Houghton Mifflin Company. All rights reserved.

Excerpt from "North American Time," copyright © 2002, 1986 by Adrienne Rich; excerpt from "Aunt Jennifer's Tigers," copyright © 2002, 1951 by Adrienne Rich; excerpt from Poem V of "Twenty-One Love Poems," copyright © 2002 by Adrienne Rich, copyright © 1978 W. W. Norton & Company, Inc.; excerpt from "Power," copyright © 2002 by Adrienne Rich, copyright © 1978 by W. W. Norton & Company, Inc., from *The Fact of a Doorframe: Selected Poems 1950–2001* by Adrienne Rich. Reprinted by permission of the author and W. W. Norton & Company, Inc.

Excerpt from "Riprap" by Gary Snyder. Reprinted by permission of the author.

Excerpt from "The Secret Garden" from *The Yellow House on the Corner* by Rita Dove. Carnegie-Mellon University Press, copyright © 1980 by Rita Dove. Reprinted by permission of the author.

Excerpt from "Thomas at the Wheel," and "Daystar," from *Thomas and Beulah* by Rita Dove. Carnegie-Mellon Press, copyright © 1986 by Rita Dove. Reprinted by permission of the author.

Every effort has been made to trace copyright holders and to obtain their permission for the use of copyright material. The author and publisher will gladly receive any information enabling them to rectify any error or omission in subsequent editions.

# How To Use This Book

This book is one of the series Blackwell Guides to Literature, and consistent with the design of that series is intended both as a guide to the independent reader who wishes for an introduction to the major writers, texts, and issues of twentieth-century American poetry, and also for graduate students and upper-level undergraduates taking courses that focus upon this subject area. The book should also be helpful to students studying twentieth-century American literature, as well as modern or contemporary poetry in English.

After reading this book the reader will be aware of the major figures in twentieth-century American poetry and some of its central texts – as well as some of the issues behind canon formation, the impact of modernism upon American poetry, and the split between the international modernism of a writer like H.D. and the aggressively nativist version of a writer such as William Carlos Williams. The reader will be acquainted with the influence of T. S. Eliot's poetry and criticism in the decades leading up to the middle of the century, of the various kinds of rebellion against its principles in the 1950s, of the formalist response in turn to that rebellion, and of the relatively recent prominence of feminist, multi-cultural, and Native American poetry.

As the reader will see from the contents page, the information within the book is organized in a number of ways. A chronology sets out the major social, political, and literary events of the century as they provide a broad context for the poetry. In the introduction I set out the thinking behind the choice of writers and texts for individual essays, and introduce the themes that are the subject of the longer essays in the subsequent section. Before the individual essays on writers and texts begin, a more focused history follows the introduction. This history treats the broad developments in the century's American poetry – from the dominance of New England and the east coast academies at the turn of the century, to the major strands and multiple voices of American poetry 100 years later. The reader who has little familiarity with the subject would do best starting with this general essay.

The individual essays on writers and texts can be read as two perspectives upon the same story. The reader may choose to switch between individual writers and texts, to juxtapose larger groupings based upon chronology or such categories as modernism, formalism, or other shared concerns, or to read each section as a separate narrative. Not all writers who are the subject of individual essays are represented by an essay in the section on texts. Further discussion of the relationship between the two sections can be found in the introduction.

The essays that follow the sections on writers and texts take up more specialized topics: the broad impact of the other arts on poetry, versions of the long poem, the complexities of nationality and continuity, poetry and war, and canon formation as it has been impacted by the century's anthologies. These essays are designed for a reader already familiar with the general subject of the volume, but may be read as individual, self-contained introductions to their topics.

Finally, the guide to further reading is designed to point the way to further discussion of a century of writing which this one volume cannot hope to fully represent, but about which – if this book has achieved one of its primary aims – the reader will wish to know more.

# Chronology: Significant Dates and Events, 1900–2000

1900   US population around 75 million; death of Stephen Crane (1871–1900)

1901   First transatlantic radio transmissions; President McKinley assassinated; Theodore Roosevelt at 42 becomes the youngest president in the nation's history

1902   William Carlos Williams meets Ezra Pound, a fellow student at the University of Pennsylvania; in 1905, Pound introduces Williams to H.D.

1903   Wright Brothers make the first successful airplane flight; Leo and Gertrude Stein settle in Paris and begin to collect modern art

1904   Pacific cable completed

1908   Ezra Pound arrives in London from Venice

1909   National Association for the Advancement of Colored People (NAACP) founded; Henry Ford begins production of Model "T" automobile

1911   H.D. leaves for Europe for what was intended as a short summer visit; only returns to the US twice in the next 45 years; in London renews her earlier friendship with Pound. Robert Frost sells his Derry, New Hampshire, farm, and moves with his family to England the following year

1912   *Poetry* magazine publishes its first issue, in Chicago

1913   The Armory Show exhibit of modern painting opens in New York; Robert Frost publishes his first book, *A Boy's Will*, in London, having failed to find an American publisher

1914    T. S. Eliot, studying at Oxford, decides to settle in England, meets
        Pound in London; Panama Canal opens

1915    Ezra Pound begins working on *The Cantos*; Marcel Duchamp among
        the European artists in New York because of the war in Europe

1917    US enters the First World War

1919    Alcock and Brown make the first non-stop flight in an aircraft across
        the Atlantic

1920    18th Amendment to the US Constitution prohibits the manufacture,
        sale, and transportation of alcoholic beverages ("Prohibition"); 19th
        Amendment grants the vote to women

1922    T. S. Eliot publishes *The Waste Land*; Claude McKay publishes *Harlem
        Shadows*; Allen Tate, Robert Penn Warren, and John Crowe Ransom
        begin publication of *The Fugitive* (1922–5); the first Pulitzer Prize for
        Poetry goes to Edwin Arlington Robinson for his *Collected Poems*

1923    William Carlos Williams publishes *Spring and All*; Wallace Stevens
        publishes *Harmonium*; Jean Toomer publishes *Cane*; Hart Crane
        begins work on *The Bridge* (published 1930)

1925    *Collected Poems of H.D.* published in New York

1926    Marianne Moore takes over as editor of *The Dial*, until it ceases
        publication in 1929; Langston Hughes publishes *The Weary Blues*

1927    Transatlantic telephone service begins; T. S. Eliot becomes a British
        citizen; Bliss Carman edits *The Oxford Book of American Verse*, includes
        one poem by Pound, but nothing by Eliot, H.D., Stevens, or Williams

1928    Edwin Arlington Robinson wins his third Pulitzer Prize for Poetry
        in seven years, for *Tristram*

1929    Stock market crash, beginning of the Great Depression; New York's
        Museum of Modern Art opens

1930    Novelist Sinclair Lewis becomes the first American to win the Nobel
        Prize for Literature; over 4 million unemployed

1931    Objectivist issue of *Poetry* edited by Louis Zukofsky

1933    "Prohibition" repealed; James Joyce's *Ulysses* allowed to be published
        in the US

1934    Academy of American Poets founded

1935    Robert Penn Warren and Cleanth Brooks found the *Southern Review*; in 1938 they publish their influential textbook *Understanding Poetry* (revised 1950)

1936    Spanish Civil War (1936–9) begins; James Laughlin founds New Directions and begins to publish Pound and Williams, who now have their first regular US publisher

1939    John Crowe Ransom founds *The Kenyon Review*, a major literary journal of the 1940s and 1950s; W. H. Auden arrives in the US, becomes a citizen in 1946; regular transatlantic air service begins

1941    US enters the Second World War following Japanese attack on Pearl Harbor

1943    Ezra Pound indicted for treason for his Italian radio broadcasts. He is arrested in May 1945, and begins writing *The Pisan Cantos* while imprisoned; Robert Frost wins his fourth Pulitzer Prize for Poetry, for *A Witness Tree*

1944    US Supreme Court rules that no citizen may be denied the vote on grounds of color

1948    T. S. Eliot awarded the Nobel Prize for Literature

1949    Ezra Pound, in St. Elizabeths Hospital, Washington, DC, after being judged criminally insane, is awarded the first Bollingen Prize for Poetry for *The Pisan Cantos*

1950    Gwendolyn Brooks becomes the first African American writer to win a Pulitzer Prize, for *Annie Allen*; US population 150 million; Korean War (1950–3) begins; F. O. Matthiessen re-edits *The Oxford Book of American Verse*: he includes Eliot, H.D., Stevens, and Williams, and expands the selection by Pound, but includes no black poets

1951    Charles Olson becomes Rector of Black Mountain College, Robert Creeley and Robert Duncan teach there (closes 1956)

1953    Lawrence Ferlinghetti and Peter Martin open City Lights bookstore in San Francisco

1954    US Supreme Court rules that racial segregation in schools is unconstitutional; the Poetry Center founded at San Francisco State University with an inaugural gift from W. H. Auden

1955    October 13, Allen Ginsberg gives first reading of "Howl," in San Francisco

1957    US Customs agents seize 520 copies of *Howl* on the grounds of obscenity; judge rules in favor of the book

1959    Robert Lowell publishes *Life Studies*

1960    Beginning of the Civil Rights movement with a sit-in at the Woolworth's lunch counter, Greensboro, North Carolina; H.D. becomes the first woman to receive the American Academy of Arts and Letters Medal; Donald Allen edits *The New American Poetry*

1963    Suicide of Sylvia Plath; Civil Rights March on Washington; assassination of President Kennedy; William Carlos Williams awarded his first and only Pulitzer Prize, posthumously

1964    Race riots in Harlem and Philadelphia; T. S. Eliot and Carl Sandburg awarded the Presidential Medal of Freedom, the nation's highest civilian award

1965    Vietnam War (1965–73); Malcolm X assassinated; Amiri Baraka moves to Harlem, founds the Black Arts Repertory Theater/School; Congress establishes the National Endowment for the Arts; in protest at the escalation of the Vietnam War, Robert Lowell publicly refuses an invitation from President Johnson to attend a White House Arts Festival; Sylvia Plath's *Ariel* published posthumously

1966    National Organization for Women founded

1967    Protest against Vietnam War grows; race riots in major cities continue

1968    Martin Luther King and Robert Kennedy assassinated

1969    Stonewall riots in New York City lead to beginning of Gay Liberation Movement; Apollo moon landing

1970    Native American Rights Fund established

1971    Adrienne Rich's essay "When We Dead Awaken: Writing as Re-Vision"; National Poetry Foundation founded, University Of Maine

1972    Suicide of John Berryman; Watergate break-in, President Nixon resigns in 1974; Ezra Pound dies in Venice

1974    Suicide of Anne Sexton; Amiri Baraka rejects Black Nationalism as racist

1976    US Bicentennial; John Ashbery's *Self-Portrait in a Convex Mirror* wins the Pulitzer Prize, the National Book Award, and the National Book Critics Circle Award

1978    Carolyn Forché working for Amnesty International in El Salvador, *The Country Between Us* published 1982

1980    Robert Penn Warren awarded the Presidential Medal of Freedom

1981    US begins military aid to El Salvador government

1982    Sylvia Plath's *Collected Poems* wins the Pulitzer Prize for Poetry 19 years after her death

1987    *Poetry* publishes its seventy-fifth anniversary issue

1988    Yusef Komunyakaa publishes *Dien Cai Dau*, having served in Vietnam from 1969 to 1970

1989    US invades Panama, first use of American military force since 1945 unrelated to the Cold War; fall of the Berlin Wall; collapse of the Soviet Union

1991    Rita Dove becomes the first African American Poet Laureate of the US; Iraq invades Kuwait, leading to Gulf War; World Wide Web introduced

1992    End of the Cold War (1945–92); US intervention in Somalia

1994    US intervention in Haiti

1996    Electronic Poetry Center goes online at State University of New York, Buffalo, <http://epc.buffalo.edu>

1997    Adrienne Rich awarded the Academy of American Poets $100,000 Tanning Prize, the largest annual literary prize in the US, but declines the National Medal for the Arts, writing "the very meaning of art, as I understand it, is incompatible with the cynical politics of this Administration"

1999    US part of Nato-backed military intervention in former Yugoslavia

2000    2000 census shows US population is 281 million: 69.1% white, 12.5% Hispanic, 12.1% black, 3.7% Asian and Pacific Islander, 0.7% American Indian; Hispanic population the fastest-growing group

# Introduction

The story of American poetry in the twentieth century begins with the dominance of one region and the legacy of one tradition – New England, and English Romantic verse. But by the end of the century one of the major characteristics of American poetry is its geographical diversity, while the range of its traditions reflects the diverse cultural origins of its writers, and their differing or complementary sense of heritage. Such a development makes far more complex at the start of the twenty-first century the once simpler issue of trying to define the particular characteristics of American poetry and its origins. While a single volume covering twentieth-century American poetry can tell and illustrate this story, it can hope to do no more than sketch something of the range. The scope and richness of twentieth-century American poetry rise beyond any selection of authors, texts, or thematic essays that try to encompass it, and my hope in this volume is to indicate enough of that scope and richness that the reader will want to explore further.

But it was not only by the end of the century that American poetry became international and that some of its writers eluded national categories. Claude McKay arrived in the United States in 1912 from Jamaica and became an important early figure in the Harlem Renaissance. The London avant-garde poetry scene just before the First World War was virtually taken over by Americans, with Ezra Pound, H.D., and T. S. Eliot actively involved in publishing and editorial work, work that stretched across the Atlantic to find an audience in the pages of the little magazines that sprang up in Chicago and New York. Eliot remained in London, for most of his career the dominant poet of his own and arguably the next generation, and wielding an important influence as editor at the publishing house of Faber & Faber.

In later generations, W. H. Auden, Denise Levertov, and Thom Gunn began their careers in England and took up residence in the United States.

The American Sylvia Plath wrote much of her best-known work in England, and the international scope of the academic world in recent decades has meant that poets can sometimes live and work on different continents, problematizing cultural, if not national, identity, all the more.

One earlier response to such blurring of borders was to see Anglo-American poetry as a single entity, and thus avoid the question of how to treat such figures as British citizen Eliot, and American citizens Auden and Levertov – and also making room for the impact of writers such as Yeats and D.H. Lawrence upon American poetry as well as English. Such a category would recognize the impact of Eliot's criticism via the New Critics on the poetry of both countries, and Auden's work would be a convenient continuation of the story. But while such a focus might hold together for the years of Frost and Robinson, both influenced by the English Georgian poets, and the international modernism of 1912–30, and even for the neo-Romantic Hart Crane, it starts to be particularly problematic in the 1950s. In that decade a more open form of poetry began to be asserted through the work of the Black Mountain College poets Charles Olson and Robert Creeley, and to a lesser extent through the meditative poetry of New York poets John Ashbery and Frank O'Hara, while Allen Ginsberg's long lines looked to the work of Walt Whitman for their foundation. All of these movements, reacting to various degrees against the New Critics and Anglo-American formalism, saw the major figures of twentieth-century American poetry in terms that suited their particular modes. Much of this view of history involved revising the story of modernism to bring to the fore poets seen as particularly emphasizing American themes, and forms that challenged the traditions of English verse.

The Anglo-American compromise becomes even more problematic when considering the impact of black poets on American poetry, a central issue of which is the history of slavery and racism in American culture. Even in the 1920s the question of which heritage – English or black – was an issue among the Harlem Renaissance poets. In the late 1950s an important figure in the Black Arts movement of the next decade, Amiri Baraka, was publishing his early poetry and formulating his own answer. In addition to the role of America's racial history, recent events, such as the influx of Asian immigrants into the United States following the Korean and Vietnam wars, the changes in the formerly Euro-centered immigration laws, and the growing influence of US neighbors Canada and Central and South America, have all left their mark. Such developments in American poetry, while international, are also directly related to the history and geographical position of the United States itself, and would be misrepresented by a predominantly Anglo-American focus.

Instead I have tried to take up the challenge posed by such issues to stay focused on American poetry, while also taking account of the increasingly international scope within which it has been written – and to draw attention to some of the issues and compromises involved in such a focus. One of the longer essays in this book, on nationality and continuity, introduces some of these issues. Meanwhile some practical, if arguably arbitrary, decisions needed to be made. I have treated Eliot as an American poet. I have not treated Auden as an American writer for the purposes of the author-centered essays, but his name and his work are very much a presence in the book. I have treated Levertov as an American poet because for the majority of her career she wrote and published in the United States. But her incorporation of European writers into her work in the later part of her career, along with her interest in religious poetry, point up again the arbitrariness of pinning a national category on some poets. Levertov herself, like McKay, was a very disaffected American citizen to some extent, but such disaffection is too in many ways a characteristic of American poets. The charge of treason leveled by the US government against Ezra Pound for his views and actions during the Second World War is perhaps only the most famous illustration.

The international context of American poetry in the twentieth century is shown nowhere more than in that poetry's relationship with the visual arts. A number of critics have pointed to the impact of the famous 1913 Armory Show, which opened in New York, on American poetry – a show that was the first major introduction of modernist painting to the United States. Meanwhile, in London Pound found affinities for a while with such vorticist painters as Wyndham Lewis, while in Paris Gertrude Stein's famous salon was the forerunner of the interest that 1920s writers – and not just expatriates – would have in the work of Picasso, Braque, Matisse, and others. In the 1930s and 1940s surrealism interested a number of American poets, while in the 1950s such writers as John Ashbery and Frank O'Hara were art critics as well as poets, although they were particularly associated with a home-grown avant-garde movement, abstract expressionism. Some later poets have been very concerned with the visual material that accompanies their poems, or the graphic design of a volume itself. Anthologists have recently grappled with the problem of how to represent this particular context, and some of the more ambitious have incorporated visual material into their selections. The role of other arts, including drama, the novel, and music, as well as the visual arts, is taken up in the extended essay on "Twentieth-Century American Poetry and the Other Arts," while the essay on anthologies includes a discussion of some of these attempts to incorporate visual material (along with a more historical summary of the role and impact of anthologies on the developing canon of modern American poetry).

The relationship of American poetry to other traditions and cultures, and the increasingly global reach of the United States economically and politically, are also issues that are part of two other extended essays, those on the long poem and on war poetry. American poets have been among the great innovators of the long poem in the century, such innovation often being foregrounded as a theme in the work. One only has to consider the long poems of, for example, Williams, Pound, H.D., Crane, Hughes, Olson, Ginsberg, Lowell, Merrill, and Rich to discover a remarkable range of inventiveness. With such experiment, challenges are raised about whatever principles might be holding such a poem together, and whether their role is to suggest an underlying unity that the more dispersive poem is acting to undermine, or a unity to which the poet and poem seek some kind of return – perhaps a cultural or historical loss, or one associated more specifically with identity. Other long poems, however, might stress the arbitrariness of any such unifying principles, fragmented or not. Such tensions are acted out in various ways in various texts, the net result by the end of the century being a challenge to the assumed characteristics of the whole genre itself. And this is not to forget the remarkable achievement, by such writers as Frost, Robinson, Stevens, and the later Eliot, of long poems that by comparison are closer to an earlier tradition.

The global reach of United States' foreign policy, and the global presence of its military, was a given by the end of the century, but earlier in the century the country went through the periods of isolationism that produced an initial reluctance to get involved in either of the century's two world wars. In addition, there has always been – inevitably, given its history as a one-time colony – an anti-imperialist streak in American thinking. But this characteristic clashes with another dominant strain, often evoked by the country's political leaders, that the American way is the best way, whether that way is defined in secular terms such as "democracy," or a more vaguely spiritual way that invokes "good" and "evil." Such varied characteristics surface in the war poetry of the century written by Americans: the doggedness of the poets of the two world wars fulfilling a distasteful but necessary duty (little of the shock and despair of Wilfred Owen or Siegfried Sassoon), the broader cultural criticism of Pound and Eliot, and the protests of the poets of the Vietnam and later eras. The role of the media, and of the politicians and corporations who control it, is a particular issue in some of the later poetry, because of the international dominance of the American communications networks and their attempts, sometimes, to represent only a majority view – a danger of democracy particularly noted by de Tocqueville at the beginning of the nineteenth century.

The opening essay in this volume summarizes some of the major developments in twentieth-century American poetry and puts them into the broad contexts of artistic, social, and political history. The writers who are the subjects of the individual essays that follow have been selected on the grounds of their importance to the history of twentieth-century American poetry, and their influence upon their contemporaries or upon future poets. These two criteria do not always go together. An account of the poetry of Frost, for example, is essential to a history of American poetry in the twentieth century, but Frost has had relatively little influence upon subsequent American writers. The work of the much lesser known George Oppen and Louis Zukofsky, on the other hand, is considered essential by a number of prominent contemporary poets. Critics and poets do not all agree on what the major currents of such a history are. Different anthologies that pick up the history of American poetry since the middle of the century, for example, might start with Robert Lowell and Elizabeth Bishop, or they might start with Charles Olson – the figures who lead off the selection probably signal a good deal about the names in the subsequent pages.

The same criteria that governed the selection of writers for individual essays has governed my selection of texts for individual notice – texts that have had prominence and influence, whether at a particular moment in time, with later recognition, or consistently since publication. I have imposed upon myself the arbitrary limitation of letting a particular poet only be represented by one text, although clearly a case could be made for two or more texts by a number of the poets: *The Waste Land* and *Four Quartets*, for Eliot, *Hugh Selwyn Mauberley* and the *Pisan Cantos*, for Pound (or for that matter all of the *Cantos*), *Spring and All* and *Paterson*, for Williams, and *The Dream of a Common Language* and *An Atlas of the Difficult World*, for Rich. Such a list could go on. On the other hand, some poets produced only one obviously central text, for example, Claude McKay's *Harlem Shadows*. And some important poets have gained their importance more through the accumulated body of their work than a particular text, as in the cases, for example, of H.D. and of Langston Hughes. These latter poets are treated in individual author essays and inevitably feature in the essays treating broader topics. The one exception that I have permitted myself to the rule of one is to allow Ezra Pound another entry, as an editor, for his role in the publication of *Des Imagistes*, a text that had an important impact upon a number of significant poets. In addition, to limit the concept of an influential volume to works by an individual figure seemed to me to be too restrictive if it disallowed this volume, or the landmark volume edited by Donald Allen in 1960, *The New American Poetry*. Otherwise, collections – their purposes and polemics, and their impact – are discussed in the essay on anthologies in the final section of this book.

# Some Historical and Cultural Contexts of Twentieth-Century American Poetry

# The Romantic Legacy and the Genteel Tradition

At the beginning of the century the American poetry that found most favor in general circulation magazines, and in magazines devoted entirely to poetry, largely conformed to the expectations firmly established in the nineteenth century as to what a poem should be about, and how it should express itself. Rhymed lyric poetry was to the fore, and such poetry was directly addressed to the reader, usually expressed the feelings of the poet – feelings that were heightened in some way – and, even if the emotions conveyed were not entirely those of pleasure, the lyric quality of the poem, its rhyme, and its summary conclusion, were intended to make reading it a pleasurable, uplifting experience. Arthur Davison Ficke, in a poem titled "Poetry," and as late as 1912, demonstrated many of the qualities that had been to the fore in the American poetry of the previous two decades, and against which by 1913 many of the modernist poets would rebel. The modernist poets were helped a great deal in this rebellion by the very journal, *Poetry*, published in Chicago, that carried this poem as the first poem of its first issue:

> It is a little isle amid bleak seas –
> An isolate realm of garden, circled round
> By importunity of stress and sound,
> Devoid of empery to master these.
> At most, the memory of its streams and bees,
> Borne to the toiling mariner outward-bound,
> Recalls his soul to that delightful ground;
> But serves no beacon toward his destinies.
>
> It is a refuge from the stormy days,
> Breathing the peace of a remoter world
> Where beauty, like the musking dusk of even,
> Enfolds the spirit in its silver haze;

> While far away, with glittering banners furled,
> The west lights fade, and stars come out in heaven.[1]

In this definition of poetry, expressed in the traditional form of the sonnet, poetry has no power to direct or comment influentially upon the "stress and sound" of the modern industrial world. Poetry offers instead an escape from that world, via a series of sentimental and conventional abstractions, to a now diminished but nevertheless unsullied island of culture where the pleasures of poetry are appreciated. Some of the same late Romantic imagery had appeared in Yeats's much more distinguished "The Lake Isle of Innisfree" (1890), where, homesick on a busy London street, the poet longs for an island with "a hive for the honey-bee" where he can "live alone in the bee-loud glade."

As James Breslin has pointed out, Ficke's sonnet was the kind of poetry that William Carlos Williams was reading in the first years of the century as he prepared to write his first self-financed book of poems, locally published in Rutherford, New Jersey, in 1909. Williams's "On a Proposed Trip South," which, like his other 1909 poems, he never collected and in fact preferred to forget, reproduces the same landscape. The poet will shortly be leaving the cold north for "a southern flight" – and "shall shortly view / The lush high grasses, shortly see in air / Gay birds and hear the bees make heavy droon."

Williams sent this volume of poems with pride to his friend Ezra Pound, by then in London and moving into the center of the London avant-garde. Pound replied unsparingly that the poems were decades out of date and that Williams needed to modernize himself, and Pound included a list of writers for his friend to read, none of whom was American. There was nothing for a modernist writer to learn, for Pound, from the American poets of the previous generation. In his poem "The Return" (1912), Pound writes of the "pallid" classical gods returning from decades of neglect, to bring poetry back into the present rather than retreating from it. His near-contemporary poem "Surgit Fama" offers a similar prophecy. Wallace Stevens, in his "Sunday Morning," of 1915, pointed out that all such islands of retreat, including for Stevens in this poem the Palestine of Christianity, are cultural constructions that become eventually merely rhetorical souvenirs. For Stevens, there is no

> isle
> Melodious, where spirits gat them home,
> Nor visionary south, nor cloudy palm

---

[1] Quoted in James Breslin, *William Carlos Williams: An American Artist* (New York, 1970), 29, and Robert Buttel, *Wallace Stevens: The Making of Harmonium* (Princeton, 1967), 47.

> Remote on heaven's hill, that has endured
> As April's green endures; or will endure

Again the present world returns to poetry. One way this happens is the American poets' embrace of the concrete pictorialism of imagist poetry, by Williams as much as anybody, as a way to dispel the "haze" of a vision such as Ficke's.

The situation at the turn of the century in American poetry did not give any hint of the extraordinary achievement of American poets that was to come in the 1920s. Nationally, the newspapers and magazines with the highest status and circulation generally treated poetry as a filler item for the corner of columns, and preferred to print formal, uplifting, uncontroversial verse. For reasons connected with the historical development of the continent, the main base of the literary establishment in 1900 was the northeastern seaboard. The main publishers were in Boston and New York, and the oldest universities (any rivals in the South still recovering from the devastation of the Civil War) were also in that region. The universities, writers, and publishers generally looked to England for the standards they wanted to be seen as upholding with equal rigor, and were viewed by writers in much of the rest of the country as in effect a powerful, if provincial, extension of the London scene. A group of poets associated with Harvard, George Santayana, William Vaughn Moody, Trumbull Stickney, and George Cabot Lodge, exemplified the most refined versions of the genteel style. Written in traditional forms, their verse was inspirational, earnest, and carefully crafted, vaguely spiritual, and usually confined to abstractions. Moody is usually considered the most ambitious of the group, although uneven in his execution, while Santayana (in old age many years later the subject of a well-known poem by Wallace Stevens) the most intellectually rigorous. A blander version of this group existed in New York, with E. C. Stedman its leading figure.

The reactions against the genteel style were usually light-hearted, humorous poems by writers who were largely entertainers and newspaper poets. These poems would make fun of the formality and Anglophile values of the genteel style by being in rollicking ballad or regional conversational style, expressly about "American" characters and pursuits – such as farming, fishing, hunting, or baseball. Humor and sentiment ruled the day in these poems, and their most famous exponent, James Whitcomb Riley (1849–1916) was the best selling poet of his day. The African American poet Paul Dunbar (1872–1906) had more serious ambitions, but the racial climate of the time was such that serious verse from a black writer was not particularly welcome, and his audience demanded "plantation" lyrics from him which painted a sentimental, nostalgic, and largely fictitious account of life for black slaves in the pre-Civil War South or later. Dunbar's reputation has risen since the 1960s with the rediscovery of his many lyric poems outside of the "plantation" vein. But it would take the Harlem Renaissance and Langston Hughes in the 1920s to present American black speech stripped of the dialect stereotypes expected of Dunbar. Other poetic forms that found some favor around the turn of the century were the social protest poems of Edwin Markham, and the "vagabond-style" Romantic wanderer verse of such poets as Bliss Carman and Richard Hovey.

A factor that handicapped the development of American poetry was the vast distances between poets who showed some talent and may have thrived in a center which allowed writers to communicate with one another. London was such a center in England, but the United States saw no movement at the end of the century to resemble the 1890s poets in London who rebelled against the Victorian moralities and the late nineteenth-century version of Romanticism. Outside of the Harvard and New York centers, American poets worked alone, educating themselves on anthologies of English poetry, and finding most publishing outlets wanting verse that conformed to the established conventions expected by their readers. Frustration with the cultural climate of the United States had already by the turn of the century contributed to the exodus to Europe of the painters Whistler and Mary Cassatt, and the writers Henry James and Gertrude Stein – as it would a few years later to the exodus of Pound, H.D., and T. S. Eliot, and in the 1920s to a generation of expatriates, including Ernest Hemingway and F. Scott Fitzgerald.

But there were other developments in nineteenth-century American poetry which produced poets whose work would be recognized in the coming century as major. Although Walt Whitman had published the first edition of *Leaves of Grass* in 1855 and had died in 1892, his achievement was still questioned into the 1940s in some academic circles. As an undergraduate at Columbia University, Allen Ginsberg had found hostility to Whitman's work among the English faculty. Nevertheless, for more radical poets of the 1910s Whitman's work offered a possible direction for American poetry: it sanctioned both free verse and a frankness about physical matters that was alien to the genteel tradition. Even Pound accepted, in his poem "A Pact," that he had "one sap and one root" with Whitman. Another poet whose work became important in the new century was Emily Dickinson, whose poetry began to be published in 1890. Her wit, verbal inventiveness, and ambiguity were a sharp contrast to the hopeful, formal pieties of mainstream verse, while her sophistication was quite different from the academic formality of the Harvard poets. The poetry of Stephen Crane also prefigured some aspects of the modernist style to come. Although best known for his prose writing, the two volumes of poetry that he published around the turn of the century ridiculed conventional religious piety, condemned the material values of the age, and used a direct, prosaic form of address borrowed from his fiction writing and from journalism.

Two other poets who borrowed techniques from prose writing, and whose work would produce major contributions to American poetry in the first two decades of the new century, were Edwin Arlington Robinson and Robert Frost. Both used narrative in their tales of individual characters, community, and hardship, and both initially had trouble finding publishers and an audience. Both developed their styles largely by reading English poets, and separate from urban centers – Robinson in Maine, and Frost in New Hampshire. Robinson finally found success when he moved to New York, and Frost when he moved to England and found a publisher in London willing to print his work. Both writers worked within the subject matter of Romantic poetry – human potential, the relationship of man to nature, man's place in the universe, and the relations between men and women. But theirs is poetry which, like the poetry of Hardy in England, questions the assumptions of Romanticism. In the case of Robinson's work, ideals and hope function as fantasies to allow his characters to escape for a time the realities of their defeated lives. For Robinson much remained unknown about the spiritual condition of mankind, an uncertainty that his poetry dramatized the difficulties of facing.

Frost, in a quieter but more varied way, wrote poetry about the limitations imposed upon the human desire for limitless possibility – limitations imposed by a nature probably indifferent to human wishes, and by the physical and intellectual limits of the human condition, limitations all the more quietly tragic when set against the boundless reach of human imagination. Such poetry set Frost and Robinson against the poetry of genteel spiritual comfort. Once the poetry of Frost and Robinson found an audience in the early decades of the century, they, more than the modernist poets who soon followed, were awarded the literary prizes and embraced by the wider poetry-reading public. The formal qualities of their poetry still appeared, for some readers, to suggest the possibilities of an order, even if it were only Frost's "momentary stay against confusion." But this "stay" became a more contingent order in a poet like Wallace Stevens, whose order was self-consciously a necessary fiction, and even more problematic in poets such as Pound, H.D., and T. S. Eliot, where such possibilities seemed to be located in the past, if at all, and certainly not an immediate past for which a reader might feel the indulgence of a sentimental nostalgia.

# Transatlantic Connections

Pound, writing from England, had urged Williams to acquaint himself with the London writers in order to modernize himself. The letter, and the reading list that accompanied Pound's advice, were part of his tireless attempts to bring news of the London avant-garde to his home country, which he saw as hopelessly provincial. But in the years leading up to the outbreak of war in Europe in 1914, in the war years themselves, and in the decade that followed, the United States increasingly became more integrated politically, economically, and artistically into world, and particularly European, concerns. In addition, the growing wealth of the United States helped to produce more publishing outlets for poetry, a greater readership for the volumes produced, a growing university system, an economic environment of opportunity for foreign writers and artists to visit or settle, and the economic means for more and more American writers and artists to travel and live abroad.

The isolation of American poets also began to be mitigated by movements in various urban centers that challenged – or ignored – the New England and New York establishment. These centers fostered cheaply produced or subsidized "little magazines" that published modern writing, and, through an act as simple as sending in a subscription, a writer could read the work and – as was often the case – travel to the city to join the group.

The two most important centers to emerge were in Chicago and a revitalized New York, although there were important movements in New Orleans, San Francisco, and Philadelphia too. In Chicago Carl Sandburg applied what he learned from Whitman to celebrate the commercial activities and ruthlessness at the heart of the city's wealth, bringing a prosaic directness and concreteness into modern poetry. When a writer such as Sherwood Anderson looked for an alternative to the business world of Ohio he looked to Chicago, and, adding to what was quickly becoming a recognizable regional literature, published a volume of somewhat forgettable

Whitmanesque lyrics, although a few years later he became much better known for his prose volume *Winesburg, Ohio*. Out of the Chicago avant-garde emerged two important "little magazines," non-commercial, low-paying, limited circulation, and committed to printing modern writing. *Poetry*, the first of these, was started by Harriet Monroe, whose own poetry was not particularly modern. But she published the work not only of the Chicago poets, but of Williams, Wallace Stevens, Marianne Moore, and other east coast writers too, and, with Ezra Pound sending in manuscripts from London, she also published Pound, H.D., Yeats, and early poems by T. S. Eliot. *Poetry* appeared regularly every month – and still does; the poets were actually paid for their contributions thanks to a group of wealthy sponsors gathered through Monroe's social contacts. The magazine also offered a series of prizes annually. *Poetry* retained for a few years a certain stuffiness that finally alienated Pound, and that led Williams to complain that if Monroe continued to print the first letter of each of his lines in upper case against his will he would send in no more poems; but its existence was central in putting poets in touch with one another and in bringing American poetry on to the international scene.

The other magazine to come out of the Chicago Renaissance was a more intermittent, ragged, and radical affair, *The Little Review*, published by Margaret Anderson and Jane Heap. With such journals as *Poetry* and *The Little Review*, Monroe and Anderson redefined the role of the salon hostess that had been satirized in Pound's poem "Portrait d'une Femme" and took it into the twentieth century. *The Little Review* took more chances than *Poetry*, and Pound eventually shifted his support and contacts to Anderson's journal. Along with publishing the Chicago writers and modernist poets, Anderson published the early chapters of James Joyce's *Ulysses* as they became ready for print, and thus ran into legal troubles for publishing what the authorities deemed obscene. For one issue subscribers received a magazine consisting almost entirely of blank pages, with a complaint by Anderson that submissions were inadequate for the kind of radical work that she wanted to publish. Like *The Egoist* in London, which at different times boasted H.D. and T. S. Eliot as associate editors, *The Little Review* had a parallel agenda of promoting greater political and moral freedoms for women (denied the vote until 1920 in the US). *The Little Review* followed its editors to New York, and subsequently to Paris, its location almost a barometer of where avant-garde activity was most centered. And its final issue in 1929 also mirrored the end, with the Wall Street crash, of the financial well-being that had allowed such journals to survive.

A thriving avant-garde movement began towards the end of the century's first decade in New York City, one important focus of which were the painters and photographers centered around the work of Alfred Stieglitz. Stieglitz's 291 Gallery brought the work of the Paris impressionists and cubists to New York, and encouraged such American first-generation modernist painters as John Marin, Marsden Hartley, Charles Demuth, and Georgia O'Keefe. Writers mixed with visual artists at 291, and also in the salons of wealthy patrons such as Walter Arensberg and Mabel Dodge. Many American modernist poets looked to the radical activity of the painters, sculptors, and photographers for direction rather than to the previous generation of poets. A high-profile culmination of this activity was the 1913 Armory Show, which gathered together in New York the paintings of such artists as Gauguin, Matisse, Cézanne, and Duchamp. So much did this exhibition become in retrospect a foundation event in American modernism that William Carlos Williams convinced himself in a number of interviews years later that he had attended, although his wife was sure that he was recalling a later exhibition.

With the outbreak of war in Europe in 1914, a number of European painters retreated to New York, supported by such patrons as Arensberg. Thus New York itself became a center for international avant-garde activities. Two of the most important artists to turn up in New York were Marcel Duchamp and Francis Picabia. Duchamp's "ready-mades," such as his snow shovel and his urinal "sculptures," challenged the authority of viewer-imposed conventions upon the artist's activities, insisting that the qualities of what could be called "art" rested solely on the authority of the artist. Such prefabricated objects also challenged other Romantic assumptions about the relationship of the artist to his or her material, particularly the Romantic foregrounding of originality and emotional expression. Arensberg purchased from Duchamp a photographic reproduction of his painting *Nude Descending a Staircase*. The original had been a sensation of the Armory Show. Duchamp painted over the photograph, had it framed, and it took its place in Arensberg's collection. In addition to the general ethos of creative rebellion produced by such gestures, Duchamp's "ready-mades" – and Picabia's machine-like drawings – promised an industrial-based art particularly suited to the artists of what had become the world's foremost industrial economy. Such icono-clastic gestures signaled the irrelevance of the prestigious European heritage of past achievements, and emphasized instead the primacy of subject matter not connected to historic themes, places, or narratives.

Imagism, developed initially in the pages of *Poetry* and *The Egoist*, and demonstrated in the poetry of Pound and H.D. among others, had a similar appeal to a number of American poets. Its emphasis upon non-traditional rhythms, the primacy of the moment, free verse, and economy of expression also made the legacy of English verse largely irrelevant. The manifestos of imagism invoked modern painting as a parallel. Here was a sanction for

American poetry to take its own direction, and imagism had much more of an impact upon subsequent American poetry than upon verse in England.

The various art exhibitions that accompanied New York's emergence as an avant-garde center produced their own short-lived little magazines, and there was often room for poetry. One of the most important literary magazines in these years was *Others*, which originated out of the activities of an artists' colony in Grantwood, New Jersey, just across the Hudson from Manhattan, and which was at one point financed by Arensberg. Behind the magazine were such figures as painter and photographer Man Ray, and poets William Carlos Williams and Alfred Kreymborg. The tireless Pound sent over a sheaf of imagist poems for the journal to publish. *Others* set itself up as an alternative and complement to Chicago's *Poetry*. It carried more belligerent manifestos than its Chicago rival, appeared more erratically, and was much less well funded. In its pages appeared early work by Williams, Wallace Stevens, and Marianne Moore.

The end of the war in 1918 left western Europe in a financial quagmire, but the United States at the beginning of an economic boom. The artists and writers who had taken shelter from the war in New York returned to Paris, and they were followed by a new generation of American writers, artists, editors, and hangers-on, who flocked to Paris, where the dollar's buying power against the devalued franc allowed a lifestyle that bought leisure to write, and allowed journals to publish cheaply – with time left to play in a country where moral rectitude had not led to Prohibition as it had in the United States. Journals such as *Broom* and the *transatlantic review* offered opportunities for modernist poets, and Americans Robert McAlmon and William Bird set up publishing houses in France that offered small print runs and quality printing for writers whose work could not find a commercial press. Meanwhile the London poetry scene lost some of its most promising poets in the war, and D. H. Lawrence began travels that took him anywhere but England, looking in his poetry to Whitman as a guide to what poetry could be. Pound moved to Paris, and later to Italy, declaring England to be in the last stages of a fading and corrupt empire.

But the centers of activity for American poetry split rather than shifted. Chicago, where Edgar Lee Masters and Carl Sandburg appeared to be repeating themselves, became less important, but in New York an alternative to the international modernism of the prose and poetry writers in Paris asserted itself. Critics such as Van Wyck Brooks and Paul Rosenfeld argued, much as Emerson had done in the previous century, for America to find its own writers and themes. A vibrant economy, an increased interest in new kinds of arts, and progress in promoting racial equality were behind the explosion of talent in the Harlem Renaissance, with such figures as Claude

McKay, Countee Cullen, and Langston Hughes leading the way. *Others* folded, but Williams began a new magazine titled *Contact* which emphasized, as its title suggests, the need to stay connected to America and American things; but his co-editor McAlmon joined the exodus to Paris. However, a well-financed takeover turned a moribund journal titled *The Dial* into an important New York outlet for modernist work – although the journal was international in its scope. A $2,000 annual prize indicated the resources of the magazine. The first award went to Sherwood Anderson. The second went to T. S. Eliot, whose *The Waste Land* had its first US publication in *The Dial*. Eliot had remained in London, and his influence on poetry and criticism on both sides of the Atlantic went on to become immense.

With the success of *The Waste Land*, and with much modern American prose and poetry being written or published in Europe, the provincial isolation of the American poet was over, something even the nativist apologists in New York conceded in their subject matter and styles. Despite the movement in New York, international modernism became the predominant style of modern American writing, the allusions and models coming from the European and Eastern traditions rather than from the legacy of American writing, with the exception of the increasing recognition of the achievement of Whitman. Eliot's style had been developed largely from his reading of nineteenth-century French poetry. Back in New Jersey, Williams ruefully imagined in a prose essay introducing his *Kora in Hell: Improvisations* (1920) an international congress of poets where translations of French medieval poetry would be offered as representative American verse. This period – in which Continental Europe seemed an extension of the American literary scene, publication outlets abounded, and little magazines could be started in Europe for relatively few dollars – came to an end with the Wall Street crash of 1929. By the end of the decade *The Dial*, *Broom*, *the transatlantic review*, and the presses of McAlmon and Bird had all folded.

# Tradition and the Rise of the Universities

The economic troubles of the 1930s gave birth to a number of politically radical magazines whose pages were open to poetry, but which preferred poetry in line with their own political views. "Relevance" became an issue for some editors and critics, and high modernism was viewed with suspicion by some for what were regarded as its insular concerns with questions of form, and its elitist sense of audience. Of prominent poets, Robert Frost and Wallace Stevens particularly encountered criticism for writing poetry cut off from current events, although from the perspective of more than 50 years later critics can link their work convincingly to cultural and political events of the decade. When it didn't refer to a political position, "relevance" often meant writing about a recognizable contemporary world outside of the poem, as well as writing in a more inviting – usually traditional – way.

Two ways in which poetry returned to more traditional concerns that had been marginalized by modernism but that were not necessarily rooted in the contemporary world, and even marked a retreat from it, were in a revival of the poetry of meditation, and an associated claim for the moral duties of poets and poetry. Following *The Waste Land*, T. S. Eliot's poetry moved, with *Ash-Wednesday* and later *Four Quartets*, towards a more meditative vein, and following Eliot's conversion to the Anglican Church in 1927 his poetry became more explicitly concerned with linking moral and spiritual issues, and finding redemption through intellectual, spiritual, and physical discipline. Eliot's London journal *The Criterion* had an important influence on US as well as British poetry, and his editorial position at publishers Faber & Faber also governed which US poets received that important international distribution. Faber & Faber published the verse of Marianne Moore, for example, the volume carrying an introduction by Eliot.

The second contrast to high modernist concerns also owed a great deal in one of its aspects to the work of Eliot. The 1930s saw the rise of a group of poets centered in the South, including Allen Tate, John Crowe Ransom, and Robert Penn Warren, who argued for a return to the virtues of a more rural way of life, and a poetry that in its content and craft reflected that order and its disciplined moral focus. The claims for rural virtues were in part a response to the perceived failure of cities, industry, and the complex economic developments that had produced the Depression. These poets were professional educators, associated with English departments, and their views – shaped by Eliot and the work of English critics I. A. Richards, F. R. Leavis, and William Empson, and later articulated by American Cleanth Brooks along with Warren – became the foundation of the New Criticism that had important influence in English departments well into the second half of the decade. The association of these figures with the academies led to their being on important prize-awarding committees and thus to their being able to confer further prestige on the poetry endorsed by New Criticism – such as the early poems of Robert Lowell.

The more radical modernist writers still kept on writing, although publishing opportunities were fewer and their work often appeared in limited editions. Frost, Stevens, Langston Hughes, and Moore had commercial publishers; H.D.'s work was privately printed, but Pound and Williams had to wait until the end of the 1930s for James Laughlin to found New Directions before they found a regular US publisher. At the beginning of the decade objectivism reformulated some of the principles of imagism, and the movement found a publishing outlet when George Oppen started the Objectivist Press. The movement advocated precision and a careful attention to the function of language that produced a line of American poetry, including the work of Louis Zukofsky, Oppen, Charles Reznikoff, and Charles Olson, whose achievement is still debated by some literary critics.

Poetry in England in the 1930s became even more politically charged because of events on the Continent. For W. H. Auden, the foremost English poet of the 1930s, the political litmus test finally became too confining. Auden came to the United States at the end of the decade, and became an American citizen in 1946. His poetry remained formal and moral in character, and his US residence arguably did not change his work in significant ways, but he became an ever-present voice on the New York literary scene through his reviews and introductions as well as his verse, and in the 1950s introduced a whole new generation of American poets, including John Ashbery and Adrienne Rich, to the public through his association with the annual volumes of the Yale Younger Poets series. Auden's was only one example of the continuing internationalism of American poetry.

New Criticism itself, for all its local agrarian and racial issues connected to the southern United States, was an international movement. T. S. Eliot took up British citizenship, and in a later generation English poets Thom Gunn and Denise Levertov came to the United States, while American Sylvia Plath lived and wrote in England. Such cases raise complex issues of literary nationality. These issues would be further complicated by the rise of multi-cultural voices in the US as a result of post-war waves of immigration in the last decades of the century, and by the parallel rise of the poetry of ethnicity.

The political disruption in Europe in the 1930s brought European artists to New York for much the same reasons as in 1914, although it was a measure of the international scope of American culture in the 25 years up to 1939 that these visitors had less of a visible impact than the earlier wave. Most prominent of the artistic refugees on the east coast were the surrealists (many prominent French and German film directors went to Hollywood, with mixed fortunes). The surrealist emphasis upon the vocabulary of the subconscious and the unmediated expression of the subconscious in artistic expression received a welcome among avant-garde journals, and appeared to give a renewed boost to the modernist claims that the conventions of form – now dominant again with the rise of New Criticism – were an anachronism. But its foremost legacy was its contribution to abstract expressionism, the first international art movement with American origins, and a movement which itself had an influence upon some important poets in the 1950s. A case can also be made that surrealism contributed to the climate that produced the Confessional poets of the 1950s, and it was certainly an influence upon the Deep Image poets of the 1960s, represented by the work of James Wright and Galway Kinnell. As for the Second World War itself, although it produced no poetry to equal the impact of Norman Mailer's *The Naked and the Dead*, or James Jones's *From Here to Eternity*, in contrast to the First World War many current and future American poets served in the armed forces and the war figured in some of their verse, or had an impact upon their attitude towards later armed conflict, particularly the Vietnam War.

# Rebellion in the Fifties and Sixties: The Two Anthologies

The formal, crafted style endorsed by the New Criticism continued to shape the poetry of some important poets into the 1950s, including Allen Tate, Richard Wilbur, Howard Nemerov, and Melvin Tolson. The early poetry of John Berryman, Adrienne Rich, and Robert Lowell was also in this style, but they, along with a number of other poets, began to regard it as too constricting and artificial and their later work moved in different directions.

The divisions emerging in American poetry in the 1950s were captured by the appearance towards the end of the decade by two anthologies of current poetry that each offered quite a different emphasis: Donald Hall, Robert Pack, and Louis Simpson's *New Poets of England and America* (1957) and Donald Allen's *The New American Poetry* (1960). The multiple directions that American poetry took in the 1950s, and the rising student marketplace, made the kind of sorting process offered by an anthology attractive, although each of these volumes had its particular perspective to defend, and simplifications of similarities and differences were inevitable.

The Hall, Simpson, and Pack anthology carried a short introduction by Robert Frost, who had never forsaken the formal qualities of verse. Frost was a household name in the 1950s, and more popular than ever with the general poetry-reading public. The anthology included the work of English and American poets, because, in terms of the style that the anthology represented, the poetry of the two countries was similar. These poets had abandoned the extreme fragmentation and discontinuity of the modernist style, but had retained an emphasis upon economy, wit, impersonality, and craft. English poetry had arrived at a similar point in its reaction against a new Romantic revival (a revival represented, for example, in the poetry of Dylan Thomas). Poets receiving their first anthology appearance in the volume included Robert Bly, John Hollander, Donald Justice, Reed Whittemore, and Adrienne Rich. Also included were James Merrill and Robert Lowell.

The poets in the Allen anthology, by contrast, had returned to many of the high modernist qualities rejected by the writers in the 1957 collection. The 1950s saw a new interest by some contemporary poets in the work of Williams, Stevens, Pound, and H.D., who were looked to as providing possible alternative models to the qualities of formalist verse, including a more spontaneous speaking voice that in a general way could be traced back to Whitman. This speaking voice was not, as New Criticism insisted, a persona invented by the poet, but was understood to be the poet speaking directly. Such a style, along with an emphasis upon process rather than craft, and an occasional return to myth and archetype, seemed to such contemporary poets more American, more democratic, more contemporary, and less academic.

Allen's anthology divided its new American poets into five categories, and although the division was inevitably reductive and somewhat arbitrary, it provided a useful map of one set of contemporary trends in American poetry and proved very influential in later criticism and histories. In addition, it gave the first national exposure to a number of emerging writers. Allen was assisted in his selection and planning, as he acknowledged, by Charles Olson. Olson was a tireless theorizer of open, organic form, and for a time principal of the radical Black Mountain College. The poets associated with the school and/or its journal, including Olson himself, Robert Creeley, Robert Duncan, and Denise Levertov, formed one of Allen's groupings. Olson's essay "Projective Verse" was an important statement of their principles (in a gesture that recognized some of the continuities, William Carlos Williams had quoted from it and discussed it in his 1951 *Autobiography*). Another of Allen's groups was the Beat writers, most notably Allen Ginsberg, whose reading and subsequent publication of "Howl" made him first a local then a national celebrity almost overnight. The San Francisco poets, most of whose work as individuals was not sustained in future years but who represented an important center for contemporary writing that had arisen in the early 1950s, formed another group. Writers associated with New York, including John Ashbery and Frank O'Hara, writing verse that was urban, sophisticated, and concerned with the moment, formed another. In a miscellaneous group for which Allen claimed no common characteristic he included LeRoi Jones, later, as Amiri Baraka, to be a central figure in the protest voice of the Black Arts movement.

To varying degrees Allen's poets set themselves against the prevailing political conservatism of the United States in the 1950s, arguing overtly or implicitly for a different set of values to those associated with the suburban, materialistic lifestyle produced by America's post-war wealth, and foregrounded in the growing medium of television and by the popular magazines of the day. The rebellion against the impersonality of the New Critical mode also combined with a rejection of the highly specific gender roles of popular post-war culture and helped to produce the sexual frankness and open homosexual themes of a poet like Ginsberg. Sexual frankness and the questioning of gender roles would become even more central to the work of the Confessional poets, some of the most important of whom were women. Anne Sexton and Sylvia Plath are most associated with the style, and the poetry of Elizabeth Bishop and the later work of Adrienne Rich have affinities with it. These poets rejected many of the attitudes associated with the claims of male authority, as well as, in various ways, the conventions of literary decorum and romance. Male poets who adopted characteristics of the style were Robert Lowell, whose *Life Studies* in 1959 marked a major change of direction in his writing, and John Berryman in his *Dream Songs*. As a measure of the shifting allegiances, and the qualifications that need to be attached to categories, Lowell and Rich, as noted above, had appeared in the 1957 formalist anthology, while Berryman had appeared in neither.

In the decades that followed, the personal lyric, and the assertion of identity and political rights against the homogenizing pressures of a dominant Euro-American culture – along with changes in the immigration laws that scrapped quotas favoring northern Europeans – would lead to the beginnings of a rich poetry of cultural and ethnic diversity, including poetry in English by Native American writers. These trends would find full expression in the last two decades of the century.

# The Poetry of Change

One of the most prominent poets of the 1960s, Denise Levertov, was one of the most active politically. Levertov's first volume, published in her native London, had been in the neo-Romantic vein of the time, but upon moving to the United States in the 1950s she turned to the poetry of Williams and Black Mountain College, and later to Stevens and H.D. too, for models. In the 1960s, as the Vietnam War increased in intensity, Levertov's poetry became more overtly political, emphasizing less the nuance and quiet mystical intensity for which it had been admired, and engaging directly the images and consequences of war. For some of her readers and fellow poets this was an inappropriate, even naive, role for poetry. To this charge Levertov, and some of the other poets who wrote and demonstrated against the war, replied that poetry had a duty to address such a vital contemporary issue. One way that Levertov included the war in her poetry was through the "notebook" form of some of her volumes (e.g. *To Stay Alive* [1971]), emphasizing organic process and the contemporary moment. Another poet who wrote of and actively opposed the war, Robert Lowell, published his *Notebook 1967–68* in 1969 and revised it the following year. Adrienne Rich, Muriel Rukeyser, and Galway Kinnell also wrote against the war, although of course from the point of view of non-combatants hostile to the actions and values of those running the war, and responding to the images carried by the media. The closest such poets could get to the first-hand authority of such First World War British poets as Wilfred Owen and Siegfried Sassoon was to visit Vietnam, which Levertov and Rukeyser did in 1972. Yusef Komunyakaa, awarded the Bronze Star for his service in the conflict, brought the details of war directly into his poetry in *Dien Cai Dau* (1988), but he has said that he had to wait 14 years before he was able to write poetry about his experiences in Vietnam.

Two other important groups of poets who sought to distance themselves from the actions and authority of the establishment were poets of the Black

Arts movement, and poets associated with the feminist movement. LeRoi Jones was the most prominent voice in black poetry in the 1960s and into the 1970s, changing his name to Amiri Baraka with his conversion to the Black Muslim faith, basing himself first in Harlem and then in the racially troubled city of Newark. His move away in the early 1960s from the racially mixed artistic world of New York's Greenwich Village to these predominantly black urban centers signaled his intent to write for an exclusively black audience. The shift marked his giving up on attempts at integration, at convincing the white majority to share power, wealth, and opportunity, to a focus on raising the political consciousness of his black audience through his writing. Baraka published with black presses, as did Gwendolyn Brooks in Chicago, her poetry chronicling the empty, often short and violent, lives of youth in the decaying black areas of the city, histories otherwise buried in crime reports or rows of statistics. Audre Lorde also wrote of racial injustice, but from a more personal, physical perspective. Into the 1980s, Rita Dove's poetry reached back into recent black history for an act of personal and historical recovery that carried wide social significance. The poetry of Brooks, Lorde, and Dove, and of Baraka after the mid-1970s, when it addressed the possibilities of integration rather than division, insisted that that integration be more than merely well-intentioned laws and idealistic rhetoric. It insisted that the history of past and present America include the specific history and condition of those whom the fine rhetoric could too readily make merely abstract. For these poets, poetry had a role in connecting to and giving voice to community, and in insisting upon that community's place, rights, and needs in the United States of the late twentieth century. Such poetry, as with the anti-war poets, made claims for the continuing relevance of verse, for the role of the poet as community leader, and for the importance of respecting the power of language to serve the truth.

Similar concerns governed feminist poetry, most centrally voiced in the 1980s in the work of Adrienne Rich, following in the tradition of the poetry of H.D., Bishop, Sexton, and Plath. The community addressed here was women denied by male-centered conventions and social mores the opportunity to experience the real power of motherhood, to freely love another woman, and to discover and live by values other than those praised in the conventional rhetoric of politics, economics, history, and romance. More than black poetry after the mid-1970s, poetry that led and responded to the feminist movement retained a tone of anger and a determined self-sufficiency, but without the sometimes explicit violence of the black poetry of the 1960s. The poetry argued that violence was a crime committed against, not by, women.

Another role claimed for poetry in the 1970s and 1980s was not to advocate change but record it. Here the poet was again the seer, seeing what went otherwise unnoticed, but hesitant to claim that noticing such things brought the power to do more than move with the flow of time and sensation out of which human experience is composed. Such poetry posited the relativity of all moments of lived experience, examined the problems with claiming a perspective that went beyond the experience of such moments, and faced living with the probability that human perspective was inevitably limited. The range of such poetry, articulated within contemporary versions of the meditative tradition and following on in particular from the poetry of Wallace Stevens, W. H. Auden, and the later work of T. S. Eliot, can be seen in the poems of John Ashbery and James Merrill. Ashbery's poetry records the moment-by-moment engagement of consciousness with the outside world and with memory. Merrill's *The Changing Light at Sandover* sought to put the limited human perspective into the context of the wider vision offered by the world of spirits and angels speaking to mortals through the medium of the poet and his poetry. But, whether recording the hesitations of a moment or the descent of an archangel, the poetry emphasized the process of change and the limited ways in which humans could affect its direction. Such poetry did not advocate change, but saw it as the central condition of late twentieth-century existence. In some ways such a view is a particularly American one, coming out of a culture that in important ways defines itself in terms that insist upon constant change.

# A Rich Diversity

In the last 20 years of the century the presence of contemporary poets and poetry in the universities became even more visible, with creative writing programs offering faculty positions for poets, and the development of an extensive poetry-reading circuit. The prevailing style in mainstream poetry journals and graduate creative writing programs was the neo-confessional personal lyric, usually in free verse. Another prominent group of American poets, the new formalists, argued for a return to meter and rhyme as part of what it saw as a return to craft and discipline in writing, and the movement brought some English and American poets together under at least one banner, another being the common interests of poets writing on post-colonial themes.

A more radical group of poets developed around the journal $L=A=N=G=U=A=G=E$; they saw themselves as the inheritors of a line from high modernism through objectivism, the Black Mountain poets, and poststructuralist critical theory. For the Language poets, the concept of the self was not a coherent basis upon which to center the voice and meaning of a poem, but only an ideological construction, created solely by language, and a construction which should be taken apart and exposed by a poetry that foregrounds its own status as an artefact composed of words. In the poetry of such writers as Charles Bernstein, Ron Silliman, and Susan Howe, discourse is not rational and linear, but jagged, elliptical, and a reminder always to the reader of the poem's construction, and of the act of the reader in responding to it. Even the Language poets have been assimilated by the academy, the State University at Buffalo being an important center for their writing and teaching.

The most visible development in American poetry by the end of the century was the explosion of writing in English from various ethnic groups, sometimes immigrant writers and sometimes the children of immigrants.

American poetry thus began more fully to represent the country's diverse ethnic and immigrant population. Trends in literary and cultural criticism raised awareness of ethnic literatures and contributed to the increased attention to and support of ethnic writing in the academy – where the prevailing style of the personal lyric was particularly suited to the work of poets writing of their ethnic origins.

In broadening their concept of what "literary study" entails, English departments have re-evaluated what constitutes and constituted "American literature." Within the different ethnic groups themselves – the most prominent being the Chicano and Chicana writers of Mexican origin in the south-west, and Asian American writing that emerged from the immigration following the Vietnam War and the rise of the South-East Asian economies – there is great diversity, as different poets use different elements from their native traditions. A common theme, however, is a sense of cultural displacement or fragmented identity within the pressures of the dominant culture. This theme is also central to the Native American verse that was also finding its voice more and more by the end of the decade, in the writing of such poets as Leslie Marmon Silko, Louise Erdrich, and Joy Harjo, and of course displacement had for some decades been a major theme of African American writing.

While many ethnic poets may view the mainstream culture as monolithic, American poetry by the end of the century was anything but. The very trends that contribute to what for many poets is the oppressive power of that culture, including the global reach of its multi-national corporations, technology, rhetoric, and media, have heightened such poets' awareness of the distinctive features of their own origins. The threat of homogenization through what is seen as the imperialist and military ethic of the dominant culture has reopened the debate about poetry and politics, figured in the work of a poet like Carolyn Forché. The result, the assertion by poets of the distinctive features of a particular culture and its accompanying traditions, and the insistence upon what would be lost by its dying, has brought a rich diversity and a powerful set of voices to contemporary American poetry. These voices, along with the others outlined above, sometimes complementing one another and sometimes in opposition, together hold the promise of multiple and fruitful directions for American poetry in the new century.

# Writers

# Edwin Arlington Robinson (1869–1935)

Robinson has a claim to be the most important immediate forerunner of modernist American poetry, although he appears to have influenced few later poets, and much of the later work in his 20 published volumes is probably more respected than it is read. He remained throughout his career committed to formal qualities of verse, but the sometimes bleak, always questioning direction of his poetry marks his work as modern, and he brought some novelist devices into American poetry through his narratives, and a bold, sympathetic characterization which has some similarities to the portraits by Edgar Lee Masters in *Spoon River Anthology* (1915). His work was a marked break from the genteel tradition and newspaper verse of the late 1890s and early part of the century, verse which tended towards bland uplift or familiar stereotypes. Robinson's verse reflects to varying degrees a balance between the evolutionary theories of Herbert Spencer and the transcendentalism of Ralph Waldo Emerson. The questioning, open-ended issues in his verse move away from the sentimental escapist pieties of such genteel poets as Trumbull Stickney (1874–1904) and William Vaughn Moody (1869–1910), or the romantic, political, or rural generalities of Bliss Carman (1861–1929), Edwin Markham (1852–1940), and James Whitcomb Riley (1849–1916). He was some years ahead of Robert Frost in linking the stories and characters of his poems to a particular region, although Robinson's adhering to more formal qualities of verse meant that he never demonstrated Frost's interest in adapting regional, colloquial speech to his meters. For a period in the early 1920s Robinson was one of the country's best-selling poets, although that popularity came through a sentimentality in his later work that has contributed to its receiving less critical attention. In general, there has been relatively little recent critical work on this important poet.

Robinson was born in Head Tide, a small village in Maine, although soon afterwards his family moved the short distance to the equally rural Gardiner – the "Tilbury Town" of many of his poems. Robinson attended Harvard as a special student for two years, leaving when his father died in 1892. He published his first book, at his own expense ($52), in 1896, titled *The Torrent and the Night Before*. Neither this nor the books that followed, *The Children of the Night* (1897) and *Captain Craig* (1902), gained him much notice. Around the time of his first book Robinson moved to New York, where he often lived in poverty, and took a succession of jobs including work on the city's subway. But in 1905 President Theodore Roosevelt wrote a notice praising his work, and found him a sinecure in the New York Custom House for the next five years. From 1911 onwards Robinson began to spend his summers at the MacDowell Writers' Colony in New Hampshire, where he did most of his writing.

During the 1910s and 1920s Robinson published the books that established his reputation, including *The Man Against the Sky* (1916) and his *Collected Poems* (1921) – the latter bringing him the first of his three Pulitzer prizes (the others were for *The Man Who Died Twice* in 1925 and *Tristram* in 1928). *Tristram* is the third of an Arthurian trilogy of long poems that Robinson began in 1917 with *Merlin* and continued with *Lancelot* (1920). In the second half of his career Robinson published more than a dozen book-length narrative poems in blank verse. In his final months he worked on his last poem, *King Jasper*, while in hospital suffering from cancer. When published the book carried a preface by Robert Frost.

Robinson is now best known for his shorter poems, especially such character studies as the frequently anthologized "Mr. Flood's Party," "Miniver Cheevy," "Ruben Bright," "Bewick Finzer," and "Richard Cory." The early "Luke Havergal" is representative of Robinson's dense, suggestive symbolic lyrics, while "Eros Turannos" demonstrates his ability to condense into an unsentimental representative portrait – here of a woman trapped in a failed marriage – his frequent themes of inexorable fate reinforced by a desperate psychological need, the final unknowability of others (often accompanied in the poems by the use of an objective narrator to distance the powerful emotions that the poem dramatizes), and the need for a kind of stoic endurance, by both the subjects and the narrator, in the face of such inevitability and exposure:

> We'll have no kindly veil between
> Her visions and those we have seen, –
> As if we guessed what hers have been,
> Or what they are or would be.

This need for a stoic attitude towards endurance is the final position of "The Man Against the Sky," which Robinson once said came "as near as anything to representing my poetic vision." The dramatic situation in the poem presents a figure moving ahead of the narrator, towards "the sunset / . . . his last desire," upon whose life, character, attitude, and final fate the narrator speculates as a way to try to understand his own coming journey. The man may have been courageous, may have had an easy life where all comforts fell into place, may equally well have been a gloomy, bitter man, or a man whose faith was lost through adversity, or again he may have been a scientist seeing "with his mechanic eyes / A world without a meaning." The second half of the poem, some 140 lines, then examines the human condition in more general terms. Where "this man against the sky" was going "You know not, nor do I." Typically for Robinson the poem deals in questions not answers: "If there be nothing after Now, / And we be nothing anyhow, / And we know that, – why live?" The abstractions, especially in the second half of the poem, reveal the side of Robinson that would drive the long narrative poems of his later career and that are now of less interest than his treatment of such issues in the poems centered upon the lonely inhabitants of his "Tilbury Town."

Robinson does not use the idea of "fate" as any kind of pat resolution to the issues that his poems raise. Where "fate" is invoked by a character in one of his poems – "Miniver Cheevy" for example "coughed, and called it fate" that he was born after his time, his beloved medieval period – the attitude is gently mocked as self-indulgent, a self-indulgence that accompanies Miniver's alcoholism. This gentle ridicule, reinforced by the short lines and heavy rhyme, is accompanied by a genuine sympathy for a man unable to live in what his life has made of his personal present, and this range of perspective is part of what gives such short character poems their continuing power. In this case the perspective extends to some of Robinson's own tendencies, for he too had his bouts of drinking to excess, and, as his Arthurian trilogy indicates, could share Miniver's fascination with Camelot (although in Robinson's case as a way to treat the contemporary world rather than escape from it).

A similar sympathy is extended to "Richard Cory." A habit of viewing some others in terms of a finally meaningless romantic awe forms the basis of the townspeople's fascination with Cory who, only a set of imposed associations to others, isolated and self-isolating, "one calm summer night, / Went home and put a bullet through his head." In "Mr. Flood's Party" the isolation of age and having outlived his "many friends" is what confronts "Old Eben Flood" in his "hermitage" outside of town. In this poem drinking and an imagination that allows a dialogue with an invented other is what allows Mr. Flood "amid the silver loneliness / Of night" to lift up his voice and sing, and thus to mitigate his isolation for some moments under a moon that becomes "two moons listening." Such a poem demonstrates what Robinson at his best can do with what, in another poet of his generation, would have been a general lament of the poet as outcast, adrift in an uncaring modern world.

## Bibliography

*Collected Poems of Edwin Arlington Robinson* (New York, 1937).

Wallace L. Anderson, *Edwin Arlington Robinson: A Critical Introduction* (Boston, 1967).
Ellsworth Barnard, ed., *Edwin Arlington Robinson: Centenary Essays* (Athens, GA, 1969).
Emery Neff, *Edwin Arlington Robinson* (New York, 1948).

# Robert Frost (1874–1963)

Writing in a preface to Edwin Arlington Robinson's posthumously published last work, the long poem *King Jasper*, in 1935, Frost praised Robinson's commitment to "the old fashioned way to be new," although privately he had some years earlier called Robinson's later poems "Arthurian twaddle" (quoted in Pritchard 1984: 196–7). The two views mark something of Frost's similarities with and differences from Robinson. Like Robinson, Frost was determined to adhere to the formal qualities of poetry against the more iconoclastic strategies of the imagists and the complex, highly allusive poetry of Pound and Eliot. But far more than was the case with Robinson he wanted to get away from the bookish and literary in his poetry, to root his subject matter and diction in contemporary life, albeit largely the self-restricted range of New England rural life. And this interest in getting away from the literary gave a flexibility to his verse, as he played off speech rhythms against meter, and sound against sense, that Robinson rarely attained. Frost's poetry is "new" in its questioning of central Romantic assumptions, questions often more embedded in the poem than in Robinson's work, and often taking the direction of undermining a statement offered in a pithy tone of certitude earlier in the poem. Frost produced a body of work that won him most of the major literary prizes of his day short of the Nobel Prize, and in the 1950s and 1960s national stature as an icon that would have Congress noting his birthday and have him reading at the inauguration of President John F. Kennedy in 1961.

Robert Frost was born in San Francisco, but, following the death of his teacher and journalist father when Frost was 11, he moved with his mother to his father's native New England. After attending Dartmouth College for a semester in fall 1892 and Harvard as a special student in 1897–9 (where Wallace Stevens was a fellow student) Frost, now married with a family, began poultry farming, purchasing with his grandfather's assistance a farm in Derry, New Hampshire, in 1900. Here the family lived for the next nine years and he wrote many of the poems that were to appear in his first published books. The farming enterprise not being the success he had hoped for, or perhaps not something to which he could commit the necessary time and effort (Frost was never completely the farmer-poet of the public image he later cultivated), he began full-time teaching in the fall of 1906. Initially he taught at Pinkerton Academy, during which time he began to publish poems in local and regional magazines, and in 1911 he taught for a year at the New Hampshire State Normal School at Plymouth, a teachers' college for young women.

Frost sold the Derry farm in 1911 and with the proceeds, and an annuity from his grandfather's will, at the age of 38 sailed with his family to England the following summer, determined to try and make his mark as a poet. Frost's difficulty in getting his poetry published outside of minor periodicals in the United States illustrates the conservative nature of poetry readers and publishers at the time, the same conservatism that had driven Ezra Pound, H.D., and later T. S. Eliot to London. Settling in a cottage in Beaconsfield, just outside London, Frost soon met Pound, Yeats, and other central figures of the bustling London poetry scene, and was able to get his first book, *A Boy's Will*, published in 1913, and a second, *North of Boston*, the following year. The former, a volume of lyrics, appeared with a contents page that provided something of a narrative commentary upon the poems' relationships and themes. The first poem, "Into My Own," for example, carries the commentary: "The youth is persuaded that he will be rather more than less himself for having forsworn the world," while the best-known of these poems, "The Tuft of Flowers," is more briefly "about fellowship." *North of Boston*, which contains blank verse dramatic poems, and was, Frost told a correspondent, "more objective" than the first volume (Pritchard 1984: 74), includes a number of famous titles, including "Mending Wall" (which Frost noted "takes up the theme where 'A Tuft of Flowers' in *A Boy's Will* laid it down"), "The Death of the Hired Man," "Home Burial," and "The Wood-Pile." Because of his long apprenticeship, Frost's books appeared on the poetry scene with his mature style close to being fully developed.

In March 1913 Pound wrote characteristically to Alice Corbin Henderson of Chicago's *Poetry* that he had "discovered another Amur'kn. VURRY Amur'k'n, with, I think, the seeds of grace" (Pound, *Selected Letters*, 14). This was just one of a number of attempts by Pound to get Frost's poetry published more widely. In his reviews of Frost's two books, Pound berated American editors for forcing the country's best poets abroad, but along with this familiar theme he also noted Frost's avoidance of literary tricks in his presentation of New England life, the humor in his verse, and his integrity as an artist. By early 1915, writing to H. L. Mencken, he thought Frost "dull perhaps, but has something in him" (*Selected Letters*, 51), but by 1918 he was placing Frost along with Edgar Lee Masters and Vachel Lindsay as "out of the Wild Young

American gaze already" (*Selected Letters*, 135–6). For Pound, Frost was no part of the modernist revolution. In turn, although Frost respected Pound as an artist and was grateful for the generous efforts on behalf of his early work, he was wary that Pound's aggressive rhetoric might alienate American editors and possible future publishers. Many years later, in the 1950s, Frost would play an important role in obtaining Pound's release from confinement in St. Elizabeths Hospital.

In the London of 1913–14 Frost was in fact much more comfortable in the company of such Georgian poets as Wilfred Gibson, Lascelles Abercrombie, W. H. Davies, and especially Edward Thomas, with whom he became particularly close and who reviewed *North of Boston* three times. Though Frost's work was generally much more accomplished than the work of these poets, they shared an interest in a reflective poetry centered upon familiar or at least recognizable sights and happenings, accurate and detailed presentation of the – usually rural – scene, and a direct and colloquial speaking voice.

At the same time that Pound was qualifying his praise of Frost to Mencken in February 1915, Frost and his family were returning to the US from Liverpool. A combination of the war breaking out in August the previous year, suggesting possible danger for his family and reducing the possibility of publishing a third book, the many excellent reviews of *North of Boston* that had appeared, and Henry Holt in New York agreeing to bring out both *A Boy's Will* and *North of Boston* and possibly future volumes suggested that a return home would be propitious.

Frost purchased a farm in Franconia, New Hampshire, upon his return, and also began his long association with Amherst College. The next ten years saw a steady increase in his reputation, augmented by a third book, *Mountain Interval*, in 1916, and a fourth that brought him his first Pulitzer Prize, *New Hampshire* (1924). By the mid-1920s Frost's reputation was established, although for most critics the work in subsequent volumes – *West-Running Brook* (1928), *A Further Range* (1936), *A Witness Tree* (1942), *Steeple Bush* (1947) and *In the Clearing* (1962) – is marked by a gradual hardening of attitude and a more didactic tone than the rich, suggestive possibilities of the earlier work.

In the 1930s Frost came under increasing criticism from liberal and left-leaning literary journals for his opposition to President Roosevelt's New Deal, and his literary and political conservatism generally, but he remained committed to his own principles. This decade also saw a series of personal tragedies for the poet: the death following childbirth of his favorite daughter in 1934, the death of his wife in 1938, and the suicide by gunshot of his son Carol in 1940. By 1950 Frost had become a revered American institution, his occasional teaching and his public appearances taking over from his now intermittent writing of poetry. This comfortable image was disturbed by an influential three-volume biography of the poet by Lawrance Thompson, which appeared between 1966 and 1976, and which portrayed Frost as quarrelsome, sometimes ruthlessly ambitious, manipulative – of his family and of his public image – and at times consumed by self-doubt and guilt. A number of biographies since have taken positions on the fairness or otherwise of Thompson's picture. The tendency to read Frost as mainly the producer of such comfortable pieties as "good fences make good neighbors" was complicated most notably by Randall Jarrell in 1953, and again by Lionel Trilling in 1959, both of whom pointed out the tentative, questioning direction of many of the poems, and the ways that any final statements remained suspended rather than being asserted. This issue too has continued to generate critical debate.

Frost was never comfortable writing public prose, and left behind relatively few statements beyond a rich correspondence about his poetry. In the most important of these statements, "The Figure a Poem Makes" from 1938 and included for many years as an introduction to his *Collected Poems*, he argues for an organic theory of poetry, and for a qualified, although necessary, role for verse:

> it assumes direction with the first line laid down, it runs a course of lucky events, and ends in a clarification of life – not necessarily a great clarification, such as sects and cults are founded on, but in a momentary stay against confusion. It has denouement. It has an outcome that though unforeseen was predestined from the first image of the original mood – and indeed from the very mood.

This "confusion" is often very close to the surface of a Frost poem, and is examined in poems which explore the human relationship to nature, and definitions of home, marriage, community, and even sanity, often illustrating a quiet desperation in the attempt to impose order upon a finally alien world capable of sudden and unpredictable actions. For example, in the well-known "Stopping by Woods on a Snowy Evening," the threat of annihilation in the pull of the "lovely, dark, and deep" woods is set against the superficiality of real-estate contracts ("Whose woods these are I think I know"), and the limitations of human domestication of nature ("My little horse" with his "harness bells"). Against this the woods threaten to expose and dissolve all such attempts to measure nature in merely human terms. "And miles to go before I sleep," is repeated at the poem's end as assertive reiteration of such human measure, as if the experience of glancing outside such measure had raised disturbing questions about its efficacy and status.

In this poem, as in many others, Frost uses the formal qualities of the poem itself, the closure provided by sound and sense and rhyme scheme, to reinforce the role of the poem as a way to order the world in human terms, "a momentary stay." This role for poetry is sometimes made explicit, as in "The Silken Tent" (1942), on one level a poem in praise of its own sonnet form, and even more explicitly in the "verse" of the famous "The Need of Being Versed in Country Things" which closes the *New Hampshire* volume.

## Bibliography

*The Poetry of Robert Frost*, ed. Edward C. Lathem (New York, 1969).

Jay Parini, *Robert Frost: A Life* (New York, 1999).
Richard Poirier, *Robert Frost: The Work of Knowing* (New York, 1977; rev. 1990).
William H. Pritchard, *Frost: A Literary Life Reconsidered* (New York, 1984).
Mark Richardson, *The Ordeal of Robert Frost: The Poet and his Poetics* (Urbana, IL, 1997).
*The Selected Letters of Ezra Pound: 1907–1941*, ed. D. D. Paige (New York, 1971); originally published as *The Letters of Ezra Pound* (New York, 1950).

# Carl Sandburg (1878–1967)

Carl Sandburg's poetry came out of the literary movement centered in Chicago around the time of the First World War that sought a direct, usually celebratory, often urban realism in contrast to the genteel sentimentalities of much late Romantic magazine poetry. Out of this movement also came the prose of Sherwood Anderson, Edgar Lee Masters's *Spoon River Anthology*, and *Poetry* magazine, but of all these Sandburg's poetry was most quintessentially the poetry of the city and the people. He lived for most of his life in Chicago.

Sandburg was born in Galesburg, Illinois, to Swedish immigrant parents, and left school at 13 to pursue a variety of jobs and an itinerant life, including serving as a private in the Spanish–American War. He then attended Lombard College, but left in 1902 without a degree. The following years saw him holding various journalist positions, and working for the socialist causes that would remain an important part of his work. In 1914 Harriet Monroe published a group of Sandburg's poems in *Poetry*, and their aggressive Whitmanesque celebrations of the city caught the attention of many readers. His first book, *Chicago Poems*, appeared in 1916, and was followed in 1918 by *Cornhuskers*, which took the prairie as its general theme. In the best of these poems of direct or evocative celebration – whether of the city or the prairie or in tender, generalized portraits of their inhabitants – the broad sweep of the lyrical free verse is set against a degree of particularized detail. Thus his most frequently anthologized poem, "Chicago," begins:

> Hog Butcher for the World,
> Tool Maker, Stacker of Wheat,
> Player with Railroads and the Nation's Freight Handler;
> Stormy, husky, brawling,
> City of the Big Shoulders:

> They tell me you are wicked and I believe them, for I have seen
>     your painted women under the gas lamps luring the farm boys.

Such verse had claims to be contemporary for its directness, its rooting of poetry in the modern industrial landscape, its breaking of traditional meter, and generally its affinities to the iconoclasm of Whitman. The poetry's lack of serious intellectual challenge, and Sandburg's platform skills in performing his work, helped to make the poet a popular figure. But despite more than half a dozen subsequent volumes over a long career, his poetry did not develop a great deal beyond these early books. Sandburg also collected and published two admired volumes of folk songs. But as far as poetry was concerned, he became a marginal figure, by 1968 one of the six examples of the fleetingness of poetic fame in Hyatt Waggoner's *American Poets from the Puritans to the Present*. However, a measure of Sandburg's personal stature, a stature enhanced by his six-volume prose biography of Abraham Lincoln published between 1926 and 1939, is that his *Complete Poems* won him a second Pulitzer Prize in 1951 (the final part of the Lincoln biography had already been honored in 1940). The long, chanting lines of a poem like "Chicago" has affinities with some Beat poetry of the 1950s, for example Allen Ginsberg's "Howl," and Sandburg is listed in Ginsberg's *Kaddish* as one of the figures inspiring dreams in the poet of being an "honest revolutionary labor lawyer . . . President, or Senator." In his old age as much of an icon as Frost, three years before he died Sandburg received the Presidential Medal of Freedom from President Lyndon Johnson.

## Bibliography

*The Complete Poems of Carl Sandburg* (New York, 1970).

Richard Crowder, *Carl Sandburg* (New York, 1964).
Penelope Niven, *Carl Sandburg: A Biography* (New York, 1991).
Philip R. Yannella, *The Other Carl Sandburg* (Jackson, MS, 1996).

# Wallace Stevens (1879–1955)

When Wallace Stevens published his 1951 book of essays *The Necessary Angel* he subtitled the collection "Essays on Reality and the Imagination," and the terms sum up the two central concerns of his poetry throughout his career. His poetry explores the role that imagination plays in our engagement with, understanding of, and interpretation of the world outside of the self, and conversely the role of the "facts" in that world – what we can know and say about those facts. "The poet," Stevens wrote in his essay "The Noble Rider and the Sound of Words," "gives to life the supreme fictions without which we are unable to conceive of it." In his poem "The Plain Sense of Things" Stevens asserts: "Yet the absence of the imagination had / Itself to be imagined." And in "The World as Meditation," centered upon Penelope's long wait for the absent Ulysses to return, she senses that he may be "moving // On the horizon." Yet the question: "But was it Ulysses? Or was it only the warmth of the sun / On her pillow? The thought kept beating in her like her heart. / The two kept beating together" is answered characteristically: "It was only day. // It was Ulysses and it was not. Yet they had met . . ." again insisting upon the role of "imagination" in shaping "reality."

Stevens took no firm position on the final relationship of the two; his poems instead explore propositions and suppositions about the balance, more playfully in his earlier work, and more meditatively in the poems of his last 15 years. Sometimes two poems taken together explore the extremes of the spectrum, almost as companion pieces. "The Emperor of Ice-Cream" and "Cortège for Rosenbloom," both poems about funeral rituals, is one such pairing; "The Snow Man" and "Tea at the Palaz of Hoon" is another. The pairing of the physical and the imaginative are illustrated in the title and narrative of "Peter Quince at the Clavier." The bumbling mechanical's earthy response to female beauty (Quince is a character from a play, *A Midsummer Night's Dream*, itself about the interplay of the physical and the dream) is articulated lyrically and musically through his playing an instrument normally associated with lightness and order.

Stevens's theme was the poem recording the mind searching, weighing, and balancing, a meditation upon degrees of attention, order, and projection, as well as upon the making of metaphor. This search, for Stevens, was necessary because past systems of belief no longer provided an adequate framework for understanding and interpreting our world.

Thus poetry had a role. Stevens writes, in his essay "Imagination as Value": "the great poems of heaven and hell have been written and the great poem of the earth remains to be written." "Why should she give her bounty to the dead?" asks the narrator of the woman in "Sunday Morning," who is pulled away from the present by "The holy hush of ancient sacrifice. / . . . Over the seas, to silent Palestine." For Stevens, the poet needed to invent a "supreme fiction" for the age, or at any rate to describe that fiction's characteristics, acknowledging among them the relative nature of its truths, and thus the need for them to be discarded at some future date when they too had served their use. As Stevens put it in "Of Modern Poetry":

> The poem of the mind in the act of finding
> What will suffice. It has not always had
> To find: the scene was set; it repeated what
> Was in the script.
> > Then the theater was changed
> To something else. Its past was a souvenir.

Characteristically, the claim for the end result is an understated one, "what will suffice." Equally characteristically, the theme is set in terms of performance, the "script" and "theater" now replaced by the performance of the mind upon the stage of the poem. Often in Stevens's poems, the issues are distanced from the poet himself, in this case through the performance metaphor and by the emphasis upon the act of thinking and writing rather than upon the particular writer of the poem.

This distance and emotional restraint in the poems has often been coupled in discussion of Stevens with his two apparently disparate careers, as poet and as a vice-president of the Hartford Accident and Indemnity Company, although recent work has argued for a more integrated reading of his business and writing interests. Born in Reading, Pennsylvania, Stevens's interest in poetry was displayed in his years as a special student at Harvard (1897–1900), where, like T. S. Eliot a few years later, he was associated with and published in *The Harvard Advocate*. After a short career as a journalist in New York, Stevens attended New York Law School and was admitted to the New York bar in 1904. He began his career as an insurance lawyer in 1908, married Elsie Kachel from Reading in 1909, joined the Hartford company in 1916, and moved to Hartford, where he lived for the rest of his life. He was made a vice-president in 1934. Apart from a couple of short business trips to Cuba, Stevens never traveled outside of the United States, although an interest in French painting, Havana cigars, and postcards and news sent from abroad by friends and acquaintances were among his most important pleasures.

Stevens remained close to a number of his Harvard friends in his New York years, and with them published some poems in the journal *The Trend* and some subsequent short-lived magazines that reflected the group's interest in turn-of-the-century exoticism and dandyism, and also in such modern iconoclastic movements as Dada. His association with avant-garde literary and artistic circles grew to incorporate members of the *Others* group, which included Alfred Kreymborg, Marianne Moore, and William Carlos Williams. This group of writers, loosely centered around the artists' colony of Grantwood in New Jersey and the apartment of Walter Arensberg in New York (one of Stevens's Harvard friends) saw themselves and their sporadic journal *Others* (which was financed by Arensberg) as an alternative to the sometimes conservative pages of Chicago's *Poetry*. The group's association too with Alfred Stieglitz and the artists connected to his gallery and the journal *291* illustrates their closer ties to the European avant-garde than was the case with the Chicago movement. Marcel Duchamp was only the most famous of the many European artists who fled to New York with the outbreak of the First World War, reinforcing the impact upon the city of the ground-breaking Armory Show exhibit of European painting in 1913.

From 1915 to 1923 Stevens wrote the poems that make up his 1923 volume *Harmonium*. The themes of reality and imagination are displayed through an exuberant, sometimes comic, playfulness of language and through shifting points of view. "Le Monocle de Mon Oncle" captures these elements in the dandified rhetoric and fastidiousness of its narrator, who is concerned about the possible crisis of turning 40, in his turn-of-the-century eyepiece, and in the title itself being a French schoolchildren's handwriting exercise. A playful poem about language, a way of life, and appearance, its subtext concerns aging, insecurity, and fears of impotence. "Thirteen Ways of Looking at a Blackbird" displays Stevens's awareness of the experiments of imagism as well as the analytical cubism of Picasso and Braque. While this poem displays what the onlooker brings to an understanding of the object, "The Snow Man" argues that without this human-centered framework of interpretation (which, for example, would construct a human figure out of the blankness of snow) we would see only "Nothing that is not there and the nothing that is." And while "Sunday Morning" in its final stanza echoes Keats's celebration of change in his ode "To Autumn," Stevens's rewriting foregrounds the inevitable coming "darkness" that is the corollary of the imagination's freedom to inventively engage the earth's ever-changing present.

When *Harmonium* appeared in 1923, in an edition of 1,500 copies, it was little noticed. Stevens, then 44, apparently wrote little for the next few years, offering as an excuse to editors who asked for poems that he was focused for the moment on career and family (his daughter Holly had just been born). But the book garnered more attention when reissued in 1931 with the addition of 14 poems (three others were omitted), and Stevens began to write and publish volumes regularly for the rest of his life, beginning with *Ideas of*

*Order* (1935). The poems of the 1930s address their philosophical issues more directly than the more exuberant poems of *Harmonium*, and in a barer style, although their concerns are similar. In "The Idea of Order at Key West," a poem that echoes Wordsworth's "Stepping Westward" and "The Solitary Reaper," the idea of order produced through witnessing the girl's singing by the sea is as immediately present as, but more temporary than, the sound carried away by Wordsworth's narrator. For Stevens it is an *idea* of order rather than order itself, but it can be a communal force, one between observers as well as between nature and man. Nature, its essence finally unknowable although always being interpreted, is merely the "place by which" the girl sings:

> For she was the maker of the song she sang.
> The ever-hooded, tragic-gestured sea
> Was merely a place by which she walked to sing.
> Whose spirit is this? we said, because we knew
> It was the spirit that we sought and knew
> That we should ask this often as she sang.

Stevens's response to criticism in the 1930s that his poetry was remote and more concerned with abstractions than the real world of the Depression and political debate led to his volume *Owl's Clover* (1936), which deals with the social responsibility of art, but Stevens and most of his readers were dissatisfied with the result. Returning to themes more congenial to him, Stevens went on to a series of volumes that, particularly in the 1940s with *Parts of a World* (1942), *Transport to Summer* (1947), and *The Auroras of Autumn* (1950), consolidated his reputation as a major poet. He was elected to the National Institute of Arts and Letters in 1946, awarded the Bollingen Prize in 1950, and his *Collected Poems* published in 1954 won him his second National Book Award in Poetry as well as a Pulitzer Prize. Stevens is sometimes cited more by critics and scholars than contemporary poets, but at least two major poets of later in the century, James Merrill and John Ashbery, are important inheritors of his work.

## Bibliography

*The Collected Poems of Wallace Stevens* (New York, 1954).

Milton J. Bates, *Wallace Stevens: A Mythology of Self* (Berkeley, 1985).
Harold Bloom, *Wallace Stevens: The Poems of our Climate* (Ithaca, NY, 1977).
James Longenbach, *Wallace Stevens: The Plain Sense of Things* (New York, 1991).
Glen MacLeod, *Wallace Stevens and Modern Art* (New Haven, 1993).

# William Carlos Williams (1883–1963)

William Carlos Williams, like Wallace Stevens, had a successful professional career outside of poetry, in Williams's case as a small-town physician in Rutherford, New Jersey. The two were also both members of the *Others* group centered around New York City at the time of the First World War, and remained lifelong if intermittent correspondents and generally respected each other's work. But whereas recognition and awards began to come Stevens's way from the 1940s, Williams had to wait until the 1950s for similar attention. But in that decade, with some of his books having been out of print for years, he became a major influence upon younger poets looking for alternatives to the tenets of formalist verse and New Criticism. Williams's range of correspondents became extensive, and visiting the by then largely housebound Williams in Rutherford became in effect an act of pilgrimage in the mid- to late 1950s for such poets as Robert Lowell, Allen Ginsberg, Denise Levertov, and Robert Creeley.

The central ideas of imagism had a major impact upon Williams's poetry around 1914, and his work explored for the next five decades some of the implications of its principles in ways that had not interested Pound or its other original practitioners. This interest marks another major contrast with Stevens. Whereas Stevens was interested in the role of the mind and of codes of language in the interpretation and articulation of the world beyond the self, for Williams such pre-existing constructs only obscured what should be the poet's attempt at a direct encounter with the world of objects. Thus a frequent metaphor in Williams's work is that of the body (rather than the mind), and such terms as "contact" and "rooted" are central. The call for "No ideas but in things," as he put it in his long poem *Paterson*, had its roots in the imagists' "direct treatment of the thing." But Williams's poetry is far more than the pictorial vignettes by which he is too often represented in anthologies, or the anti-intellectual gesture that "no ideas but in things" might imply. As Denise Levertov felt the need to point out more than once in writing of Williams, the phrase did not mean "no ideas."

This poet who demanded that poetry record the "local" as a necessary first step to presenting the "universal" was born, lived his life in, and died in Rutherford. Williams's father had left his native England at the age of 5, but on his commercial travels in Central and South America kept "a British passport / always in his pocket," as Williams puts it in "Adam," a poem about his father. Williams's mother was born in Puerto Rico, and Williams raised this English/Spanish division to a mythic level in his work. Although the pattern was complicated in various ways, males, English heritage, and formalism together represented to Williams what America, to fulfill its literary and cultural promise, needed to resist; while women, Latin (and Native American) heritage, and a freedom often portrayed as sexual license represented liberation and possible fulfillment of that potential.

While an undergraduate at the University of Pennsylvania School of Medicine from 1902 to 1906, Williams met and formed lifelong friendships with Ezra Pound, Hilda Doolittle, and the American modernist painter Charles Demuth. Williams's poems at this time were largely watery imitations of Keats and Whitman, while his first book, the self-financed *Poems* of 1909, contains verse modeled on the genteel Romanticism of such writers as Bliss Carman and Arthur Davison Ficke. (Williams never reprinted these poems in his collected volumes.) Pound, now in London, as was H.D., responded to the book's derivative poems frankly, and sent the "out of touch" Williams the first of what would over the years be many reading lists (Williams, sometimes exasperated with them, reproduces an example in *Paterson*). Williams visited Pound in London in 1910, following six months of studying pediatrics in Leipzig, and Pound continued to keep Williams informed about the latest movements and journals in London. This international source, coupled with Williams's associations with *Poetry* and *The Little Review* in Chicago, and (again through an introduction by Pound) with Alfred Kreymborg and the *Others* group in New York, meant that Williams, although now established as a doctor in a provincial town, could keep abreast of the central movements in modernist poetry and art. In 1912 Williams married Florence Herman, the "Flossie" of a number of his poems, whose childhood figures centrally in his 1937 novel *White Mule*. (Williams's publications in addition to poetry include not only four novels, but also short stories, essays, improvisatory prose, plays, and even an opera libretto.)

Williams's poems in the years immediately following his 1909 volume on the whole followed in the wake of developments in Pound's work, although Williams's "Hic Jacet" from his 1913 volume *The Tempers* prefigures his poetry's later use of his medical experience and concrete, observed detail. Williams's mature style is more evident in his next volume, *Al Que Quiere!* (1917), and is fully developed in *Sour Grapes* (1921) and in what many consider his finest book, *Spring and All* (1923).

Between these volumes of poetry Williams published his *Kora in Hell: Improvisations* (1920), with a prologue that declared his separation from the international modernist style being developed by Pound and the now London-based Eliot. In this essay, central to an understanding of Williams's poetry, he took issue with Eliot, Pound, H.D., and Wallace Stevens, arguing that

American poetry needed to get back to beginnings – which for Williams meant a pictorial emphasis, fragmented and loosely associative verse forms, and local subject matter. The prose improvisations were written spontaneously each night, according to Williams's account, as he returned home exhausted during the influenza epidemic of 1917–18. They illustrate for Williams the "more flexible, jagged" patterns of form and syntax that could counter the habitual associations of thought hindering the promise of a nativist poetics, and stopping Americans from seeing the unique landscape in front of their eyes.

Williams's sense of embattled isolation was reinforced by the exodus of the European artists to Paris following the end of the war, and their being followed by many American writers and artists. Among those leaving was Robert McAlmon, with whom Williams had edited the journal *Contact* following the demise of *Others*. However, Williams's hostility to Europe and the expatriate movement was not a one-dimensional response. His 1928 novel *A Voyage to Pagany*, based upon his 1924 trip to Paris, Rome, and Vienna, reveals the challenge and fascination that Europe held for him. And he was obliged to rely upon expatriate publication for his poetry volumes in the 1920s. Among these, *Spring and All* contains many of his most frequently anthologized poems, although in the original volume they are surrounded by pages of thematically related, manifesto-like prose.

In the early 1930s Williams was associated with the objectivist movement, which also included Louis Zukofsky, George Oppen, and Charles Reznikoff. Objectivism was in effect a development of imagism's insistence upon precision and concrete presentation, but with more emphasis upon the formal construction of the poem. Williams had no regular publisher in this period, and his books came out in small, special editions, until James Laughlin founded New Directions at the end of the decade and committed the press to publishing the work of both Williams and Pound. At the same time Williams began to struggle with the formal problems of his long poem *Paterson*, and an initial experiment, his manuscript "Detail & Parody for the poem *Paterson*," although unpublished as a whole, was the source of many of his published poems in these years.

Williams finally settled on a collage-like form for *Paterson* that included, along with the poetry, such prose documents as extracts from histories, letters from friends and from readers of the poem (including letters from Pound and the then unknown Allen Ginsberg), leaflets, transcribed speech, and extracts from newspapers. Sometimes these items were reproduced verbatim, sometimes they were edited by Williams, and occasionally he made them up. Williams originally conceived of the poem as having four books, and they appeared separately from 1946 to 1951, but a fifth book appeared in

1958, while fragments of a sixth were found among his papers at his death. The New Jersey city that is the poem's focus has a long and rich history, from its early settlement, to its heyday as a silk and manufacturing center in the second half of the nineteenth century, to its economic decline following a pivotal textile workers' strike in 1913 – all of which Williams brings into the work. The poem also incorporates episodes from the history of the famous Paterson Falls that provided the water power driving the industry, and that was itself a well-known tourist attraction. The Falls serve as an example of the single-minded exploitation of landscape that the poem decries, and the roar of its crashing waters becomes the foundation of the poem's attempt to discover and articulate a language rooted in the native landscape.

With the publication of the first four books of *Paterson* Williams's poetry began to receive more attention, including a National Book Award in 1950. Between 1949 and 1951 Williams's publications included two volumes of *Paterson*, his *Selected Poems*, two volumes of collected poetry, his *Autobiography*, and a book of short stories. Unhappy with the marketing of his books by New Directions, Williams shifted to commercial publisher Random House in 1950 (he returned to New Directions by the end of the decade). But in 1951 he suffered the first of a number of debilitating strokes and had to retire from his medical practice. He was unable to take up an appointment as Consultant in Poetry to the Library of Congress, initially because of health problems and then because of questions raised about his political leanings, particularly in the 1930s. The poems in his next two volumes, *The Desert Music* and *Journey to Love*, are poems of memory and reflection, written in a long triadic line that Williams argued in a number of essays at the time allowed for recording the voice of "the American idiom." These poems are at once more conventional and more accessible than Williams's earlier style and contributed to his widening readership. After *Paterson V*, Williams's final volume of poems *Pictures from Brueghel* appeared in 1962. A measure of his late recognition as a major poet is the posthumous award for this volume in 1963 of his first, and only, Pulitzer Prize.


## Bibliography

*The Collected Poems of William Carlos Williams*, vols. I and II, ed. A. Walton Litz and Christopher MacGowan (New York, 1986, 1988).

William Carlos Williams, *Imaginations*, ed. Webster Schott (New York, 1970).
—— *Paterson*, ed. Christopher MacGowan (New York, 1992).
James Breslin, *William Carlos Williams: An American Artist* (New York, 1970).
Paul Mariani, *William Carlos Williams: A New World Naked* (New York, 1981).

# Ezra Pound (1885–1972)

Ezra Pound was at the center of the modernist avant-garde in London, Paris, and even – from a distance – in New York. He was a recognizer of major talent in others (including Henry James, William Carlos Williams, James Joyce, H.D., and T. S. Eliot), a selfless entrepreneur on their behalf in such journals as *Poetry* and *The Little Review*, and a remarkable editor (most memorably helping Yeats and Eliot). His critical principles continue to be influential, and the triumphs and tragedies of his life are still debated; all this in addition to the range and achievement of his own poetry.

Pound was born in Hailey, Idaho, but at the age of 2 moved east with his family, eventually to the suburbs of Philadelphia. He first attended the University of Pennsylvania, where he met Williams and Hilda Doolittle (who was later a student at Bryn Mawr) before transferring to Hamilton College. He returned to the University of Pennsylvania with a fellowship for graduate work in Romance languages and literature, receiving an MA in 1906. His fellowship was not renewed for the following year, and from September 1907 to February 1908 he taught Romance Languages at Wabash College, Indiana, from which he was fired over a disputed incident concerning a woman in his room. Determined on a career as a writer, in 1908, with his father's financial help, Pound traveled first to Venice, where he published his first book, *A Lume Spento*, at his own expense, and then at the end of the summer to London.

*A Lume Spento* and the next four books that appeared over as many years, *A Quinzaine for this Yule*, *Personae*, *Exultations*, and *Canzoni*, show Pound's interest in the medieval and Renaissance poets of the Romance cultures he had been studying since his college years. These included the troubadour poets of Provence, and early Tuscan poetry, and in particular Dante, Guido Cavalcanti, Arnaut Daniel, Rabelais, and Villon. His *The Spirit of Romance* (1910) is a prose study of the medieval poets of southern Europe. Pound's interest in the way that the values of a culture are reflected in its dominant figures, its literature, and its treatment of its major artists – a theme central to his *Cantos* – is also part of these early volumes. But for Pound this was not merely a nostalgic return to the past, although these were poets that Pound felt any serious reader and writer should know. His concern was with the present state of poetry in particular, which he came to feel was behind the novel, music, and painting in modernizing itself. For Pound, writers of the present, and the wider culture within which they wrote, could learn from the significant achievements of the past.

In these volumes sometimes the poems not only reflect the style of the particular historical poet, but present the poet as speaking the lines, bringing the poem closer to the poet's state of mind and to the quality of his time. (This mode also reveals Pound's admiration for Browning, although he had little time for most other Victorian poets.) In the poems as in his criticism Pound emphasizes the difficult craft of poetry, as against Romantic ideas of "inspiration," and also the importance of writer and reader being informed about work in languages other than English.

Pound's use of the past can be illustrated in his version of the Anglo-Saxon *The Seafarer*. Pound's poem parallels the original's alliterative line, thus opening with "May I for my own self song's truth reckon." But his interest is not in a literal rendering of the original, but in capturing something of the poet's voice and the reading experience of the original poem for the present-day reader. Thus he renders the Anglo-Saxon *wrecan* as "reckon," it being closer in sound to the original than the literal "to make or compose." *The Seafarer* is one of the first known poems in English, and thus marks a return to one set of beginnings (Pound begins Canto I with alliterative lines, perhaps an allusion to this poem and to his version of it). The subject matter is an anonymous poet who chooses exile over compromising with the mercenary values of his "lord," just as Pound felt he had been driven into exile by the commercial values of American publishers and readers. "The Return" (1912) dramatizes the tentative and weakened return of a force once powerful, associated as in Pound's later poetry with a rediscovery of latent powers in "Gods" too long displaced by the Christian tradition.

Pound threw himself into the Edwardian literary scene, but as he met some of the figures, such as Yeats, T. E. Hulme, and Ford Madox Ford, who advocated alternatives to it, his attitude became less reverential and more critical. He worked as Yeats's secretary for three years, became the foreign correspondent of *Poetry*, the poetry editor of *The Egoist*, later was associated with *The Little Review*, and worked tirelessly to promote himself and the writers whom he believed in through the pages of these and any other journals open to modern work. His passionate interests included music, painting, sculpture, and philosophy, and these all contributed, aided in particular by Hulme's theories on "images," "accuracy," and their relationship to language, to his development around 1912, along with Richard Aldington, H.D., and F. S. Flint, of the ideas of imagism. The principles stressed compression, complexity, concrete presentation, economy of language, and variety of rhythm. The two-line poem "In a Station of the Metro" is the example most often printed. This pictorial style dovetailed with Pound's work on the manuscripts that the widow of orientalist scholar Ernest Fenollosa gave him in 1913, and which resulted in the translations of *Cathay* in 1915. In both the oriental translations and the imagist poems economy of language worked with a pictorial focus, a lack of explicit connectives, and juxtaposition, to produce a heightened moment of emotional intensity. Meanwhile, through his interest in the vorticist movement, particularly the writing and painting of Wyndham Lewis, Pound was associated with the two issues of the aggressively iconoclastic journal *Blast*. Vorticism stressed dynamic force rather than the pictorial stasis of imagism. The poetry of Yeats and the theories and writing of Ford Madox Ford continued to be major interests of Pound's, and he met T. S. Eliot for the first time in September 1914. Out of this mix of developments came *Lustra* (1916), a volume of free verse poems which also included the poems of *Cathay*.

But with the coming of war, opportunities to promote a revolution in the arts dried up. A particular blow to Pound was his close friend vorticist sculptor Henri Gaudier-Brzeska being killed in France in June 1915. Pound moved towards what would become a career-long interest in alternatives to the contemporary economic and political systems that he saw on both sides of the conflict as stifling the arts, and producing the needless and self-serving destruction of the war. "There died a myriad, / And of the best, among them," he wrote in *Hugh Selwyn Mauberley*, "For an old bitch gone in the teeth, / For a botched civilization."

Pound left London permanently in 1920 for France, settling in Paris in 1921. In the three years before this move his important publications included *Homage to Sextus Propertius* (1919) and *Hugh Selwyn Mauberley* the following year. Both marked steps towards what would after 1920 become Pound's life's work, *The Cantos* (although he had begun publishing a version of the earliest cantos in 1917). Both the *Homage* and *Hugh Selwyn Mauberley* find a way to bring together in a longer sequence contemporary concerns and recent and distant history, using irony and shifting styles, attitudes, and responses to represent the poem's full temporal and historical reach. The method of the *Cantos* is a development of this discovery, while the structure of Eliot's *The Waste Land* is also indebted to their achievement. *Homage to Sextus Propertius* is Pound's version of the *Elegies* of the first-century BC Roman poet. In 1931 he wrote of the poem that it "presents certain emotions as vital to me in 1917, faced with the infinite and ineffable imbecility of the British Empire, as they were to Propertius some centuries earlier, when faced with the infinite and ineffable imbecility of the Roman Empire" (*Selected Letters*, 231). These shared concerns, as Pound saw them, included trying to remain a writer with integrity in a time of war when under pressure to write what amounted to imperialist propaganda. The poem was also another of Pound's blasts at the academic establishment, this time for its neglect as he saw it of Propertius.

*Hugh Selwyn Mauberley* foregrounds more contemporary cultural and political history, although tracing its theme of present philistine decadence back to what Pound saw as the influence and decline of Christianity. "Christ follows Dionysus // . . . Even the Christian beauty / Defects – after [i.e. as did the cult of] Samothrace." The poem is divided into two halves and within them into sections. Although it is not reducible to easy parallels with Pound's life, it is often read as reflecting two aspects of his interests and career up to that point. "E.P.," the persona of the first half, is presented as a writer of good intentions ("born / In a half savage country, out of date"), who tried to bring the best of the past's literary achievements into contemporary writing and culture. He finds only a philistine audience preferring to settle for something much less demanding. E.P.'s failure to find a wider readership or to extend his work beyond sophisticated pastiche of past masters is put into the context of the failure of the Pre-Raphaelite painters and writers, the failure of the poets of the 1890s such as Ernest Dowson and Lionel Johnson, and the inevitable drift into war. Mauberley, on the other hand, in the poem's second half, is an imagist who fades into oblivion on the stream of his heightened and finally irrelevant intensities, a small master of a minor art. But although the poem displays the limitations of these two sides of Pound's career, broadly drawn, the poem itself helped give him an answer. It showed a way for the *Cantos* to use juxtaposition within a sentence, stanza, or section, or between cantos, to present multiple levels of time, different cultures, and the central figures that Pound saw representing them, all within a framework in which connections accumulated suggestion, rather than becoming reductively definitive. Thus the poem could demand full attention from a reader required to fill out and connect the allusions sketched sometimes only by a phrase or word.

When *A Draft of XVI Cantos* appeared in 1925 Pound and his wife had moved from Paris to Rapallo, Italy. In Paris his circuit had included Joyce and Ford Madox Ford, as well as many of the American expatriates, including Hemingway. In 1921 Eliot left with him the draft of *The Waste Land* for suggestions, and the poem was published the following year much as Pound had left it after cutting it down considerably in length, and eliminating many surface continuities. As a mark of gratitude Eliot dedicated the landmark poem to him.

Pound's interests in the late 1920s and the 1930s increasingly focused on economics, particularly the social credit theories of Major C. H. Douglas, and on politics, although his root concern was always the impact upon writing and a culture's treatment of its writers. In his tendency to view an age as summed up in the actions of a single figure, he came to see Mussolini's policies as representing the kind of social and monetary reform that he was advocating. This attraction to fascism, combined with an increasing tendency on Pound's part to equate what he condemned as the parasitical effects of usury (see Canto XLV) with world Jewry, led to his sometimes virulent anti-Semitism. Such views come into the Cantos of these years, for this "poem including history" was to include also the history of its maker. Pound began broadcasting his literary and political views over Rome radio in 1941 and was arrested by the US army on charges of treason at the war's end and imprisoned near Pisa.

The *Cantos* start with a series of beginnings: the descent to the underworld of book XI of the *Odyssey*, a ritual blood-drinking with prophet Tiresias, a voyage, and a search. The general themes of the poem take up the first seven cantos. Cantos VIII–XI explore the career and impact of the fifteenth-century Venetian soldier and art patron Sigismundo Malatesta, and, after a passage through the modern hell of London, in Canto 17 medieval Venice serves as a vision of paradise. The middle cantos, XXXI–LXXI, explore the policies of some early US presidents (Jefferson, John Quincy Adams, Van Buren, and John Adams), and the history of ancient China, which Pound saw as at its most prosperous and peaceful when governed by Confucian ethics. Cantos LXXIV–LXXXIV, the Pisan Cantos, were written under the extreme conditions of Pound's arrest and confinement. He was initially held in a cage, and later housed in a tent, with the loan of a typewriter for a few hours in the evening and just a handful of books to consult. For many readers these are the finest cantos. In them the destruction of the poet's personal life (he faced execution) and of his literary and social hopes are at the center of a remarkable sequence that blends sharp observation of the camp and its surroundings, memories of friendships, plans and achievements in worlds now irrevocably past, and a sometimes humble, sometimes defiant personal reflection. The sequence was published in 1948 and the following year awarded the first Bollingen Prize for Poetry by a jury that included T. S. Eliot, W. H. Auden, and Robert Lowell. Pound was by now housed in St. Elizabeths Hospital in Washington, DC, having been declared insane and thus not fit for trial. The resulting political controversy over Pound winning the prize resulted in its future management being taken away from the control of the Library of Congress and given to Yale University.

Pound continued his reading and translations in St. Elizabeths, received many visitors, and increasingly became a figure whose work was looked to by those seeking an alternative to the tenets of formalism. He also continued *The Cantos. Section: Rock-Drill* (LXXXV–XCV) appeared in 1955, and *Thrones* (XCVI–CIX) in 1959, the year after he was released from St. Elizabeths and the charges of treason dropped. However, *The Cantos* were never finished, and Pound sometimes expressed the opinion late in his life that his massive and ambitious project had failed. *Drafts and Fragments* of cantos 110–17 was published in 1968. Pound spent most of his last years in Venice, where he died and is buried, having outlived all of the major modernist peers upon whom his life and work had such an impact.

## Bibliography

*Personae: The Shorter Poems of Ezra Pound*, ed. Lea Baechler and A. Walton Litz (New York, 1990).
*The Cantos of Ezra Pound* (New York, 1995).
*The Selected Letters of Ezra Pound: 1907–1941*, ed. D. D. Paige (New York, 1971); originally published as *The Letters of Ezra Pound* (New York, 1950).

Christine Froula, *A Guide to Ezra Pound's Selected Poems* (New York, 1983).
Hugh Kenner, *The Pound Era* (Berkeley, 1971).
Lawrence Rainey, *Ezra Pound and the Monument of Culture* (Chicago, 1991).
Carroll F. Terrell, *A Companion to the Cantos of Ezra Pound* (Berkeley, 1993).

# H.D. (Hilda Doolittle; 1886–1961)

For much of her writing career and for some years after her death H.D. was often associated first and foremost with her own particular mythologically grounded form of imagism, but her achievement – particularly as viewed in the United States – has since come to be seen much more broadly, and has been the subject of much critical discussion. Her later poetry, especially the *Trilogy* that she wrote in London during the Second World War, is now viewed as a remarkable act of poetic renewal, and a poem to be discussed alongside *The Cantos*, *Paterson*, and *The Waste Land*. H.D.'s prose work offers the bonus of striking portraits of some of the central figures important at various points in her life, including D. H. Lawrence, Richard Aldington, Ezra Pound, and Sigmund Freud.

Hilda Doolittle was born in Bethlehem, Pennsylvania, and grew up in the Moravian Church. Her father was a professor of astronomy, first at Lehigh University and subsequently at the University of Pennsylvania. In 1896 the family moved to a suburb of Philadelphia. H.D. attended Bryn Mawr briefly, but dropped out in 1906 after three semesters. By that time she had met two University of Pennsylvania students interested in poetry, Ezra Pound and William Carlos Williams, and for a brief period was engaged to Pound. In 1911 she settled in London, and became part of the imagist group alongside Pound, Richard Aldington, T. E. Hulme and F. S. Flint. In 1912 Pound sent a batch of her poems, signed "H.D. Imagiste," along with some of Aldington's, to *Poetry* in Chicago, where they were published by Harriet Monroe. H.D.'s poems then began to appear in *The Egoist*, where Aldington served as literary editor until he went off to war, upon which H.D. herself took over the position, to be followed by T. S. Eliot.

H.D. married Aldington in 1913, but the marriage was not successful. A daughter, Perdita, born in 1919, was not Aldington's, and in that year the couple split up, although they were not divorced until 1938. In 1914 H.D. began a close, apparently platonic, personal friendship with D. H. Lawrence that covered four years and is recorded in her novel *Bid Me To Live* (written in 1939, published in 1960), although the narrative centers upon her relationship with Aldington. But the crucial personal meeting in these years was with the writer Bryher (Winifred Ellerman) in 1918. After the break-up with Aldington, the wealthy Bryher became variously friend, companion, lover, and financial protector to H.D. for the rest of the poet's life, although they did not live together after 1946.

In these years of dramatic change in her personal life H.D. published her first books of poems, *Sea Garden* (1916), *Hymen* (1921), and *Heliodora and Other Poems* (1924). The poetry of these books conforms broadly to imagist principles, and often uses figures from classical myth to give a voice to the commands, evocations, or descriptions within the poem. There is typically more dynamic movement and emotional intensity in the poems than in Pound's imagist work. As some critics have noticed, the undercurrent of powerful emotion seems barely contained by the ostensible subject or speaker in a number of the poems written after 1916–17. The subject might appear more straightforward in the earlier work. In "Oread," for example, the mythological mountain nymph of the title who is the speaker of the short poem calls for the sea's "pointed pines" – imagined as a parallel to the forested mountain – to "cover us." But while the concrete detail and pictorial transference within the poem justify its place as one of the most anthologized examples of imagism, the call to be covered has led a number of critics to note additionally the recurring theme of a "buried life" in H.D.'s poems. Similarly, other poems present pictorially a "border" existence, between extremes (see for example the early "Sea Rose"). The poems in the second and third books more overtly concern gendered authority and the repression of female sexuality and Otherness, both heterosexual and homosexual: poems such as "Helen," "Leda," and "At Baia," and the series of poems that amplify and comment upon Sapphic fragments. Three of the Sappho poems "Fragment Forty-one," "Fragment Forty," and "Fragment Sixty-eight," all from *Heliodora*, are revisions of unpublished poems much more personally revealing in their earlier versions. Sappho, like many of the classical and mythological speakers in these poems, serves to expand through allusion the poet's voice and themes across time and circumstance, but also in a sense to bury them. Some more explicitly autobiographical poems, such as "I Said," a poem written to Bryher in winter 1919, remained unpublished for many years after H.D.'s death. Responding to this aspect of H.D.'s poetry, Lawrence urged her to bring the emotion of the poems more to the surface, to make them less abstract, but H.D. in turn thought Lawrence's poems too artless and often too fragmentary.

In the early 1920s H.D. traveled extensively with Bryher, including trips to Greece, California, and Egypt, and worked on her first novels. In 1927 she began a personal and professional relationship with filmmaker Kenneth Macpherson and appeared in his silent films *Foothills* (1928) and *Borderline*, the latter in 1930 alongside Paul Robeson. She began psychotherapy in London in 1931, and became a patient of Sigmund Freud's in 1933 and 1934, crediting him with helping the renewal of her creative powers and self-confidence. H.D. wrote a good deal of poetry in the 1930s, and continued her translations from the Greek, but published relatively little of the results.

What for many readers and critics is a remarkable creative renaissance began when H.D. spent the years of the Second World War in London. At this time she wrote a memoir, *Tribute to Freud*, of the figure who became both mentor and male antagonist to her, and the autobiographical prose work *The Gift* (1941–3) which concerns her family history and Moravian origins. But most significant is the *Trilogy* (1942–4), a long poem consisting of *The Walls Do Not Fall*, *Tribute to the Angels*, and *The Flowering of the Rod*. Here the trials of the London Blitz are paralleled to the history of ancient Egypt, while the poem synthesizes the Judaeo-Christian tradition and the Egyptian and Greek pagan traditions in its assertion of faith that love and hope will bring resurrection out of the ruins. In the poem's final lines the Magi present their gifts in acknowledgment of this hope.

The years following the war were difficult but continued to be productive for H.D. She moved to Switzerland, but mental and physical difficulties necessitated her residence at a sanitarium. Her *Selected Poems* appeared in 1957, and she completed a long poem, *Helen in Egypt* (1961) and the prose volume *End to Torment: A Memoir of Ezra Pound* (published in 1979). In 1956 she visited the United States for the first time in 35 years, and again in 1960 when she received the Gold Medal Award from the American Academy of Arts and Letters, the first woman to receive it. Since her death in 1961 she has become for many the central female modernist poet, a figure who was unfairly neglected in her lifetime. Her former consignment to a historical role as an associate of the imagists is seen as a result of her subject matter and gender. The experimental fiction and personal essays have received almost as much attention as the poetry. Denise Levertov, Adrienne Rich, and Robert Duncan are among the poets who have acknowledged a debt to her work. The *Collected Poems 1912–1944* (1983), as well as the later long poems, reveal a poet much more diverse and complex than the handful of imagist poems once so frequently anthologized as representative of her work might suggest.

## Bibliography

H.D., *Collected Poems 1912–1944*, ed. Louis L. Martz (New York, 1983).
—— *Trilogy*, with notes by Aliki Barnstone (New York, 1998).

Rachel Blau DuPlessis, *H.D.: The Career of that Struggle* (Bloomington, IN, 1986).
Susan Edmunds, *Out of Line: History, Psychoanalysis, & Montage in H.D.'s Long Poems* (Stanford, CA, 1994).
Susan Stanford Friedman, *Psyche Reborn: The Emergence of H.D.* (Bloomington, IN, 1981).

# Robinson Jeffers (1887–1962)

Robinson Jeffers was committed to writing of modern life in his poetry, but saw in the example of the modernists a limitation both of theme and technical possibility that he was determined to avoid in his own work. In long narrative poems, shorter lyrics, and plays, often written in a long Whitmanesque line, he articulated his theme of the final insignificance of human life alongside the power of nature and of the corruption of what was inevitably a doomed civilization. He wrote his poems while living his life on the edge of the Pacific, in a stone cottage and tower that he built with his own hands. Many of the poems are filled with the surrounding landscape and people, although Jeffers's poems also often apply his view of the human condition to national and international politics. In his self-imposed isolation and self-sufficiency Jeffers lived an alternative to the "gathered vast populations incapable of free survival, insulated / From the strong earth" that he condemned in his poem "The Purse-Seine."

Jeffers was born in Pittsburgh, where his father was a professor at the Western Theological Seminary, and he received a cosmopolitan education including training in the classics, knowledge of French, German, and Italian, and stints at a number of boarding schools in Europe. His family moved to California in 1904, where Jeffers graduated from Occidental College at the age of 18. He continued graduate study for a number of years, variously at the University of Zurich, the University of Southern California, and the

University of Washington, undecided between his interests in medicine and in forestry. He published two early books of derivative poems, *Flagons and Apples* in 1912, and *Californians* in 1916, before finding his own voice with the 1924 volume *Tamar, and other Poems*.

Jeffers went on to a good deal of critical and popular success in the 1920s and 1930s with a series of volumes that articulated his theme, influenced by his reading of Nietzsche, of a necessary stoicism against the power, violence, and beauty of nature. His adaptation of Euripedes' *Medea* (1946) was a great success in New York, with the title role played by Judith Anderson, and this triumph brought him national attention. But his view of the Second World War as a prime example of the human propensity to self-destruction was not a popular one. His 1948 volume, *The Double Axe and Other Poems*, now considered by some critics his finest, appeared with a disclaimer from the publisher, who had also insisted upon some of the intended poems being removed. He insists in his late poem "Carmel Point": "We must uncenter our minds from ourselves; / We must unhumanize our views a little, and become confident / As the rock and ocean that we were made from." And his stoic pessimism is summed up in the lines from "The Deer Lay Down their Bones" (1954): "We have been given life and have used it – not a great gift perhaps – but in honesty / Should use it all. Mine's empty since my love died –."

The "love" in these lines is Jeffers's wife, Una Kuster, who had died of cancer in 1950. The two met in 1906 when she was already married, and married in 1913 following her divorce. She became an important muse and subject in his work. Together they moved to what was then the village of Carmel, and Jeffers designed Tor House on Carmel Point for their home, apprenticing himself to the building contractor and thus learning stonemasonry. Electricity was not installed until 1949. Between 1920 and 1924 Jeffers added, entirely by himself, the 40-foot Hawk Tower, and both stone structures figure largely in his poetry. Following the death of his wife, Jeffers lived on in Tor House with his family, although increasing illness forced him to give up writing in 1958. The house and tower are now preserved as a historic landmark.

Commentators have often noted the recurrence of the rock and hawk symbols in Jeffers's verse, and their significance has been variously described. In his poem "Rock and Hawk" Jeffers juxtaposes a number of the qualities:

> bright power, dark peace;
> Fierce consciousness joined with final
> Disinterestedness:
>
> Life with calm death; the falcon's
> Realist eyes and act
> Married to the massive

> Mysticism of stone,
> Which failure cannot cast down
> Nor success make proud.

The unblinking look at what he saw as the powerlessness of humanity against the forces of nature, and the sense of perspective that he argued for in the light of this reality, characterize Jeffers's poems at their best. Along with this theme, Jeffers's poems emphasize the inevitable suffering inherent in nature and in the human condition, and he wrote poems rivaling those of D. H. Lawrence in their treatment of violence and their frankness about sexuality. Jeffers's achievement, both in his longer narrative poems and his short lyrics, is one that, while having comparatively little influence upon later poets, nevertheless demands recognition as one significant alternative to the direction taken by the modernist poets.

## Bibliography

The Collected Poetry of Robinson Jeffers, ed. Tim Hunt, 5 vols. (Stanford, CA, 1988–2001).

William Everson, The Excesses of God: Robinson Jeffers as a Religious Figure (Stanford, CA, 1988).

William Henry Nolte, Rock and Hawk: Robinson Jeffers and the Romantic Agony (Athens, GA, 1978).

Robert Zaller, The Cliffs of Solitude: A Reading of Robinson Jeffers (Cambridge, 1983).

—— ed., Centennial Essays for Robinson Jeffers (Newark, DE, 1991).

# Marianne Moore (1887–1972)

Marianne Moore's poetry was greatly admired by her fellow poets. William Carlos Williams often praised the precision of her observations and language, while T. S. Eliot, in his introduction to her Selected Poems, cited her as "one of those few who have done the language some service in my lifetime." W. H. Auden also wrote admiringly of her work, as did Ezra Pound. But it was not until her Collected Poems (1951) garnered the National Book Award and the Pulitzer and Bollingen prizes that she gained a wider fame. She became something of a national celebrity in later years through her much-reported and photographed enthusiasm for baseball.

Moore's poetry exhibits many standard modernist characteristics: allusion through quotation, economy of expression, fragmentation, and elliptical statement. But the result, when combined with her distinctive use of syllabic verse, her subject matter, her wit and reticence, and poems that variously are discursive, cumulative, or meditative in their development, is a body of work entirely her own and like that of no other modernist.

Moore was born in Kirkwood, a suburb of St. Louis, but grew up in Carlisle, Pennsylvania. She graduated from Bryn Mawr College in 1909, and spent a year at Carlisle Commercial College. Following four years teaching at the United States Indian School at Carlisle, she moved with her mother to New York City, where she worked from 1921 to 1925 at a branch of the New York Public Library. She became editor of the important literary magazine *The Dial* in 1926, staying until its demise in 1929.

Outside of college publication, Moore's poems first appeared in 1915 in *The Egoist*, *Others*, and *Poetry*. From the first the poems display the precision of language and close observation that characterize all of her work. The opening lines of "Poetry" show many of these characteristics:

> I too, dislike it: there are things that are important
> beyond all this fiddle.
> Reading it, however, with a perfect contempt for it,
> one discovers that there is in
> it after all, a place for the genuine.

The lines capture the voice of many of Moore's poems, personable but reticent, and the disciplined perspective – making no grandiose, unsupported claims, but looking carefully at and celebrating what is there. The lines also display Moore's precision and economy in another way, for a version of these three lines of what was in 1924 a poem ten times as long are all that she published of "Poetry" in her *Complete Poems* (1967), while the rest of the poem appeared in a note.

Such economy and precision are characteristics of the imagism dominant at the time that Moore's poems first appeared, but she is no imagist. Equally, her treatment in "A Grave" of a theme characteristic of Robinson Jeffers, the power of the sea against the arrogance of mankind trying to tame it and use it, marks the very different qualities of her work. In Moore's poem there is some sympathy for human ambition, and for human fear, and her emphasis is finally upon the multitudinous and insouciant ocean life rather than its elemental power and endurance. Many of Moore's poems begin with close observation of a plant, bird, or animal, and move from the close analytical inspection of appearance and movement to a meditation upon the larger significance of the particular qualities. Often there is comparison to social and moral values, to human behavior, or to the act of writing itself. For example, Moore's famous poem "The Pangolin" begins "Another armored animal – scale / lapping scale with spruce-cone regularity until they / form the uninterrupted central / tail-row!" This careful record is subsequently juxtaposed to an example of religious decoration, a "wrought-iron vine" in Westminster Abbey. This brings a meditation upon spiritual and physical grace, decoration, and the importance of self-deprecating wit and self-knowledge to the contradictory, fearful, but finally celebrated "being we call human, writing- / master to this world."

Moore spent many hours in such places as the American Museum of Natural History and the Bronx Zoo observing and gathering the factual detail that fills her poems. But these facts are taken in a Moore poem into an unfolding series of shifting and enriching contexts, and are thus the starting point of connections explored with a rigor both logical and imaginative. Poetry presents "imaginary gardens with real toads in them," as she put it in one of the excised lines in "Poetry." In another part of the poem also relegated to the notes in later publication, she characterizes poets as "literalists of / the imagination." This phrase is itself, as Moore's note to the line points out, a paraphrase of Yeats commenting upon Blake, and gives an example of the way quotation adds to the levels and to the play of wit in Moore's poems. But quotation is not only for providing literary context in Moore's work; it is more often a mode of inclusion, albeit qualified by being set off in quotation marks. Sometimes it is remembered conversation: "My father used to say . . ." in "Silence." Or it provides an example from the multitude of written and printed material in the world, the "business documents and / / school-books," a combination cited, again, in lines excised later from "Poetry." As with the summary from Yeats, Moore's notes point out that this is itself a quotation, in this case from the diary of Tolstoy, where he argues in contrast that such material is not poetry. Sometimes the quoted material is apparently invented by Moore herself.

Moore's influential editorship of *The Dial* followed her winning the prestigious Dial Award in 1925 for her volume *Observations* published the previous year. Friends in London had published an earlier collection, *Poems*, in 1921 without her knowledge. The *Selected Poems* with Eliot's introduction appeared in 1935, and three further volumes before the multiple-prizewinning *Collected Poems*. In 1954 she published a translation of the *Fables* of La Fontaine, and in the same year was elected to the American Academy of Arts and Letters. She continued to publish prolifically into her seventies. The poetry volumes were augmented by a book of essays, another book of two lectures, and even a play, *The Absentee* – a comedy in four acts. A *Complete Poems* appeared in 1967. Among the poets who have acknowledged her influence on their work are Elizabeth Bishop, Ted Hughes, and Robert Lowell.

### Bibliography

*The Complete Poems of Marianne Moore* (New York, 1967).

Bonnie Costello, *Marianne Moore: Imaginary Possessions* (Cambridge, MA, 1981).
Jeanne Heuving, *Omissions Are Not Accidents: Gender in the Art of Marianne Moore* (Detroit, 1992).
Cristanne Miller, *Marianne Moore: Questions of Authority* (Cambridge, MA, 1995).
Robin G. Schulze, *Becoming Marianne Moore: The Early Poems, 1907–1924* (Berkeley, 2002).

# T. S. Eliot (1888–1965)

Thomas Stearns Eliot was born in St. Louis, Missouri, the youngest son of Henry Ware Eliot, a successful businessman, and Charlotte Stearns, but the family's roots were in New England. Eliot's grandfather, William Greenleaf Eliot, a Unitarian minister, had come to St. Louis from Massachusetts in 1834 and his activities included founding the school that became the University of Washington. Eliot's education at Milton Academy in 1905–6, followed by undergraduate and graduate study at Harvard (1906–10, 1911–14), reinforced the importance of New England to his development. But he was to spend most of his adult life in England, in 1927 becoming a British citizen and joining the Anglican Church. On both sides of the Atlantic, for about thirty years following the publication of *The Waste Land* in 1922, he became probably the most influential writer in English. Initially this impact was upon his fellow poets, but subsequently it was upon the dominant modes of criticism practiced in the universities. Not until the mid-1950s did important alternatives emerge to the authority and prestige of his literary criticism.

Eliot was writing both before and while at Harvard, but his verse, hitherto derivative, began a dramatic change when in 1908 he discovered Arthur Symons's *The Symbolist Movement in Literature*. This book introduced him to a number of contemporary French writers, including Rimbaud, Verlaine, and, most importantly, Jules Laforgue. In a series of poems written between 1909 and 1911, culminating in "Portrait of a Lady" and "The Love Song of J. Alfred Prufrock," Eliot adapted and developed such aspects of Laforgue's style as his incongruous juxtapositions of imagery and of diction, his detached irony and lack of emotional commitment, and his dramatic vignettes. Additionally, drawing from models in fiction, particularly the manner of Henry James, the poems present their central figures in terms of selective, concentrated, external impressions. These poems also introduce the theme common in Eliot's later work of a figure or figures in transition between states or conditions. In the case of "Portrait of a Lady" and "The Love Song of J. Alfred Prufrock," the central figure in each poem is frozen into inaction by an acute self-consciousness. The theme subsequently expands to become a social and cultural stasis in *The Waste Land*, before receiving expression as the stages of a spiritual journey in the poems following Eliot's conversion.

Eliot's introduction to contemporary French poetry was reinforced by a year in Paris, his first visit to Europe. He sailed in October 1910, and his interests included attending weekly lectures by the relativist philosopher Henri Bergson (whose views may have influenced "The Love Song of J. Alfred Prufrock"). In the fall of 1911 he returned to Harvard as a graduate student, where he studied Buddhism and a number of sacred Eastern texts, and decided to write his dissertation on the philosophy of F. H. Bradley. Bradley's skepticism invites some comparison to Eliot's own positions, most particularly Bradley's assertion of the absolute, interrelated completeness of all knowledge, a knowledge, however, which can only be apprehended partially and subjectively by any individual. In 1913 Eliot became a teaching assistant in Harvard's philosophy department, and he completed his dissertation by 1916. But by then his life had taken a direction away from that of an academic career.

The achievement of the still unpublished "Prufrock" gave way to a series of poems in these years, never subsequently collected by Eliot, which illustrate the confusion caused by the personal conflicts within the poet, largely concerning his religious views and the future direction of his life. In the summer of 1914 he again traveled to Europe, intending to complete his studies at Merton College, Oxford. He arrived in London in August 1914, and at the urging of Conrad Aiken introduced himself to Ezra Pound the following month. Pound, then at the height of his influence in the London pre-war avant-garde, brought Eliot into the circles of a number of writers and artists, and upon seeing examples of his work recognized its importance immediately. Urging Harriet Monroe of *Poetry* in Chicago to publish it, Pound declared of "The Love Song of J. Alfred Prufrock" that Eliot "has sent in the best poem I have yet had or seen from an American. . . . He has actually trained himself *and* modernized himself *on his own*." The poem eventually appeared in the June 1915 issue.

Eliot was not particularly happy at Oxford, and gradually felt the attraction of the London literary scene. He published some lighter poems based upon his life in Boston, and Wyndham Lewis published "Preludes" and "Rhapsody on a Windy Night" in the July 1915 *Blast*. The month before, in June, Eliot's circumstances changed dramatically when he married Vivien Haigh-Wood in London. The somewhat sudden marriage soon became difficult for both. Vivien had a nervous, unpredictable personality, which alongside Eliot's formality and emotional reticence produced increasing torment for both. Eliot's marriage to Vivien has been seen as the source of a number of scenes between couples in Eliot's poetry and plays, and more generally as reinforcing Eliot's distant and often ironic treatment of the emotional and physical elements of sexual attraction in his work.

Newly married in 1915, needing an income not least for Vivien's medical expenses and soon for his own, and with his interest in an academic career waning, Eliot spent two years as a schoolmaster. In 1916 the couple decided firmly to settle in London. Eliot gradually became more of a presence in the wider social and literary world there, book-reviewing extensively, and offering courses of evening lectures. Writing little verse at this time, he continued to be encouraged by Pound, but feared that "Prufrock" might turn out to be his major achievement in poetry.

In March 1917, having resigned his teaching post, Eliot joined the Colonial and Foreign department of Lloyds Bank, where he remained until joining publishers Faber & Gwyer in 1925. At the same time as joining the bank he began writing poetry again, and became particularly interested in exploring the possibilities of the quatrain form. Largely thanks to the efforts of Pound, Eliot's first book, *Prufrock and Other Observations*, was published in June, although it gained little attention. In the same month Eliot took over from H.D. as assistant editor of *The Egoist*. The Hogarth Press published his volume *Poems* in 1919, containing most of the quatrain verses, including the well-known "Sweeney Among the Nightingales." The rapid shifts within these quatrain poems are set off powerfully against the tight form, but moving on again, in this same year he began the more expansive "Gerontion." The poem is a dramatic monologue in the voice of an isolated old man who argues for the futility of history and of action. Pound later dissuaded him from using the poem as a prologue to *The Waste Land*, for which it is something of a dress rehearsal.

*The Sacred Wood* appeared in 1920: it was the first of a series of essay collections that would establish Eliot's authority as a literary critic. Three of his most influential concepts appeared in this volume or soon after. The essay "Tradition and the Individual Talent" asserts, against the Romantic tradition, the essential impersonality of the poet, and stresses the shifting but necessary relationship between contemporary expression and the record of achievement ("tradition") within which it takes its place. The idea of the "objective correlative" is developed in the essay on *Hamlet*, and argues for a necessary correspondence between the emotion generated within a work and its narrative or dramatic equivalent. In *Hamlet*, for Eliot, Shakespeare had not achieved this correspondence. Thirdly, Eliot claimed that a "dissociation of sensibility" had occurred in the seventeenth century separating thought from feeling, a separation that for Eliot characterized the condition of the contemporary Western world. Such generalizations and others became highly influential in the newly formed English departments of the major universities, suggesting both a critical vocabulary and a methodology for analyzing contemporary writing and relating it to work of the past.

In 1921 Eliot began writing in earnest the poem that was to become *The Waste Land* when published the following year. The history of the poem's composition, and Pound's vital excisions and suggestions made when Eliot left the manuscript with him in Paris, can be traced in the manuscript, a facsimile of which was published in 1971. Behind the poem is Eliot's personal collapse from overwork and from the emotional strain of his marriage (he was given three months' leave from the bank, and thus had time to write the much-delayed poem). Equally important is the political, economic and social chaos in the years following the end of the First World War, and also Eliot's ideas about the relationship of the contemporary world to the history and values of a broad range of past cultures as expressed through the poem's multiple and complex allusions to anthropology and literature. Different readings of the poem give different weight to these various components. Readings range from seeing the poem as arguing the impossibility of any coherence on a personal or a cultural level beyond the disintegration that the poem enacts, to arguing that its final pages suggest a framework for resolution that is present within the poem, although not achieved by its characters. The former reading emphasizes more the immediate personal and cultural circumstances of the poem's composition; the latter views it more in the light of the spiritual search that Eliot's subsequent poems were to enact.

*The Waste Land* appeared in the first issue of *The Criterion*, a literary journal that Eliot was to edit from this first issue to its last in 1939. The following month, November 1922, it was printed in the New York journal *The Dial*. When the poem appeared in book form in Britain and the United States shortly afterwards, Eliot added "Notes" on some of its sources, a radical gesture that initially almost captured as much attention as the poem itself.

Along with editing the increasingly authoritative *Criterion*, Eliot began writing what turned out to be an unfinished play, *Sweeney Agonistes*, although he was to return to this interest in drama as a main preoccupation of the second half of his career. The chief poem from these years, "The Hollow Men," has a directness in its fusion of meter and speech that comes out of this work on playwriting. These years also marked Eliot's joining Faber & Gwyer, and thus becoming an influential figure in the publication of contemporary work, and his search for faith, which culminated in 1927 in his joining the Anglican Church. The major poem of the years immediately following his conversion, *Ash-Wednesday* (1930), reflects this spiritual search. Within its echoes of Dante and Beatrice there is also the search for a physical and emotional discipline missing in Eliot's increasingly difficult domestic life.

Eliot could not undertake sustained poetic composition for five years following *Ash-Wednesday*, although they were years that saw the continuing consolidation of his reputation as a major critic and poet. Such fallow periods in his poetry writing occurred throughout his career. In 1932, during a year teaching at Harvard, his first visit to the United States in 17 years, and after many years of mutual unhappiness, he finally took the difficult decision to take out a deed of separation from Vivien Eliot. Increasingly disoriented and upset, she was committed to a private mental hospital in 1938 for her own protection at the instigation of her personal doctor, and died suddenly in 1947 at the age of 58. Eliot had not seen her since 1935, when she approached him after he had delivered a public lecture. In his political and social views Eliot became increasingly conservative, most evidently in a series of lectures given during his American trip, at the University of Virginia in April 1933. Collected as *After Strange Gods: A Primer of Modern Heresy*, the book was later disavowed by Eliot, and he did not permit any part of it to be reprinted.

In the middle of the decade Eliot began the poems that were to become his last major poetic work, *Four Quartets* (1943), made up of "Burnt Norton," "East Coker," "The Dry Salvages," and "Little Gidding." They again reflect Eliot's interest in a poetry closer to direct speech than the dense, allusive fragmentation of *The Waste Land* – in fact, the first of the series, "Burnt Norton," developed from some passages that Eliot took out of his 1935 play *Murder in the Cathedral*. The sequence is structured around four locations important to the poet. East Coker, for example, was the village from which his ancestor Andrew Eliot had traveled across the Atlantic more than two centuries earlier, while the Dry Salvages are a ledge of rock off Cape Ann, Massachusetts, where Eliot sailed as a boy. Each quartet is also based upon one of the four elements. The poems meditate upon time, history, language, and the spiritual condition, and while for some readers the sequence is the culmination of Eliot's work, for others its discursiveness represents a retreat into abstraction and away from the intensity and originality of his earlier work.

Much of Eliot's major writing in his final years was devoted to his interest in verse drama, and his plays met with varying degrees of success. Although *Murder in the Cathedral* concerned the twelfth-century murder of Thomas Becket, Eliot wanted his later plays to deal with contemporary life. *The Family*

*Reunion* (1939) was followed by *The Cocktail Party* (1950), *The Confidential Clerk* (1954), and *The Elder Statesman* (1959). The plays represent Eliot's attempt to combine verse with the popular stage, and in *The Cocktail Party* he came closest to commercial success.

In 1948 Eliot was awarded the Nobel Prize for Literature. A measure of his fame in the 1950s is the crowd of 14,000 that gathered to hear him lecture on April 30, 1956, in a baseball stadium at the University of Minnesota. In 1957 he married his secretary of eight years, Valerie Fletcher. By all accounts these last years before his death in 1965 and burial at East Coker were the happiest emotionally of a complex man often suffering and isolated beneath his appearance of order and formality.

### Bibliography

*The Complete Poems and Plays of T. S. Eliot* (London, 1969).
*Selected Prose of T. S. Eliot*, ed. Frank Kermode (London, 1975).

Ronald Bush, *T. S. Eliot: A Study in Character and Style* (New York, 1983).
Maud Ellmann, *The Poetics of Impersonality: T. S. Eliot and Ezra Pound* (Cambridge, MA, 1987).
Helen Gardner, *The Composition of Four Quartets* (New York, 1978).

# John Crowe Ransom (1888–1974)

In the title of his 1941 book of critical essays *The New Criticism*, John Crowe Ransom supplied a name to a movement. "New Criticism" argued for discovering meaning in close textual analysis of the internal relationships within a work (usually a poem), rather than its context within a period, or within its author's oeuvre. Such a view of the function of criticism, and the writing of poetry that mirrored its values, had been developing out of Ransom's work and that of others since the 1920s, and in 1941 was about to enter the two decades of its greatest influence. The critics whom Ransom discussed in the book, along with his own views, were among the most influential in the movement: I. A. Richards, William Empson, Yvor Winters, and T. S. Eliot. Ransom's immediate affinities, however, were with a group of southern poet-critics known as the Fugitives and centered initially upon Vanderbilt University. Ransom's own poetry mostly had been written by 1927, when he published his third volume of verse, although in turning to criticism and editorial work he continued to revise his poems. In fundamental ways the poetry and critical principles of the New Critics went hand in hand, their values founded on a search for order represented, in the poetry, by formal composition. They advocated an intellectual rigor expressed through such characteristics as emotional restraint, irony, complexity, wit, and ambiguity, and contrasting with what they saw as Romantic indiscipline and excess. The multiple complexities of a poem, they argued, could mirror the multiple complexities of the world itself, and the job of the poet was to supply such complexity, and that of the ideal reader/critic to discover and respond to it.

Ransom was born in Pulaski, Tennessee, the son of a Methodist minister. After graduating from Vanderbilt in 1909 he attended Christ Church, Oxford, as a Rhodes scholar, returning to Vanderbilt to begin teaching in 1914. His education included extensive study in Greek and Latin texts in the original languages. He returned to Europe for two years with the United States army, finishing in 1919, the year in which he published the first of his three books of poems, *Poems About God*. However, Ransom chose never to republish these early poems.

Back at Vanderbilt, along with a group that included Donald Davidson and Allen Tate, Ransom founded *The Fugitive* in 1922. In this journal, which ran until 1925, he published many of his mature poems. These were later collected in *Chills and Fever* (1924) and *Two Gentlemen in Bonds* (1927). He later published three editions of his *Selected Poems*, in 1945, 1963, and 1969. The poems dealing with death are frequently anthologized, for they illustrate well the detached, ironic, shifting attitudes in a Ransom poem in the face of an event that could in another poet produce emotional outburst or cliché. "Here Lies a Lady" recounts in language successively tender, colloquial, elegant, concrete, sympathetic, and self-consciously archaic the illness of "a lady of beauty and high degree." The suffering and loss is summarized in the last line as "six quick turns of quaking, six of burning," but the serious intent of the poem is never far away, including its religious dimension. The range of responses embedded in the poem's language is held together by the speaker's tolerance for and even interest in such intellectual and emotional complexity, just as the poem itself is held together by its rigorous rhyme scheme. There are similar effects in the well-known "Bells for John Whiteside's Daughter," where vitality in life is contrasted with a death that looks like merely a temporary repose. The concluding emotional response, "vexed," in "vexed at her brown study, / Lying so primly propped" is curiously formal and restrained, although for reasons, the poem implies, connected with the mystery of life and death which is itself at the heart of the poem's concerns. Archaic diction in "Dead Boy" works similarly: "But the little man quite dead, / I see the forbears' antique lineaments." Importantly, none of these moments are representative of their poem's whole stance and tone, but are part of the play of interrelated perspectives held together by the poem's structure. Similarly, in his criticism Ransom distinguished between the "structure" and "texture" of a work.

The characteristics of such poems owed something to the practice of John Donne, and the New Critics followed Eliot in arguing for the importance of Donne and the school of metaphysical poetry, prizing its wit, religious grounding, and intelligence. But although Ransom shared this and a number of other important critical and social concepts with Eliot, his criticism did not, any more than his poetry, advocate the direction of high modernism represented by *The Waste Land*. Ransom did not share any of Tate's enthusiasm for Eliot's poem. Ransom's values were tied to an agrarian vision of an ordered, racially segregated, aristocratic South set against the chaos of the industrialized North. His prose volume *God Without Thunder* (1930) tied this order to a return to religious values, although by his 1938 *The World's Body* poetry is offered as a possible alternative to religion.

In 1937 Ransom began teaching at Kenyon College in Ohio, and in 1939 founded *The Kenyon Review*, which he edited until his retirement in 1959, and which he turned into a major literary journal. *The Kenyon Review* thus became part of Ransom's important legacy, which, along with his poems, included his influence upon such students of his as Tate, Randall Jarrell, Robert Penn Warren, Cleanth Brooks, and Robert Lowell. Later poets who are seen as following his direction include John Berryman, W. S. Merwin, Howard Nemerov, Melvin Tolson, and James Merrill. Ransom's multiple contributions were recognized by his being awarded the Bollingen Prize for Poetry in 1951.

### Bibliography

John Crowe Ransom, *Selected Poems*, 3rd edn. (New York, 1991).

Mark Jancovich, *The Cultural Politics of the New Criticism* (Cambridge, 1993).
Mark G. Malvasi, *The Unregenerate South: The Agrarian Thought of John Crowe Ransom, Allen Tate, and Donald Davidson* (Baton Rouge, 1997).
Miller Williams, *The Poetry of John Crowe Ransom* (New Brunswick, NJ, 1972).

# Claude McKay (1890–1948)

Claude McKay was born in Jamaica of a farming family, but received an education from an older brother who was a school teacher, with whom he went to live at the age of 6. He went on to spend most of his adult life in the

United States and Europe, and is best known for his volume *Harlem Shadows*. The book is one of the foundation texts of the Harlem Renaissance, and has also been seen as one of the inspirations for the 1960s Black Arts movement. He was the most militant of the Harlem Renaissance writers.

McKay's first two books of poems were published while he still lived in Jamaica. Both *Songs of Jamaica* and *Constab Ballads* appeared in 1912. The poems in both are written in dialect, and include local folklore and, in the case of the latter, material from McKay's brief service as a policeman. These books brought him some local recognition and the resources to journey to the United States. He studied farming briefly at Tuskegee Institute, and then at Kansas State College from 1912 to 1914, following which he moved to Harlem. Supporting himself by odd jobs, he became interested in socialist causes and gradually his poems began to be published regularly in the US and England. By 1920 he had been living in England for a year when he published the poems of *Spring in New Hampshire* in London. He returned to Harlem the following year, and in 1922 published *Harlem Shadows*.

Like another founding figure of the Harlem Renaissance, Countee Cullen, McKay wrote his poems of the black experience in traditional verse forms, usually sonnets or short lyrics in the English Romantic mode. Thus their importance comes from their content rather than, as with Langston Hughes, any formal innovation. Not all of the poems concern the Harlem scene; some are nostalgic recollections of and yearning for a homeland left behind, while others conventionally extol nature or love. But those on Harlem combine a concreteness of description and a militancy that were liberating for some young black writers. His "The Harlem Dancer" brings out the distance and alienation felt by the young performer behind the seductive pleasures offered by her dance, and enjoyed and then questioned by the poem's observer. The well-known "If We Must Die" is a response to the anti-black race riots in Chicago and other cities in 1919 and calls for "fighting back!" and not passively accepting the violence. "The Lynching" concerns, as well as the violence of the murder, the indoctrination of race hatred into the next generation; "America" articulates a response both fascinated and appalled at the "cultured hell" that surrounds him, while "The Negro's Tragedy" insists that "Only a thorn-crowned Negro and no white / Can penetrate into the Negro's ken. . . . / There is no white man who could write my book."

McKay's interests led him to work on the left-wing magazines *The Liberator* and *New Masses*, and he also traveled to Moscow in 1922 as a representative of the American Workers' Party at the Third Internationale, where he met Lenin and Trotsky. Following this trip he remained in Europe for the next

12 years, mainly in France and North Africa. His interests turned to writing prose and he published a number of novels and two autobiographical works in these years, the most notable being the novels *Home to Harlem* (1928), *Banjo* (1929), and *Banana Bottom* (1933).

In his last years McKay wrote less, and he repudiated his earlier interest in communism. He became a US citizen in 1940, converted to Catholicism in the early 1940s, and taught for Catholic organizations in Chicago until his death. The late sonnets "Look Within" and "Tiger" illustrate McKay's continuing commitment to revealing the injustices of race. His *Selected Poems* were published posthumously in 1953.

### Bibliography

Claude McKay, *Selected Poems* (New York, 1953).
*The Passion of Claude McKay: Selected Poetry and Prose, 1912–1948*, ed. Wayne F. Cooper (New York, 1973).

Heather Hathaway, *Caribbean Waves: Relocating Claude McKay and Paule Marshall* (Bloomington, IN, 1999).
*Claude McKay: Centennial Studies*, ed. A. L. McLeod (New Delhi, India, 1992).
Tilley Tyrone, *Claude McKay: A Black Poet's Struggle for Identity* (Amherst, 1992).

# E. E. Cummings (1894–1962)

The popularity of Edward Estlin Cummings's poetry has never been fully matched by his critical reputation. For unsympathetic readers, the visual and syntactic complications of his verse are undercut by the simplicity, even naivety, of its themes and sentiments. For the New Critics of the 1940s and 1950s, Cummings's visual and verbal inventiveness masked a sensibility essentially late Romantic rather than modernist. But for some readers Cummings achieved a fresh, expressive vocabulary which, while unlike that of any other modernist poet, explored the possibilities of free verse in significant new ways, ways that, it can be argued, have been influential upon some later poets.

Cummings was born in Cambridge, Massachusetts, the son of a Unitarian minister who also taught sociology at Harvard. In 1915 Cummings graduated from Harvard with a BA, gaining an MA in 1916. When the United States entered the European war he served as a volunteer in France in the Norton Harjes Ambulance Corps and was imprisoned for three months on suspicion of espionage, out of which experience came his successful novel *The Enormous Room* (1922). The poetry that Cummings had been writing during and following his college years appeared soon afterwards in three books, *Tulips and Chimneys* (1923), *XLI Poems* (1925), and & (1925). His popular reputation now established by the novel and the poetry volumes, Cummings settled into a routine of living in New York and spending his summers in New Hampshire. His creative work included painting as well as writing, and his paintings were frequently exhibited in galleries over the following decades.

Although Cummings continued to publish collections of poetry up to his death, there was little substantial change in his style and themes. *Viva* (1931), *50 Poems* (1940), and *Xiape* (1950) are just three of the many volumes. Of the various collected editions, a *Collected Poems* was published in 1963, the year after the poet's death, and a scholarly edition appeared in 1991 (revised 1994), edited by George J. Firmage. The poems show the strong influence on Cummings of the first phase of modernist experiment as practiced in New York around 1915, particularly imagism and the experiments with typography. Cummings's poems praise concreteness, spontaneous feeling, eccentricity, and individualism, and scorn mass movements, consumerism, nationalism, and what he saw as the monolithic abstractions of scientific and religious thought. His poem "O sweet spontaneous," for example, excoriates "prurient philosophers," "the naughty thumb / of science," and "religions / . . . upon their scraggy knees," and demands that all be answered "with / spring." Cummings's famous poem on his father, "my father moved through dooms of love," praises him for his emotional spontaneity: "Scorning the pomp of must and shall / my father moved through dooms of feel." Similarly, timid respectability is mocked in the well-known poem beginning, "the Cambridge ladies who live in furnished souls / are unbeautiful and have comfortable minds."

Most of the poems are short lyrics either in praise of the qualities that Cummings admired, nature poems, or witty satirical pieces. Formally, the poems might break up words into syllables and sometimes into individual letters, or words may be run together with spacing eliminated, techniques that contribute to the celebration of unpredictability, and the refusal to obey set notions of form. Punctuation is used expressively rather than to demarcate thematic, grammatical, or rhythmic units. The syllables of a word might be scattered across a line between or within other words, or scattered across a poem. Parts of speech might change their conventional grammatical function, verbs becoming nouns, adverbs becoming adjectives, for example. Idiosyncrasies of spelling and capitalization might be used for punning, or to reflect speech, emphasis, or variety of rhythm, and such formal inventiveness and play sometimes also extends to a poem's visual pattern on the page.

Among Cummings's best-known poems are his praise of the lost, rugged individualism of Buffalo Bill ("Buffalo Bill's / defunct"), and another that celebrates the refusal to conform of conscientious objector "Olaf glad and big." Cummings's celebration of feeling over the abstractions of "wisdom," and the role he gives to language, love, and the seasons, is captured in the opening lines of "since feeling is first":

> since feeling is first
> who pays any attention
> to the syntax of things
> will never wholly kiss you;
>
> wholly to be a fool
> while Spring is in the world
>
> my blood approves,
> and kisses are a better fate
> than wisdom
> lady i swear by all flowers.

Cummings's publications also include his Dadaist play *Him* (1927), and *Eimi* (1933) an account in experimental diary form of his visit to Russia in 1931. In 1952 Cummings was invited to deliver the Charles Eliot Norton lectures at Harvard, and these appeared as *I: six nonlectures* in 1953.

**Bibliography**

E. E. Cummings, *Complete Poems, 1904–1962*, rev. edn., ed. George J. Firmage (New York, 1994).

Norman Friedman, *(Re)valuing Cummings: Further Essays on the Poet, 1962–1993* (Gainesville, FL, 1996).
Richard S. Kennedy, *E. E. Cummings Revisited* (New York, 1994).
Rushworth Kidder, *E. E. Cummings: An Introduction to the Poetry* (New York, 1979).

# Hart Crane (1899–1932)

The self-destructive spiral of Crane's last years, coupled with the epic ambitions of his work, have contributed to making him a figure fascinating to later American poets, most notably Robert Lowell and Allen Ginsberg. Crane appears as one of the tortured exiles in the third section of Lowell's *Life Studies*, where he speaks as "the Shelley of my age." And the continuing presence of Crane's work and spirit is asserted a number of times in Ginsberg's *Collected Poems*. Marsden Hartley and Jasper Johns have both paid tribute to him in paintings centered upon his suicide at sea.

Crane's poetry brings together the expansive, celebratory side of the poetry of Whitman on the one hand (reinforced by his admiration of Melville's prose in *Moby-Dick*), and the blend of French symbolist and seventeenth-century English metaphysical poetry that he found in the work of T. S. Eliot on the other. The resulting poetry is dense, complex, allusive, and emotionally charged, the diction sometimes archaic, but incorporating the language, sounds, and landscape of the contemporary world, especially the modern city. The poetry develops through successive juxtapositions and transformations of its central images and symbols rather than through a more conventional narrative. Crane wants to move his language beyond referentiality towards possibilities musical, symbolic, and metaphysical, his packed phrases and fragments heightening unexpected, fluid possibilities of meaning. As Crane wrote in 1925 in his "General Aims and Theories," "the terms of expression employed are often selected less for their logical (literal) significance than for their associational meanings. Via this and their metaphorical inter-relationships, the entire construction of the poem is raised on the organic principle of a 'logic of metaphor,' which antedates our so-called pure logic." Not surprisingly, Crane often found himself having to explain his use of particular words or phrases to friends and editors. Where his ambition is unsuccessful, the verse can seem forced, be almost impossibly obscure, and its expansive celebration appear driven largely by declamatory rhetoric. But where he is successful, as in parts at least of each of his major sequences and in a number of his shorter poems, the result is a texture dense, complex, and of a visionary intensity; amongst twentieth-century poets he is surpassed in these qualities only by Eliot himself.

Crane was born in Garrettsville, Ohio, the son of a successful candy manufacturer. The marriage of his parents was an unhappy, often stormy, one, and following one of their many quarrels he was sent to the home of his maternal grandmother in Cleveland, where he attended high school and began to write verse. His parents, temporarily reconciled, came to live in Cleveland, and his father introduced him to the widow of poet William Vaughn Moody. She encouraged his early interest in poetry. In 1916 Crane published his first poem, "C33," in *Bruno's Weekly*, a Greenwich Village journal friendly to modern writing, and in the same year he left for New York and met some of the writers associated with poet and editor Alfred Kreymborg. In 1918 he became associate editor of *The Pagan*, which had printed most of the dozen or so poems for which he had found publication. But this year also began the series of wanderings, with periodic returns to New York City, that were to characterize the rest of his life. Over the next five years he moved between Cleveland, Akron, and Washington, DC, working for his father until they quarreled, and variously as a reporter, as a salesman, and writing advertising copy. In 1923 he returned to New York and Greenwich Village.

An early example in Crane's mature poetry of his ability to suggest a whole history from a contemporary moment and a particular object is his short lyric "Black Tambourine." This poem dates from Crane working for his father in a Cleveland store-room in 1921 alongside a black porter. The isolation of the cellar, the insects on its floor, and the fables of Aesop come together in the last stanza to suggest a world both expansive and constricted:

> The black man, forlorn in the cellar,
> Wanders in some mid-kingdom, dark, that lies,
> Between his tambourine, stuck on the wall,
> And, in Africa, a carcass quick with flies.

In "Chaplinesque," from the same year, Crane uses Chaplin's famous tramp figure to suggest the complex emotions – the responses to pain and to authority, and the need for continued hope – that he saw at the center of the comedian's films. "Episode of Hands," a poem of controlled, quiet intensity and careful description, also dates from this period. The poem remained unpublished in Crane's lifetime, no doubt because of the generally hostile climate surrounding homosexuality at the time.

When he returned to New York Crane found employment writing advertising copy, but his drinking and his many casual sexual encounters began to border on the compulsive. Despite this dissipation, which sometimes resulted in violence or his being locked up for drunkenness, the next three or four years were among the most productive of his short career. He had read and been impressed by Eliot's *The Waste Land*, but was determined to write a poem that countered what he saw as its pessimism. In 1923 he completed and began publishing a long poem, "For the Marriage of Faustus and Helen," that demonstrates the dense, symbolic style that he was to develop most fully in "Voyages" and *The Bridge*. Crane wrote to his friend Waldo Frank in 1923 that Helen represented the "abstract 'sense of beauty,'" while Faustus was "the symbol of myself, the poetic or imaginative man of all times." He explained that the contemporary detail of the poem (which includes riding the subway, dancing to jazz music, and piloting a plane) is an attempt to display "the transition of the imagination from quotidian details to the universal consideration of beauty – the body still 'centered in traffic.'" A quieter, more personal tone governs the earlier sections of "Voyages," whose six parts were composed over the five-year period 1921–6. In these poems – their source a passionate love affair with a merchant seaman, Emil Opffer – the lover's ocean voyages are transformed by the poem's series of multiple associations into journeys that become broadly psychological and spiritual.

Both of these sequences appeared in Crane's first book of poems, *White Buildings*, published by Horace Liveright in December 1926. This was also the year in which Crane composed many of the sections of *The Bridge*, assisted by financial support from New York banker and patron of the arts Otto Kahn. Most of this composition took place at his grandmother's plantation in July and August, on the Isle of Pines in the West Indies, but the devastation of a hurricane later in the year forced him to return to New York.

By now, the excesses of Crane's behavior had begun to alienate some of his closest friends and supporters. He had shared a house with Allen and Caroline Tate, for example, in 1925, until they could take the chaotic disruptions no longer. In 1927 Crane lived for a period in Paterson, New Jersey, still working sporadically on his epic poem, and in 1928 served as traveling secretary to a stockbroker on a trip to California. At the end of the year Crane sailed for Europe, intending to settle in Majorca, but became caught up in the temptations offered by Paris. He returned to New York, made a number of other unproductive trips, but finally in the summer and fall of 1929 he completed the "Cape Hatteras," "Quaker Hill," and "Indiana" sections of *The Bridge* and revised the others. The poem was published the following year.

The title refers to New York's famous Brooklyn Bridge, completed in 1883. Crane's ambitious vision transforms the bridge into an all-inclusive symbol. This vision is centered first and foremost on the engineering triumph of the bridge itself, uniting sea and land, space and time, history and the future. But it also includes, for example, in the Cape Hatteras section, an imagined flight over the east coast made possible by the achievement of the Wright Brothers at Kitty Hawk, and in "The River" a train ride alongside the Mississippi. Conversely, in "The Tunnel" section of the poem the city's subway functions as a kind of mechanistic hell, and is haunted by the sad spirit of Edgar Allen Poe. But more characteristically the poem invokes the ecstatic vision of Whitman. In the concluding section, "Atlantis," the "cordage" of the bridge itself vibrates, its music the central accompaniment to the poem's final lyrical affirmation of inclusion: "– One Song, one Bridge of Fire!" Critical reaction upon publication of *The Bridge* was mixed, and opinion since, while always recognizing the importance of the poem, has often tended to see it as flawed, and suffering inevitably from the range of time and the differing circumstances behind the composition of its various sections.

Following the publication of his epic, Crane resolved to return to the more personal lyrics of *White Buildings*, and after another brief stint at a writing job, this time at *Fortune* magazine, he applied for a Guggenheim Fellowship. But when in spring 1931 he heard that he was successful, he decided to move to Mexico in order to research and compose an epic poem on the conquest of that country. However, his alcoholism was now seriously debilitating, and he could be drunk for days on end. This behavior continued in Mexico, where he lived in Mixcoac, near Mexico City, and sometimes at the artists' colony in Taxco. One important poem to come out of this final year that recaptures Crane's particular quality of lyrical intensity is "The Broken Tower," centered upon the church tower in Taxco's village square.

Crane began a short-lived heterosexual relationship at this time, although this did little to bring stability to his life. He threatened to commit suicide more than once, and continued to appall and alienate friends by his dissipation. In the last months of his life his father died, and two days out on a voyage back to the United States, a return trip made at the request of his stepmother to help settle the estate, and in front of a number of passengers, he threw himself into the sea from the stern of the ship. His body was never found.

### Bibliography

*The Complete Poems of Hart Crane*, ed. Marc Simon (New York, 2000).

Maria F. Bennett, *Unfractioned Idiom: Hart Crane and Modernism* (New York, 1987).
Warner Berthoff, *Hart Crane: A Re-Introduction* (Minneapolis, 1989).
R. W. B. Lewis, *The Poetry of Hart Crane: A Critical Study* (Princeton, 1967).
Thomas E. Yingling, *Hart Crane and the Homosexual Text: New Thresholds, New Anatomies* (Chicago, 1990).

# Langston Hughes (1902–1967)

Langston Hughes was the most influential and innovative of the writers associated with the Harlem Renaissance, and his prolific output included 15 volumes of poetry, as well as novels, short stories, plays, children's books, biographies, two autobiographies, histories, opera librettos, essays, articles, radio scripts, and songs for musicals. He also translated works from Spanish and French, and edited several anthologies. Hughes was the first black writer to make a living entirely from his writing, and a vital inspiration and mentor for many young black writers of the 1960s.

"Most of my own poems are racial in theme and treatment, derived from the life I know," Hughes wrote in his 1926 essay "The Negro Artist and the

Racial Mountain." In this essay Hughes describes the cultural pressures that he felt black writers faced to conform to white norms, and to see writing about black customs and black artistic expression as inferior subject matter to the white equivalents. He goes on to defend the characteristic use in his own poems of language and forms derived from jazz, blues, and other musical forms – an interest that he was to develop in innovative ways in his writing over the next 40 years. In an introductory paragraph to his 1951 long poem *Montage of a Dream Deferred* he described one version of this synthesis:

> In terms of current Afro-American popular music and the sources from which it has progressed – jazz, ragtime, swing, blues, boogie-woogie, and be-bop – this poem on contemporary Harlem, like be-bop, is marked by conflicting changes, sudden nuances, sharp and impudent interjections, broken rhythms, and passages sometimes in the manner of the jam session, sometimes the popular song, punctuated by the riffs, runs, breaks, and disc-tortions of the music of a community in transition.

Hughes was born in Joplin, Missouri, but his parents separated shortly afterwards and he grew up with his mother and maternal grandmother in Lawrence, Kansas. Upon his mother's remarriage, he went to school in Illinois, and then Cleveland, Ohio, where he began publishing verse and short stories in the school magazine. Upon graduation Hughes spent a year living with his father, now a successful businessman in Mexico, although the two clashed about Hughes's ambition to be a writer. His father supported him when he enrolled at Columbia University in September 1921, but Hughes withdrew after his first year. Hughes's poem "Theme for English B" recalls his time at Columbia and his living in Harlem. Given an assignment to write a "page" that will "come out of you," the resulting poem is an exploration of difference and similarity between black student and white instructor, the associated cultural and community tensions, and the implications for America itself as a multi-cultural community.

In his essay, "When the Negro was in Vogue," Hughes claimed that "the main reason I wanted to go to Columbia" was to see the black musical review *Shuffle Along* (among the many names associated with the show later to become famous, Eubie Blake co-wrote the music and Josephine Baker was in the chorus). Certainly the sojourn in New York proved important for Hughes's introduction to some figures associated with the Harlem Renaissance. He published one of his best-known poems, "The Negro Speaks of Rivers," in *The Crisis* the summer before attending Columbia, and met its editors Jessie Fauset and W. E. B. Du Bois, as well as meeting Countee Cullen. This poem reflects Hughes's reading of Carl Sandburg, whose work, along with that of Paul Laurence Dunbar, was an important early influence.

In a series of lines both celebratory and elegiac, the poem traces a proud heritage back to "the Euphrates when dawns were young," and the building of the pyramids alongside the Nile, while also incorporating the narrative of forced displacement, slavery, and emancipation marked by "the singing of the Mississippi when Abe Lincoln went down to New Orleans."

After withdrawing from Columbia, Hughes continued to publish poems in *The Crisis*, supporting himself with various jobs. 1923–4 saw him take two voyages as a seaman, the first on a steamship trading along the west coast of Africa, and a second during which he jumped ship to spend some months in Paris and Italy. In 1925 Hughes lived for a year with his mother in Washington, DC. He had already written and published some of his best-known early poems when he left a few examples beside the plate of Vachel Lindsay at the Wardman Park Hotel, where he was working as a busboy, and Lindsay, impressed, went on to help publicize his work.

With the assistance of New York literary figure Carl Van Vechten, Hughes found a publisher for his first book of poems, *The Weary Blues*, which appeared in 1926. The title poem concerns a blues singer on Harlem's Lenox Avenue, and the narrator's response to the performance and the emotion behind it. The poem incorporates, through repetition, sound, and stanza form, elements of the blues genre itself. The performance brings an exhausted relief to the singer, but also produces a community of suffering and release for both performer and narrator. Another well-known poem from the mid-1920s is "I, Too," in which the speaker, the "darker brother," looks forward confidently to a future when "Nobody'll dare / Say to me, / 'Eat in the kitchen,' / Then." This poem, like others in the volume and in volumes to come, allows the colloquial voice to govern the language and structure of the poem, moving black poetry and poetry about black people away from the conventions of dialect and minstrelsy stereotypes into a greater degree of realism. Such speakers also moved Hughes's poetry away from the more conventional diction of such poets as McKay and Cullen. In "Brass Spittoons," for example, the musings of the lowly hotel worker are constantly interrupted by the demands of customers, but the poem conveys in less than 40 lines the pressures of a life lived in near poverty, and the escapes – women, drink, and religion – that make it almost bearable. In his later work Hughes created the memorable Alberta K. Johnson in a series of poems in which she asserts her right to be treated with dignity even within the difficult world of menial employment, greedy landlords, and faithless lovers that her monologues reveal. In prose Hughes created a male counterpart in Jesse B. Semple.

In the same month in which his first book appeared, Hughes enrolled in the historically black Lincoln University, in Pennsylvania, graduating in 1929.

In 1927 he met Charlotte Mason, a wealthy supporter of the arts, who became his patroness for the next three years. In 1931, following his break with Mason, Hughes's work took a marked turn to the left in a series of essays and poems that he published in the radical journal *New Masses*. He began to take an interest in communism and its commitment to civil rights. He also began the work in a variety of genres that was to mark his output for the rest of his career. His first novel, *Not Without Laughter*, appeared in 1930, and he began writing plays, as well as poems and stories intended for children, and undertaking some translations. In 1932–3 he traveled to the Soviet Union and China, and in 1936 began a Guggenheim Foundation Fellowship. The year 1937 found Hughes in Europe covering the Spanish Civil War for the Baltimore *Afro-American* and other black newspapers.

Hughes's radical shift in the 1930s produced attacks upon his work in subsequent decades from various conservative groups. One of his most radical poems, "Goodbye Christ," written in the Soviet Union and first published in 1932, became material for a long racist and anti-communist campaign against him in the 1940s and early 1950s. He repudiated the poem in the period of Joseph McCarthy's congressional inquiries into "subversive activities," and was himself called before the McCarthy committee in 1953. In the poem, the church, "kings, generals, robbers, and killers –," the rich, and the mass media are all dismissed as corrupt and manipulative. "Make way for a new guy with no religion at all – / A real guy named / Marx Communist Lenin Peasant Stalin Worker ME – // I said, ME!" But Hughes's anger and militancy even in the 1930s is tempered by an idealistic strain that is essentially amelioratist. In his well-known "Let America Be America Again," even though "America never was America to me," the loss is also that of the "poor white, fooled and pushed apart," as well as "the Negro" and "red man." The promise of "the dream the dreamers dreamed" is reaffirmed. "And yet I swear this oath – / America will be!"

Hughes's verse collection *Shakespeare in Harlem* (1942) moved away from the radicalism of the previous decade, returning to the themes and forms of his 1920s poetry. But his career over the next 25 years was marked by the continuing attacks upon his work, initially by conservative, anti-communist forces – and later even by some of the more radical black writers of the 1960s for what they saw as too much compromise. Hughes himself objected to what he saw as the obscenity and profanity of much militant black writing, although he was also opposed to the high formalism of such writers as Melvin B. Tolson. He defended the moderate civil rights approach of the NAACP and Martin Luther King against their more militant critics. Meanwhile Hughes's stature as writer and public figure continued to increase.

He lectured and traveled widely both within the United States as well as in Africa and Europe. The American Academy of Arts and Letters recognized him in 1946 for his distinguished service as a writer, in 1961 he was inducted into the National Institute of Arts and Letters, and in 1964 he was honored at the annual dinner of the Poetry Society of America. His prolific and varied literary work continued right up to his death – from complications following prostate surgery in May 1967.

Among Hughes's later work in drama, musicals, and opera libretti, two notable successes were his collaboration on Kurt Weill's *Street Scene* (1947) and later his own *Black Nativity* (1961), a musical steeped in gospel music. His *Selected Poems* appeared in 1959, largely omitting his more radical work, and was criticized in a review by James Baldwin for what he saw as the poetry's too distant stance. Important poetry volumes from these years were *Montage of a Dream Deferred* (1951) and *Ask Your Mama: 12 Moods for Jazz* (1961), although both were initially published to poor reviews. Both books continue Hughes's experiments with combining literary and popular – particularly black – musical forms. Since his death has come broad recognition of his vital contribution, both to African American poetry and to twentieth-century American poetry in general.

### Bibliography

*The Collected Works of Langston Hughes*, vols. 1–3, ed. Arnold Rampersad (Columbia, MO, 2001).

Richard Barksdale, *Langston Hughes: The Poet and his Critics* (Chicago, 1977).
R. Baxter Miller, *The Art and Imagination of Langston Hughes* (Lexington, KY, 1989).
Arnold Rampersad, *The Life of Langston Hughes*, 2 vols. (New York, 1986, 1988).
Steven C. Tracy, *Langston Hughes and the Blues* (Urbana, IL, 1988).

# Louis Zukofsky (1904–1978)

Louis Zukofsky was born on Manhattan's Lower East Side of Russian immigrant parents, and grew up reading Yiddish as well as English. He graduated from Columbia University at the age of 20, and later supported himself by a variety of jobs including teaching English for many years at the Polytechnic Institute of Brooklyn, New York. His writing includes poetry, fiction, criticism, and translations, although he is best known for his long collage-like poem of 24 sections, *"A"*, which he published in parts over 50 years, and for his association with the objectivist movement in the 1930s and the principles that developed from it.

In February 1931, having been recommended to editor Harriet Monroe by Ezra Pound, Zukofsky guest-edited an issue of *Poetry* within which he published a group of poets whose work incorporated the principles that he outlined in two accompanying essays "Program: 'Objectivists' 1931," and "Sincerity and Objectification." These poets included, along with Zukofsky himself, William Carlos Williams, George Oppen, Kenneth Rexroth, Charles Reznikoff (the main subject of the second essay), and Carl Rakosi. The journal noted that Ezra Pound "gave over to younger poets the space offered him." The objectivists were scarcely a group, and the term itself did not carry much beyond the early 1930s, in which time there was an associated Objectivist Press, which published Pound and Williams, and *An "Objectivists" Anthology* (1932), edited by Zukofsky. But the emphasis upon the linguistic properties of the poem that the poets shared received renewed interest in the 1950s from such poets as Robert Creeley, Robert Duncan, and Cid Corman, and this renewed interest increased still further with the importance of Zukofsky's work for the Language poets in the 1970s and 1980s.

As Zukofsky's "Program" explains the goals of objectivism, the poets aim for two particular kinds of achievement, which Zukofsky terms "sincerity" and "objectification." "Sincerity," he argues, is "preoccupation with the accuracy of detail in writing" which can be for example in the detail of objects or, again, "in the rendering of character and speech." "Objectification" refers to structural unity, at the level of the sound, syllables, and the relationships of words within the line and the poem as a whole. "Sincerity" thus provides the building blocks of "objectification," unifying the poem through the very close relationship between the properties of language properly used and the detail that it expresses.

Zukofsky argued that this resulting unity within a poem must also have a historical basis. In a note accompanying the part of his long poem *"A"* which he included in the 1931 issue of *Poetry* he summarized two of its "themes":

I – desire for the poetically perfect finding its direction inextricably the direction of historic and contemporary particulars; and II – approximate attainment of this perfection in the feeling of the contrapuntal design of the figure transferred to poetry.

In the case of Zukofsky's own poetry the resulting work is often extremely difficult – even for such readers as William Carlos Williams – the difficulty caused by a density of allusions literary, historical, and personal, and a sustained wit operating on multiple levels and incorporating sound, sense, and form. Sometimes Zukofsky's own notes, or comments in interviews, are essential to a full engagement with a particular poem. Zukofsky has never had a wide general readership, but to the modernist and postmodernist poets who were and are strong admirers of his work this "dangerous sort of writing," as Williams put it in a 1942 review of *55 Poems*, when it succeeds, more than justifies its method and difficulties. "Their successes," Williams affirms of the poems, "are of a superlative quality when achieved."

Some of Zukofsky's best-known poems include the witty "To My Washstand," which narrates the action of close attention that Zukofsky's poetry demands, "Mantis," with its series of bold associations of history and social comment, and "Ferry," which shows the close affinities to imagism that some critics see in objectivist verse. In the objectivist issue of *Poetry* Zukofsky published the seventh section of *"A"*, which illustrates well the close relationship of language properties to detail that he argued for, as his description of seven sawhorses fencing off a construction site turns into a dance of sound and movement through the multiple possibilities offered by the poem's multilevel connections.

In addition to *55 Poems* (1941) Zukofsky's major volumes include *Anew: Poems* (1946), the critical study *A Test of Poetry* (1948), and the publication of the complete *"A"* in 1978. His ambitious and wide-ranging prose study of Shakespeare *Bottom: On Shakespeare* (1963) has been seen variously as a neglected masterwork, eccentric, and baffling. Zukofsky's extensive and often illuminating correspondence with Williams and with Ezra Pound has also been published, and his relationship with these two major modernist figures has, like his own work, become a subject of interest to a widening group of scholars and poets since his death.

## Bibliography

Louis Zukofsky, *"A"* (Berkeley, 1978).
—— *Complete Short Poetry* (Baltimore, 1991).

Barry Ahearn, *Zukofsky's "A": An Introduction* (Berkeley, 1983).
Sandra Kumamoto Stanley, *Louis Zukofsky and the Transformation of a Modern American Poetics* (Berkeley, 1994).

# Robert Penn Warren (1905–1989)

Robert Penn Warren made distinguished contributions to American letters in the fields of the novel, poetry, and criticism, although his major achievements in poetry came in the last 30 years of his life. Warren was born in the small town of Guthrie, in Kentucky, and had to abandon a planned naval career because of an eye injury. He entered Vanderbilt University in 1921, and became a member of the Fugitives group, which included John Crowe Ransom and Allen Tate, sharing a room for a period with Tate. Warren absorbed their commitment to the culture and history of the South and their conservative program for a return to agrarian values. Before he graduated from Vanderbilt in 1925 he had published his first poems in the journal *The Fugitive*. Warren's studies continued with graduate work at Berkeley and Yale, and in 1928 he entered Oxford University on a Rhodes scholarship. While at Oxford he published his first book, *John Brown: The Making of a Martyr* (1929).

Returning to the United States in 1930, Warren embarked upon a highly successful academic career, teaching in Memphis and at Vanderbilt, before joining Louisiana State University in 1934. There he co-founded the influential *Southern Review*, which he also helped edit until 1942, and with fellow faculty member Cleanth Brooks he published *Understanding Poetry* in 1938. This volume, along with its companion *Understanding Fiction* (1943) had an enormous impact upon the teaching of literature in high schools and colleges well into the 1960s. Intended as textbooks, but also serving to inform generations of teachers, the anthologies synthesized in practical and readable form the ideas of what became known as New Criticism, emphasizing close reading to reveal the complex technical and thematic relationships within a text.

Warren published *Night Rider*, the first of his ten novels, in 1939. These novels, like his poetry, are centrally concerned with autobiographical and historical themes. The best known of the novels is *All the King's Men* (1946), which won a Pulitzer Prize and was made into a highly successful film in 1949 starring Broderick Crawford. Warren based the powerful story upon the career of Louisiana governor Huey Long.

In 1935 Warren had published his first book of poetry, *Thirty-Six Poems*. *Eleven Poems on the Same Theme* (1942) followed, and subsequently *Selected Poems 1923–1943* (1944). Although accomplished, these poems are generally viewed as derivative, well-crafted poems in the style of the major influences on his poetry at this time – Tate, and, through Tate and the work of T. S. Eliot, seventeenth-century metaphysical poetry. "Bearded Oaks" is a representative poem from these years. From a concretely evoked landscape scene the poem moves to a series of oracular abstractions ("If hope is hopeless, then fearless fear") that take the poem out of a diminished present, and move it towards the moral urgency and the "eternity" with which the poem ends:

We live in time so little time
And we learn all so painfully,
That we may spare this hour's term
To practice for eternity.

Following the *Selected Poems* Warren published no poetry for nine years. Then in 1953 appeared the book-length verse narrative *Brother to Dragons: A Tale in Verse and Voices*, in which a number of speakers narrate and reflect upon the 1811 murder of a young slave in Kentucky by a nephew of Thomas Jefferson. This combination of narrative and history characterizes the poetry that marked the rest of Warren's career – along with a more vernacular, less rhetorical, language, a more open formal structure, and more autobiographical content than in his earlier period. Some critics have suggested parallels to the work of Robinson Jeffers. Poetry collections followed regularly after *Promises: Poems 1954–1956* (1957), which won Warren his second Pulitzer Prize and a National Book Award. He was awarded a third Pulitzer for *Now and Then: Poems, 1976–1978*. In later volumes Warren's poems often look back to his Kentucky boyhood. "Amazing Grace in the Back Country" (1978), concerning the experience of a camp meeting when he was 12, is an example.

Although in his earlier career Warren's racial views had been segregationist, after he left the South in 1942 to take up a position at the University of Minnesota, and later, in 1950, a position at Yale University, his views became more liberal. In 1956 he published *Segregation: The Inner Conflict in the South*, and in 1965 *Who Speaks for the Negro?*, a series of interviews with leaders of the civil rights movement. Warren taught at Yale until his retirement in 1973, and his wide-ranging publications continued to include fiction and literary criticism as well as poetry. The remarkable achievement of the major phase of his poetry was recognized by his being appointed in 1986 the first Poet Laureate of the United States.

## Bibliography

*The Collected Poems of Robert Penn Warren*, ed. John Burt (Baton Rouge, 1998).

William Bedford Clark, *The American Vision of Robert Penn Warren* (Lexington, KY, 1991).

Lesa Carnes Corrigan, *Poems of Pure Imagination: Robert Penn Warren and the Romantic Tradition* (Baton Rouge, 1999).

James A. Grimshaw, *Understanding Robert Penn Warren* (Columbia, SC, 2001).

# George Oppen (1908–1984)

George Oppen's is one of the more remarkable stories of twentieth-century American poetry. After an early career in which he was associated as publisher and poet with a movement that won the support of Ezra Pound and William Carlos Williams among others, he wrote no further poetry for 24 years, working as a political activist. Then in 1969 he won the Pulitzer Prize for Poetry, his *Collected Poems* was later nominated for the National Book Award, and he received lifetime recognition awards from the American Academy and Institute of Arts and Letters, and from the National Endowment for the Arts. By the end of the century a number of contemporary poets were acknowledging his influence on their work.

Oppen was born in New Rochelle, New York, but grew up in San Francisco, where his father became a successful businessman. In 1926 he enrolled at what is now Oregon State University, at Corvallis, and met his future wife Mary Colby. The two left the university shortly afterwards, following his suspension and Mary's expulsion for violating the girl's dormitory curfew.

Married in Dallas, Texas, in 1927, they moved to New York and became associated with the objectivist poets, a group which included Louis Zukofsky, William Carlos Williams, Charles Reznikoff, and Carl Rakosi. Although only very loosely a "movement," the poets agreed on emphasizing the materiality of the poem, economy, and the close connections of the properties of language to what it describes. Many critics have noted the relationship of objectivist ideas to the intensity of vision advocated by the earlier imagists. Oppen was included in the February 1931 issue of *Poetry* edited by Zukofsky, in which Zukofsky laid out some of the central tenets of objectivism as he saw them.

In 1929 the Oppens moved to France, where they set up TO Publishers in Toulon, and where the publications of the press included Williams's *A Novelette and Other Prose*, Pound's *How to Read*, and *An "Objectivists" Anthology* edited by Zukofsky. Returning to the United States, in 1933 they established the Objectivist Press, which published Williams's *Collected Poems 1921–31* (with a preface by Wallace Stevens that greatly irritated Williams), three volumes by Charles Reznikoff, and, in 1934, Oppen's own first book *Discrete Series*.

*Discrete Series* carried a preface by Pound, termed "irrelevant" by Williams in a 1934 review in which he nevertheless praised the discipline and commitment of the poems themselves. The poem "1930's", which had also appeared in the objectivist issue of *Poetry*, is representative of what Williams called the poems' attempt at "an irreducible minimum in the means for the achievement of their objective, no loose bolts or beams sticking out unattached at one end or put there to hold up a rococo cupid or a concrete saint":

Thus

Hides the

Parts – the prudery
Of Frigidaire, of
Soda-jerking –

Thus

Above the

Plane of lunch, of wives,
Removes itself
(As soda-jerking from
The private act

Of
Cracking eggs);

big-Business.

By the following year, 1935, however, the Oppens decided to devote themselves fully to political work on behalf of those suffering from the economic consequences of the Depression. They joined the Communist Party and involved themselves for the rest of the decade in pressing for basic social services for the unemployed, and as strike organizers. In 1942 Oppen was working as a factory machinist when he was drafted into the army, being seriously wounded on April 22, 1945 – an event he refers to in a number of later poems.

The Oppens moved to California after the war, where Oppen worked as a carpenter, but, feeling hounded by the anti-communist sentiments of the time, and following two interviews from the FBI, they moved to Mexico City in 1950, where they remained until 1958. In May 1958 Oppen wrote his first poem in 24 years, "Blood from a Stone." In 1962, now living in New York City, he published his second volume, *The Materials*, 28 years after *Discrete Series*. The book was well received, as were *This in Which* (1965) and the volume which won the Pulitzer Prize, *Of Being Numerous* (1968) – which is generally seen as his finest work. Michael Heller has summarized the book as "concerned with the deepest notions of community and with the basis on which community might be established: with the meaning of humanity, ethics and love." Like all of Oppen's work, Heller argues, the poems are an interrogation of language, "an attempt to discover whether these words can truthfully be retained in the light of what humanity has become."

*Alpine: Poems* (1969) followed, and then *Seascape: Needle's Eye* (1972), poems centered on San Francisco, where the Oppens moved in 1967. A volume of *Collected Poems* appeared in 1973 with a fuller edition appearing in 1975. Oppen's final volume, *Primitive*, was published in 1978. In his last years Oppen suffered from Alzheimer's disease, and he died in California.

Critics differ on whether Oppen's later career reflects a synthesis of his political and artistic concerns, or whether it acknowledged that neither could finally bring fundamental change. But in returning so successfully to verse, Oppen provided an important link for younger poets to the work of Williams and Pound, and the restraint, clarity, craftsmanship, and emphasis upon essentials in his work remain an important influence on many poets. His *Selected Letters* (1990) provide an invaluable record of objectivism and its influence; also valuable is Mary Oppen's biography of the couple's relationship and political activities, *Meaning A Life: An Autobiography* (1978).

## Bibliography

George Oppen, *New Collected Poems*, ed. Michael Davidson (New York, 2002).

Burton Hatlen, ed., *George Oppen: Man and Poet* (Orono, ME, 1981).

Michael Heller, *Conviction's Net of Branches: Essays on the Objectivist Poets and Poetry* (Carbondale, IL, 1985).

# Theodore Roethke (1908–1963)

Theodore Roethke was born in Saginaw, Michigan, where his father owned a commercial greenhouse business. Roethke's childhood memories of the greenhouses and of his father are frequent subjects of his poetry, alongside the related theme of descending into the self to discover an elemental life force at one with the growing plants of the greenhouse and the life that surrounds it. Thus towards the end of "North American Sequence," a long meditative sequence in his posthumously published *The Far Field*, the poet thinks:

> of roses, roses,
> White and red, in the wide six-hundred-foot greenhouses,
> And my father standing astride the cement benches,
> Lifting me high over the four-foot stems, the Mrs. Russells, and his own
> elaborate hybrids,
> And how those flowerheads seemed to flow toward me, to beckon me,
> only a child, out of myself.

A little later, almost in the poem's final lines, that self emerges in lines that echo two key influences on Roethke's later work – Whitman and Dylan Thomas:

> Among the half-dead trees, I came upon the true ease of myself,
> As if another man appeared out of the depths of my being,
> And I stood outside myself,
> Beyond becoming and perishing,
> A something wholly other,
> As if I swayed out on the wildest wave alive,
> And yet was still.

This interest in adapting the long lines and catalogue narratives of Whitman was just the final stylistic development of a number that characterize Roethke's career. Some of the influences that have been suggested for his first book, *Open House* (1941), include W. H. Auden, William Blake, Emily Dickinson, and John Donne, while he consciously based some poems in the 1950s on the work of Yeats. But Roethke is far more than an imitator of other poets' styles, and he used these poetic "fathers" in innovative ways as part of exploring his ambivalent attitude towards his childhood and towards his own father. This autobiographical search is combined with an intense feeling of affinity with the oneness of living things and natural processes that he felt with even the most neglected and lowly forms of nature. He has been seen by some readers as a latter-day transcendentalist.

Roethke's father died of cancer in 1923, two years before the poet entered the University of Michigan. Upon his graduation in 1929 he briefly attended graduate school at the University of Michigan and then at Harvard, before beginning his teaching career at Lafayette College. At Lafayette Roethke found a strong supporter and colleague in poet Stanley Kunitz, and later he formed an important friendship with Kenneth Burke while teaching at Pennsylvania State University (1936–43). He then went on to teach at Bennington College. But between holding the positions at Lafayette and Pennsylvania State, while teaching at Michigan State in 1935, Roethke was hospitalized for what were to become recurring bouts of mental illness. These breakdowns, and a drinking problem that sometimes produced violent mood swings – alternate feelings of self-doubt and of bravado – haunted Roethke for the rest of his life, but became part of the intense exploration of self (Fishing "in an old wound" as he put it in "The Flight") that is central to many of his poems.

Roethke began publishing his poetry at the beginning of the 1930s, and established a growing reputation that was reinforced by the 1941 publication of *Open House*. In 1948, the year in which he took a position as poet-in-residence at the University of Washington, he published what many critics consider his finest volume, *The Lost Son and Other Poems*. The book uses the sometimes repressed memories of lost youth, including memories of the greenhouses and of the poet's father, to explore a visionary connection between the self, imagination, memory, and nature. The volume contains such well-known poems as "Frau Bauman, Frau Schmidt, and Frau Schwartze" (three of Otto Roethke's employees), "My Papa's Waltz," and the two poems titled "Cuttings." The poet's close identification with the elemental life forms around him is expressed dramatically rather than meditatively, as in the second of the "Cuttings" poems, " I can hear, underground, that sucking and sobbing, / In my veins, in my bones I feel it, – / . . . I quail, lean to beginnings, sheath-wet."

Some of the poems of *The Lost Son* use forms and rhythms associated with childhood as part of their attempt to capture early memories and responses, and this strategy is developed more fully in *Praise to the End!* (1951). But the new poems in his subsequent volume, *The Waking: Poems 1933–1953* (1953), mark Roethke's return to the more formalist verse of his earlier career, now with a particular interest in the work of Yeats. This volume, which won the 1954 Pulitzer Prize, contains the often anthologized "Four for Sir John Davies." The continuity of Roethke's themes is illustrated by the poem's explicit echoes of Yeats's "Among School Children," itself an exploration of memory, age, and youth. In the same year as this book appeared, 1953, Roethke married a former student from Bennington, Beatrice O'Connell, who provided invaluable support through the poet's continuing mental and alcoholic crises.

The 1950s saw Roethke's reputation continue to grow. In addition to the Pulitzer Prize, he was awarded a Guggenheim Fellowship in 1950, two Ford Foundation grants, and a Fulbright grant. He received many awards for his 1957 volume *Words for the Wind*, including the Bollingen Prize and the National Book Award. In this volume Roethke published "Meditations of an Old Woman," a commemoration of his mother, as well as some children's verse and the often reprinted "I Knew a Woman." Now at the height of his fame, Roethke lived a life of teaching, reading, writing, and travel until suffering a fatal heart attack at the age of 55.

Following the publication of his last poems in *The Far Field* in 1964 – which won another National Book Award – his *Collected Poems* appeared in 1966. Among the many notable poets who have been influenced by his work are James Dickey, Seamus Heaney, Ted Hughes, Sylvia Plath, Anne Sexton, and James Wright.

**Bibliography**

*The Collected Poems of Theodore Roethke* (Garden City, NY, 1966).

Peter Balakian, *Theodore Roethke's Far Fields: The Evolution of his Poetry* (Baton Rouge, 1989).
Don Bogen, *Theodore Roethke and the Writing Process* (Athens, OH, 1991).
Jay Parini, *Theodore Roethke: An American Romantic* (Amherst, 1979).

# Charles Olson (1910–1970)

Charles Olson consciously cast himself as furthering and developing the work of the modernist generation of poets, especially Ezra Pound and William Carlos Williams, although for some critics his work never fully emerges from their shadow. Nevertheless, in his essays, letters, and poetry, and in his work as an educator, he served as an important bridge between the modernist innovators and such younger poets as Robert Creeley, Robert Duncan, Paul Blackburn, Ed Dorn, and Amiri Baraka. Williams himself endorsed Olson's theory of "Projective Verse" by reprinting a sizeable section of the essay in his 1951 *Autobiography*. Olson was one of Pound's first visitors at St. Elizabeths following the older poet's incarceration in the Washington, DC, mental hospital, and in frequent meetings over the next two years struggled to reconcile his deep respect for Pound's work, his interest in his economic philosophy, and his disgust at his politics. Following their break in 1948 (although there may have been at least one further meeting) the two did not meet again until 1965, seven years after Pound's release.

Olson, the son of a postal worker, was born and grew up in Worcester, Massachusetts, although he spent his summers in Gloucester – the site of his later *Maximus* sequence. He attended Wesleyan University, and completed the course work for a doctoral degree at Harvard. He was awarded a Guggenheim Fellowship in 1940 for his research on Melville, work that eventually lead to his first book, *Call Me Ishmael* (1947). But before committing himself to a career as a writer Olson spent five years (1941–5) working in New York and Washington, first for the American Civil Liberties Union, and then, from 1942 to 1944, in the Office of War Information. In 1945 he was working for the Democratic National Committee as director of the Foreign Nationalities Division, but, following the death of Franklin Roosevelt, he gave up this burgeoning career in politics. He had advanced to the point of being informally offered the posts of Assistant Secretary of the Treasury and the Post Office Generalship.

In the years that followed Olson published his prose study of Melville and his first poems began to appear – in such magazines as *Harper's* and *Atlantic Monthly*. He won a second Guggenheim Fellowship, began his visits to Pound, and in 1948 began lecturing at Black Mountain College in North Carolina. In the same year he published his first collection of verse, *Y & Z*, and in 1949 he wrote one of his most important poems, "The Kingfishers." In 1950 he published the influential statement on "Projective Verse," and began an extensive correspondence with Robert Creeley, an exchange that over the years produced almost a thousand letters, some of which are included in Olson's *Mayan Letters* (1953); the two did not meet until 1954. In 1951 he took over as rector of Black Mountain College, a position he held until the college closed down in 1956. Olson turned the college into a writing and arts laboratory that focused on the poetics laid down in the work of Pound, Williams, and Olson himself. There were never more than 16–20 students at any one time, faculty were paid little if any salary, the college tried to be self-supporting as much as possible, growing its own food for example, and classes were held at erratic hours. Histories of the college recount stories of students descending on a local bar to bring a professor to class, and of Olson himself feeling most inspired to teach in the small hours of the morning, and then speaking for hours in an energetic roar. The legacy of Black Mountain College includes, along with later work of such students as Ed Dorn, Jonathan Williams, and John Weiners, its journal *The Black Mountain Review*, which published the work of Creeley, Olson, Robert Duncan, and Denise Levertov among others, and in its final issue in 1957 a number of San Francisco and Greenwich Village Beat writers such as Allen Ginsberg, Jack Kerouac, and Gary Snyder.

The absence of an imposed conventional structure on the educational project at Black Mountain has its equivalent in Olson's own poetic practice. He advocates in his poetry and critical statements a theory of "open" form or "composition by field," as he put it in "Projective Verse," as opposed to "inherited line, stanza, over-all form." Olson viewed the poem as a "high energy-construct," the energy coming from the poet's charged encounter with the outside world or "where the poet got it," and transferred via the poem to the reader. In Olson's poetry this concept of open form results in frequent dislocation of syllables, words, lines, and stanzas, their having no predetermined positions within the poem or on the page as the work unfolds. For Olson, the structure of a poem takes its shape from the content of the material itself. In "Projective Verse" he quoted as a central thesis of his work Creeley's "Form is never more than an extension of content." And time and history are also fluid and spatial for Olson. Thus, for example, his researches into Mayan culture at Yucatan in the late 1940s and early 1950s enter his poems as a series of active gestures in response to the living but hidden promise of a particular place, a search for true origins. Appropriately, "I hunt among stones" is the last line of "The Kingfishers," while his poem "At Yorktown" concludes: "time is a shine caught blue / from a martin's / back." In the latter poem, the phrase "At Yorktown" begins 11 of the poem's 35 lines, reflecting, as a further aspect of Olson's emphasis upon process, that the poem must recognize the immediacy of each of its discrete encounters. For Olson, the "energy" within such dislocation of conventional patterns of time and space breaks up potentially restrictive systems of thought and form – or any other patterns that may be rooted in unexamined convention. In addition to their formal strategies of disjunction, Olson's poems also shift between lyricism, vatic statement, historical, literary, and mythic allusion, and detailing such facts (for example topographical data) that are part of the archaeologist-poet's exploration of site and history.

Olson published volumes of poems regularly, mainly with small presses, from the late 1940s on, but he devoted much of his later career to his long sequence *Maximus*, dedicated to Creeley, which he began in 1950 as a series of "letters" to Vincent Ferrini about a proposed new journal. Sections 1–10 appeared in 1953, followed by 11–22 in 1956, a further volume in 1968, and a posthumous volume in 1975. Like Pound's *Cantos*, the poem accumulates meaning through juxtaposition of history, allusion, and autobiography, and, like Williams's *Paterson*, Maximus is an inclusive figure who represents, as well as place, a man composing, and the poem as process and discovery. It begins:

> Off-shore, by islands hidden in the blood
> jewels & miracles, I, Maximus
> a metal hot from boiling water, tell you
> what is a lance, who obeys the figures of
> the present dance

For Olson, *The Cantos* were often too restricted by the presence of Pound's own ego, while Williams's poem was too local in its focus and too sentimental in its vision. The Gloucester, Massachusetts, of Olson's poem is a community formerly rooted in the craft, history, and courage of its farmers and fishermen, but now being taken over by absentee proprietors, commercialism, and thoughtless redevelopment. The poet-historian searches for and seeks to revive and express the vital origins of the community (a vision of community that the poem terms "polis"), and in doing so to counter the "pejorocracy" (literally "worse-rule") of the present – a term borrowed from Pound's *Pisan Cantos* that Olson first used in "The Kingfishers." The later sections of the poem tend to move away from the detailed history and topography of Gloucester that characterize the earlier sections, and concern themselves more with myth – myth in Olson's work is always a potential source for rediscovering the origins of language, place, and history.

Olson lived in Gloucester following the closing of Black Mountain College, and lectured and read across the country as his work became more widely known. He taught at the State University of New York in Buffalo for two years from 1963, but returned to Gloucester in 1965 following the death of his wife in an automobile accident the previous year – a tragedy which affected him deeply for the rest of his life. He had begun teaching at the University of Connecticut in the fall of 1969, only weeks before his death in January 1970.

### Bibliography

*The Collected Poems of Charles Olson*, ed. George F. Butterick (Berkeley, 1987).

Charles Olson, *The Maximus Poems*, ed. George F. Butterick (Berkeley, 1983).
Robert von Hallberg, *Charles Olson: The Scholar's Art* (Cambridge, MA, 1978).
Thomas F. Merrill, *The Poetry of Charles Olson: A Primer* (Newark, DE, 1982).
Libbie Rifkin, *Career Moves: Olson, Creeley, Zukofsky, Berrigan, and the American Avant-Garde* (Madison, WI, 2000).

# Elizabeth Bishop (1911–1979)

The respect in which Elizabeth Bishop's work was held in her lifetime is reflected in the many awards and honors that came her way, but her stature has further increased in the years since her death. Despite a relatively small output of poems – just over a hundred in her *Complete Poems 1927–1979* (1983), and a total of four individual volumes of verse – she has increasingly been viewed as one of the major American poets of the century. Her combination of Romantic sensibility, restraint, wit, moral vision, and narrative craft produced a voice which, while having affinities with such early influences as Marianne Moore and the seventeenth-century poet George Herbert, is one wholly her own.

Bishop was born, like Charles Olson, a year her senior, in Worcester, Massachusetts. Her father died before her first birthday, and her mother suffered a series of breakdowns that eventually led to her being permanently institutionalized by the time Bishop was 5. Bishop was initially brought up in these early years by her mother's family in Nova Scotia, and then by her father's relatives in Massachusetts. This early rootlessness was a prelude to a life often spent traveling and living abroad, and to poetry that often takes travel as one of its central themes. Not so fully to the surface of her poetry, but nevertheless informing it in crucial ways, was a lifelong battle with asthma, alcoholism, and depression.

Bishop had planned a medical career upon entering Vassar, but by the time she graduated in 1934 she had decided to become a writer. At Vassar, with fellow students Mary McCarthy and Muriel Rukeyser, she founded the student literary journal *Con Spirito*, and published there a number of her earliest poems. The Vassar librarian arranged a meeting for her with Marianne Moore, which lead to a lifelong friendship. Her poem "Invitation to Miss Marianne Moore" is one well-known tribute. With the income from a small trust fund (her grandfather and father's construction company had overseen the building of the Boston Public Library and the city's Museum of Fine Arts) she lived for the next few years in New York, in Europe, and in Key West, Florida.

The first of her four books of verse, *North & South*, appeared in 1946, and contains some of her best-known poems, including "The Man-Moth" and "The Fish." The former displays the quality of imaginative transformation that characterizes many of her poems, a transformation – often of mundane objects – that never completely leaves behind the careful recording of detail and the associated wonder that is the poem's foundation. "The Man-Moth" is a creature resembling a compulsive artist, driven from underground to rise up to the light to inevitably fail and try again. The poem balances description of the everyday, the subway and its electric "third rail," with fable. The "man-moth" of the title is viewed from multiple perspectives and degrees of scale, and is variously distanced or identified with. "The Fish" shows something of Bishop's response to the work of Moore; 75 lines of absorbed, intricate, restrained observation, before the last line's "And I let the fish go" confirms that the detailed description of the captured fish was anything but distanced and clinical, but was an intense admiration of and identification with its power, beauty, and history – "five big hooks / grown firmly in his mouth" from earlier escapes.

*North & South* was greeted with a number of reviews which recognized that an important new poet had arrived on the scene, and two of the most perceptive were those of Randall Jarrell and Robert Lowell. Jarrell, writing in *Partisan Review*, noted the affinities with the work of Moore, the balance of "outlandish ingenuity" with a tone "grave, calm, and tender at the same time," and added that "in her best work, restraint, calm and proportion are implicit in every detail of metre or organization or workmanship." "She is," Jarrell concluded, "morally so satisfactory."

Lowell, who like Jarrell went on to form a lifelong friendship with Bishop, characterized the poems in a *Sewanee Review* essay as "unrhetorical, cool, and beautifully thought out." Lowell also noted a tension between motion, "weary but persisting, almost always failing . . . and yet, for the most part, stoically maintained," and "terminus, rest, sleep, fulfillment or death." This tension remained a characteristic of many later poems too. For example, "Over 2000 Illustrations and a Complete Concordance," describes a wide-ranging journey within which the various stops contribute memorable images of this or that particular place. In "The Moose" tired, sleepy bus travelers riding through "moonlight and mist" are stopped "with a jolt" by a moose in the middle of the road that carefully investigates the bus before the driver can move on – leaving as legacy the mystery of its appearance out of the mist and "a dim / smell of moose, an acrid / smell of gasoline."

The publication of *North & South* helped Bishop to win a Guggenheim Fellowship in 1947 (she won a second in the last year of her life). From 1949 to 1950 she served as Consultant in Poetry at the Library of Congress. But her life took a sudden turn in 1951 when she was taken ill while on a trip to South America. She then made Brazil her home for more than 16 years, until the suicide of her female companion, Brazilian architect Lota de Macedo Soares. She stayed informed of developments in American poetry, assisted greatly by her extensive correspondence with Moore, Lowell, Jarrell, and May Swenson.

In the books following *North & South* the poems become more direct, more autobiographical, and less metaphysical. Bishop's second volume, *A Cold Spring*, appeared in 1955 and included the poems of *North & South*. The book won Bishop a Pulitzer Prize. Two years later she translated (from Portuguese), and wrote an introduction for, *The Diary of "Helena Morley,"* a diary kept by a young girl at the end of the nineteenth century in rural Brazil. In a review in *Poetry* Moore noted a quality that both diarist and translator had of a "gift for fantasy . . . use of words and hyper-precise eye." Bishop's subsequent translations included work from French and Spanish, as well as Portuguese, sources, and included collaborating with Emanuel Brasil on *An Anthology of Twentieth-Century Brazilian Poetry* (1972). In 1962 she published a book on Brazil with the *Life World Library*. Brazil is the setting for many of the poems in the third collection of her own work, *Questions of Travel*, which appeared in 1965. This was followed in 1969 by the first *Complete Poems*, which won a National Book Award, by which time, following Soares's death in 1967, Bishop had left Brazil and begun increasingly to live in the United States. The title poem of *Questions of Travel* concludes with a traveler's entry in "a notebook":

> "Continent, city, country, society:
> the choice is never wide and never free.
> And here, or there . . . No. Should we have stayed at home,
> wherever that may be?"

In 1969 Bishop became poet-in residence at Harvard University, and went on to teach there for seven years. Her fourth volume of poetry, *Geography III*, appeared in 1976, the same year in which she became a member of the American Academy of Arts and Letters. This volume further cemented her reputation, and contains some of her best-known poems, including (in addition to "The Moose") "Crusoe in England," and "One Art." She died on October 6, 1979, at 68, in Cambridge, Massachusetts, of a ruptured cerebral aneurysm. One of her last pieces of writing was a foreword for a bibliography of her work prepared by Candace MacMahon. With characteristic restraint, she noted, "I am rather pleased to see I've written so much when I've always thought I'd written so little."

**Bibliography**

Elizabeth Bishop, *The Complete Poems, 1927–1979* (New York, 1983).

Bonnie Costello, *Elizabeth Bishop: Questions of Mastery* (Cambridge, MA, 1991).
Susan McCabe, *Elizabeth Bishop: Her Poetics of Loss* (University Park, PA, 1994).
Anne Stevenson, *Five Looks at Elizabeth Bishop* (London, 1998).
Thomas Travisano, *Elizabeth Bishop: Her Artistic Development* (Charlottesville, 1988).

# John Berryman (1914–1972)

John Berryman was born John Smith in the town of McAlester, in south-eastern Oklahoma. His parents' marriage was a troubled one, and in 1926 his father, John Alleyn Smith, shot himself near the window of his son's room. The event haunted Berryman for the rest of his life, and appears often in his poetry, particularly in his later work. One of the *Dream Songs* (235) pleads:

> Mercy! my father; do not pull the trigger
> or all my life I'll suffer from your anger
> killing what you began.

And earlier, in no. 76:

> – *If* life is a handkerchief sandwich,
>
> in a modesty of death I join my father
> who dared so long agone leave me.
> A bullet on a concrete stoop
> close by a smothering southern sea
> spreadeagled on an island, by my knee.

In the penultimate "Song" of the sequence (no. 384), the response is one of anger, "I stand above my father's grave with rage ... // I spit upon this dreadful banker's grave / who shot his heart out in a Florida dawn." The stanza goes on to plead that "indifference come," but it never did for Berryman. A life filled with a tormenting variety of moods, three marriages, and heavy drinking – as well as a unique contribution to the poetry of the century – was itself ended by suicide. In the last years of his life, however, Berryman had risen to the first rank of American poets, creating out of his own torments an exhilaration of language and a starkness of exposure rarely matched by his contemporaries.

Three months after his father's death, Mrs. Smith married John McAlpin Berryman, and the son took the new surname. The family moved to New York, and although the marriage did not last, Berryman's stepfather provided for his stepchildren, and Berryman attended a preparatory school in Connecticut and entered Columbia University, graduating with a BA in 1936. While at Columbia he published poetry in the *Columbia Review* and *The Nation*, and came under the mentorship of poet Mark Van Doren. Two years' study at Clare College, Cambridge, followed, before he began an academic career that took him to teaching posts at Wayne State, Princeton, Harvard, Iowa (where he was dismissed for public intoxication), and finally in 1955 to the University of Minnesota. Although he was evidently a remarkable teacher, Berryman was often contemptuous of this side of his career. "A Professor's Song" describes a class marked by clock-watching, rote repetition of literary catchphrases, and student disinterest. Dream Song 35, subtitled "MLA," indicating the annual Modern Language Association convention, exhorts the gathered professors to "forget your footnotes" and "dance around Mary" – one of the professor's wives.

Berryman's poetry was in a formal mode into the 1950s, and important early influences were Yeats and Auden. His first two book publications, however, were with New Directions, the publishers of Ezra Pound and William Carlos Williams. *Five Young American Poets* (1940) was followed by *Poems* (1942). From 1939 to 1940 he served as the part-time poetry editor of *The Nation*. Berryman married his first wife, Eileen Mulligan, in 1942, but before publication of his next book, *The Dispossessed* (1948), he had begun what was to be the first of the many extra-marital affairs that marred his marriages. A series of 115 sonnets that Berryman wrote about this affair in 1947 was published 20 years later as *Berryman's Sonnets*. Although affecting at times some of the characteristics of Elizabethan sonnet sequences, the verses are more direct and frank than the academic poetry that Berryman was writing at the time for publication. He separated from Eileen Mulligan in 1953 and they divorced in 1956. Her novel *The Maze* (1975) is based upon their marriage, while her *Poets in their Youth* (1982) is a biography (both written under her later married name, Eileen Simpson).

Berryman published articles and reviews on many writers as part of his academic work, and a psychological biography, *Stephen Crane*, in 1950. But he became famous for his sequence *Homage to Mistress Bradstreet*, first published in the *Partisan Review* in 1953, and in book form in 1956. The poem imagines the life of the seventeenth-century New England poet, and at times directly addresses her. The poem is learned and difficult, but also often concrete in its depiction of Anne Bradstreet's physical and spiritual struggles with what the poem sees as her repressive world. The 57 eight-line stanzas open with the modern poet speaking to her, but, as Berryman's notes to the poem explain, by stanza 4 his voice modulates into hers. Some of the second section of the poem is a dialogue with Bradstreet, although her voice takes over again until the final four-stanza coda. Berryman's interest did not extend to an endorsement of Bradstreet's poetry. When he annotates an early reference in the poem to Joshua Sylvester and Francis Quarles, he adds "her favorite poets; unfortunately." Writing in 1964, Robert Lowell characterized the work as "the most resourceful historical poem in our language."

*Homage to Mistress Bradstreet* was nominated for a Pulitzer Prize, which Berryman eventually won for the first volume of *The Dream Songs* (1964). Between the two books he had married Ann Levine in 1956, divorced in 1959, and married again in 1961, to Kate Donahue. From the late 1950s Berryman began to be hospitalized at least once a year for alcoholism and exhaustion. *The Dream Songs* – 385 "songs" in all, in three-stanza, 18-line rhymed units – were completed by *His Toy, His Dream, His Rest* (1968). This volume, to complete which Berryman had been awarded his second Guggenheim Fellowship (the first was in 1952), won the National Book Award and a shared Bollingen Prize (with Karl Shapiro).

*The Dream Songs*, published complete in 1969, took Berryman completely away from the academic poetry of his early career. The subject and sometimes speaker is "Henry," a white middle-aged man who has suffered an irreversible loss, and who is also spoken to in Negro dialect by a white friend wearing blackface who calls him at times "Mr. Bones." The reference is to one of two minstrel characters, a duo that would appear between acts in vaudeville shows. The diction is variously slang, dialect, pig Latin, archaisms, baby talk, the language of the minstrel shows, and standard English, but the free-ranging diction is contained strictly within the regular stanza arrangement. Much of Henry's character, thoughts, and fantasies clearly come from Berryman's own life and views, although he insisted in a 1972 interview that "Henry is accused of being me and I am accused of being Henry and I deny it and nobody believes me." *The Dream Songs* contain elegies for various poets close to Berryman in one way or another who had died in recent years, including Frost, Randall Jarrell, Roethke, Delmore Schwartz, Yvor Winters, Louis MacNeice, Sylvia Plath, and William Carlos Williams. Dream Song 153 summarizes bitterly:

> I'm cross with god who has wrecked this generation.
> First he seized Ted, then Richard, Randall, and now Delmore.
> In between he gorged on Sylvia Plath.
> That was a first rate haul.

The views and experiences recounted in Berryman's next book, *Love & Fame* (1970), are not expressed through alter egos but are autobiographical and explicit, and thus lack the wit and variety of the *Dream Songs*. In this same year Berryman returned to the Catholicism in which he had been raised as a child, and his last book of poems, *Delusions, etc. of John Berryman* (1972) reflects the spiritual struggles that now occupied him. He left unfinished a prose fiction, *Recovery* (1973), that came out of his sporadic attempts to conquer his alcoholism. On January 7, 1972, he jumped to his death from the Washington Avenue Bridge in Minneapolis, above the Mississippi.

## Bibliography

John Berryman, *Collected Poems, 1937–1971*, ed. Charles Thornbury (New York, 1989).
—— *The Dream Songs* (New York, 1969).

Joel Conarroe, *John Berryman: An Introduction to the Poetry* (New York, 1977).
John Haffenden, *John Berryman: A Critical Commentary* (New York, 1980).
Helen Vendler, *The Given and the Made: Strategies of Poetic Redefinition* (Cambridge, MA, 1995).

# Robert Lowell (1917–1977)

Robert Lowell is considered by many to be the foremost American poet of the two decades following the mid-century. From a distinguished New England family, Lowell's subject was often his estrangement from the promise of comfort and security offered by this heritage, and a related subject was often the torments and anxieties of his own life – a life which in his poetry he paralleled to the larger history and events of his own time.

Lowell was related on his mother's side to the Winslows, who arrived in the *Mayflower*, and on his father's to the poet James Russell Lowell and to imagist poet Amy Lowell. Another relative, cousin A. Lawrence Lowell, was president of Harvard from 1909 to 1933 – Lowell entered the university in 1935. At St. Mark's School (where a tutor had been Richard Eberhart), and in his first months at Harvard, Lowell determined on a career as a poet. In 1937, after meeting Allen Tate, he transferred to Kenyon College to study with Tate's mentor John Crowe Ransom, and in his first year Randall Jarrell was a room-mate. At Kenyon, Lowell took Ransom's advice to study philosophy and the classics. Under the tutelage of Ransom, a pioneer of New Criticism – and later, upon graduation in 1940, of Cleanth Brooks and Robert Penn Warren in classes at Louisiana State University – his poetry developed the qualities of thematic complexity, compression, and ambiguity advocated by his teachers. Even Ransom found them rather too forbidding, and only accepted two of them for the *Kenyon Review*.

In 1940 Lowell married novelist Jean Stafford, the first of his three troubled marriages. In the spring of 1941 they remarried in a Catholic church, Lowell having converted to Catholicism in the previous months. This further rebellion against his family's Protestant roots lasted until 1947, by which time he was divorcing and had renounced Catholicism (although he would return to the faith with fervor from time to time for the next two or three years).

Lowell worked on the galleys of his first book, *Land of Unlikeness* (1944) while serving a prison sentence in Danbury, Connecticut, for declaring himself a conscientious objector to the world war when he had received his induction papers. The first ten days of his one year and one day sentence (of which he served six months in prison) was spent in New York City's West Street jail. That experience later formed the subject of his well-known poem "Memories of West Street and Lepke" in *Life Studies* (1959).

*Land of Unlikeness* met with mild critical success, but Lowell's second volume, *Lord Weary's Castle* (1946) received great acclaim, winning him a Pulitzer Prize, and leading to a Guggenheim Fellowship and an award from the American Academy of Arts and Letters. In October 1947 he took up for a year the post of Consultant in Poetry at the Library of Congress.

*Lord Weary's Castle* contains many of the finest poems of Lowell's early style, poems marked by a vision of apocalypse and a plea for a *deus ex machina* resolution to the torment of human history. "I ask for bread, my father gives me mould" he records in "Christmas Eve Under Hooker's Statue," and the poem ends: "But we are old, our fields are running wild: / Till Christ again turn wanderer and child." Two other well-known poems, "Mr. Edwards and the Spider," and "After the Surprising Conversions," stem from Lowell's interest in the eighteenth-century divine Jonathan Edwards, while Lowell's continuing concern with integrating the rituals and images of

Catholicism into his own New England heritage are evident throughout the book, most vividly in "The Quaker Graveyard in Nantucket."

The same compressed, allusive style, developed from the poetry of Tate and, through T. S. Eliot, the seventeenth-century metaphysical poets, characterizes the poems in *The Mills of the Kavanaughs* (1951). Religious, classical, and personal themes run through the poems, most of them placed in the mouths of speakers set in historical or contemporary scenes. Reviews of this book were respectful but much less enthusiastic than for *Lord Weary's Castle*, and Randall Jarrell's view that "Falling Asleep Over the Aeneid" is the most successful poem, certainly more so than the long title poem, has generally been borne out by time.

Lowell did not publish another book until the ground-breaking *Life Studies* in 1959. Through that decade he continued to have bouts of hospitalization that had begun with a nervous breakdown in 1949, and the introspection occasioned by his treatments contributed to a growing dissatisfaction with the formal surface of his poetry. This dissatisfaction was compounded by a correspondence Lowell began with William Carlos Williams, and by his experience on a west coast reading tour in 1957 of hearing Allen Ginsberg reading "Howl." In *Life Studies* Lowell confronts much more directly than in his earlier work, and in a style much looser than he had written in before, his family background, and his own troubles as a writer and husband (in 1949 he had married writer Elizabeth Hardwick). But as well as this autobiographical element, which led M. L. Rosenthal to coin the term "Confessional" for such self-revealing poetry, Lowell successfully maintains the ambitious historical sweep that he had sought in his earlier books. The book is effectively a record of Lowell's shift in style. The first section is in the manner of his early 1950s work and includes "Beyond the Alps," his farewell to Catholicism.

The second section is a long prose account of his childhood, developed from a journal that he kept during a period of hospitalization. Section 3 presents four writers defeated and exiled in various ways, Ford Madox Ford, George Santayana, Delmore Schwartz, and Hart Crane. The final section describes a series of losses, family deaths and Lowell's own electric shock treatment, culminating in the poet's facing the Maine night watching skunks foraging and surviving. In *Life Studies* Lowell's father is presented as weak and ineffectual, his mother as oppressive, and the Boston hierarchy into which the poet was born as no more a preparation for the modern world than was his own education for Henry Adams. In such landmark poems as "My Last Afternoon with Uncle Devereux Winslow," "Waking in the Blue," "Memories of West Street and Lepke," and "Skunk Hour" a personal voice is heightened and modulated by the most delicate of formal restraints –

occasional rhyme, stanza forms and line lengths that are varied and open but not with the expansiveness of Ginsberg or the aggressiveness of Williams.

Lowell followed *Life Studies* with a volume of *Imitations* (1961) for which he was awarded the Bollingen Poetry Translation Prize. The original authors range from Homer to Boris Pasternak, and, as Lowell noted in his introduction, "my licenses have been many." The poems based on Pasternak's work, for example, come from other translations, while Lowell cuts or adapts the work of some other sources in various ways.

*Imitations* served as a stepping-stone for Lowell to his next volume. His achievement in *Life Studies* became something of a model for a number of poets, including Sylvia Plath, Anne Sexton, and Adrienne Rich, but although *For the Union Dead* (1964) kept many of his stylistic innovations, it was not so centrally autobiographical, and some poems come closer to his earlier formality. The title poem, one of his most admired, is a condemnation of a New England devoid of heroism or causes, and lacking any values beyond those behind building the underground car park that has displaced the aquarium of his childhood, and that threatens to topple "St. Gaudens' shaking Civil War relief," a memorial to Colonel Shaw and his black regiment. The poem concludes with an image conflating childhood memory and social criticism:

> The Aquarium is gone. Everywhere,
> giant finned cars nose forward like fish;
> a savage servility
> slides by on grease.

The poems in this book, for many reviewers, confirmed Lowell's status as the most important poet of his generation.

Lowell strongly opposed the Vietnam War, and his stature ensured that his public protests for this cause made news. As one form of protest he publicly refused an invitation from President Johnson to participate in a White House Festival of the Arts, and in 1967 he participated in the massive march on the Pentagon to protest the war. In his *The Armies of the Night* Norman Mailer, a fellow participant, describes the audience applauding Lowell at a poetry reading that proceeded the march "for his talent, his modesty, his superiority, his melancholy, his petulance, his weakness, his painful, almost stammering shyness, his noble strength." The theme of rebellion, whether against a heritage that he saw as irrelevant or oppressive, or against an immoral war, has been noticed in the plays that he wrote at this time. A trilogy, *The Old Glory* (1965), based upon some short stories by Hawthorne and Melville, and a version of Aeschylus' *Prometheus Bound* (1967) are the most notable of his dramas.

The poems of Lowell's last decade are generally viewed as less of an achievement than his previous work. *Near the Ocean* (1967) opens with his important "Waking Early Sunday Morning," but on the whole the book, although thematically linked, is somewhat loosely written. *Notebook 1967–68* (1969), revised and expanded in 1970, is Lowell's record of a tumultuous two years written in what he characterized in a note as "fourteen line unrhymed blank verse sections." Lowell wrote entirely in this unrhymed sonnet form for seven years, until 1973. The poems in the two *Notebook* volumes formed the basis of two books Lowell published in that year, *History* and *For Lizzie and Harriet*. The latter, like a third volume published at the same time, *The Dolphin*, contains a good deal of personal material, including quotations from Elizabeth Hardwick's letters. Lowell and Hardwick had divorced in 1972, and Lowell had subsequently married English novelist Lady Caroline Blackwood.

Lowell's attacks of manic depression, and his consequent hospitalization, continued through the 1960s and up to the end of his life. The attacks contributed to the failure of his third marriage, and memories of old and more recent personal troubles are the subject of his final volume, *Day by Day* (1977). On September 12 of the same year he suffered a fatal heart attack during a taxi-ride from New York's Kennedy Airport into the city, where he had planned to visit Elizabeth Hardwick.

### Bibliography

Robert Lowell, *Selected Poems* (New York, 1977).

Steven Gould Axelrod, *Robert Lowell: Life and Art* (Princeton, 1978).
William Doreski, *Robert Lowell's Shifting Colors: The Poetics of the Public and the Personal* (Athens, OH, 1999).
Henry Hart, *Robert Lowell and the Sublime* (Syracuse, 1995).
Paul Mariani, *Lost Puritan: A Life of Robert Lowell* (New York, 1994).

# Gwendolyn Brooks (1917–2000)

Gwendolyn Brooks was born in Topeka, Kansas, but lived most of her life in Chicago. The people and stories of Bronzeville on Chicago's South Side are the subjects of many of her poems. Brooks was the first black writer to win a Pulitzer Prize. She was also the first black woman to be elected to the National Institute of Arts and Letters, and the first black woman to be selected as Consultant in Poetry to the Library of Congress. Her poetry covers a wide range of forms and styles – including free verse, dramatic monologues, lyrics, and objective presentations driven by a controlled but powerful rage. The poetry is always rooted in the concrete experience and the localities of the characters whose stories she tells. The culture in which the characters of her poetry live out their lives is by turns oppressive, dynamic, and dangerous. Within this culture, the mundane details of an individual life can be lifted by Brooks through accumulation of detail and sympathetic rendition to a poem that celebrates as it mourns.

Brooks attended high schools in Chicago that ranged from largely white, to all black, to integrated. She graduated from the city's Wilson Junior College (now Kennedy–King College) in 1936, and was encouraged early in her publishing career by James Weldon Johnson and Langston Hughes. She published many of her early poems in the *Chicago Defender*, where she was an adjunct member of the staff, and later in *Poetry*. In 1938 Brooks married Henry Blakely and moved to Chicago's South Side.

Her first book of poems, *A Street in Bronzeville*, was published in 1945 and was received with critical acclaim. In this book appeared such characteristic poems as "A Song in the Front Yard," where the speaker wants to break free from respectability and convention ("I want to peek at the back . . . / A girl gets sick of a rose"), and "Of De Witt Williams on His Way to Lincoln Cemetery," detailing the haunts and truncated life of "a / Plain black boy." These poems echo the narrative vein and novelistic style of a poet such as Edwin Arlington Robinson, or the *Spoon River Anthology* poems of Chicago poet Edgar Lee Masters. The characters are sympathetically treated even as their limitations are exposed. "The Sundays of Satin-Legs Smith" is another often anthologized poem from this first book. From a different perspective, the dramatic monologue "The Mother" explores the emotions of the speaker towards the children she has aborted, aware of their presence through their absence, offering a love which can only reach out to their memory, for "Abortions will not let you forget."

Brooks's second book, *Annie Allen* (1949), won her the Pulitzer Prize, and was followed by a regular output of essays and reviews, the novel *Maud Martha*, as well as poetry volumes that continued to be well received: *Bronzeville Boys and Girls* (1956), *The Bean Eaters* (1960), and *We Real Cool* (1966).

The poetry in these earlier volumes often protests against the injustice of the limited lives imposed upon her characters by poverty and segregation. "Gay Chaps at the Bar," from 1945, is a series of 12 sonnets based in part upon letters that Brooks received from black soldiers fighting in the Second World War in the segregated US army. "The Lovers of the Poor" (1960) recounts the patronizing distaste felt by "The Ladies from the Ladies' Betterment League" for the prospective recipients of their charity, as they look for "The worthy poor. The very very worthy / And beautiful poor. Perhaps just not too swarthy?" From 1961, "The Ballad of Rudolph Reed," tells the story of a black man and his family who, in search of better housing and a better life, move into a white neighborhood, resulting in a series of violent confrontations that lead to the man's death. The title poem from *We Real Cool* captures in its eight lines, its monosyllables, and its rhymes the inevitability of its speakers' self-destruction. The speakers' "we" is an assertion of communal strength which in its repetition reinforces the shared limitation, and in its absence in the final line, the shared doom.

These themes of protest and of social and racial oppression in Brooks's poetry up to 1967 intensified in her work following what she came to see as a defining moment in her career that occurred in that year. When attending the Second Fisk University Black Writers' Conference she was impressed with the activism of many of the participants, and particularly with the work of Amiri Baraka (then known as LeRoi Jones). In her first volume of autobiography she recalled, "Until 1967 my own blackness did not confront me with a shrill spelling of itself." Following this conference Brooks began active community work with the Chicago wing of the Black Arts movement. She founded a poetry workshop for young black writers, and promoted the work of black writers to the wider community. She left her commercial publisher, Harper & Row following *In the Mecca* (1968), and began publishing with small minority-owned presses. In 1981, with *Primer for Blacks*, she began to publish her own work. Brooks's two volumes of autobiography appeared in 1972, *Report from Part One*, and 1996, *Report from Part Two*.

Later poems include "The Blackstone Rangers," a sequence based on the various members of a street gang from Chicago's black ghetto, and "The Boy Died in My Alley," in which the shooting death of a particular black boy echoes many similar deaths. The speaker's foresight of the doom of such lives is matched only by a frustrated sense of powerlessness. "To Those of My Sisters Who Kept Their Naturals" celebrates those black women who "have not bought Blondine," who "never worshipped Marilyn Monroe," and who "say: Farrah's hair is hers." A sequence from 1981, "To the Diaspora," includes a section on Steve Biko, murdered by the South African police, and regrets the rote and passionless memorials that will inevitably ensue, the "organized nothings / . . . the weep-words." Such a characterization indicates as well as anything what the tough, unsentimental voices and stories in Brooks's own poetry sought to avoid.

Honors continued to come Brooks's way right up to her death, on December 3, 2000. In 1968 she was named Poet Laureate for the state of Illinois, following Carl Sandburg. From 1985 to 1986 she served as Consultant in Poetry to the Library of Congress. Adrienne Rich, writing the citation when Brooks was awarded the Academy of American Poets Fellowship in 1999 "for distinguished poetic achievement," praised both the technical range of her work and its variety, "from precise microcosmic narratives of the human condition to apocalyptic meditations." The poetry, she concluded, "holds up a mirror to the American experience entire, its dreams, self-delusions and nightmares."

## Bibliography

Gwendolyn Brooks, *Selected Poems* (New York, 1963).
—— *Blacks* (Chicago, 1991).

B. J. Bolden, *Urban Rage in Bronzeville: Social Commentary in the Poetry of Gwendolyn Brooks, 1945–1960* (Chicago, 1998).
Harry B. Shaw, *Gwendolyn Brooks* (Boston, 1980).

# Robert Duncan (1919–1988)

Born in Oakland, California, Robert Duncan was an early figure in the San Francisco Renaissance, and was also associated with the Black Mountain College poets of the 1950s. In the 1960s he established himself as an important poet with three books of poetry characteristically learned, intense, and visionary. His critical reception has nevertheless been mixed, with some contemporary poets viewing him as a major voice in postmodern poetry, while others have found his work too studied and even pretentious. Important influences on his poetry are the work of Pindar, Dante, Blake, Gertrude Stein, Pound, and H.D.

Duncan's mother died soon after his birth (a powerful later poem on his sense of connection to her is "My Mother Would Be a Falconress"). His father was forced to put him up for adoption, and he was brought up by devout theosophists who changed his name from Edward Howard Duncan to Robert Edward Symmes. In 1941 he returned to his birth surname. His Theosophist upbringing informs the power that Duncan's poetry gives to dreams, myths, visions, and what he calls in *The Truth and Life of Myth* "a kind of magic." The visionary scope of Duncan's poetry is captured in the title of his first book, *Heavenly City, Earthly City* (1947).

Duncan enrolled at the University of California, Berkeley, in 1936, but left in 1938 and moved to the east coast to join his male lover. In 1940 Duncan joined a small commune in Woodstock, New York, whose members included

Henry Miller and Anaïs Nin. He was an assistant and contributor to the commune's journal *The Phoenix*, and edited the *Experimental Review* – where one of his correspondents was Kenneth Rexroth, who was to become an important contact when Duncan returned to the west coast. In 1941 he was briefly drafted into the military, but was discharged after declaring his homosexuality. In 1943 he married Marjorie McKee, although they were divorced after a few months. In 1944 he published a pioneer essay "The Homosexual in Society" in the journal *Politics*, and paid the price for such a forthright statement at a time when the subject was still largely taboo. An immediate outcome was that John Crowe Ransom refused to print Duncan's "An African Elegy" in *The Kenyon Review*, even though the poem had been scheduled for publication. Duncan's essay is a plea for tolerance on all sides, both from those who condemned homosexuality, whether on racial, religious, or sexual grounds, and from homosexuals themselves. The essay, he noted in a 1959 introduction to its reprinting, was "as far as I know . . . the first discussion of homosexuality which included the frank avowal that the author was himself involved; but my view was that minority associations and identifications were an evil wherever they supersede allegiance to and share in the creation of a human community good – the recognition of fellow-manhood" (*Selected Prose*, 38).

Duncan returned to San Francisco in 1945 and subsequently resumed his studies at Berkeley, focusing upon medieval and Renaissance civilization. Resuming contact with Rexroth, and with fellow poets Jack Spicer and Robin Blaser, Duncan began to formulate his concept of a collage or "serial form" for poems, allowing for a maximum of inclusiveness and sometimes drastic discontinuities, while retaining an inner coherence through the repetition of motifs, sounds, images, and phrases. Duncan's well-known poem from 1960, "Often I am Permitted to Return to a Meadow," articulates this sense of form and its relationship to creativity and the world outside the poem. It concludes:

> Often I am permitted to return to a meadow
> as if it were a given property of the mind
> that certain bounds hold against chaos,
>
> that is a place of first permission,
> everlasting omen of what is.

And in "Poetry, a Natural Thing," also from 1960, he wrote that "The poem / feeds upon thought, feeling, impulse, / to breed itself, / a spiritual urgency at the dark ladders leaping."

In the same year that Duncan published his first book he met Charles Olson, whose theory of "projective verse" bears some resemblance to Duncan's concepts; he also visited Ezra Pound at St. Elizabeths Hospital ("Old man, early / devoted voice," as he described him in the poem "Homage and Lament for Ezra Pound in Captivity May 12, 1944"). *Poems 1948–49* appeared in 1949 and *Medieval Scenes* in 1950, but the new decade saw important developments in both Duncan's personal life and his literary associations. In 1951 he began his lifelong relationship with visual artist Jess Collins, with whom he collaborated in the visual design of a number of his subsequent books of poems. In 1952 he began publishing in Cid Corman's *Origin* and in the *Black Mountain Review*. *Caesar's Gate: Poems, 1949–1950* appeared in 1955 and two further books in the late 1950s. Meanwhile Duncan taught briefly at Black Mountain College in 1956, and helped to found the Poetry Center at San Francisco State University, where he served as assistant director from September 1956 to June 1957.

The 1960s saw Duncan's emergence as an important figure with the publication of *The Opening of the Field* (1960), *Roots and Branches* (1964) and *Bending the Bow* (1968). The achievement brought such recognition as a major prize from *Poetry* magazine, grants from the National Endowment for the Arts, and in 1963 a Guggenheim Fellowship. This decade also saw the republication of Duncan's earlier poems. Duncan took a forceful stand against the Vietnam War, treating it in the "Passages" poems of *Bending the Bow* in a broad mythological context. In "Up Rising: Passages 25" he described the agony and destruction inflicted by the war as:

> in the line of duty, for the might and enduring fame
> of Johnson, for the victory of American will over its victims,
> releasing his store of destruction over the enemy,
> in terror and hatred of all communal things, of communion,
> of communism

In the early 1970s Duncan declared that he would not publish a new book of poems for 15 years, in order to be able to focus more fully on his writing. He continued to be increasingly involved in the printing and distribution of his books, and when his next volume of poetry, *Ground Work: Before the War*, appeared in 1984 it carried notice that the volume was "typeset under Duncan's direct supervision." *Ground Work II: In the Dark* appeared in 1987, and the following year Duncan died in San Francisco from a long-standing kidney disease.

## Bibliography

Robert Duncan, *Selected Poems*, rev. and enlarged, ed. Robert J. Bertholf (New York, 1997).
—— *A Selected Prose*, ed. Robert J. Bertholf (New York, 1995).

Robert Bertholf and Ian Reid, eds., *Robert Duncan: Scales of the Marvelous* (New York, 1979).
Michael Davidson, *The San Francisco Renaissance: Poetics and Community at Mid-Century* (Cambridge, 1989).
Mark Johnson, *Robert Duncan* (Boston, 1988).

# Richard Wilbur (b. 1921)

Throughout his writing career Richard Wilbur has emphasized the importance of meter and form in the poem. In a 1995 interview, for example, he argued that "in free verse one loses all sorts of opportunities for power, emphasis, and precision, especially rhythmic precision." On the other hand "meters and forms" are for a poet "instruments or contraptions which heighten and empower his words – underlining the shape and steps of the argument, giving it an appropriate music, honing the colloquial movement, hitting the important words hard, changing the utterance in every way." Wilbur's output has been variously seen as a major achievement despite taking a direction abandoned after the 1950s by many of his contemporaries, or as the work of a poet who is elegant but essentially minor, despite his unquestioned craftsmanship. In this latter view Wilbur's poetry is limited in its development and scope. What has been universally praised is his skill as a translator in his versions of plays by Molière and Racine, particularly in his translations of *The Misanthrope* (1955) and *Tartuffe* (1963).

Wilbur was born in New York City and grew up in New Jersey. He graduated from Amherst College in 1942, and entered the army, where he first began writing verse seriously. He received an MA from Harvard in 1947 and in the same year published his first book, *The Beautiful Changes and Other Poems*. This was followed by *Ceremony and Other Poems* in 1950 and *Things of This World* (1956) – which was awarded the Pulitzer Prize and the National Book Award. All three contributed to place Wilbur's reputation in the 1950s on a level with Robert Lowell's. Meanwhile Wilbur taught at Harvard until 1954, moved on to teach at Wellesley, and then at Wesleyan University. From 1977 to 1986 he was writer in residence at Smith College. At Wesleyan he played a central role in founding the Wesleyan University Press poetry series, which since 1959 has been important in supporting the work of many emerging and established poets.

In Wilbur's poetry the independent existence of things in the world is important, but his vision is also one that emphasizes the spiritual and imaginative quality that engagement with those things can produce. In his well-known "Love Calls Us To the Things of This World" the speaker awakens to the sound of pulleys sending full laundry lines out into the morning air, but while the laundry consists of "bed-sheets," "blouses," and "smocks," the items are also imagined as "angels." As James Longenbach has written of this poem, "Wilbur's point is that a devotion to laundry alone – to the world's sensual pleasures, physical and linguistic – may be as world-denying as the most ascetic spirituality." The parallels in this image to the wit of seventeenth-century metaphysical poetry are a feature of Wilbur's verse, and illustrate his affinities with the poetry and criticism of T. S. Eliot and of the major New Critical poets of the 1940s. "A World Without Objects Is a Sensible Emptiness" takes its title from a Meditation of Thomas Traherne's and similarly explores the very full world of spirit and grace that surrounds the world of objects. The language here and in Wilbur's verse generally is at once precise, carefully crafted, and accessible, a poem's use of allusion always maintaining a careful balance with its grounding in the everyday.

*Advice to a Prophet and Other Poems* (1961) was followed by *Walking to Sleep: New Poems and Translations* (1969), which was awarded the Bollingen Prize. Wilbur had already won a Bollingen translation prize for his *Tartuffe*. *The Mind-Reader: New Poems* appeared in 1976 and a *New and Collected Poems* in 1988 (which won him his second Pulitzer). *Mayflies: New Poems and Translations* (2000) collects Wilbur's poems of the 1990s. His publications also include editions of poems by Shakespeare and Poe, and books of verse for children. His collections of prose essays include pieces on such contemporaries as Elizabeth Bishop and John Ciardi. Among the other honors that have recognized his achievement have been two Guggenheim Fellowships, and his being named the second Poet Laureate of the United States in 1987, following Robert Penn Warren.

## Bibliography

Richard Wilbur, *New and Collected Poems* (San Diego, 1988).

Rodney Stenning Edgecombe, *A Reader's Guide to the Poetry of Richard Wilbur* (Tuscaloosa, 1995).

John B. Hougen, *Ecstasy within Discipline: The Poetry of Richard Wilbur* (Atlanta, GA, 1995).

James Longenbach, *Modern Poetry after Modernism* (New York, 1997).

# Denise Levertov (1923–1997)

Denise Levertov was born in Ilford, England, a suburb of London, and became a US citizen in 1955. Her mother was Welsh, and her father of Russian Jewish ancestry who converted to Christianity and became an Anglican priest. Levertov's work in the 1950s responded to the examples of William Carlos Williams and of the Black Mountain College poets, especially Robert Creeley and Robert Duncan, but by the 1960s she had found her own powerful voice. Her poetry combines visionary mysticism with a focus on the everyday, and often with urgent social and political concerns. She was strongly opposed to the war in Vietnam and later to the Gulf War, and was active in the environmental and anti-nuclear movements. Her later books explore religious faith more explicitly, and towards the end of her life she converted to Catholicism. For some critics Levertov's poetry of the 1960s is her major achievement, and they find the anti-war poetry in particular to be crudely rhetorical in comparison with her earlier work. But for many Levertov remained an important figure, as poet, teacher, and critic, offering her own particular perspective upon the country that she – not always contentedly – had chosen as her own, and bringing to that perspective her own multi-cultural heritage and moral vision.

Levertov was educated mostly at home. Her first published poem, "Listening to Distant Guns," somewhat similar in tone to the poems of Hardy, appeared in 1940, and her first book, *The Double Image*, in 1946. In 1947 she married American writer Mitchell Goodman, who would go on to be a major anti-war activist in the 1960s. In France and Italy in the next few years Levertov began reading Williams and Wallace Stevens, and in 1951, at the instigation of Creeley, who had known Goodman at Harvard, she began a correspondence with Williams. Kenneth Rexroth included six of her poems in his anthology *The New British Poets* (1949), a volume designed to illustrate the new British Romanticism (with Dylan Thomas as its major figure) that was reacting against the work of Auden and the poets of the 1930s.

From 1952 until the late 1960s – when she moved to the Boston area – Levertov was based in New York. She began to publish in such journals as *Origin* and the *Black Mountain Review*. During two years living in Mexico (1957–8), she published her first two American books, *Here and Now* and *Overland to the Islands*. In these volumes and in *With Eyes at the Back of Our Heads* (1960) she responded to the open form poetics of Williams, Duncan, Creeley, and Charles Olson. Like Williams and Creeley, her poetry emphasized a full engagement with the world of objects. But in Levertov's poetry the object, properly engaged, reveals an almost magical essence beneath its surface. This is Levertov's version of Williams's phrase "No ideas but in things" from his *Paterson*, which she insisted when writing of Williams's own poetry did not mean "no ideas." This direction is to go "beyond the end," as she put it in a poem of that title. In the title poem of *Overland to the Islands* a dog "keeps moving, changing / pace and approach but / not direction – 'every step an arrival.'" This visionary aspect of her work gave her an especial affinity to the poetry of Robert Duncan. Dreams were an important area of experience for Levertov, and the journals among her papers at Stanford University contain many descriptions and possible interpretations reflecting this interest.

In three volumes in the 1960s Levertov found her own particular voice, *The Jacob's Ladder* (1961), *O Taste and See* (1964), and *The Sorrow Dance* (1967). In "September 1961," from the 1964 volume, she wrote of her sense of the heritage bestowed by the aging Williams, Pound, and H.D.: "This is the year the old ones, / the old great ones / leave us alone on the road." These figures "have told us / the road leads to the sea, / and given / / the language into our hands." The poem concludes:

> But for us the road
> unfurls itself, we count the
> words in our pockets, we wonder
>
> how it will be without them, we don't
> stop walking, we know
> there is far to go, sometimes
>
> we think the night wind carries
> a smell of the sea . . .

Levertov's public role grew in the 1960s too. In 1961 and again from 1963 to 1965 she was poetry editor of *The Nation*, and she held a series of teaching and writer-in-residence positions which included Vassar, City College of New York, Berkeley, and MIT.

Her opposition to the Vietnam War began in earnest in 1965, culminating with a visit to Hanoi with poet Muriel Rukeyser in the fall of 1972. Poems in *The Sorrow Dance* begin to reflect this concern, which became central to Levertov's next volumes. "What Were They Like?" is a particularly well-known poem from the 1967 volume, and "Advent 1966" an example from a little later.

Another important event for the poet in the 1960s was the death in 1964 of Levertov's older sister Olga, who is remembered in the sequence first published in *The Sorrow Dance* titled "Olga Poems." These poems and the late autobiographical essays in *Tesserae* reveal the importance of the sometimes difficult relationship between the sisters.

Levertov and Mitchell Goodman separated in 1973 and divorced in 1975. Marriage is a theme in a number of poems in Levertov's volumes, and love continued to be a subject that she often returned to subsequently, although never in the confessional mode of some of her peers – a mode that she depreciated in her essays and interviews. From 1972 to 1978 she taught at Tufts University. In 1980 she was elected to the American Academy and Institute of Arts and Letters, and in 1981 began a period teaching a semester each at Brandeis and Stanford. Subsequently she moved to Seattle in 1989, and retired from Stanford as a full professor in 1993.

Levertov continued her social activism in the 1980s and into the last years of her life. Her poetry in the 1980s began to foreground the interest in religious faith that became characteristic of her later work, but that was also one with the visionary emphasis in all of her poetry. *Candles in Babylon* (1982) illustrates the integration of many of her interests, since it includes poems on political action, a speech for an anti-draft rally, a eulogy of Williams, and also "Mass for the Day of St. Thomas Didymus." Another direction in Levertov's work in these years was the broadening of her sense of heritage to include English and other European poets, especially Rilke, that her 1950s and 1960s poetry had given less attention to. She published three volumes of essays on such topics as her impressions of contemporaries, reflections on the challenge of teaching, the craft of writing, and the nature of political poetry.

Levertov's final volumes, *Evening Train* (1992), *Sands of the Well* (1996), and the posthumous *This Great Unknowing: Last Poems* (1999), reflect her continuing faith, her sensitive response to the seasons around Mount Rainier and Lake Washington where she lived her last years, and meditations and memories from the perspective of her terminal illness – lymphoma, complications from which ended her life just before Christmas 1997. The quality of Levertov's most successful work is informed by a keen eye and a visionary passion, and – for sympathetic readers – driven by a political and moral commitment that is always balanced by a concern for craftsmanship.

## Bibliography

Denise Levertov, *Selected Poems*, ed. Paul A. Lacey (New York, 2002).

Linda A. Kinnahan, *Poetics of the Feminine: Authority and Literary Tradition in William Carlos Williams, Mina Loy, Denise Levertov, and Kathleen Fraser* (Cambridge, 1994).

Anne C. Little and Susie Paul, eds., *Denise Levertov: New Perspectives* (West Cornwall, CT, 2000).
Harry Marten, *Understanding Denise Levertov* (Columbia, SC, 1988).

# James Dickey (1923–1997)

James Dickey was born in Atlanta, Georgia. After a year at Clemson College he enlisted in the air force and was posted to the Pacific. Upon his return he studied at Vanderbilt, graduating with an MA in 1950, and having determined to be a writer. In that same year he had his first important publication when *The Sewanee Review* accepted his poem "The Shark at the Window." He began teaching at Rice University with the initial intention of finishing his doctorate, but was recalled to the air force during the Korean War – although, contrary to some of his own later accounts, he stayed in the US, working at a number of military bases in the south. Dickey had a tendency to inflate biographical details, exaggerating his flying exploits in the Pacific in the Second World War, for example. Upon his return to Rice, Dickey struggled to publish his poetry and creative prose, and lost interest in completing his doctoral dissertation. Dickey's poems in these years mirror the formal vein of Allen Tate, John Crowe Ransom, and the early work of Robert Lowell, although a few years later his work became more experimental in form. He left Rice in 1954 when he won a *Sewanee Review* Fellowship, and spent a year in Europe before taking another teaching position, this time at the University of Florida. He left the Florida job abruptly, before his contract had finished, oppressed for the moment by the world of academe. From 1956 to 1961 he worked as a copywriter for advertising agencies, first in New York and then in Atlanta.

During his business career Dickey continued to work hard at his writing, working on the novel that would become his best known, *Deliverance* (1970), and on the poems that went into his first two books, *Into the Stone and Other Poems* (1960), and *Drowning with Others* (1962), both of which were well received. His poems began to appear in *The New Yorker* and other prestigious journals, and he began to receive invitations to read his poems at colleges and high schools. The award of a Guggenheim Fellowship in 1961 prompted him to leave advertising. After another year in Europe, Dickey taught at a number of colleges, and published *Helmets* (1964) which was a finalist for the National Book Award. He won the award with his next book, *Buckdancer's Choice* (1965), usually considered his finest volume of verse, and this led to his appointment as Consultant in Poetry to the Library of Congress from 1966 to 1968, a National Institute of Arts and Letters Award, and the Melville

Cane Award of the Poetry Society of America. *Babel to Byzantium: Poets and Poetry Now*, a book of essays and reviews, appeared in 1968. At this point in his career Dickey could make serious claim to be one of the two or three most important poets of his generation.

Dickey's poems have been described as "gothic" and "surrealist" in their treatment of nature, fear, and human sexuality. These qualities are represented in his well-known "The Sheep Child." The poem opens describing the legends held by "farm boys wild to couple" about a "sheep-child" preserved in alcohol "in a museum in Atlanta / Way back in a corner somewhere." The poem then goes on to imagine the short, intense experience of such a creature's *"blazing moment"* of birth and death *"In the summer sun of the hillside."* Equally powerfully imagined is "Falling," based upon the actual incident of a 29-year-old flight attendant falling to her death after being sucked out of the plane when an emergency door sprang open. In the long fall to her death, Dickey imagines her going through a series of intense emotions, stripping off her clothes in a kind of ecstasy, and serving in her fall from the sky as a fantasy love goddess to the dreaming farmers below.

Following his Library of Congress appointment Dickey began teaching at the University of South Carolina, where he stayed until his death, even continuing to teach his classes when barely able to breathe in his last illness. The popular success of *Deliverance* when it was published in 1970, and its subsequent filming – for which Dickey wrote the screenplay – made him a celebrity, and a large sum of money. But he never received the same kind of critical acclaim or popular success in his poetry or prose work again. He developed a serious drinking problem, which became part of the boisterous, aggressive persona he brought to his many poetry readings in the 1970s. His celebrity was reinforced when he read his poem "The Strength of Fields" at President Carter's inauguration in 1977, but by the late 1970s his poems appeared less and less frequently in prestigious magazines and his reputation as a poet began a long decline. However, for some years he continued to command high fees for his popular readings and large advances for his novels, and was often called upon by northern literary journals to represent the voice of southern writing in essays and reviews.

Dickey continued to be productive in the 1980s and 1990s, although his reputation became more regional and his following more local. Nevertheless he was elected to the American Academy of Arts and Letters in 1988. His last new book of poetry, *The Eagle's Mile* (1990), contained many poems that had been written in the early 1980s. His collection *The Whole Motion: Collected Poems 1945–1992* did not garner a great deal of attention, and where it did the main consensus was that Dickey's strongest period had been 1947–57, and that his writing since then had suffered from a lack of discipline.

In 1994 Dickey became seriously ill, a condition brought on by his many years as an alcoholic, and he never fully recovered his health.

## Bibliography

James Dickey, *The Whole Motion: Collected Poems, 1945–1992* (Middletown, CT, 1992).

Robert Kirschten, *Struggling for Wings: The Art of James Dickey* (Columbia, SC, 1997).
Ernest Suarez, *James Dickey and the Politics of Canon: Assessing the Savage Ideal* (Columbia, MS, 1993).
Gordon Van Ness, *Outbelieving Existence: The Measured Motion of James Dickey* (Columbia, SC, 1992).

# A. R. Ammons (1926–2001)

Archie Randolph Ammons was born in Whiteville, North Carolina, the son of a tobacco farmer, and began writing poetry while serving in the navy in the Second World War. He studied biology and chemistry at Wake Forest University, and following his graduation in 1949 pursued graduate study in English for two years at the University of California, Berkeley. After a year as principal of a small elementary school in Hatteras, North Carolina, and a period as a real estate salesman, he went on to manage his father-in-law's glass-making company in southern New Jersey. The publication of his first book of poems, *Ommateum* (1955), was self-financed and barely noticed, but the appearance of his second, *Expressions of Sea Level*, in 1964 coincided with his appointment to a position teaching writing at Cornell University. In his subsequent career he published more than 25 books of poetry, and his honors included two National Book Awards, a Bollingen Prize, the National Book Critics Circle Award, and fellowships from the Guggenheim Foundation, the MacArthur Foundation, and the American Academy of Arts and Letters.

Ammons's poetry is primarily meditative. His interest in the relationship of humans to nature, and in the possibilities of transcendence, has led his work to be compared to that of Emerson. Both formally and in its subject matter Ammons's poetry is concerned with process, with an organic set of relationships that allows for open possibilities and a series of ongoing, connected encounters. Within this concern his work sometimes juxtaposes science and aesthetics – not to suggest a dichotomy, but rather two related ways of looking at phenomena.

The often anthologized "Corson's Inlet" is probably Ammons's most characteristic poem. The opening lines describe setting out for a walk over the landscape of dunes in south-east New Jersey that give the poem its title. The subsequent lines and stanzas, varying in length and in position on the page, parallel the varied encounters that fill the journey and – equally important – the variety of responses within the poet. Boundaries disappear, and thought is made concrete:

> the walk liberating, I was released from forms,
> from the perpendiculars
>     straight lines, blocks, boxes, binds
> of thought
> into the hues, shadings, rises, flowing bends and blends
>     of sight:

The poem's flux and process is held together by the poet's responsiveness: "the possibility of rule as the sum of rulelessness: / the 'field' of action / with moving, incalculable center:" and form is not imposed upon the poem or the surroundings:

>             no arranged terror: no forcing of image, plan,
>     or thought:
> no propaganda, no humbling of reality to precept:
>
>     terror pervades but is not arranged, all possibilities
>     of escape open: no route shut, except in
>         the sudden loss of all routes:
>
>         I see narrow orders, limited tightness, but will
>     not run to that easy victory:

As these examples illustrate, the colon is a favorite mark of punctuation for Ammons to signify these balanced relationships. In another characteristic poem, "The City Limits," the boundlessness is, as with the meditative walk across the dunes, immediately associated with the mind's response. The poem begins:

> When you consider the radiance, that it does not withhold
> itself but pours its abundance without selection into every
> nook and cranny not overhung or hidden; when you consider

Ammons is the author of five long poems. The first of these, *Tape for the Turn of the Year* (1965) he typed onto a roll of adding machine tape, in part as an exercise in responding to the physical demands of such a restricted space. *Sphere: The Form of a Motion* (1974) consists of 155 sections each of four three-line stanzas, the whole organized around the central image of earth as viewed from outer space. The whole poem is one continuous sentence. The other book-length poems are *The Snow Poems* (1977), *Garbage* (1993) – which won Ammons his second National Book Award, following that for his *Collected Poems: 1951–1971* in 1973 – and *Glare* (1997). Ammons's occasional prose appears in *Set in Motion: Essays, Interviews, and Dialogues* (1996). Ammons retired from Cornell in 1998, and he died in Ithaca on February 25, 2001, of cancer.

### Bibliography

A. R. Ammons, *The Selected Poems: Expanded Edition* (New York, 1986).

Alan Holder, *A. R. Ammons* (Boston, 1978).

Steven P. Schneider, *A. R. Ammons and the Poetics of Widening Scope* (Rutherford, NJ, 1994).

—— ed., *Complexities of Motion: New Essays on A. R. Ammons's Long Poems* (Madison, NJ, 1999).

# Allen Ginsberg (1926–1997)

Allen Ginsberg was as renowned for his poetry readings as for his poetry itself, although his work had an important impact upon his own and subsequent generations and reached a wide readership. He was at the center of the 1950s Beat Movement that included William Burroughs, Jack Kerouac, and Gregory Corso. He was probably the best known American poet of the second half of the century.

Ginsberg was born in Newark, New Jersey, and grew up in nearby Paterson. His father Louis was a high-school teacher and locally well-known poet who wrote in a formal vein, but had associated with the avant-garde New York school of the 1920s. Louis was the author of three books of poetry, his posthumously published *Collected Poems* (1992) running to over 400 pages. Naomi Ginsberg, Allen's mother, was a Russian immigrant whose family left in 1905 to avoid a pogrom. Naomi, a committed communist, suffered from severe persecution paranoia for much of her adult life, for which she had to be hospitalized, and her suffering, and death – confined in Pilgrim State Hospital – is the subject of one of her son's best known poems, *Kaddish*.

Allen Ginsberg attended Columbia University, where he was briefly suspended in 1945 as the result of allowing Kerouac to spend the night in his dormitory room. His early poetry at Columbia was in the vein of such seventeenth-century poets as Sir Thomas Wyatt and Andrew Marvell. But his most important literary education came from his growing friendship with Kerouac, Burroughs, and other radical writers centered in New York's Greenwich Village. Yeats, Baudelaire, and Blake were the key figures informing the Romantic sensibility of the group. In 1948, the year in which he graduated from Columbia, Ginsberg had a mystical vision which he later recalled many times as central to his growth as a writer, and which he particularly associated with William Blake.

Ginsberg's late 1940s poems also owe a good deal to Whitman, but his work became more concrete, less visionary, and the language of his poems more contemporary, as a result of his response to the work of William Carlos Williams. Ginsberg wrote to Williams in the late 1940s, while the older poet was completing the later books of his long poem *Paterson*, and Williams included two of these early letters in book IV of the poem, and a later letter from Ginsberg in book V. Writing from Paterson, the 23-year-old Ginsberg told Williams in the first of these letters: "I know you will be pleased to realize that at least one actual citizen of your community has inherited your experience in his struggle to love and know his own world-city, through your work, which is an accomplishment you almost cannot have hoped to achieve." Williams was never comfortable with the visionary and chant-like side of Ginsberg's poetics, but he went on to write the introduction to Ginsberg's *Empty Mirror: Early Poems*, which remained unpublished until 1961, and to *Howl and other Poems* (1956), the book that made Ginsberg famous.

Upon graduating from Columbia, Ginsberg worked as a local journalist, and also in the merchant marine, spent some time in Mexico, and in 1954 moved to San Francisco, where such writers as Kenneth Rexroth, Robert Duncan, and Gary Snyder were part of the city's active poetry scene; Lawrence Ferlinghetti opened the City Lights bookstore in June 1953, and Ruth Witt-Diamant founded the San Francisco Poetry Center at the end of 1954 – both important meeting places for poets.

For a few months Ginsberg worked as a market researcher, but his company closed down its San Francisco office in May 1955. In August of that year Ginsberg began writing "Howl," returning to his long, Whitman-like lines, combining them with the visionary intensity that he brought from his interest in Blake, and the concrete detail and contemporary focus that characterized his short poems written under the influence of Williams.

Ferlinghetti published *Howl and other Poems* as number 4 in his Pocket Poets series, and Ginsberg began reading the poem on the West Coast, where it was received with great enthusiasm. Richard Eberhart wrote an influential review in *The New York Times* on September 2, 1956, identifying

Ginsberg as a major new poet, and noting of "Howl" that it "has created a furor of praise or abuse whenever read or heard." On the other hand, John Hollander in the *Partisan Review* called the book a "dreadful little volume," "a very short and very tiresome book," and deplored its "hopped-up and improvised tone." The book's success was helped greatly by further controversy when the police unsuccessfully prosecuted it as obscene in August 1957. The American Civil Liberties Union took up the defense. By the end of the trial there were more than ten thousand copies of *Howl* in print.

The poem is both a frontal assault on the reader, with its long lists of lives broken, acts of rebellion, and destructive sexual and cultural oppression, and also an attempt to transcend ordinary consciousness, through accumulation, repetition, lyrical intensity and the breaking of conventional connectives. The aim of the poem's chant-like lyricism is to produce a condition of consciousness and understanding in which logic, reason, and confining social and creative categories are left behind in a visionary celebration of suffering community. Section I displays the cultural breakdown, opening with its famous declaration:

> I saw the best minds of my generation destroyed by madness, starving
>   hysterical naked,
> dragging themselves through the negro streets at dawn looking for an
>   angry fix,
> angelheaded hipsters burning for the ancient heavenly connection to the
>   starry dynamo in the machinery of night,

Section II offers a series of definitions of "Moloch" to illustrate the pervasiveness of the oppressive force both in the culture and the creative process itself. Section III turns to Carl Solomon, whom Ginsberg had met when they were fellow patients in the late 1940s at Columbia Presbyterian Psychiatric Institute (and who received a not entirely welcome fame from his role in the poem). In this section the poem offers its vision of community: "I'm with you in Rockland" the poem repeats, concluding:

> in my dreams you walk dripping from a sea-journey on the highway across
> America in tears to the door of my cottage in the western Night

Ginsberg added a "Footnote to Howl" which declares "Holy" – and celebrates – many of the poem's characters and values, ending with an assertion of the soul's freedom, or potential freedom, from the forces of "Moloch." The poem's urgency, and the richness of detail with which it portrays its generation of victims, heroes, and outcasts, brought a new frankness to American poetry, including its open celebration of homosexuality and of experiments with drugs. Some of the other poems in the volume are also some of Ginsberg's best known, including "A Supermarket in California" – where the poet records a vision of meeting Walt Whitman – "Sunflower Sutra," and "America." A section of "Earlier Poems" includes some of the tight, short poems written in the vein of Williams.

Ginsberg soon became the perceived spokesman for the Beat generation, and began the world travels that he undertook for the rest of his life, and also his generous career-long efforts on behalf of other poets to use his fame to get their work published. In 1959 he began writing *Kaddish*, experimenting with heroin, liquid Methedrine, and Dexedrine tablets as a way to explore the painful memories of his mother's suffering. The poem, published in 1961, is a sometimes harrowing tribute and funeral lament for Naomi Ginsberg, who had died in 1956. The long elegy is modeled on the traditional Jewish memorial service for the dead. For some commentators, for whom "Howl" has retreated into being something of a historical document, "Kaddish" remains a powerful personal lament, and Ginsberg's finest sustained poem.

Ginsberg's poetry became somewhat diffuse in the 1960s, although he became if anything an even more prominent figure. He continued to advocate sexual freedom and experimentation with drugs, and became more involved in political activism. His poem "Wichita Vortex Sutra" is an indictment of the war in Vietnam. In this decade Buddhism and the practice of meditation began to play an important role in Ginsberg's explorations of consciousness, eventually replacing drugs, a realization that is recorded in his poem "The Change." In 1974 with poet Anne Waldman he co-founded the "Jack Kerouac School of Disembodied Poetics," based at Tibetan Buddhist teacher Chogyam Trungpa Ripoche's Naropa Institute in Boulder, Colorado, and he began teaching there regularly in the summer. Ginsberg's environmental concerns and anti-nuclear activities are represented in the poems of his *Plutonian Ode* (1982). His characterization of the title poem, on the volume's back cover, is that it: "combines scientific info on 24,000-year cycle of the Great Year compared with equal half-life of Plutonium waste, accounting Homeric formula for appeasing underground millionaire Pluto Lord of Death, jack in the gnostic box of Aeons, and Adamantine Truth of ordinary mind inspiration, unhexing Nuclear ministry of fear."

In the 1970s Ginsberg's work began to be recognized by the literary establishment. He won the National Book Award for *The Fall of America: Poems of These States 1965–1971* (1973), which was dedicated to Walt Whitman. In 1979 he was inducted into the American Academy and Institute of Arts and Letters. In the 1980s he began to publish with Harper & Row, who brought out his widely reviewed *Collected Poems 1947–1980* in 1984. He was able to obtain some relief from the necessity of reading tours (he had lived on his earnings as a writer since 1955) when appointed as a Distinguished Professor, teaching one day a week, at Brooklyn College in 1986.

Ginsberg's readings, usually with his own musical accompaniment provided by a portable harmonium, continued to draw large audiences up to the end of his life. Three further books of poems followed the *Collected Poems*. The title poem of *White Shroud* (1986) he described as a "dream epilogue to 'Kaddish'" while another poem in the volume, "Written in My Dream by W. C. Williams" showed the continuing importance to Ginsberg of this early mentor. *Cosmopolitan Greetings* appeared in 1994, and *Death & Fame: Last Poems 1993–1997* in 1999, two years after his death from liver cancer.

### Bibliography

Allen Ginsberg, *Collected Poems, 1947–1980* (New York, 1984).

Lewis Hyde, ed., *On the Poetry of Allen Ginsberg* (Ann Arbor, 1984).
Barry Miles, *Ginsberg: A Biography* (New York, 1989).
Marjorie Perloff, *Poetic Licence: Essays on Modernist and Postmodernist Lyric* (Evanston, 1990).
Paul Portugés, *The Visionary Poetics of Allen Ginsberg* (Santa Barbara, CA, 1979).

# Robert Creeley (b. 1926)

Robert Creeley has been an important editor and teacher as well as poet, forging an individual path in his work out of the open-ended poetics advocated by Charles Olson and the concentration upon the everyday world stressed by William Carlos Williams. This poetry records in minimalist, sometimes cryptic, terms an interior drama usually concerned with intimate emotional feelings – about love, loss, aging, or the poet's craft itself. Creeley's poetry rejects traditional rhyme and meter, and his view of form is organic. Olson often quoted Creeley's assertion that "Form is never more than an extension of content."

Creeley was born in Arlington, Massachusetts. Before his fifth birthday his father, a doctor and the head of a local hospital, had died, and Creeley had lost the sight of his left eye in an accident. The family moved to a farm in West Acton. Attending Holderness School, in Plymouth, New Hampshire, Creeley edited the school's literary publications before entering Harvard in 1943. His studies at Harvard were interrupted for a year when he served as an ambulance driver in 1944–5 for the American Field Service in India. He returned to Harvard, published his work in the Harvard *Wake*, married, and left before graduating with only a semester left to complete.

Like Frost before him, Creeley tried farming in New Hampshire for the next couple of years. He made plans to start a literary magazine and began a correspondence with Cid Corman and later with Charles Olson. Corman founded *Origin* after Creeley's plans fell through and the journal became an important outlet for poets interested in the alternatives to New Critical formalism, alternatives that they saw represented in particular by the work of Pound and Williams. Creeley's correspondence with Olson has become legendary. The two wrote to each other sometimes daily, and the complete correspondence when published took up ten volumes. The two did not meet until 1954, four years after the correspondence began.

In 1951 the Creeleys moved to Aix-en-Provence in France, where their neighbors included Harvard friend Mitchell Goodman and his wife Denise Levertov. Creeley's poems began to appear in *Origin*, and his first book of poems, *Le Fou*, published by Golden Goose Press, appeared in 1952 – the same year that the family, now including two sons and a daughter, moved to Mallorca. *The Kind of Act Of* and *The Immoral Proposition*, two further books of poems, appeared in 1953.

From the Spanish island in the western Mediterranean, where printing was cheap, Creeley set up the Divers Press, publishing Robert Duncan, Charles Olson, and his own 1954 book of short stories, *The Gold Diggers*. From March to July he taught at Black Mountain College, where Olson was principal, and in the same year began to edit *The Black Mountain Review*. He returned to teach at Black Mountain College in 1955, and the following year began teaching at a boys' school in New Mexico. Divorced by 1956, he remarried in 1957, and continued his teaching in various locations – in Guatemala, the University of New Mexico, and the University of British Columbia. Black Mountain College had granted him a BA in 1956, and the University of New Mexico followed with an MA in 1960. Creeley continued to publish volumes of poetry with small presses regularly in the 1950s, but he became well known with the wider publication of *For Love: Poems 1950–1960* in 1962, which offered an opportunity to review his achievement.

"I Know a Man," from 1962, is often anthologized. The poem records a moment of intimate, stressful exchange while driving with a friend, concerned that "the darkness sur / rounds us," and suggesting that one comfort might be to "buy a goddam big car." The friend replies:

> drive, he sd, for
> christ's sake, look
> out where yr going.

In the ordinariness of the central activity and the everyday language, the wit, economy, compression, the focus on the present rather than an abstraction, and the quiet but intense anxiety motivating the short narrative, this is a quintessential Creeley poem. But sometimes the poems are more cryptic and illogical in their movement, while still retaining the characteristics of interior drama. "The Door," a longer poem, dedicated to Robert Duncan, is an example. Creeley's emphasis upon immediacy, and its relationship to language and poetry, receives explicit statement in his poem "I Keep to Myself Such Measures . . ."

*The Island*, Creeley's only novel, appeared in 1963. In the 1960s Creeley began to receive some major grants and awards, including, in 1964, the first of two Guggenheim Fellowships. In 1966 he taught for the first time at the State University of New York, Buffalo, where in 1970 he accepted a permanent teaching position. In 1991 he became the founding director of the university's important Poetics Program, which now includes in its core faculty poets Charles Bernstein and Susan Howe.

In his more than 60 books of poetry, Creeley has remained a central figure in the line that finds its roots in the work of Pound, Williams, and Louis Zukofsky, and later Olson, Duncan, and Levertov. In recent years his work has begun to include responses to death and aging, although the theme appeared at least as early as "Self Portrait" in 1983 and "Age" in 1988. A 1998 collection is titled *Life & Death*. Creeley was elected a Chancellor of the Academy of American Poets in 1999, and won the 1999 Bollingen Prize in Poetry.

## Bibliography

Robert Creeley, *Selected Poems* (Berkeley, 1991).

Tom Clark and Robert Creeley, *Robert Creeley and the Genius of the American Commonplace: Together with the Poet's own Autobiography* (New York, 1993).
Cynthia Edelberg, *Robert Creeley's Poetry: A Critical Introduction* (Albuquerque, 1978).
John Wilson, ed., *Robert Creeley's Life and Work: A Sense of Increment* (Ann Arbor, 1987).

# Frank O'Hara (1926–1966)

Although Frank O'Hara was fairly well known in his lifetime, having been prominently featured as one of the "New York Poets" in Donald Allen's *The New American Poetry* (1960), his reputation became firmly established when, five years after his early death in 1966, his *Collected Poems* appeared, edited by Allen and with an introduction by John Ashbery. Many of the unpublished poems had survived only because O'Hara had sent them in letters to friends, the poet himself being very casual at times about keeping copies.

O'Hara was born in Baltimore, but grew up in Grafton, near Worcester, Massachusetts. For two years following high school, in 1944–6, he served in the US navy, and then entered Harvard. He began to publish poems in *The Harvard Advocate*, and after graduating in 1950 spent a year at the University of Michigan where he finished an MA. O'Hara then moved to New York, took a job at the publications and ticket desk of the Museum of Modern Art, and began writing seriously.

O'Hara had many friends at the center of the contemporary New York art world. His poetry shares many qualities with the 1950s and 1960s work of Ashbery (a friend from Harvard), and fellow poets Kenneth Koch, Ted Berrigan, and James Schuyler, and the group's work is often associated with such painters as Larry Rivers, Jackson Pollock, Willem de Kooning and Jasper Johns. O'Hara wrote reviews and essays for *Artnews*, and in 1953 became an editorial associate at the journal. He returned to the Museum of Modern Art in 1955, and by the time of his death was an associate curator.

Larry Rivers provided two drawings for O'Hara's first book of poems, *A City Winter and Other Poems* (1951). The title reveals O'Hara's fascination with and love of New York City, and its sounds, signs, smells, and people fill his poems, although nearby Long Island is sometimes the setting. For *Stones* (1957–60) O'Hara contributed 12 poems for a series of lithographs by Rivers. Sometimes he wrote his poems in his lunch hour, and *Lunch Poems* (1964) is the title of one of his best-known volumes. His poem "A Step Away From Them" begins: "It's my lunch hour, so I go / for a walk among the hum-colored / cabs. First down the sidewalk" and the poem then begins its detailed account of a stroll around midtown Manhattan. *Lunch Poems* and the earlier *Meditations in an Emergency* (1957) were the two books, of the six that he published, for which O'Hara was best known in his lifetime.

O'Hara's poems emphasize spontaneity, wit, variety, and an openness to the rich density of lived experience. He called such poems "I do this I do that" poems, and the description conveys the inclusive, accumulating power of such a poem as it records the poet's often mundane activities in his usually urban world. Political and social themes rarely enter the poetry explicitly. The associations in the earlier volumes are sometimes illogical and surrealist, but in the later poems work more to emphasize process and surface arrangement – qualities that critics have compared to those in abstract expressionism. Elements from high and popular culture – for example avant-garde French poets and advertising billboards – range side by side in O'Hara's poems.

In one of O'Hara's most admired poems, "The Day Lady Died," the detail of a lunchtime ritual comes to a halt with the discovery, from a newsstand display, of Billie Holiday's death. "It is 12:20 in New York a Friday" the poem begins, and the poet is looking forward to a weekend on Long Island. Concrete detail records a series of everyday actions on a lunch break:

> I walk up the muggy street beginning to sun
> and have a hamburger and a malted and buy
> an ugly NEW WORLD WRITING to see what the poets
> in Ghana are doing these days
> I go on to the bank
> and Miss Stillwagon (first name Linda I once heard)
> doesn't even look up my balance for once in her life

The poem's open-ended accumulation continues as the poet enters a bookstore and purchases a book by Paul Verlaine (after considering a variety of choices), and on to "the tobacconist in the Ziegfeld Theatre" where the poet discovers the news of Holiday's death. The heightened present gives way to a memory of hearing the singer and her accompanist perform, "she whispered a song along the keyboard / to Mal Waldron and everyone and I stopped breathing."

O'Hara's well-known "Why I Am Not a Painter" is a witty exploration of the painter's relationship to language and the poet's to color. His "A True Account of Talking to the Sun at Fire Island" is an engaging account, following a similar poem by Vladimir Mayakofsky, of a dialog with the Sun about poetry. The Sun delivers its judgment of O'Hara's work – enjoying the poems' lack of grand claims, the poet's idiosyncratic confidence, and gently chiding the writer for sometimes being inaccessible "between buildings" in the Manhattan "I know you love."

It was at the Fire Island of this poem's title that on July 24, 1966 O'Hara was accidentally struck by a dune buggy. Only 40, he died the following day of his injuries.

## Bibliography

*The Collected Poems of Frank O'Hara*, ed. Donald Allen (New York, 1971).

Brad Gooch, *City Poet: The Life and Times of Frank O'Hara* (New York, 1993).
Marjorie Perloff, *Frank O'Hara: A Poet among Painters*, rev. edn. (Chicago, 1998).
Hazel Smith, *Hyperscapes in the Poetry of Frank O'Hara: Difference, Homosexuality, Topography* (Liverpool, 2000).

# James Merrill (1926–1995)

James Merrill was born in New York City, the son of wealthy financier Charles Edward Merrill one of the founders of the highly successful brokerage firm Merrill, Lynch, and Company. When he was 13 his parents separated, a traumatic event for Merrill that is recalled in a number of his poems. His mother was Charles Merrill's second wife. The poet writes of his father's marriages in "The Broken Home":

> Each thirteenth year he married. When he died
> There were already several chilled wives
> In sable orbit – rings, cars, permanent waves.
> We'd felt him warming up for a green bride.
>
> He could afford it. He was "in his prime"
> At three score ten. But money was not time.

Merrill's undergraduate studies at Amherst College were interrupted for a year in 1944 when he served in the US army. He graduated in 1947 having written an undergraduate thesis on Marcel Proust – a writer who was to have influence upon the reflective, meditative mode of Merrill's mature poetry in which, as in the lines above, time and death are frequent themes. Following his graduation, Merrill taught occasionally at colleges and universities, but thanks to his inherited wealth he was able largely to live a life of writing and traveling, eventually publishing more than 25 volumes of verse and proving himself a master of a wide variety of poetic forms.

Merrill's first two books of poetry were privately published, with the help of his father: *Jim's Book* in 1939 while he was at preparatory school, and *The Black Swan* in 1946 while he was still in college. After a short period living in New York, and some years traveling in Europe and Asia, Merrill purchased a house in Stonington, Connecticut, and settled there. He later purchased additional homes in Athens – spending much of each year in Greece until the late 1970s – and in Key West, Florida.

Merrill's first commercial volume of poems, *First Poems*, appeared in 1951 and was praised for its craft and elegance, with some admiration of its high symbolist rhetoric, but the book produced little excitement. A later volume, *The Country of a Thousand Years of Peace* (1959), garnered more attention, but the work for which he is best known was still to come. Between the two books he published two plays, and the first of his two novels, *The Seraglio* – in which a central character is based upon his father.

*Water Street* (1962) marked Merrill's emergence as an important poet, and many of its poems exhibit the qualities that characterized his work for the rest of his career. To the wit, polish, and elegance of the earlier work was added an increased interest in narrative and a relaxed conversational style and emotional depth. "An Urban Convalescence," the first poem of *Water Street*, is often cited as marking the change. For the first time Merrill writes in an overtly autobiographical mode. The poem begins, "Out for a walk, after a week in bed, / I find them tearing up part of my block," and goes on to be a meditation on, among other things, the nature of time and home. Characteristic themes in Merrill's mature poetry are the description of a past love, or of lost childhood. The poems are often structured around a particular motif that takes on emotional and narrative resonance through the poem. In "The Broken Home" the memories of his parents' marriage coming apart return a number of times to a remembered scene with the family's Irish setter. In "Lost in Translation" a complex jigsaw puzzle from "a New York / Puzzle-rental shop" replaces the child's absent mother and father. The poem narrates the piecing together of the puzzle as the adult poet tries to piece together the actions and feelings of "A summer without parents." "The Victor Dog" takes the old trademark of RCA Victor Records as the starting point for musing upon a world of music and art, pleasure and work.

Merrill's poetry of the 1960s and later was significant and highly regarded. His 1966 volume *Nights and Days* won a National Book Award; in 1971 he was elected to the National Institute of Arts and Letters; in 1973 he won the Bollingen Prize for his volume *Braving the Elements* (1972); and from 1979 until his death he served as a Chancellor of the Academy of American Poets. But Merrill's book-length poem *The Changing Light at Sandover* (1982) was the work that firmly established him as a major poet. The result ostensibly of many years at a Ouija board, shared with his long-time companion David Jackson, the ambitious poem, running to 560 pages, is populated by figures from the spiritual world. These include the medium Ephraim (a figure from the first century), W. H. Auden, and dead friends and family members of Merrill's and Jackson's. The poem lays out a complex system of earthly and spiritual levels, and its voices range from the intimate to the cosmic. Parts of the poem are presented as "dictation" from the Ouija board itself.

*Divine Comedies* (1976) includes the first section of the poem "The Book of Ephraim," and the volume won Merrill a Pulitzer Prize. Two subsequent sections followed, *Mirabell: Books of Number* (1978), which won the poet a second National Book Award, and *Scripts for the Pageant* (1980). When the complete poem appeared in 1982 Merrill added to the three sections a Coda in which he begins to read the poem to an assembly of gathered spirits. For some reviewers, the poem's visionary qualities invite comparison with the work of Yeats, Blake, Milton, and Dante.

Following *The Changing Light at Sandover* Merrill returned to the style of his shorter poems in *Late Settings* (1985) and *The Inner Room* (1988). The former contains "From the Cutting-Room Floor" – material that did not finally appear in *The Changing Light at Sandover*, including the voices of William Carlos Williams, Marianne Moore, Gertrude Stein, and Wallace Stevens. Merrill's final volume, *A Scattering of Salts*, was published a month after his death. *A Different Person* (1993) is a prose memoir which includes much biographical information that is relevant to the poems. *Recitative* (1986) collects Merrill's shorter prose pieces.

## Bibliography

James Merrill, *Collected Poems*, ed. J. D. McClatchy and Stephen Yenser (New York, 2001).

Don Adams, *James Merrill's Poetic Quest* (Westport, CT, 1997).
Timothy Materer, *James Merrill's Apocalypse* (Ithaca, NY, 2000).
Stephen Yenser, *The Consuming Myth: The Work of James Merrill* (Cambridge, MA, 1987).

# John Ashbery (b. 1927)

John Ashbery would be the choice of a significant number of critics for the title of most important poet writing at the end of the century. The author of more than 20 volumes, he has won all of the nation's major poetry prizes and fellowships, including the Bollingen Prize, and a fellowship from the MacArthur Foundation, as well as many international honors. His verse of constantly shifting possibilities is difficult, "a recurring wave / Of arrival" as he describes the painting that is the subject of his best-known poem, "Self-Portrait in a Convex Mirror," or "pure / Affirmation that doesn't affirm anything," to quote a later part of the same poem. His poetry is in the meditative tradition of Wallace Stevens and W. H. Auden, but without the confident claims that Stevens could make for the imagination, or Auden for a moral constant. Such claims, and many others, become problematic and speculative in Ashbery's work.

Ashbery was born in Rochester, New York, and graduated from Harvard in 1949 having written his senior honors thesis on Auden. In 1951 he received an MA from Columbia University. While at Harvard he met Kenneth Koch and Frank O'Hara, and the three became central figures in what was later termed the "New York School" of the 1950s, a group particularly interested in the relationships between poetry and painting, and often using witty, surrealist images in their poetry. Ashbery's first book, *Turandot and Other Poems*, was published by the Tibor de Nagy Gallery in 1953 in only 300 copies. His first major publication was *Some Trees* (1956) in the Yale Younger Poets series, with an introduction by Auden. In the best known of this volume's poems, "The Instruction Manual," singled out for comment by Auden, the speaker drifts away from the routine demands of his task writing the manual to imagine a quietly extravagant visit to Guadalajara, Mexico. Ashbery had worked on such manuals for his New York publisher employers in the years following his Columbia degree. The volume also includes a sestina, "The Painter," which demonstrates Ashbery's skill with formal verse, although his usual mode is open form. In his introduction, Auden recognized that Ashbery's subject matter – no firm definitions of the self or its relationship to a world that is itself always shifting – would create difficult poetry. The poet "must accept strange juxtapositions of imagery, singular associations of ideas, he is tempted to manufacture calculated oddities as if the subjectively sacred were necessarily and on all occasions odd. At the same time," Auden continues, "he cannot avoid the question of how to reconcile truth to nature with accuracy of communication, for the writing of poetry presupposes that communication is possible; no one would write it if he were convinced to the contrary." Thus, Auden concludes, Ashbery is strongly interested in the creative process itself.

In Ashbery's work this creative process is usually represented by poetry or painting. In 1955 Ashbery won a Fulbright scholarship and spent most of the next ten years in France. From 1958 to 1965 he wrote art criticism for the *New York Herald Tribune*'s European edition and for *Artnews*, and following his return to New York he edited *Artnews* until 1972. Ashbery's poetry received some important attention when he had three poems included in Donald Allen's *The New American Poetry* (1960), where his work was grouped with that of Koch, O'Hara, Barbara Guest, James Schuyler, and Edward Field.

Some of Ashbery's poems in his next book, *The Tennis Court Oath* (1962), are collage-like in their severe disjunction and fragmentation, particularly the longest poem in the book, "Europe." For some of Ashbery's readers this was taking virtuosity too far, but for some others the book's experimentation represents an achievement they prefer to his more characteristic discursive work. Ashbery himself said in a 1985 interview with John Tranter that he wrote these poems "to shake my mind up, to get out of my habitual ways of thinking and writing. I had intended at some point to go back and put things together again, and indeed I began doing that while I was still living in France."

Ashbery's reputation continued to grow with the publication of *Rivers and Mountains* (1966) which includes his well-known long poem "The Skaters," and with *The Double Dream of Spring* (1970), in which he first displays what has become his mature style of open-ended, discursive meditation, sometimes with shifting pronouns or subjects, in which all stages of a poem's narrative rest upon statements and premises that are momentary and tentative, and end with conclusions that deny any closure. The three poems of *Three Poems* (1972) are in prose, with occasional pieces of verse interspersed. In this same year, 1972, *Artnews* folded and Ashbery went on to write art criticism for *Newsweek* and began teaching at Brooklyn College, some years later taking the position of Charles P. Stevenson, Jr., Professor of Languages and Literature at Bard College.

Ashbery's next book following *Three Poems*, *Self-Portrait in a Convex Mirror* (1975) is his best known and its title poem is probably his most widely read work. The poem takes as its starting point sixteenth-century artist Parmigianino's well-known painting now in the Kunsthistorisches Museum in Vienna, which he painted on a curved surface. It is more accessible than many of Ashbery's poems because its examination of his familiar themes of the passing of time, of selfhood, narrative coherence, love, art, language, creativity, perception, and judgment often return to the painter, whose aims and work on the portrait form an ongoing framework within the poem. There is always a danger in quoting Ashbery that out of context the sentences appear more conclusive than his work ever allows, but in this poem there are a number of helpful summaries within the narrative of meditation, even if they too remain tentative.

*Self-Portrait in a Convex Mirror* won three major literary prizes for Ashbery, the Pulitzer, the National Book Award, and the National Book Critics Circle Award. A volume from the same year, *The Vermont Notebook*, was more light-hearted, although he returned to his characteristic mode with *Houseboat Days* (1977) – one of the poet's own favorite books. This volume includes the often anthologized "Daffy Duck in Hollywood," a good example of the way that Ashbery's poetry can mix popular and high culture – here including advertising slogans and opera, comic strips and allusions to *Paradise Lost*. Ashbery's own "Self-Portrait in a Convex Mirror" becomes "me mug's attenuated / Reflection in yon hubcap." (An earlier poem, from 1970, "Farm Implements and Rutabagas in a Landscape," had been peopled with characters from E. C. Segar's Popeye comic strip.) *As We Know* (1979) included a poem, "Litany," which has provoked much discussion. The poem consists of almost 70 double-column pages, and invites multiple strategies for trying to read it, none of them definitive. "It was sort of an experiment that didn't really work," Ashbery said of the poem in the 1985 interview, and he included very little of "Litany" in his *Selected Poems* in 1985. The 50 poems of *Shadow Train* (1981) are all 16 lines long, each with four stanzas, further illustrating Ashbery's interest in formal inventiveness. The title poem of *A Wave* (1984) is one of Ashbery's finest love poems. He has continued to publish well-received volumes fairly regularly, every one or two years in the 1990s, including a book-length poem, *Girls on the Run: A Poem* (1999), based upon the disturbing paintings of recluse Chicago artist Henry Darger.

A selection of Ashbery's art criticism appeared in *Reported Sightings* (1989). His *Other Traditions: The Charles Eliot Norton Lectures* (2000) contains essays on six writers important to Ashbery: John Clare, Thomas Lovell Beddoes, Raymond Roussel, John Wheelwright, Laura Riding, and David Schubert. Ashbery edited *The Best American Poetry 1988*, which offers a revealing glimpse of his taste in contemporary poetry. He has published three plays, and also a novel, *A Nest of Ninnies* (1969) with James Schuyler.

## Bibliography

John Ashbery, *The Mooring of Starting Out: The First Five Books of Poetry* (Hopewell, NJ, 1997).
—— *Selected Poems* (New York, 1985).

David Herd, *John Ashbery and American Poetry* (New York, 2000).
Susan M. Schultz, ed., *The Tribe of John: Ashbery and Contemporary Poetry* (Tuscaloosa, 1995).
John Shoptaw, *On the Outside Looking Out: John Ashbery's Poetry* (Cambridge, MA, 1994).

# Galway Kinnell (b. 1927)

In his poem "On the Oregon Coast," Galway Kinnell describes a conversation with fellow-poet Richard Hugo in which the two agree "that as post-Darwinians it was up to us to anthropomorphize the world less and animalize, vegetable-ize, and mineralize ourselves more. / We doubted that pre-Darwinian language would let us." This attempt to make language express the self's folding into the elemental world around it produces the subjects frequent in Kinnell's poetry: the primal rhythms of birth and death, transcendence and mortality, raw confrontations of survival, sexual love, memory, and time. Kinnell's poetry is first and foremost personal. Sometimes his subject is a member of his family – perhaps a son's birth or a young daughter's nightmare – but the poetry is rooted in the poet's response to and meditation upon what the experiences might reveal of the human place in a world outside of human order and understanding. The poet for Kinnell is finally an isolated figure, as he depicts William Carlos Williams (a major influence, along with Whitman) in "For William Carlos Williams," a poem describing hearing Williams reading to a largely inattentive campus audience:

> You seemed
> Above remarking we were not your friends.
> You hung around inside the rimmed
> Circles of your heavy glasses and smiled and
> So passed a lonely evening. In an hour
> Of talking your honesty built you a tower.

Kinnell was born in Providence, Rhode Island, and entered Princeton in 1944, where he first began writing poetry seriously and where W. S. Merwin was a fellow undergraduate. After spending time in the US navy and the summer of 1947 at Black Mountain College, he graduated from Princeton in 1948. In 1949 he received an MA from the University of Rochester. He spent a year (1955–6) in France on a Fulbright Fellowship, and in 1963 worked in a voter registration campaign for the Congress of Racial Equality in Louisiana. He has taught at more than 20 colleges and universities, his first tenured position being at New York University in 1985, where he is currently the Erich Maria Remarque Professor in Creative Writing.

Kinnell's first book, *What a Kingdom It Was*, appeared in 1960 and displays a more traditional Christian sensibility than his subsequent work. The most notable poem, "The Avenue Bearing the Initial of Christ into the New World," in its 14 sections blends memories of the Holocaust with a description of Manhattan's Avenue C ghetto, reproducing many of the city's voices and signs. (When Kinnell collected his earlier books in 1974 this poem provided the volume's title.) *Flower Herding on Mount Monadnock* (1964) and *Body Rags* (1968) furthered Kinnell's interest in elemental situations. *Body Rags* contains two of his best-known poems, "The Bear" and "The Porcupine," both of which explore the communality between man and animal in situations involving death. In "The Bear," the narrator wounds a bear and then trails the slowly dying animal for days. When the bear dies, he cuts it open and climbs inside for shelter and in his exhausted sleep relives the bear's experience of its last days and hours.

*The Book of Nightmares* (1971) is usually considered Kinnell's finest book. One of its best-known poems, "Little Sleep's-Head Sprouting Hair in the Moonlight" describes his daughter Maud wakened from a nightmare, and his comforting of her leads to a meditation upon time, instinctive childhood knowledge, and future love. In this book and in other volumes Kinnell also writes of his son Fergus. One of these is the often anthologized "After Making

Love We Hear Footsteps." Fergus appears in his parents' bedroom, as "one whom habit of memory propels to the ground of his making." Kinnell has also written poems about the impact of dropping the atomic bomb on Japan in 1945, and about the Vietnam War, but on the whole he sees poetry as having the status of personal expression, a human cry, rather than, except for a brief period in the 1960s, a direct agent for social change or protest.

In addition to volumes of his own poems that continue to explore the relationship of the self to forces primal and elemental, including *When One Has Lived a Long Time Alone* (1990) and *Imperfect Thirst* (1994), Kinnell has published a number of books of translations. These include the poems of François Villon, Yves Bonnefoy, Yvan Goll, and Rainer Maria Rilke (whose *Duino Elegies* influenced *The Book of Nightmares*). He has also translated a novel by René Hardy. His own novel, *Black Light*, appeared in 1966, and a book of interviews, *Walking Down the Stairs*, in 1978. *How the Alligator Missed Breakfast*, a children's book, appeared in 1982. Kinnell's *Selected Poems* (1982) won the National Book Award and Pulitzer Prize the following year, and his *A New Selected Poems* (2000) was a finalist for the National Book Award. In 1984 Kinnell was awarded a MacArthur Fellowship, and he is a Chancellor of the Academy of American Poets.

**Bibliography**

Galway Kinnell, *A New Selected Poems* (Boston, 2000).

Richard J. Calhoun, *Galway Kinnell* (New York, 1992).
Howard Nelson, ed., *On the Poetry of Galway Kinnell: The Wages of Dying* (Ann Arbor, 1987).
Lee Zimmerman, *Intricate and Simple Things: The Poetry of Galway Kinnell* (Urbana, IL, 1987).

# W. S. Merwin (b. 1927)

William Stanley Merwin was born in New York City but grew up in Union City, New Jersey, and Scranton, Pennsylvania. His father was a Presbyterian minister, and Merwin has said that his first experience of writing poetry came from writing hymns. He attended Princeton University, where he studied with R. P. Blackmur and John Berryman, graduating in 1948. He stayed on for a graduate year, studying Romance languages, his first preparation for later translations from Latin, French, and Spanish poetry that are much admired. In 1950 he moved to Europe, where he would remain, in Spain, England, and the south of France, for much of the next two decades. In 1950 he spent a year tutoring for the family of Robert Graves, and some of Merwin's interest in myth has been attributed to this association with Graves. Through much of the decade Merwin made his living as a translator.

In 1952 W. H. Auden selected Merwin's first book, *A Mask for Janus*, for the Yale Younger Poets series. Merwin's poems in this book, like those he published later in the decade, are formal and highly wrought, and characterized by detachment and technical virtuosity. "Leviathan," for example, from 1956, is modeled on the Anglo-Saxon alliterative line and is similar in its dense complexity to some of the poems Robert Lowell was writing in the late 1940s and early 1950s. In the mid-1950s Merwin also wrote a number of plays. The 1960 poem "The Drunk in the Furnace" from the volume of that title, its central figure creating a wild music behind his "cosily bolted" door, is often seen as signaling the more personal voice and open verse forms of Merwin's later poetry. But this development found its most consistent expression in his next three books, *The Moving Target* (1963), dedicated to Blackmur and winner of the National Book Award, *The Lice* (1967), and *The Carrier of Ladders* (1970) – which won Merwin the Pulitzer Prize. These books were among the most influential poetry volumes published during the 1960s. Merwin's pacifist views led him to take a stand against the war in Vietnam. From 1961 to 1963 he served as poetry editor of *The Nation*, writing in its pages in 1962 that the poet who recognized such responsibilities to speak out would "not have been another priest of ornaments." Poems such as "When the War is Over" and "The Asians Dying" express his contemplative but firm opposition.

Merwin's poems, particularly those of the 1960s, have an elegiac tone, and often contain dream-like, surreal images. The language, like the images, can take unexpected directions while remaining within the almost private logic established by the poem itself. Peter Davidson has written that Merwin's poetry seems "to flow up from an underground river that lies beneath mere speech, as though written in some pre-verbal language of which all later languages have proved to be a mere translation." Edward Hirsch, reviewing Merwin's *Selected Poems* (1988) in *The New York Times*, has termed him "a master of erasures and negations, a visionary of discomfort and reproof." Merwin himself often speaks about language in interviews and in his poetry with a kind of mystical reverence. The interest in process (sometimes connected by commentators to the influence of Frost and Stevens) extends to a refusal to burden the subject matter with definitive claims for the experience or emotion explored. Merwin clearly endorses the advice that he describes John Berryman giving him in his undergraduate days at Princeton. His 1983 poem "Berryman" concludes:

I had hardly begun to read
I asked how can you ever be sure
that what you write is really
any good at all and he said you can't

you can't you can never be sure
you die without knowing
whether anything you wrote was any good
if you have to be sure don't write

Concern for the environment and sensitivity to the threats to animal, insect, and plant life have been frequent subjects of Merwin's poetry since the late 1970s, as are the intimate ways in which language and landscape are intertwined. This direction has led some commentators to see a more positive outlook in Merwin's later work, although the vision can still be quietly apocalyptic. Since 1975 Merwin has lived on the island of Maui in Hawaii, where his garden contains a large number of tropical plants, many of which are threatened with extinction elsewhere. The poems of *The Folding Cliffs* (1998) are subtitled "A Narrative of 19th-Century Hawaii."

He has continued publishing poetry volumes regularly, including acclaimed translations, particularly of Spanish and French poetry, but also including *Four French Plays* in 1985, and in 2000 a translation of Dante's *Purgatorio*. His volume *Feathers from the Hill* (1978) won the Bollingen Prize for Poetry. In April 1999 Merwin was named Special Consultant in Poetry to the Library of Congress, a position he held jointly with Rita Dove and Louis Glück. Merwin's prose works are also highly regarded. These include the short stories of *The Miner's Pale Children* (1970), the autobiographical *Unframed Originals* (1983), *Regions of Memory* (1987) containing his selected prose writings, and *The Lost Upland* (1992) a memoir of his life in the south of France in the 1960s.

## Bibliography

W. S. Merwin, *Selected Poems* (New York, 1988).

Jane Frazier, *From Origin to Ecology: Nature and the Poetry of W. S. Merwin* (Madison, NJ, 1999).

H. L. Hix, *Understanding W. S. Merwin* (Columbia, SC, 1997).

Cary Nelson and Ed Folsom, eds., *W. S. Merwin: Essays on the Poetry* (Urbana, IL, 1987).

# Anne Sexton (1928–1974)

Anne Sexton, née Harvey, was born in Newton, Massachusetts, the daughter of a prosperous wool merchant. She attended Garland Junior College, a Boston finishing school, for a year, and until she some years later began attending poetry workshops that remained the extent of her formal education. By the time of her suicide in 1974 she was a full professor at Boston University, had also taught at Harvard, Radcliffe, and Colgate, and had won fame for her poetry and such recognition as a Guggenheim Fellowship, honorary doctorates, and a Pulitzer Prize. Sexton is usually associated with the "Confessional" poets of the 1960s, along with Sylvia Plath, the early poetry of W. D. Snodgrass, and the Robert Lowell of *Life Studies*, but some critics have argued that such a classification limits her achievement and significance. In Sexton's later work, for these readers, the personal difficulties which she experienced in her own life as a woman, daughter, and mother, and out of which come many of the subjects of her poems, become more universally the problems of identity and social role in a middle-class culture intent on erecting stereotypes of women, and gender barriers to their achievement and emotional expression.

In 1948, after the year at Garland, Sexton eloped with and married Alfred Sexton, who later went to work in her father's business (they were divorced in 1973). A woman of striking appearance, she worked briefly as a model before giving birth in 1953 to the first of two daughters. Following the birth she suffered a mental breakdown and began the first of a number of hospitalizations for depression, anxiety, and suicidal impulses. The birth of her second daughter in 1955 was followed by another breakdown, a suicide attempt, and institutionalization. Out of her time in hospitals come such later poems as "Music Swims Back To Me," "Ringing the Bells," and "Unknown Girl in the Maternity Ward," poems that deal directly with feelings of chaos, despair, and alienation.

One of the doctors treating her suggested that she take a poetry workshop, and in the fall of 1957 she enrolled in John Holmes's class at the Boston Center for Adult Education. There she met poet Maxine Kumin, who became a lifelong close friend, and with whom she co-authored four children's story books. The following year she won a scholarship to the Antioch Writers' Conference to work with W. D. Snodgrass, whose poems in *Heart's Needle* (1959) she always acknowledged as an important influence. She subsequently enrolled in Robert Lowell's writing seminar at Boston University (at the beginning of 1959 Sylvia Plath also began attending the class). In the middle of the year both of Sexton's parents died, within four months of each other. Her 1962 poem "The Truth the Dead Know" records her feelings at her father's funeral, and begins:

> Gone, I say and walk from church,
> refusing the stiff procession to the grave,
> letting the dead ride alone in the hearse.
> It is June. I am tired of being brave.

Sexton's ambivalent feelings about her father, variously angry and forgiving, form the subject of a number of her poems. "And One for My Dame," for example, from her second volume, parallels the selling careers of her father and husband, the nursery-rhyme title and subsequent narrative suggesting her reliance upon, and resistance to, a "master."

Sexton's first book, *To Bedlam and Part Way Back*, appeared in 1960 and was nominated for a National Book Award. Often centered upon raw, powerful emotions – connected to childbearing, hospital routines, her parents, her daughters, the presence of death, and her own breakdowns – the book gained Sexton immediate attention. In this book and subsequent poems she sometimes referred to herself as a "witch." "Her Kind," for example, begins "I have gone out, a possessed witch, / haunting the black air" and ends: "A woman like that is not ashamed to die. / I have been her kind." She continued attending workshops and classes, studying modern literature with Irving Howe and Philip Rahv at Brandeis that summer. Her second book, *All My Pretty Ones* (1962), was also nominated for a National Book Award, and in that year she won the prestigious Levinson Prize from *Poetry* magazine. *All My Pretty Ones* used as an epigraph a sentence from one of Franz Kafka's letters: "A book should serve as the ax for the frozen sea within us" indicating the kind of direct confrontation that Sexton's poems seek with their subject matter.

Her third book, *Live or Die*, won the Pulitzer Prize in 1967, and described a progress from sickness towards health that was not completely reflected in her own condition. *Love Poems* followed in 1969. The poems continued to be made out of the raw material of her life – personal difficulties, love affairs, and relationships to those closest to her – and moved towards a more open form than in her first books. She gave flamboyant, intense readings of her poetry in public, and in 1968 began accompanying her performances with a rock group, billed as "Anne Sexton and Her Kind." In 1969 her play *Mercy Street*, for work on which she had received a Guggenheim Fellowship, was produced off-Broadway.

*Transformations* (1971) retells a number of the Grimms' fairy tales in a ribald, wry manner, bringing in contemporary references, often using the stories to point up the implications of their treatment of women – as objects to worship and/or to subject to servitude. Snow White is a "china-blue doll" and none too bright in "Snow White and the Seven Dwarfs." Cinderella's story is equated with such escapist fantasies as winning the lottery or marrying a rich man, a story mocked by its lack of any connection to real life and by its questionable source – what "they say":

> Cinderella and the prince
> lived, they say, happily ever after,
> like two dolls in a museum case
> never bothered by diapers or dust,
> never arguing over the timing of an egg,
> never telling the same story twice,
> never getting a middle-aged spread,
> their darling smiles pasted on for eternity.
> Regular Bobbsey Twins.
> That story.

*The Book of Folly*, which appeared the following year, was the last book Sexton published in her lifetime, and included a number of poems that mix personal and religious themes, as did the posthumously published *The Awful Rowing Toward God* (1975). On October 4, 1974, wrapped in her mother's fur coat, she shut herself inside the garage of her home with the car engine running and committed suicide by carbon monoxide poisoning. A posthumous volume of poems, *The Death Notebooks*, was published later that year, and a number of other volumes of uncollected poems followed. A *Complete Poems* appeared in 1981. The biography by Diane Middlebrook published in 1991, *Anne Sexton: A Biography*, produced some controversy because of its use of some of Sexton's confidential early medical records.

### Bibliography

Anne Sexton, *The Complete Poems* (Boston, 1981).

Frances Bixler, ed., *Original Essays on the Poetry of Anne Sexton* (Conway, AR, 1988).
Diana Hume George, *Oedipus Anne: The Poetry of Anne Sexton* (Urbana, IL, 1987).
Caroline King Barnard Hall, *Anne Sexton* (Boston, 1989).

# Adrienne Rich (b. 1929)

One of the foremost contemporary poets in the United States, Adrienne Rich is the leading voice in poetry of the radical feminist movement, demanding that poetry be committed to necessary change, and that it be recognized as coming out of and connecting to its cultural moment and that moment's true history. Rich began to date her poems in 1956 to emphasize this last point. In her poem "North American Time" (1983) she writes:

> Poetry never stood a chance
> of standing outside history.
> One line typed twenty years ago
> can be blazed on a wall in spraypaint

And in "Poetry I" (1985) she imagines "someone young   in anger" asking "Can you remember?   when we thought / the poets taught   how to live?" Rich brings that urgent purpose and commitment into her poetry.

Adrienne Rich was born in Baltimore, "white and middle-class into a house full of books, with a father who encouraged me to read and write" as she put it in her influential essay "When We Dead Awaken" (1971). But she records in that essay that "for about twenty years" she wrote to please "a particular man," and that her early style was formed by male poets: she lists Frost, Dylan Thomas, Donne, Auden, Louis MacNeice, Stevens, and Yeats as poets from whom she learned to craft poetry. This was the canon of mainly white male writers that Rich, along with writers and critics associated with the feminist movement, was to question in the 1960s.

Rich's first book, *A Change of World*, appeared in 1951, the same year that she graduated with a BA from Radcliffe. The book was selected for the Yale Younger Poets Award, and published with an introduction by Auden. In 1952–3 she traveled in Europe on a Guggenheim Foundation award, and was first afflicted with the rheumatoid arthritis for which she since has had a number of operations. In 1953 she married Alfred H. Conrad, a Harvard economist, and they resided in Cambridge, Massachusetts, until 1966. By 1959 the couple had three children.

*A Change of World* and Rich's second volume, *The Diamond Cutters and Other Poems* (1955), were in a formal, distanced vein, a "formal order" that she argued later came at the expense of suppressing or omitting "certain disturbing elements" from the poems. They were poems, she would say later, that were "*about* experiences" rather than being experiences themselves. Nevertheless there were poems that sometimes indicated something of Rich's future themes. "An Unsaid Word" describes learning the silent support expected in marriage to "her man." "Aunt Jennifer's Tigers" contrasts the energy and vitality of a tapestry's tiger figures with the quiet, oppressed acquiescence in marriage of their creator, the poem illustrating the split between the woman artist and her art that later becomes a major theme. The poem concludes:

When Aunt is dead, her terrified hands will lie
Still ringed with ordeals she was mastered by.
The tigers in the panel that she made
Will go on prancing, proud and unafraid.

This earlier work was recognized by a National Institute of Arts and Letters Award in 1960, and a second Guggenheim Fellowship in 1961–2, among other awards. But major changes occurred in Rich's life and poetry in the 1960s, marked by the publication of *Snapshots of a Daughter-in-Law* in 1963, and *Necessities of Life* in 1966. The title poem of the 1963 collection, which Rich has identified as an important transition and which took her two years to write, seeks to recover the voice of women and women writers in history marginalized by the attitudes represented in some of the poem's quotations and allusions. "Time is male / and in his cups drinks to the fair" – but behind such male "gallantry" across history is a mocking attitude towards the intellectual and creative potential of women. The poem also marks a move towards a loosening of the formal structure of the work in the earlier two books. In the same volume, "A Marriage in the 'Sixties" documents a couple growing apart yet bound together by habit and shared memories. "A life I didn't choose / chose me" she writes in "The Roofwalker," the final poem of the volume, a poem dedicated to Denise Levertov, also a poet, wife, and mother.

In 1966 the family moved to New York when Alfred Conrad accepted a teaching post at City College. Rich and her husband began to be increasingly active in the anti-Vietnam war movement. Rich also began a teaching career which was to take her to Swarthmore, Columbia, City College in New York, Brandeis, Rutgers, Cornell, Scripps, San José State, and finally Stanford – from which she retired in 1993.

The title poem of the 1966 volume, "Necessities of Life," begins with a statement about remaking, reconnecting with a true self: "Piece by piece I seem / to re-enter the world." Another poem in this collection, "I Am in Danger – Sir – ," quotes from and praises the "single-mindedness" of Emily Dickinson, who "chose to have it out at last / on your own premises." *Leaflets: Poems 1965–1968* (1969) continued this direction of her verse. In this volume "Orion," as Rich has observed, articulates what she had come to see as the false choice between "womanly, maternal love" and "egotism – a force directed by men into creation, achievement." "Planetarium" from her 1971 volume *The Will to Change* draws attention to the scientific achievements of Caroline Herschel, sister of the better-known eighteenth-century astronomer William. In 1970 Rich left her husband, who later in the year committed suicide, an event which enters into a number of later poems. By 1971 she was increasingly identifying with the women's movement. In 1974, when she received the National Book Award for *Diving into the Wreck,* she accepted it not as an individual but jointly with fellow nominees Alice Walker and Audre Lorde for all women who are silenced. In 1976 she affirmed herself a lesbian in the sequence of sonnets "Twenty-One Love Poems" and in that year began living with Jamaican American writer Michelle Cliff. Her prose essay "Compulsory Heterosexuality and Lesbian Existence" (1980) argued that expression of the lesbian experience and achievement had been systematically silenced, as ten years earlier "When We Dead Awaken" had argued the claim for women and women's creativity generally. The fifth poem of "Twenty-One Love Poems" looks at the result of this silencing:

> the ghosts – their hands clasped for centuries –
> of artists dying in childbirth, wise-women charred at the stake,
> centuries of books unwritten piled behind these shelves;
> and we still have to stare into the absence
> of men who would not, women who could not, speak
> to our life – this still unexcavated hole
> called civilization, this act of translation, this half-world.

Rich's poetry continued to address her own involvement in and alienation from particular aspects of contemporary culture; the series of personal pressures on identity and heritage that come from her identities of being white, a woman, a lesbian, a poet, and Jewish – issues sometimes examined in poems of sexual frankness. But following *Diving into the Wreck* (1973) the wide-ranging roles of history and historical memory become increasingly important. One of Rich's aims became, as in "Planetarium," to bring the achievement and the buried voices of women in history to the fore, as a way for women to rediscover and reassert a marginalized heritage and to articulate the cultural forces that still contributed to such marginalization in the present. "For Ethel Rosenberg" (1980) examines the victimization of the woman executed with her husband in 1953 for "conspiracy to commit espionage." The potential power of women is celebrated in the poem "Power" (1974) on Marie Curie, reprinted in her 1978 collection *The Dream of a Common Language*:

> She died    a famous woman    denying
> her wounds
> denying
> her wounds    came from    the same source as her power

She rewrites John Donne, one of the early influences on her work, in "A Valediction Forbidding Mourning" (1970), and closes "From an Old House in America" with an echo of one of his famous sermons: "Any woman's death diminishes me." In her poems' undermining of imprisoning conventions she has acknowledged the influence of film-maker Jean-Luc Godard, an influence perhaps most overtly seen in the poem sequence "Shooting Script" (1970).

Rich has pointed to the importance of her move to the west coast, to Santa Cruz, in 1984 as bringing her closer to many cultures that had previously seemed far away. The move further expanded the range of history brought in to her examination of present social forces. "I am bent on fathoming what it means to love my country" Rich writes in "An Atlas of the Difficult World" – the title poem of her important 1991 volume. This poem includes extracts from the prison letters of Black Panther leader George Jackson, the author of *Soledad Brother: The Prison Letters of George Jackson*, which record Jackson's attempt to educate himself, and the psychological and physical desperation brought on by the brutalizing routine of the prison system. Jackson, shot in a prison uprising at San Quentin in 1971, questions in a quotation within Rich's poem, whether *"the world and its affairs / are run as well as they possibly can be, that I am governed / by wise and judicious men"* – which is what he is told to believe – *"if when I leave the instructor's presence and encounter / the exact opposite . . . / is it not reasonable / that I should become perplexed?"* The questioning, the refusal to accept the dictates of "the instructor," is also Rich's constant aim.

Adrienne Rich has been the recipient of many honors and awards, including honorary doctorates from across the nation, many of the leading poetry awards, and a MacArthur Fellowship. She is a former Chancellor of the Academy of American Poets, and by 2001 had published nearly 20 volumes of poetry, including *Fox: Poems 1998–2000* in 2001. She has co-edited *Sinister Wisdom*, a lesbian/feminist journal, and was a founding editor of *Bridges: A Journal for Jewish Feminists and Our Friends* in 1990. Her important prose is collected in *Blood, Bread, and Poetry* (1986), *Of Woman Born: Motherhood as Experience and Institution* (1986), *What Is Found There: Notebooks on Poetry and Politics* (1993), and *Arts of the Possible: Essays and Conversations* (2001). Perhaps the most influential of contemporary poets, she continues to be an active and highly visible campaigner for gay rights, reproductive rights, the progressive Jewish movement, and national and international social justice.

## Bibliography

Adrienne Rich, *The Fact of a Doorframe: Selected Poems 1950–2001* (New York, 2002).

Claire Keyes, *The Aesthetics of Power: The Poetry of Adrienne Rich* (Athens, GA, 1986).

Alice Templeton, *The Dream and the Dialogue: Adrienne Rich's Feminist Poetics* (Knoxville, TN, 1994).

Craig Werner, *Adrienne Rich: The Poet and her Critics* (Chicago, 1988).

Liz Yorke, *Adrienne Rich: Passion, Politics, and the Body* (London, 1997).

# Gary Snyder (b. 1930)

Gary Snyder's poetry combines the many facets of his interests and activities – writer, teacher, student of Oriental philosophy and religion, physical laborer, and concerned environmentalist. In poetry that is disciplined and focused in its language and its record of lived experience, there is a celebration of the whole grandeur of nature, from ants living in decaying wood to mountain ranges off to the far horizon. Snyder's world is one of interconnections, as he illustrates in his well-known poem "Axe Handles." In making an axe handle with his son Kai, he remembers a phrase from Ezra Pound: "When making an axe handle / the pattern is not far off," then a fourth-century Chinese "Essay on Literature," then a translation of the essay by his own teacher, Shih-hsiang Chen, to draw the conclusion:

> And I see: Pound was an axe,
> Chen was an axe, I am an axe
> And my son a handle, soon
> To be shaping again, model
> And tool, craft of culture,
> How we go on.

Snyder was born in San Francisco, but grew up in Washington State and Oregon. He graduated from Reed College in 1951 with a degree in anthropology. His first poems were published at Reed in student publications. He began graduate work in anthropology at Indiana University in the fall of 1951, but stayed only one semester. He returned to San Francisco, worked summers as a mountain forest fire lookout, and ended a short-lived first marriage. By 1953 Snyder had made a commitment to a serious exploration of Oriental culture and languages, and began three years of study at the University of California at Berkeley. He also began to meet poets associated with the San Francisco Poetry Renaissance and the Beat movement. He met Philip Whalen in 1952, Kenneth Rexroth in 1953, and Allen Ginsberg and Jack Kerouac in 1955. He shared a cabin for some months with Kerouac, and is represented as Japhy Ryder in Kerouac's account of the experience in *The Dharma Bums* (1958).

In 1956 Snyder made his first trip to Japan and studied under a Zen master. Before returning to San Francisco in 1958 he worked on board a ship as a wiper in an engine room, visiting Europe, and the Middle and Far East. The following year he returned to Japan and stayed there, with brief returns to the US, and a six-month stay in India, for most of the next decade, immersing himself in the study of Zen Buddhism.

In 1959 Snyder published the first of his more than 16 books of poetry and prose, *Riprap*, followed the next year by *Myths & Texts*. Some of the experiences behind the poems in the first book came from his work in the summer of 1955 on a trail crew in Yosemite National Park, and his work the previous summer at a lumber camp. The world of labor, language, discipline, and respectful, quietly celebratory observation is caught in the opening lines of the title poem:

> Lay down these words
> Before your mind like rocks.
> placed solid, by hands
> In choice of place, set
> Before the body of the mind
> in space and time:
> Solidity of bark, leaf, or wall
> riprap of things:

Snyder's own annotation explains that a "riprap" is "a cobble of stone laid on steep slick rock to make a trail for horses in the mountains."

In these and subsequent volumes Snyder explores such connections, sometimes in narrative, sometimes in a vignette that brings the experienced world into close-up. His work also takes up concern for the future of the earth's ecosystem, the world of nature and the outdoors so central to his poetry and way of life. This concern is sometimes accompanied by the evocation of a past that allowed a more primitive, respectful treatment of the natural world than the present. Some poems celebrate sexual desire and fertility, which for Snyder is part of what connects humans to the natural world around them (as in "Beneath My Hand and Eye the Distant Hills. Your Body" from 1968, and "It Was When" from 1969, which describes the conception of his son.)

In 1965 Snyder's second marriage ended, and in 1967 he married for a third time, to Masa Uehara, a relationship that went on to last for 20 years. In 1968 he returned to the United States. His volume *The Back Country* was published in that year, and he was awarded a Guggenheim Fellowship. The following year the publication of *Earth House Hold* told something of his travels. In 1974 he published what for some readers is his finest book, *Turtle Island*, which was awarded the Pulitzer Prize for Poetry. In 1987 he was inducted into the American Academy and Institute of Arts and Letters. His *No Nature: New and Selected Poems* (1992) was a finalist for the National Book Award, and he was awarded the Bollingen Prize for Poetry for the 1996 publication of his open form journal poem *Mountains and Rivers Without End*, the first sections of which he had begun writing in 1956, and began publishing in 1965. In addition to his own poems, he has published a number of translations from ancient and modern Japanese poets, and also *Cold Mountain Poems* (1965) from the T'ang dynasty Chinese poet Han-shan.

Snyder has lived since 1971 in "Kitkitdizze," a house he built himself in the remote foothills of the Sierra Nevada mountains in California. He has occasionally taught at colleges and universities, most recently at the University of California, Davis.

**Bibliography**

Gary Snyder, *The Gary Snyder Reader: Prose, Poetry, and Translations, 1952–1998* (Washington, DC, 1999).

Tim Dean, *Gary Snyder and the American Unconscious: Inhabiting the Ground* (New York, 1991).
Patrick D. Murphy, *A Place for Wayfaring: The Poetry and Prose of Gary Snyder* (Corvallis, OR, 2000).
Robert J. Schuler, *Journeys Toward the Original Mind: The Long Poems of Gary Snyder* (New York, 1994).

# Sylvia Plath (1932–1963)

Sylvia Plath was born in Boston, Massachusetts, where her German immigrant father, Otto Plath, taught entomology and German at Boston University and her mother was a high-school teacher. Her father published a number of books, including in 1934 *Bumblebees and their Ways* on his particular specialty. Otto Plath died in 1940, following complications from diabetes, when his daughter was 8. He emerges as a central figure in Plath's poetry, especially her final poems, where he is sometimes allied with her husband, poet Ted Hughes, from whom she had separated. Both embody a haunting, oppressive presence that she cannot set aside, one that is resented for being there and also condemned for abandoning her. The penultimate stanza of "Daddy," evoking vampire myth, reads:

If I've killed one man, I've killed two –
The vampire who said he was you
And drank my blood for a year,
Seven years if you want to know.
Daddy, you can lie back now.

The last five poems of *Ariel*, as she had planned the book she was writing in her final months, all use beekeeping as a central metaphor. Within four months of writing these poems, and two weeks after the publication of her only novel, *The Bell Jar*, Plath committed suicide. *Ariel* went on to become one of the bestselling poetry volumes in English in the twentieth century, and her *Collected Poems* when they appeared in 1981 won a posthumous Pulitzer Prize.

Plath was a prizewinning student at Smith College, publishing poems and short stories, being elected to Phi Beta Kappa, and winning a competition to serve as college editor of *Mademoiselle* magazine for a month. At the end of her junior year at Smith she had a breakdown and attempted suicide, an event recorded in *The Bell Jar*, and in "Daddy," where she writes:

At twenty I tried to die
And get back, back, back to you.
I thought even the bones would do.

But they pulled me out of the sack,
And they stuck me together with glue.

Her treatment included electric shock therapy. Plath's final year at Smith was a great success, however, and she won a Fulbright scholarship to Cambridge University for two years, where she met Ted Hughes. The two married in June 1956. Plath returned to the US with her husband to teach at Smith for a year, and the two then lived for a short period in Boston, before returning to make a home in London in late 1959. While in Boston Plath attended a poetry seminar run by Robert Lowell that also included Anne Sexton.

Plath published the only book of poems that appeared in her lifetime, *The Colossus and Other Poems*, in 1960 in London (New York publication came in 1962). The title poem, and other poems in the volume such as "Black Rook in Rainy Weather" and "The Beekeeper's Daughter," illustrate the ornate, self-conscious language which hides the voice that in the later poems bursts out with such urgency. "The Beekeeper's Daughter" opens:

A garden of mouthings. Purple, scarlet-speckled, black
The great corollas dilate, peeling back their silks.
Their musk encroaches, circle after circle,
A well of scents almost too dense to breathe in.

The last line of the opening stanza of the title poem, "The Colossus," gives an indication of the work to come within such a short time. There the ornate language of a similar opening description is deflated by the directness of a summary line: "It's worse than a barnyard." The main influences on the poems in the volume are the work of W. H. Auden, Dylan Thomas, Robert Lowell, and – in the poems written after 1959 – Theodore Roethke.

Following this first volume, Plath began work on the poems eventually published posthumously in *Crossing the Water* (1971). These include a number of poems on childbirth and on life with her two children, Frieda born in 1960 and Nicholas in 1962. These were followed by the poems of *Winter Trees* (London 1971, New York 1972) and the poems of *Ariel* – the latter written in the mood of betrayal and vengeance that followed her discovery of Hughes's involvement with another woman, a family friend. Plath and Hughes had set up house in Devon by the time the marriage broke up, and Plath remained there in the final months of 1962, often writing a poem a day, poems centered around love, death, betrayal, rage, and entrapment. In a rush of creativity in October she wrote many of the poems that are her best known, including "Daddy," "Fever 103°," "Lady Lazarus," and "Ariel" – the latter a wild ride, "Suicidal, at one with the drive / Into the red / / Eye, the cauldron of morning." Imagery of the Nazi years of Germany is frequent in these poems, often associated with her father and with oppressive, death-dealing male authority – although Otto Plath was not a Nazi. This masculine force is sometimes met with fury, "Lady Lazarus" ends famously "Out of the ash / I rise with my red hair / And I eat men like air." The magazines to which Plath sent these powerful poems for publication rejected them.

At the beginning of 1963 Plath and her children moved back to London. Critics have noted a calmer, more settled tone to some of the poems of January and early February. *The Bell Jar* was published in January under the pseudonym "Victoria Lucas." But on February 11, after sealing the doors to her children's rooms to protect them, Plath committed suicide by gassing herself.

Ted Hughes became Plath's somewhat controversial literary executor. While some commentators are sympathetic, other readers and critics have condemned him for his rearrangement of the *Ariel* poems, for destroying Plath's final diary, and for what they see as his ultimate responsibility for her suicide. He also pressed for the abridgement of Plath's journals when they were published in 1982, although an unabridged edition appeared in 2000 following Hughes's death. Among other revelations, the unabridged journals document Plath's driving ambition, and the hatred she sometimes felt towards her mother for what she saw as Aurelia Plath's role in Otto's early death. A volume of Plath's letters to her mother was published in 1975 as *Letters Home: Correspondence, 1950–1963*. Hughes waited many years to give his fullest account of the marriage, the 88 poems of *Birthday Letters* (1998). Within the narrative of the couple's meeting and later difficulties – which for Hughes were largely driven by his wife's obsessive concern with her dead father and the desire to rejoin him – some poems are direct responses to Plath's own work, for example "Night-Ride on Ariel."

*Ariel* was published in 1965, with an introduction by Robert Lowell. The mixture of a furious sense of doom barely contained within the form and language of the poems, and the directness of address, particularly in the poems written almost daily in October and early November 1962, secured Plath's early posthumous fame. In light of her suicide, the poems were understood in directly personal terms similar to the 1950s confessional poetry of such writers as Berryman, Sexton, and Lowell. More recently, however, her themes have been read within a broader context. The poems are now seen by some critics as articulating the plight more generally of talented, independent women within the gender confines of the 1950s. The Nazi allusions associated with Otto Plath in the poems, for example, that had been read as unfair, excessive and inappropriate, are sometimes read now as bringing into the poems the force of an oppressive, dictatorial male culture whose power whether consciously invoked by governments or unthinkingly accepted within a family, infects alike history, political and cultural dynamics, and the well-intentioned love within even the most intimate of relationships. Such readings have kept to the fore an appreciation of the poet's work, an appreciation which relies less on the personal legend and drama of a talented and beautiful young woman dead by her own hand at thirty, and more on a recognition of the poet's remarkable achievement itself.

## Bibliography

Sylvia Plath, *The Collected Poems*, ed. Ted Hughes (New York, 1981).

Steven Gould Axelrod, *Sylvia Plath: The Wound and the Cure of Words* (Baltimore, 1990).
Tim Kendall, *Sylvia Plath: A Critical Study* (London, 2001).
Jacqueline Rose, *The Haunting of Sylvia Plath* (Cambridge, MA, 1992).

# Amiri Baraka (b. 1934)

Amiri Baraka was born Everett LeRoy Jones in Newark, New Jersey, and adopted the spelling LeRoi in 1951. He took his Muslim name in 1967, a period when he dedicated his poetry and political activity to Black Nationalism. His poetry, as well as his plays, novels, essays, and short stories, speak with a power and commitment that have made him a prominent figure for more than 35 years. Baraka sees "art as a weapon, and a weapon of revolution," although he now sees that revolution in Marxist rather than exclusively racial terms. *The LeRoi Jones/Amiri Baraka Reader* (1991), edited by William J. Harris in collaboration with Baraka, divides the poet's career helpfully into three main stages: "The Beat Period (1957–1962)," "The Black Nationalist Period (1965–1974)," and "The Third World Marxist Period (1974– )."

Baraka initially attended the Newark branch of Rutgers University, but then transferred to Howard University. He also pursued some graduate work at Columbia. From 1954 to 1956 he served in the United States air force, and then settled in New York's Greenwich Village, joining the district's multi-racial bohemian scene. In 1958 he married his first wife, Hettie Cohn, a white Jewish writer, and together they put out the important little magazines *Yugen* and *Floating Bear*, which published the work of Allen Ginsberg and Jack Kerouac, among others. Their life together with their two daughters, and the broader Greenwich Village world of the time, is described by Hettie Jones in her 1990 memoir *How I Became Hettie Jones*.

Baraka is among the most militant of black poets, although in a 1959 statement in Donald Allen's *The New American Poetry* he records his debt to white writers: "For me, Lorca, Williams, Pound and Charles Olson have had the greatest influence." In addition, the Beat poets' social criticism and emphasis upon consciousness-raising have also been an important influence upon his work, alongside black music and jazz forms. His sense of a poem, the statement notes, is that it be open in form, "without any preconceived notion or *design* for what a poem *ought* to be."

Baraka's first volume, *Preface to a Twenty Volume Suicide Note* (1961), contains poems that show a division between two selves, a public and a personal self, as well as poems in which death is a frequent subject. These themes continue in his second book, *The Dead Lecturer* (1964). "An Agony. As Now" from 1964 begins:

> I am inside someone
> who hates me. I look
> out from his eyes. Smell

> what fouled tunes come in
> to his breath. Love his
> wretched women.

Baraka increasingly came to see the division as a racial one. This racial division became explicit in his award-winning off-Broadway play *Dutchman* (1964), the success of which brought him to national attention. The play contains a passionate claim by its leading black character that black artistic expression is a way of channeling the murderous rage that would otherwise be directed by blacks against whites. The speaker, Clay, his own anger revealed by his speech, is himself then murdered as a dangerous threat to the system of white power. Baraka writes in *The Autobiography of LeRoi Jones/ Amiri Baraka* (1984) that with the success of *Dutchman* he received many offers to work for the white media. In his view such co-opting was another way in which radical black voices were potentially silenced. *The Slave* (1964) is another of his important plays.

A visit that Baraka had made to Cuba in 1960 began his sense that the Greenwich Village artistic community was more self-indulgent than radical, and the final break came in 1965 when, following the assassination of Malcolm X, he moved from the Lower East Side of New York to Harlem, and later back to Newark. In 1965 he divorced Hettie Cohn, and in 1967 married African American poet and visual artist Sylvia Robinson. In 1967 he became a Black Muslim, taking the name Amiri Imamu Baraka (later dropping Imamu), and Sylvia Robinson took the name Amina. Baraka's art and political actions in this period were directed entirely to a black audience, conceived as a separate nation. He founded the Black Arts Repertory Theater School in Harlem, a model for many similar groups across the country. His 1969 volume *Black Magic: Sabotage, Target Study, Black Art; Collected Poetry 1961– 1967* records his journey towards Black Nationalism. Like some other black American writers and intellectuals at the time, he supported violent protest and even deadly violence as necessary for bringing about the change that would allow separate nationhood. "SOS" (1969) is a call, written to be performed as much as to be read, to "all black people, man woman child / Wherever you are, calling you, urgent, come in." "Black Art" from the same year, argues:

> We want a black poem. And a
> Black World.
> Let the world be a Black Poem
> And Let All Black People Speak This Poem
> Silently
>
> or LOUD

And "When We'll Worship Jesus" (1972) begins: "We'll worship Jesus / When jesus do / Somethin / When jesus blow up / the white house / or blast nixon down."

In 1974 Baraka concluded that Black Nationalism was narrowly racist, and became a Third World socialist, concerned more broadly with oppressed peoples everywhere regardless of race. His book of essays *Daggers and Javelins: Essays, 1974–1979* (1984) collects a number of essays that reflect this shift from a nationalist to a Marxist view of revolution. His output has remained prolific, including essays on cinema, music – including *Blues People: Negro Music in White America* (1983) following the earlier *Black Music* (1968) – and politics. However, *Wise Why's Y's* (1995), charting the record of African American movements and history, was his first volume of poetry for more than ten years. *Transbluesency: The Selected Poems of Amiri Baraka/LeRoi Jones* also appeared in 1995. In 1979 Baraka joined the African Studies department at the State University of New York, Stony Brook, retiring in 1999.

## Bibliography

Amiri Baraka, *The LeRoi Jones/Amiri Baraka Reader*, 2nd edn., ed. William J. Harris (New York, 2000).

William J. Harris, *The Poetry and Poetics of Amiri Baraka: The Jazz Aesthetic* (Columbia, MS, 1985).

Jerry Gafio Watts, *Amiri Baraka: The Politics and Art of a Black Intellectual* (New York, 2001).

Komozi Woodard, *A Nation within a Nation: Amiri Baraka (LeRoi Jones) and Black Power Politics* (Chapel Hill, NC, 1999).

# Sonia Sanchez (b. 1934)

Sonia Sanchez was born Wilsonia Driver in Birmingham, Alabama. Her mother died giving birth to stillborn twins when Sanchez was 1, and her father, a teacher, had a number of later marriages and relationships, taking the children with him when he moved to Harlem when Sanchez was 9. Sanchez attended Hunter College in New York, graduating in 1955 with a degree in political science, and then spent a year at New York University studying poetry with Louise Bogan. She is the author of more than 19 books, including poetry, plays, essays, children's books, and an anthology of poems written by one of the creative writing classes that she taught in Harlem. She has been married twice, to Albert Sanchez, and in 1968 to activist Etheridge Knight (with whom she had three children), both marriages ending in divorce.

She began a long teaching career in 1965 teaching at the Downtown Community School in New York. At San Francisco State University shortly afterwards she was a pioneer in developing Black Studies courses. From 1977 she enjoyed a long period of teaching at Temple University, retiring in 1999.

Sanchez's first two published volumes of poetry, *Home Coming* (1969) and *We a BaddDDD People* (1970) are written from a black militant, anti-white perspective influenced by the teachings of Malcolm X. In "Malcolm," from the first volume, Sanchez quotes the slain leader:

> "fuck you white
> man. we have been
> curled too long. nothing
> is sacred now. not your
> white faces nor any
> land that separates
> until some voices
> squat with spasms."

Her poem "to blk/record/buyers" begins:

> don't play me no
> righteous bros.
>            white people
> ain't rt bout nothing
> no mo.

Elsewhere she praises the jazz musician John Coltrane for not taking the route of mainstream white commercial music. The poems in these and other early books experiment with idioms and with sound arrangements, using these and slang, dialect, and profanity, to undermine conventional grammar, spelling, and syntax in an attempt to capture black speech rhythms. The poem "blk / wooooomen / chant" from her second book, for example, contains the lines:

> blk/mennnnnNN
> do u SEEEEEEE us? HEARRRRRR us? KNOWWWW us?
> black/mennnnNNN/we bes here.
> waiten. waiten. WAITEN. WAITENNNNNN
>            A long AMURICAN wait.
> hurrrrreeehurrrrreeehurrrrreeeeeeeeeee
> blacKKKKKKKKKKKKmennnnnnnnnnn/
> warriors

In the early 1970s Sanchez joined the Nation of Islam, although she left in 1976 because of the movement's treatment of women. The movement's influence is strongest in her fourth and fifth books of poetry, *Love Poems* (1973) and *A Blues Book for Blue Black Magical Women* (1974). Sanchez's later work is more feminist in its political orientation and themes, and the 1984 volume *Homegirls & Handgrenades* is particularly important. The long poem *Does Your House Have Lions?* (1997) was nominated for a National Book Critics Award. The poem is a more sympathetic treatment of her father than the earlier "A Poem for My Father" from 1970. *Shake Loose My Skin* (1999) is a useful selection from some earlier books, as well as containing a number of new poems.

### Bibliography

Sonia Sanchez, *Shake Loose My Skin: New and Selected Poems* (Boston, 1999).

Joyce Ann Joyce, *Ijala: Sonia Sanchez and the African Poetic Tradition* (Chicago, 1996).

# Audre Lorde (1934–1992)

Audre Lorde was very concerned not to have the range of her poetry limited by the application of labels, what she once called "the myth of sameness." She described herself as "a black, feminist, lesbian, mother, poet," and in her poetry intimate moments of love, for example, coexist in the same poem with the life of the city, the wider world of politics and race in the US or globally, and the myths and traditions of African heritage. Lorde's point is that these parts of her identity interconnect, as a person and as a writer.

Lorde was born in New York City, to West Indian immigrants, the youngest of three daughters, and attended Hunter College after spending 1954 at the National University of Mexico. She graduated from Hunter in 1959. In 1962 she married Edward Ashley Rollins and gave birth to two children (the couple divorced in 1970). She went on to obtain a Masters degree in Library Science from Columbia University, and worked as a librarian in and around New York City until 1968.

She had begun writing and publishing poetry in her teens, was the literary editor of her school magazine, and published regularly in the 1960s. In 1968 she published her first volume, *The First Cities*. In this same year she made the important decision to spend a year as poet-in-residence at Tougaloo

College in Mississippi. She then went on to teach at a number of colleges, including Hunter College.

Lorde's second book, *Cables to Rage* (1970), acknowledged her homosexuality, and established her style of protest poetry rooted in intimacy, love, and personal growth. A number of commentators remarked that her writing was less directly confrontational than much black poetry being written at the time. Her well-known poem "Coal" uses the metaphor of coal to suggest the honesty and self-knowledge as well as the hard work and wider awareness needed to make language productive:

> Love is a word, another kind of open.
> As the diamond comes into a knot of flame
> I am Black because I come from the earth's inside
> now take my word for jewel in the open light.

"Walking Our Boundaries" (1978) describes two lovers exploring and enjoying their own garden, while "our voices / seem too loud for this small yard / too tentative for women / so in love." They plant seedlings as part of a commitment to growth and the future. "Hanging Fire" from the same year, imagines the isolation of a 14-year-old girl, and her fears and confusion about the desires raging through her body. The sweep of "Sisters in Arms" (1986) moves from New York City to the racial violence of South Africa.

These poems are included in the volumes that regularly followed *Cables to Rage*. They include *From a Land Where Other People Live* (1973), which was nominated for a National Book Award, *New York Head Shop and Museum* (1974), and her first book to be released by a major publisher, *Coal* (1976). *The Black Unicorn* (1978) makes particular use of African tradition, particularly female African gods and matriarchal myth. The year 1986 brought *Our Dead Behind Us*, and two volumes of selected poems appeared in 1982 and 1992. *The Marvelous Arithmetics of Distance: Poems 1987–1992* was published posthumously in 1993.

Lorde's poetry is always on one level about survival, but it became an even more explicit theme when she was diagnosed with breast cancer in the late 1970s. She writes on her illness and surgery in *The Cancer Journals* (1980). Six years later she was diagnosed with liver cancer, which she discussed in the title essay of her book *A Burst of Light* (1988). She died of cancer in 1992. Other prose works are *Zami: A New Spelling of My Name* (1982), which combines autobiography, history, and myth, and which Lorde termed a "biomythography," *Sister Outsider: Essays and Speeches* (1984), and *A Burst of Light*.

**Bibliography**

*The Collected Poems of Audre Lorde* (New York, 1997).

AnaLouise Keating, *Women Reading Women Writing: Self-Invention in Paula Gunn Allen, Gloria Anzaldua, and Audre Lorde* (Philadelphia, 1996).
Cassie Premo Steele, *We Heal From Memory: Sexton, Lorde, Anzaldua, and the Poetry of Witness* (New York, 2000).

# Susan Howe (b. 1937)

"The past is the present when I write," Susan Howe has written, and an interest in history is a distinguishing feature of this poet often associated with the Language poets. Indeterminacy of meaning, open forms, disruptive syntax, the removal of an individual overseeing consciousness, and an emphasis upon language as self-referential rather than representational – these are characteristics of Howe's poetry as well as of the Language poets. To this she adds the indeterminacy of history, its inability to be assimilated into the present, and the tension which results from its pressures upon the present. Additionally, Howe sees her poetry as having its roots in the literature of modernism rather than in the Marxist and poststructuralist context of much Language poetry.

Howe was born in Boston and her early career was as a painter. She worked on collage and performance pieces following her graduation from the Boston Museum School of Fine Arts in 1961, and out of this work came her interest in words. "I used quotation in my painting," she has said, "in the same way that I use quotation in my writing, in that I always seemed to use collage." She has also observed that the lists of words that she juxtaposed with her paintings became of more interest to her than the pictures, and she began to see the lists themselves as inadequate. In the late 1960s she discovered Charles Olson's open field poetics and became particularly interested in his use of archaeology and maps.

Her first book, *Hinge Picture*, appeared in 1974, and volumes have followed regularly since, initially with small presses and in recent years from publishers with a wider distribution. A poem by Howe may quote from or summarize a historical document, as in her *Articulation of Sound Forms in Time* (1987), but where a reader might then expect a commentary, the language of the poem breaks down into fragments of sound or syntax which call attention to the constructedness of the historical account and of the whole poem, and their resistance to any imposed order. Deletions might also be included, to foreground the process of the poem's composition.

Howe was married for many years to David von Schlegell, who directed the sculpture program at Yale University, and who died in 1992. Howe's own university teaching career began in 1988. She has been a member of the faculty at SUNY Buffalo since 1989. In 1996 Howe received a Guggenheim Foundation award. She was elected to the American Academy of Arts and Sciences in 1999, and elected a Chancellor of the Academy of American Poets in 2000.

Among Howe's most recent books of poetry are *Pierce-Arrow* (1999) and *Bed Hangings* (2001). Her earlier poems have been collected as *Frame Structures: Early Poems 1974–1979* (1996) and poems from three later books appeared as *The Europe of Trusts* in 1990 (reissued 2002). In addition to the poetry, she has published the two prose studies: *My Emily Dickinson* (1985), and *The Birth-Mark: Unsettling the Wilderness in American Literary History* (1993).

## Bibliography

Susan Howe, *The Europe of Trusts* (1990; New York, 2002).

Marjorie Perloff, *Poetic License: Essays on Modernist and Postmodernist Lyric* (Evanston, 1990).
Peter Quartermain, *Disjunctive Poetics: From Gertrude Stein and Louis Zukofsky to Susan Howe* (Cambridge, 1992).

# Louise Glück (b. 1943)

Louise Glück has characterized her poetry as having an unchanging interest in love and death. Her earlier work was in the direct, "confessional" style of Sylvia Plath and the Robert Lowell of *Life Studies*, and while her later poetry retains much of the early, spare directness, it incorporates myth, legend, and history into poems that reinforce their contemporary themes within this broader context. "Myth is not formula," Glück has written, and the allusions and parallels are woven into the texture and subject of the poems, not imposed as an arbitrary addition.

Glück was born in New York City and grew up in the suburbs of Long Island. She attended Sarah Lawrence and Columbia universities – at the latter attending poetry workshops in evening courses. Her college teaching has included appointments at Columbia, the University of Iowa, and Williams College – where she now holds a permanent position.

In her first book, *Firstborn* (1968), family tensions and domestic scenes are the center of poems that explore disappointment and loss, while striving to give a larger symbolic import to the subject matter. In *The House on Marshland* (1975) she finds her own voice, as biblical and mythical allusions deepen the literal levels of meaning. The poems project a double vision characteristic of all of Glück's work, of joy or survival within despair, and threat and darkness within pleasure or illusion. In "Gretel in Darkness," for example, Hansel's sister recalls the horror of being trapped in the candy cottage and of killing the witch, and fears the even greater torment that her brother may be forgetting the terrifying experience that has been their intense common bond. Gretel's voice here is that of the distant, alienated narrator common to many of Glück's poems. In "The Mountain" the narrator describes to her students the torments of the writer's life, likening it to the myth of Sisyphus condemned for ever to roll a stone to the top of a hill only always to have it roll down again. But at the same time the end of the poem celebrates adding "height to the mountain" by the composition of the poem itself. "Cottonmouth Country" is set in the scenic beauty of North Carolina's Cape Hatteras, but is acutely aware of the threat of death by water and by land. But "Earthly Love," a poem about the pain of separation and the difficulty of facing the future, concludes with a characteristic note of acceptance of past and future happiness:

> Nor does it seem to me
> crucial to know
> whether or not such happiness
> is built on illusion:
> it has its own reality.
> And in either case, it will end.

*Descending Figure* appeared in 1980 and *The Triumph of Achilles* in 1985 – which won the National Book Critics Circle award. With *Ararat* (1990) Glück's volumes overtly took on more the characteristics of a sequence, exploring various perspectives of a theme rather than collecting individual poems that had been published separately, although Glück has commented that her interest in extended forms began as early as her 1980 book. *Ararat* concerns a family of three women, a wife, her sister, and a daughter, responding to the death of a husband/father. *The Wild Iris* (1992) for which Glück received a Pulitzer Prize, follows a New England garden from spring to late summer. *Meadowlands* (1996) examines a marriage in crisis, while simultaneously offering a reading of Homer's *Odyssey* – with Penelope very much a contemporary figure. *Vita Nova* (1999) explores life after a divorce.

In addition to the honors noted above, Glück has received many other awards, including fellowships from the Guggenheim and Rockefeller

Foundations, and the Bollingen Prize. In 1999 she was elected a Chancellor of the Academy of American Poets. She edited and introduced in 1993 that year's volume of the annual series *Best American Poetry*. In 1994 she published a collection of essays, *Proofs and Theories: Essays on Poetry*, a volume which provides some helpful biographical background to the poems. Glück's earlier work was reprinted in *The First Five Books of Poems* (1997). A recent volume of poetry is *The Seven Ages* (2001).

## Bibliography

Louise Glück, *The First Five Books of Poems* (Manchester, 1997).

Elizabeth Dodd, *The Veiled Mirror and the Woman Poet: H.D., Louise Bogan, Elizabeth Bishop, and Louise Glück* (Columbia, MO, 1992).
Lee Upton, *The Muse of Abandonment: Origin, Identity, Mastery, in Five American Poets* (Lewisburg, 1998).

# Jorie Graham (b. 1951)

Jorie Graham was born in New York City, but spent her childhood in Italy, much of it, she has said, peering into the churches of Rome and looking at the many paintings within their chapels. Graham's mother was a painter and sculptor and her father a theological scholar. Commentators have traced the combination of spiritual quest, moral purpose, and insistent claims of the importance of art in Graham's poetry to these early influences, while she has acknowledged her early and abiding interest in similar issues in the work of W. B. Yeats, T. S. Eliot, and Wallace Stevens.

Graham's higher education began at the Sorbonne in Paris, where she took part in the 1968 student uprisings. Continuing her education in the United States, she graduated with a BFA from New York University in 1973, and an MFA from the University of Iowa in 1978. She subsequently taught at Murray State University, Humboldt State University, and Columbia, before in 1983 starting to teach at the University of Iowa, where she remained for many years. She is currently the Boylston Professor of Rhetoric and Oratory at Harvard University.

The first two volumes of poetry that Graham published were part of the Princeton Contemporary Poets series: *Hybrids of Plants and of Ghosts* (1980) and *Erosion* (1983). Both concern themes of longing for spiritual attainment. This concern was merged in her book, *The End of Beauty* (1987), with some of the thematic and formal concerns usually associated with the Language poets – resisting closure, the indeterminacy of the self, the need to re-establish the contact of language and reality, and an organic theory of composition. Coupled with these concerns in Graham's work is a continued sense of the moral imperatives of the writer and poem in a world that she sees as beset by materialism and falsehood. Formally with this book her poetry became more fragmented, with ever-shifting patterns, as part of keeping questions, language, and meanings open. The extremes of the experimentation in this volume were more muted in her next, *Region of Unlikeness* (1991), the title taken from the writings of St. Augustine. One way in which the import of these concerns is connected to art for Graham is in her many poems on painters and poets. When she co-edited *The Best American Poetry, 1990* with David Lehman she used the introduction to articulate her views on the necessary direction and imperatives of contemporary poetry, particularly noting the decay of exactness in the broader uses of language, and the return of ambition and scope in the aims of contemporary poets.

More recent volumes are *Materialism* (1993), *The Dream of the Unified Field: Selected Poems 1974–1994* – which was awarded the 1996 Pulitzer Prize for Poetry – *The Errancy* (1997), *Swarm* (2000), and *Never* (2002). Her many awards include a MacArthur Fellowship, and in 1997 she was elected a Chancellor of the Academy of American Poets.

### Bibliography

Jorie Graham, *The Dream of the Unified Field: Selected Poems 1974–1994* (Hopewell, NJ, 1995).

Thomas Gardner, *Regions of Unlikeness: Explaining Contemporary Poetry* (Lincoln, NE, 1999).

James Longenbach, *Modern Poetry after Modernism* (New York, 1997).

# Gary Soto (b. 1952)

Gary Soto is a leading presence in Chicano poetry – the writing of the Mexican American community. His poetry and prose often record his childhood experiences growing up in California's San Joaquin Valley, and the struggles and hardships of the Mexican American factory and farm laborers. The stories are told in a direct, spare style in language that is clear and accessible. The lines are often short, pushing the poem on to the inevitability of its narrative conclusion.

Soto was born in Fresno, California, and his parents were American citizens, although Soto's poetry illustrates that exact status makes little difference in the challenge of assimilation. In "Mexicans Begin Jogging" the border patrol descends on a group of workers, who are told to run by the employer. "And I shouted that I was American / 'No time for lies,' he said, and pressed / A dollar in my palm." Soto's father died at the age of 27, when the boy was 5, from a work-related accident, and the uncomprehending experience of loss is recalled in a number of poems. Soto spent some time working in the fields of the surrounding farmlands before entering Fresno City College in 1970, initially intending to study geography. He transferred to California State University, Fresno, where he studied with poet Philip Levine and published his first poem, when a college senior, in the *Iowa Review*. He went on to receive an MFA from the University of California, Irvine, in 1976, and the following year began a long period teaching at Berkeley. In 1975 he married Carolyn Oda, and some of Soto's later poems attempt to explain the world to his children – for example the daughter addressed in his poem "How Things Work," where the concrete details of economic exchange are set quietly against the forces of chance and economic uncertainty.

Soto's first book, *The Elements of San Joaquin*, appeared in 1977. Its three sections begin with a series of portraits from the struggling Mexican American community of his childhood, moving on to the power of the earth – and the other classical elements of air, fire, and water – to dominate the lives of the laborers working in the fields, and finally to a focus on his own personal history. In the final poem of the book, "Braly Street," he revisits the site of the street once so full of the lives and suffering of his childhood community:

> It's 16 years
> Since our house
> Was bulldozed and my father
> Stunned into a coma . . .
> Where it was,
> An oasis of chickweed
> And foxtails.

Together with *The Tale of Sunlight*, which appeared the following year, the two books record a journey from the toil of the factory and field work of Fresno to the freedom of arriving in Central Mexico – in the second book with a companion, Molinas. The final section of *The Tale of Sunlight*, the "Manuel Zaragoza Poems," illustrates, through the experiences of tavern-keeper Zaragoza, Soto's interest in "magical realism," taking a closely observed ordinary event of human existence and putting it into an unfamiliar context, thus transforming it into the extraordinary – but with no loss of the concrete detail. In the title poem, for example, "a triangle of sunlight" takes on a magical life of its own one noontime when Manuel opens his cantina, consuming all it touches. Soto has acknowledged the influence in this aspect of his work of the Colombian writer Gabriel García Márquez.

In 1980 *Father is a Pillow Tied to a Broom* gathered together a number of Soto's previously uncollected poems, while the 1981 volume *Where Sparrows Work Hard* further explored the difficult lives of workers in urban Fresno. Following *Black Hair* (1985), poems on the themes of death, childhood, and the possibilities of community, Soto produced three prose volumes of autobiographical sketches and essays: *Living Up the Street* (1985), *Small Faces* (1986) and *Lesser Evils: Ten Quartets* (1988). He returned to poetry with *Who Will Know Us?* (1990), and a series of volumes written for children and young adults. His *New and Selected Poems* (1995) was a National Book Award finalist. Soto's many awards include a Guggenheim Fellowship (1979–80), fellowships from the National Endowment for the Arts, and, in 1999, the Literature Award from the Hispanic Heritage Foundation. He is the editor of the Chicano Chapbook series, and is currently Distinguished Professor of Creative Writing at the University of California, Riverside.

## Bibliography

Gary Soto, *New and Selected Poems* (San Francisco, 1995).

Wolfgang Binder, ed., *Partial Autobiographies: Interviews with Twenty Chicano Poets* (Erlangen, 1985).
Bruce-Novoa, *Chicano Poetry: A Response to Chaos* (Austin, 1982).

# Rita Dove (b. 1952)

Rita Dove's poetry encompasses historical events, mythic contexts, and deeply personal poems about her immediate and past family history. The connection is that the poems seek to understand history through the lives of individuals, seeing the points of view, dreams, and injustices that make up individual lives and the culture that surrounds them, in a poetry that is finally about tolerance and patience, the importance of language, understanding, and the responsibility of the poet to help stress that importance and foster that understanding. In writing such poetry, for Dove, the truth of memory – how something is recalled or imagined – can be as valid or more so than the truth of mere fact.

Dove was born in Akron, Ohio, a city dominated by its tire industry. Her father was the only one of ten children to finish high school and attend college, and like his own father he worked for the Goodyear Tire Company. His work in chemistry produced only employment as an elevator operator at Goodyear, until the protests of one of his professors led to his becoming the first black chemist in the industry. Rita Dove was a star student at Miami University, Ohio, and upon graduating in 1973 won a Fulbright scholarship to study at the University of Tübingen, in Germany. In 1977 she received an MFA from the University of Iowa. Dove has been writer-in-residence at Tuskegee Institute. She taught creative writing at Arizona State University until 1989, and now teaches at the University of Virginia. Dove has said in interviews that, while she was always reading and writing as a child and as a teenager, she knew no professional writers and had not realized that it was possible to have a writing career. As an undergraduate, she recalls, she realized that she was arranging her college course work around taking writing courses.

Dove's first two books of poetry were *The Yellow House on the Corner* (1980) and *Museum* (1983). The first volume begins in the neighborhood of her childhood in Akron, and broadens thematically and geographically as it progresses. The cosmopolitan reach is continued in the second volume. The books include poems on historical figures, such as "Banneker," the eighteenth-century African American scientist, and more generalized historical situations, such as "The House Slave" and "Kentucky, 1833," the latter poem capturing the quality of slave life in some few hours of leisure: "It is Sunday, day of roughhousing. We are let out in the woods." " 'Teach Us To Number Our Days' " details the tensions between police and inhabitants in a more contemporary scene of "alleys" and "low-rent balconies." More personal poems include the three entitled "Adolescence," where the speaker tries to understand and come to terms with the onset of sexual desire, and romantic hopes, fears, and fantasies. "The Secret Garden" continues the theme into what appears to be early adulthood, with sexual love as healing:

> I was sick, fainting in the smell of teabags,
> when you came with tomatoes, a good poetry.
> I am being wooed. I am being conquered
> by a cliff of limestone that leaves chalk on my breasts.

In the poem "Parsley," from 1983, Dove explores the motivation of then Dominican Republic dictator Rafael Trujillo in having 20,000 Haitian canefield workers killed on October 2, 1937, because they could not pronounce the Spanish word *perejil* correctly. Her aim, she has said, is to do more than merely deplore a despicable act, but to examine the role of what she has called the creativity of evil in how he came to his decision.

Dove drew national attention with her third book, *Thomas and Beulah* (1986), which won the 1987 Pulitzer Prize for Poetry. This narrative sequence tells the story of the individual lives, courtship, and subsequent life in Akron of Dove's maternal grandparents, as told by her mother, recalled from her childhood, and imaginatively rounded out as in her earlier historical poems. At the end of the sequence, a timeline of public events is set against the poems' chronology of personal milestones. The sequence is divided into two sections, one from Thomas's point of view and one from Beulah's. *Grace Notes* followed in 1989, and again focuses upon the black experience in the United States, including a section that explores the possibility of salvation through words and language. "Arrow," for example, records a patronizing and sexist presentation by an "eminent scholar," the pained response of various listeners, and the poet-narrator's determination to "learn" from the experience rather than just be appalled. *Mother Love* appeared in 1995, a contemporary retelling of the story of Demeter and Persephone. *On the Bus with Rosa Parks* from 1999 was a finalist for the National Book Critics Circle Award.

A *Selected Poems* was published in 1993, and Dove has also published *Fifth Sunday* (1985), a book of short stories, *Through the Ivory Gate* (1992), a novel, and *The Darker Face of the Earth* (1994), a verse drama. She guest-edited the annual volume *Best American Poetry* (2001). In addition to the Fulbright Award that she won as an undergraduate, she served as Poet Laureate from 1993 to 1995, the first African American poet to do so. Other honors include grants and fellowships from the National Endowment for the Arts and the National Endowment for the Humanities, and a Guggenheim Fellowship.

## Bibliography

Rita Dove, *Selected Poems* (New York, 1993).

Earl G. Ingersoll, ed., *Conversations with Rita Dove* (Jackson, MS, 2003).
Lynn Keller, *Forms of Expansion: Recent Long Poems by Women* (Chicago, 1997).
Therese Steffen, *Crossing Color: Transcultural Space and Place in Rita Dove's Poetry, Fiction, and Drama* (Oxford, 2001).

# Texts

# Robert Frost, *North of Boston*

## London: David Nutt, 1914

*North of Boston* was the second book that Frost published, the title pointing to its subject matter of the men and women living on the land in New Hampshire and Vermont, beyond the urban sophistication of Boston. Frost had arrived in England with his family in 1912, having had difficulty finding an American publisher for his poems. His first book, *A Boy's Will*, was published in London in 1913, but it was with *North of Boston* the following year that he got the attention and respect of the poets writing in London, and was able to find an American publisher, Henry Holt, eager to publish his work.

*A Boy's Will* is composed largely of autobiographical lyrics. The poems contain many features characteristic of late Romantic nineteenth-century poetry: formulaic contractions, archaic diction, and sometimes contrived inversions. Some of the poems in *North of Boston* also have origins in Frost's own life, but the incidents are conceived as dramatic monologues using colloquial diction, in the manner of Browning and Kipling, and with an earlier model in the lyrical ballads of Wordsworth – although Keats and Hardy are also important predecessors. Frost observed of this book that he "dropped to an everyday level of diction even Wordsworth kept above." Instead of stiff inversions, the lines in *North of Boston* catch the speakers' hesitations, repetitions, and second thoughts. In this book, which contains a number of Frost's best-known poems, the style and material that would characterize his poetry for the next 50 years found expression. Frost had been working on his poetry for some 20 years before these first books, and so did not go through the process of hesitant development in a series of early books before reaching his mature style, as is the case with many poets. Of the 17 poems in this book, Frost had written "The Death of the Hired Man," "The Black Cottage," and "The Housekeeper" while still farming in Derry in 1905, and "The Wood-Pile," "The Mountain," and "After Apple-Picking" before he left for England. *North of Boston* stands both as the first announcement of a major poet's distinctive style, and also the finest summation of the themes and material upon which he subsequently built the career that made him a national icon and won him four Pulitzer prizes. That material, Frost's regional subject, is the hard life of the farmers and other country people of New England, their battles with nature and with each other – neighbors, spouses – the power of their own imaginations, and also the world in which they lived, the decaying cottages and farmhouses, and the world of nature that was always ready to undo the tenuous order that human imagination, ingenuity, and need had tried to impose upon the earth.

*North of Boston* is dedicated, like Frost's first book, to "E.M.F.", his wife Elinor. On the dedication page he calls the book "This Book of People," and although the poems are more about social relations than those in *A Boy's Will*, the "people" are usually isolated, often fearful or misguided figures, although they are treated sympathetically in the poems, sometimes achieving a kind of triumph over their oppression or oppressors. In a footnote, following the invitation of the opening poem "The Pasture," Frost comments that the second poem, "Mending Wall," "takes up the theme" where the earlier book's "The Tuft of Flowers" had "laid it down," and the relationship indicates the difference between the complexity of the two books. The charming "The Tuft of Flowers" finds a comforting sense of closure and resolution beneath its surface paradox when the hay-gatherer finds that the mower has earlier spared a group of wildflowers for their beauty: "'Men work together,' I told him from the heart, / 'Whether they work together or apart.' "Mending Wall," on the other hand, takes a more complex position on the same themes of nature, community, and order. "Good fences make good neighbours" not, as the narrator's neighbor thinks, because they create a wall that divides them, but because they meet to mend it each year after nature has tried to knock it down. The narrator himself initiates this mending, and it is the repairing ritual itself – two humans trying to keep order against a nature that undermines their work – that brings them together, even if the neighbor does not recognize the wall's true communal status.

"The Death of the Hired Man" and "Home Burial" dramatize domestic strife, both centering upon definitions of "home." In the former, the wife Mary sees a more organic connection between domestic order, human community, and the broader cycles of nature, than her husband, and sees an obligation to the unreliable and dying worker Silas who has come to them. Her husband, Warren, takes a harder, more practical position, although his wife's arguments and tenderness finally win him over. In "Home Burial," based upon the death of Frost and Elinor's first-born son at the age of 3 in 1900, the wife also takes a broader view of "home," wanting to share her grief outside the home with someone other than her husband. But both husband and wife take a narrow view of the ways in which the other deals with grief, for she condemns his attempt to cope with the loss by continuing with his routine, while he insists that she keep the expression of her grief within the emotional confines of the marriage and the physical confines of the home (a position easier for him to hold, since the poem makes clear that the house is that of his family, and thus the new grave in the family burial ground outside the window is part of a larger continuity of birth and death as far as his history is concerned). These two poems begin a series of dramatic explorations of marriage and definitions of home that include, in later books, such well-known poems as "The Witch of Coös" and "West-Running Brook."

Related to "The Death of the Hired Man" and "Home Burial," two poems in which women, with varying degrees of success, confront what for them is the very real oppression of the male partner, are the female figures in "The Fear," "The Housekeeper," and "A Servant to Servants." The women in all five of these poems have powerful, sometimes potentially destructive or paranoiac, imaginations. But whereas the wife in "The Death of the Hired Man" can incorporate her broad sense of community within definitions of home that make room for the seasons, the moon, and the privacy of the marriage bed, in "The Fear" the wife finds the home a terrifying place and the source of threats that also surround it, imagining that she is being watched by a former husband. She discovers the source of what she hears, this time, to be an example of a more controlled domestic scene: two males, a father out showing his son the night, a discovery which by no means assuages her fears. The very title "A Servant to Servants" reveals the double sense of entrapped obligation that the wife of this poem feels towards her husband and the hired men she must provide for. Her sense of oppression is revealed to a traveler, one free to move on, and this oppression is paralleled in a chilling story she tells of the confinement of a lunatic and violent uncle, jailed within a home-made cage, whose nakedness and raging against "love things" can be heard in the bedroom of the new bride and husband – the speaker's parents. In "The Housekeeper," the younger oppressed woman has escaped, to the fury and puzzlement of her narrowly practical and selfish husband. He returns to demand explanations from the mother / housekeeper, who has just shared them with a visiting friend.

The clash of the practical and the imaginatively expansive is explored between male figures in "A Hundred Collars," "The Code," "The Mountain," and "The Self-Seeker." The last-named poem is based upon an accident which left Frost's friend Carl Burell crippled, and centers the conflict upon the different meanings of value and price. The crippled man refuses to put a price on the priceless – his enjoyment of the many varieties of wildflowers.

Significantly a young girl, the female imagination again, will help him counter the limitations imposed upon this joy by his handicap – her response to nature equally beyond price. The same themes of the practical and imaginative, nature and human order, become multi-layered in the justly famous "After Apple-Picking," where the imagination takes over from exhausting and unfinished labor in a poem that has been variously interpreted as about artistic creation, the possibilities of salvation following the Fall, the need to acknowledge human limitation, and the acceptance of inevitable death.

Such a poem is also concerned, in its allusions to Eden and the Fall, with origins, another theme that Frost would take up throughout his career. One way in which this exploration of origins is dramatized in his work is through abandoned and derelict houses – an inverse of the vibrant but potentially oppressive domestic spaces of the marriage poems discussed above. The two examples in *North of Boston* are "The Generations of Men," in which the extensive Stark family gathers in large numbers to explore its origins in a way that the poem gently ridicules. It is left to a young couple, meeting by a ruined cottage, to use an imagining of the past as a playful way to begin a courtship that looks to the future. The young girl's role is particularly important, as is the imagined presence of a long-dead female relative, both female presences qualifying the gender limitations of the poem's title. The other poem is "The Black Cottage," a domestic space kept vital when she was alive by a Civil War widow, the ruined cottage now viewed from the outside by two men. The cottage has been inherited by the widow's two sons, now in the west, whose plans to spend some time in the house remain only vague intentions. The real homeowners are the bees, whose presence ends the poem:

> "There are bees in this wall." He struck the clapboards,
> Fierce heads looked out; small bodies pivoted.
> We rose to go. Sunset blazed on the windows.

The final poem of the volume, "Good Hours," is a short lyric describing the narrator going out for a "winter evening walk" beyond the "cottages" whose lighted windows provide a kind of company on the outward journey. By being darkened when the walker retraces his steps they leave the narrator alone, but, the title suggests, not too disturbed. Frost would later write more threatening lyrics about such a walk beyond human habitation, for example in his "Acquainted with the Night."

The dramatic narratives in *North of Boston* explore the depths of human fears, love, needs, and despair in colloquial speech that is set against the rhythms of blank verse. The counterpoint between the syntactical stress of the speaking voice and the formal qualities of the verse parallels the narratives of an order or containment being tested, pushed, either to a greater level of incorporation or, in some of the poems, to reinforce, like an animal pacing the confines of its cage, the nature of the imprisonment. This was a theme and formal device that Frost exploited for the rest of his career.

The central theme in this book and in subsequent volumes of the role and status of human order as it confronts a nature perhaps indifferent, perhaps hostile, perhaps sympathetic to such human attempts to shape it, is paralleled by Frost's general attitude to poetic form. In a famous statement in his essay "The Figure a Poem Makes" Frost called a poem "a momentary stay against confusion." The tentative "momentary" shows the distance between Frost and the Romantic poets of a hundred years earlier, who viewed the relationship of man and nature as more harmonious. The theme is a central aspect of Frost's questioning of Romantic assumptions about the relation of nature to the human, and the possible special status of humankind. Frost accepts the parameters of the Romantic discussion, as such modernists as Pound and Eliot did not, but questions the Romantic conclusions – as well as the comfortable restatements of the Romantic relationship by the English Georgian poets – in much the way that Thomas Hardy does in his poetry. The claim also shows his distance from a modernist poet such as Wallace Stevens, who also argued with the Romantic poets, but saw the poem as bringing order to a world otherwise unknowable.

Following *North of Boston* Frost stayed with the themes and form he had found there. Pound and the other modernists soon lost patience and wrote him off as belonging to the past, but to the American public Frost came to embody the essential American poet. He went on to be feted by Congress and presidents, his reputation survived critical and political fashions, and he remained an irritant to the modernist poets throughout his career. He rejected their call for free verse, and for the urban, cosmopolitan subject matter of writers like Pound and Eliot. Perhaps it was no accident that the first poem of his next book following *North of Boston* began with "The Road Not Taken" – Frost had decided what road he wanted to take.

## Bibliography

*The Poetry of Robert Frost: The Collected Poems*, ed. Edward Lathem (New York, 1969).

Alex Calder, "Robert Frost: *North of Boston*," in Neil Roberts, ed., *A Companion to Twentieth-Century Poetry* (Oxford, 2001), 369–80.

Robert Faggen, ed., *The Cambridge Companion to Robert Frost* (Cambridge, 2001).

Matthew Parfitt, "Robert Frost's 'Modern Georgics,'" *Robert Frost Review* (Fall 1996), 54–70.

Lawrance Thompson, *Robert Frost: The Early Years, 1874–1915* (New York, 1966).

# Ezra Pound, ed., *Des Imagistes: An Anthology*

## New York: Albert and Charles Boni, 1914

*Des Imagistes*, an anthology of poems by various figures associated with Ezra Pound's London circle before the First World War, was a pivotal volume in a number of ways. The book established some important relationships, and foreshadowed the direction of international modernist poetry while at the same time providing a strategy for a more nativist modernism in the United States. While most of the poems and poets of *Des Imagistes* were familiar to readers of avant-garde magazines in London, and even to US readers of the Chicago-based *Poetry* and its rival *The Little Review*, the appearance of the book in New York galvanized one group of east coast poets. As a source book of imagism and, more broadly, of a nascent modernism, the book had a much fuller impact upon the American scene than it did in London.

The principles of "imagism" had been discussed by Pound, Hilda Doolittle (H.D.), and her future husband the English writer Richard Aldington in London in 1912, although the term always covered a broad range of different kinds of poem and the group was always a loosely knit one. In February 1912 Pound published some of its tenets in the London magazine *Poetry Review*, and produced various later formulations that were all similar in their emphasis. The imagists' argument was chiefly with late Victorian and Georgian verse, whose poets, the imagists argued, utilized only a narrow range of rhythmic possibilities, and too often indulged in wordiness or sentimentality in order to fill out a line. The imagists demanded a freer form and dispensed with rhyme. They insisted upon concision, that every word must earn its place in a poem, and argued against symbolism and poetic diction that had no clear relationship to its supposed referent ("direct treatment of the thing" as Pound put it). Pound's later summaries of the group's main principles indicated that, at any rate as far as he was concerned, it was as much an attempt at one particular moment to rid poetry of what he regarded as tired late nineteenth-century habits and excesses as it was a manifesto for future work. In fact by the time the rather diverse poems of *Des Imagistes* appeared in New York and London, Pound was ready to move on.

Pound was a tireless promoter of his own work, of those whose writing he believed in, and of modern writing generally. He had formed wide contacts from his association with the Chicago magazines, from his student days in Philadelphia, where he knew William Carlos Williams and H.D., and from his activities in London, where he knew both the younger writers of his own generation and such already established figures as W. B. Yeats and Ford Madox Ford (then Ford Madox Hueffer). The contents of *Des Imagistes* were a distillation of these contacts, and of the London scene from Pound's expatriate perspective. The volume began with ten poems by Aldington, followed by six much more distilled poems by H.D., and then continued with some impressionistic stanzas by London writer F. S. Flint. There followed poems by Americans Skipwith Cannell, Amy Lowell, William Carlos Williams, and Pound himself, and a translation in prose from John Cournos. A poem each by Hueffer and James Joyce (the latter a last-minute addition suggested by Yeats) and prose translations by Allen Upward filled out the volume. The final pages contained three "Documents": "To Hulme (T.E.) and Fitzgerald," by Pound, Aldington's "Vates, the Social Reformer," and, in Greek, "Fragments Addressed by Clearchus H. to Aldi" by Hueffer. A final page listed a "Bibliography" of the writers' published books. The sentence in this bibliography summarizing Ford's prose output, "Forty volumes of prose with various publishers," pointed to his role as an established figure, as if authorizing to some extent the activities of these younger rebels.

Alfred Kreymborg, in his *Troubadour: An Autobiography* (1925), recounts the story of how the manuscript of *Des Imagistes* turned up at his door in 1913, mailed from London by Pound with instructions to "set this up just as it stands!" (p. 204). Kreymborg, who had been involved with an earlier avant-garde journal in New York, was in the process of starting a new venture, *The Glebe*, in the summer artists' colony of Grantwood, New Jersey, with painters Man Ray and Samuel Halpert. Kreymborg had asked John Cournos in London if he could hunt up material, and Cournos had spoken to Pound. A second-hand printing press donated by Ray's employer arrived shortly after the manuscript, but the press was damaged upon delivery and Kreymborg went in search of printers in New York. He eventually teamed up with Albert and Charles Boni, proprietors of the Washington Square bookshop, who agreed to finance the journal and allow Kreymborg to edit it. The Bonis published the volume in February 1914 as the second issue of *The Glebe* and also issued a number of copies in book form between hard covers. This association continued for a number of issues until Kreymborg became discontented with the increasing number of translations by European writers appearing in the journal at the insistence of the Bonis, and resigned. Kreymborg's interest in publishing American writers was shared by William Carlos Williams, the two having been put in touch with each other by Pound, and they began to work together on a new journal that they titled *Others*. During its short life *Others* published the early work of such writers as Marianne Moore, Wallace Stevens, and Mina Loy. Meanwhile *The Glebe* folded after Kreymborg's resignation, and the Boni brothers retired from publishing, until a few years later they joined Horace Liveright to form one of the most important publishing houses of modernist American writing, Boni & Liveright.

The eclectic nature of the poems in *Des Imagistes* was revealed at a dinner that patroness and contributor Amy Lowell gave to celebrate the publication of the book in London in July 1914. In the after-dinner speeches, Hueffer declared his puzzlement over the term "imagist," and announced that his poem in the collection had quite traditional sources. Upward spoke of the Chinese sources of his work, while Aldington spoke of imagism as an outgrowth of Hellenism. Pound evidently laughed a great deal. Some of this was designed to irritate hostess Lowell, who as far as Pound was concerned was trying to take a proprietary interest in imagism, as a result of which the contributors were already splitting into two camps.

More important than particular sources, or there being relatively few "imagist" poems in the volume, was the challenge that the collection presented to the then dominant, conservative view of what the appropriate form, content, and audience of a poem should be – particularly in the United States, where such conservative ideas were more entrenched. Modern poetry, it announced, was difficult and required an educated audience. H.D.'s and Pound's poems are probably the only recognizably "imagist" work in the volume, although many of the other poems are pictorial and most are radical for their time. The translations and allusions foreshadow the international foundation of the modernism to come, as did the fact that the volume was a collaboration of poets from two continents. Pound's poem "The Return," included in the volume, illustrated his developing method (one he would apply to Eliot's *The Waste Land* ten years later) of dissolving continuities.

Pound, even at the time of Amy Lowell's London dinner party, was ready to leave future imagist anthologies to her, and to move on to the energies of vorticism and his study of the manuscripts of Chinese poetry prepared by scholar Ernest Fenollosa, whose widow gave them to Pound after having read his translations in *Des Imagistes* and elsewhere. Pound's *Catholic Anthology*, published the next year, included a number of the contributors to *Des Imagistes*, but was put together, he claimed, for the sole purpose of getting newcomer T. S. Eliot's poems into print. Williams soon dropped the classical allusions that laced "Postlude," his contribution to *Des Imagistes*, in favor of subjects drawn from his own world of New Jersey, and his most imagist poems appeared in later work. H.D. continued to develop her own style of emotional and pictorial lyrics, although the general recognition of their quality would come much later in the century. The rest of the contributors became primarily prose writers (including Ford and Joyce), anthologists, critics, and memorialists. But the principles of imagism, the seeds of which were encapsulated in this volume, maintained an appeal for American writers attracted, like Williams and Kreymborg, to a home-grown poetry, for it threw out many of the formal qualities of verse, the past achievements of which gave English poetry in particular, for them, its oppressive authority. Imagist poetry engaged the moment: its subject could be the American scene, which the poems demanded be looked at carefully. A grain elevator – or the Brooklyn ferry, as the newly appreciated Whitman had shown in the previous century – deserved to be the subject of a poem just as much as any ruined abbey or other site steeped in the literary and historical associations of a far-off and now irrelevant Europe. The book was reprinted by AMS Press in 1982.

## Bibliography

Ezra Pound, ed., *Des Imagistes: An Anthology* (New York, 1982).

John T. Gage, *In the Arresting Eye: The Rhetoric of Imagism* (Baton Rouge, 1981).
Glenn Hughes, *Imagism & the Imagists: A Study in Modern Poetry* (Stanford, 1931).
Michael Levenson, *A Genealogy of Modernism: A Study of English Literary Doctrine, 1908–1922* (Cambridge, 1984).

# Edwin Arlington Robinson, *The Man Against the Sky: A Book of Poems*

## New York: Macmillan, 1916

Edwin Arlington Robinson published his first two books of poems in 1896 and 1897, and his poems are, like Robert Frost's, modern but formed by a pre-modernist sensibility. Robinson's work, like Frost's, stayed within traditional forms, and both wrote many poems focusing upon a particular region – in Robinson's case the Gardiner, Maine, that became the "Tilbury Town" of many of his poems. But although both wrote within the framework of Romantic issues, such as the relationship of mankind to nature, what we can know of the next world, and the effects of time and change, much more to the fore in Robinson's work are the issues of failure, loneliness, and despair, and the crisis of faith. Robinson is also more likely to use Romantic rhetoric and personified abstractions than is Frost, although Robinson can also present lyrics focused upon a particular character or couple that have all the observation and quiet drama of his contemporary.

These qualities are characteristic of Robinson's poetry, but received their fullest expression in the book that cemented his reputation, *The Man Against the Sky*, published 20 years after his first volume. The poems of *The Man Against the Sky* followed a period in which Robinson unsuccessfully channeled his energies into trying to write plays, and when it appeared in 1916 its blank verse monologues, reflective lyrics, and verse portraits marked his return to significant work. The book-length poems that Robinson published after *The Man Against the Sky*, although of interest, are much less consistent in execution and have added little to his stature.

The title poem, which concludes the book, is generally considered a failure, but it marks Robinson's most ambitious expression of the human situation as he saw it. The other poems in the volume are in many ways individual examples, played out in particular lives, of the more generalized account of the human condition dramatized in the title poem. In "The Man Against the Sky," the narrator sees a figure heading towards the fiery west and death, and speculates on the way in which the man has lived his life and how it might have shaped the way that he meets his end. The poem is a series of questions and speculations, and does not pretend to offer answers. The narrator's vision of the man before him, set on the same journey that he himself and all humankind will inevitably undertake, is powerfully realized:

> Between me and the sunset, like a dome
> Against the glory of a world on fire,
> Now burned a sudden hill,
> Bleak, round, and high, by flame-lit height made higher,
> With nothing on it for the flame to kill
> Save one who moved and was alone up there

The narrator speculates upon a range of attitudes that this "dark, marvelous, and inscrutable" figure might hold – from "a faith unshaken" down to mere materialism, although the abstractions are verbose and sometimes mechanical when compared to the shorter dramatic lyrics for which the poet is now most admired. Examples of the latter in this volume are "Eros Turannos," in which habit and emotional manipulation trap a couple together, replacing love and respect, and "Bewick Finzer," which in five stanzas chronicles the rise and fall of the title character from riches to being an object of pity. The emptiness of materialism, as a value in itself, as a substitute for Romantic confidence, and, in its guise as science, as any kind of replacement for a now uncertain religious faith is a central theme of many of the poems.

The opening poem, "Flammonde," is characteristic of the poems on individual figures. Flammonde intrigues the narrator and others of the town – the narrator in Robinson's poems is by implication a member of a community, either of Tilbury Town or more generally of a fate and a curiosity he assumes are shared by the reader – but Flammonde remains, like so many other characters, at bottom a mystery. "The man Flammonde, from God knows where," the poem, and the book, opens, and towards the end of the poem the narrator is still asking: "What was it that we never caught? / What was he, and what was he not?" But questions, speculation, and inference – from what is seen or reported, and then judged through the values, fears, and sympathy of the narrator – are finally all that can be known of another:

> And this is why, from time to time
> In Tilbury Town, we look beyond
> Horizons for the man Flammonde.

The characters and narratives in the book variously illustrate the mystery of human lives, mostly through figures haunted, betrayed, worn by time, isolated, bitter, or disappointed. The poems question and sometimes comment upon the ways that the characters find to keep on living – if they do keep on living – perhaps through clinging to illusions, or by stoic acceptance, by using alcohol, or by hiding in the escape of a dulling routine. This mystery extends to the person of Shakespeare, imagined in "Ben Jonson Entertains a Man from Stratford" as the subject of a monologue by his fellow Renaissance playwright. (*The Man Against the Sky* appeared in the tercentenary year of Shakespeare's death.) Robinson rewrites "Old King Cole" to turn the title figure, bereft of a loved wife and saddled with two sons who are "a curse," into a determined stoic. In "John Gorham" the beauty of moonlight produces what is later a bitter, failed romance.

Although Robinson's poems come out of the late nineteenth century's crisis of faith, he remained an optimist himself and insisted that "The Man Against the Sky," was a poem that admired man's ability to find a purpose and to continue living and holding ambitions. The poem is not always read that way, however, and its concluding questions can be taken as a desperate search on the narrator's part for answers never to be realized within the inevitable limitations of an earthbound perspective – the limited view from this side of the sky:

> If after all that we have lived and thought,
> All comes to Nought, –
> If there be nothing after Now,
> And we be nothing anyhow,
> And we know that, – why live?

How a reader judges the final stanzas of the title poem will condition that reader's sense of Robinson's final attitude to the assorted characters who people his book – whether they are victims of a fate against which they to various degrees rage to no purpose, or whether they are characters to be admired or pitied for the ways most of them have found to continue living. The range of the book allows for both possibilities, and this is part of the continuing strength of Robinson's work at its best.

## Bibliography

*The Poetry of E. A. Robinson*, selected and ed. Robert Mezey (New York, 1999).

Richard Cary, ed., *Early Reception of Edwin Arlington Robinson: The First Twenty Years* (Waterville, ME, 1974).

Mark Jarman, "Robinson, Frost and Jeffers and the New Narrative Poetry," in R. S. Gwynn, ed., *New Expansive Poetry: Theory, Criticism, History* (Ashland, OR, 1999).

John N. Sanborn, "Juxtaposition as Structure in 'The Man Against the Sky,'" *Colby Quarterly*, 10 (1974), 486–94.

# T. S. Eliot, *The Waste Land*

## New York: Boni & Liveright, 1922

Such was T. S. Eliot's growing reputation as poet and critic in 1922 that publishers and journals were prepared to bid on publication rights to *The Waste Land* without having seen the recently completed poem. Some of this interest was generated by Eliot's earlier books, published since his decision to live in England in 1915. *Prufrock and Other Observations* appeared in 1917. A collection including more recent poems such as "Gerontion" was published in both Britain and the United States in 1920, and a book of essays, *The Sacred Wood*, in the same year. But the poem's early reputation was also helped by Ezra Pound, who along with New York lawyer John Quinn was centrally involved in the marketing of the poem, and in Pound's case also with the final stages of its arrangement. Pound's high opinion of the poem lead him to tell a correspondent in 1922: "Eliot's *Waste Land* is I think the justification of the 'movement,' of our modern experiment, since 1900." Lawrence Rainey, in an examination of the publishing history of the poem, has argued convincingly that the coming together of commercial and institutional forces to bid for the poem marks "the crucial moment in the transition of modernism from a minority culture to one supported by an important institutional and financial apparatus," and the first stage of modernism's eventual acceptance into the colleges and universities (see *The Waste Land*, ed. North, p. 106). What is certainly the case is that the publication and success of the poem established Eliot's reputation and authority so that as editor at Faber & Gwyer, later Faber & Faber, and as a critic, he became a dominant presence well into the 1950s. The high reputation of the poem in academic circles over the next decades signaled that fame could now come from the academy as well as from newspapers and magazines. Eliot's own poetry moved in a different direction after *The Waste Land*, towards the meditative verse that followed his conversion to Anglicanism in 1927 – *Ash-Wednesday* and *The Four Quartets* – and eventually towards verse drama. But for the 30 years following the poem's publication, for many poets and readers a modern poem was characterized by the kind of dense, complex, allusive, cosmopolitan, fragmented text inaugurated by *The Waste Land*.

Although Eliot's writing career was on the road to success in 1922, his personal life at the time of the poem's composition was very troubled. He had married Vivien Haigh-Wood in June 1915, but she was often ill for months at a time and, on top of Eliot's worry about her health, their living arrangements always had to take her illnesses into account. Money was also a problem, for Eliot's father disapproved of his living in England, and such vacations that the couple managed turned into stressful situations that afforded no relaxation. Eliot over-extended himself. The demands of his teaching jobs, and from 1917 his position in the Colonial and Foreign department at Lloyd's Bank, combined with the stressful domestic situation and the commitments of his writing career (which included a grueling schedule of reviews and lectures, as well as editorial duties at *The Egoist*), lead in 1921 to a mental and physical collapse that forced him to take three months' leave from the bank. But during this convalescence, much of it away from the immediate strains of his marriage, he was able to complete the composition of *The Waste Land*.

Many critics have seen these personal crises behind details and even central themes of the poem, even though Eliot argued in his critical writings for "impersonality," that poetry should not be about the emotions of the individual poet. This argument, which became very influential in the years that followed, was one of modernism's important differences from the Romantic poets. *The Waste Land* offers multiple voices, not the voice of a single narrator or character, and the literary, mythic, and anthropological allusions disperse individual voices further. Nevertheless personal details, of Eliot's own breakdown and of the difficulties of his marriage, are arguably just beneath the surface of the text, and the sexual disgust, neurotic projections, and general despair of the poem may equally have personal origins. Such readings of *The Waste Land* gained further evidence when the early drafts of the poem became available in the late 1960s, drafts which also detailed the important editorial role played by Pound.

Certainly the demands of other writing commitments, and the strains of Eliot's personal life, delayed his starting the poem. He wrote to his mother on December 18, 1919 that he hoped soon to start work on "a long poem I have had on my mind for a long time," and the following September in another letter to her he still longed for "a period of tranquility" in order to write the poem. The earliest fragments incorporated into the finished poem (lines 377–84 in section V) date from 1914.

Eliot found himself able to work on the poem in February 1921. A second period of composition came in October 1921 when he was resting at the resort town of Margate (mentioned in section III), work that he continued the following month when in Lausanne, seeing a specialist about his breakdown. Eliot then consulted with Pound in Paris in January, before returning to London. Pound suggested cutting a number of the poem's narratives, and also much of the parody and pastiche, including some of the music hall-style monologues that had lead Eliot to call the early version of sections I and II "He do the police in different voices." Pound's suggestions, most of which Eliot accepted, tightened the whole poem, substituted fragmentation for continuity and thus suggestiveness for logic, and at certain points even supplied an alternative word for a key line. One radical suggestion was to cut from section IV several pages of narrative describing a sea voyage and retain just the ten lines beginning "Phlebas the Phoenician" of the finished poem.

Pound's influence on the poem was also more generally in the poetry and criticism he had been writing for a decade or more in support of the kind of modernist principles that *The Waste Land* built upon. His own sequence *Hugh Selwyn Mauberley* from 1920 had shown how to set representative characters and voices against a larger social fabric through allusion. Eliot's recognition of Pound's help came in his generous dedication of the poem to Pound, *"il miglior fabbro"* (the greater craftsman).

Both Pound and John Quinn were anxious to negotiate a publishing arrangement for the poem that might allow Eliot the financial freedom to devote more time to his writing, and after months of discussion a deal was made. The poem appeared almost simultaneously in October 1922 in the first issue of *The Criterion* in London, and in the prestigious New York avant-garde magazine *The Dial*. *The Dial*, as part of the arrangement, awarded Eliot its important and valuable annual prize, and the award further helped the reputation of poem and poet. New York publishers Boni & Liveright issued the poem in book form in December, and it quickly went through a number of printings. Leonard and Virginia Woolf brought out an edition in England in 1923.

For the Boni & Liveright publication Eliot added three pages of notes to the poem that had not appeared in the periodical publications. Although for many years the notes were thought to be a last-minute addition because the publishers lamented the small size of the volume, recent evidence indicates that Eliot had in mind adding notes as early as February 1922 (see North, pp. 107–8). They draw attention to some of the poem's sources, particularly the anthropological work of Jessie Weston and James Frazer, and the sources in Eastern religion. Some notes are almost commentary, such as Eliot's comment that Tiresias is "the most important personage in the poem, uniting all the rest." Others are more cryptic, and for some passages a reader might wish for notes that do not appear. But the notes emphasize finally that this is a difficult poem, one not making compromises to accommodate its audience, and one requiring, for a full appreciation, the kind of awareness of literary tradition so lacking in the momentary, sensual obsessions of the poem's characters.

Some reviewers, for example Edmund Wilson and Gilbert Seldes, recognized immediately the importance of Eliot's achievement, although the poem also came in for scorn as a "hoax" and "so much waste paper." The case for the poem's significance was soon taken up by such important critics as F. R. Leavis and I. A. Richards. The poem has since produced commentary that varies a good deal in its emphasis, although, in general, discussions up until the 1960s sought to "explain" it, seeing it as presenting a degenerate post-war society. More recent commentary, while emphasizing the autobiographical elements more fully, also recognizes the open-ended nature of the poem's structure and meaning, its function as an evocative as much as a logical text.

The poem's five sections are loosely connected. Although there are recurring motifs, lines, allusions, and even characters, the relationships suggest multiple perspectives rather than a linear narrative. Eliot even thought at one point of allowing the poem to appear over a number of different issues of the journals. The poem's opening quotation, in Greek, announces the multiple languages of the poem. The Sibyl of Cumae, having been granted a long life, forgot to ask for eternal youth and lives in the kind of living/dead limbo of the characters who populate the poem. Section I, "The Burial of the Dead," begins with the evocation of spring, a traditional epic opening, and also the resistance to renewal and a resulting debased fertility that become central themes in the poem:

> April is the cruellest month, breeding
> Lilacs out of the dead land, mixing
> Memory and desire, stirring
> Dull roots with spring rain.

Section I goes on to introduce the hellish, dry landscape, evocative of Dante's Hell, that reappears in section V, while at the same time presenting the voices and landmarks of a recognizable post-war London. In the final lines of the section time becomes even more disjointed and the reader is implicated in the social and cultural breakdown that the poem has dramatized.

Section II moves from the overview of the first section to a more individualized focus through two women, one apparently rich and the other working class. Allusions to Shakespeare, both concerning water, open and close the section and emphasize the dryness that is a major motif of the poem. Throughout the poem the motif of water also accompanies the allusions from anthropology to various river-god ceremonies.

The first of the female characters sits in a dry, suffocating environment, in a room burdened with heavy, late Victorian décor. When a visitor, possibly her husband, appears, the resulting dialogue is an exercise in neurotic non-communication. The working-class woman in the London pub whose voice takes up the last third of the section reveals her superficial values and the narrow, appetite-driven lives of those around her in a self-revealing monologue stopped only by the publican's "HURRY UP PLEASE ITS TIME" – an ironic echo of the poem's vision of cultural apocalypse.

Section III, the longest, finds the River Thames empty of any meaningful rituals, and within a gloomy urban industrial landscape tells a series of sordid sexual encounters. The section ends with fragments from St. Augustine and Buddha pleading for release from the fires of passion. Section IV describes a "Death by Water" so absent from the *Waste Land* world, and offers cryptic pointers to its significance. Section V begins with an explicitly Christian framework, Christ's betrayal and sacrifice, but moves on, after more apocalyptic imagery, to a quieter attitude towards time and death, and the voice of the Thunder from the *Upanishads* with its imperatives to "Give," "Sympathize," and "Control." But the poem's final lines return to madness, violence, and the disruption of natural cycles of renewal, before the repetition of the thunder's voice and the poem's last three words: "Shantih shantih shantih" – translated by Eliot in his notes as "The Peace which passeth understanding." This ending has been read variously as offering a possibility that could be but is not realized by the inhabitants of the Waste Land, or a stark contrast intended to set into relief the unredeemable condition dramatized in the poem. In this final section the Grail Chapel is discovered, but it is empty, "only the wind's home," and the rain remains only a "damp gust," bringing no relief to the harsh dryness.

Eliot's use of allusion in the poem contributed to the subsequent re-evaluation of the two major neoclassical poets, Dryden and Pope, whose stature had been diminished by more than a century of Romantic writing. And such use of allusion became the hallmark of many a subsequent modernist poem. As Eliot wrote of James Joyce's *Ulysses* in an influential review, such allusion provided a way to set the modern world into a historical and mythic framework. But just what is the final status of history and the past in *The Waste Land* has been much debated: whether the poem condemns the modern world in particular, or whether it finally condemns human society throughout history. What is certain is that Eliot himself was looking, in this poem and others that he wrote in these years, for a way to transcend the merely earthly and physical. The idea of "tradition" in *The Waste Land* finally fails to satisfy this need, and the religious allusions, whatever their final meaning, also function ironically. Eliot was to find his own answer with his conversation to the Anglican faith in 1927. His next major poem, *Ash-Wednesday* (1930), is quite explicitly about the attempt to leave behind the material world and physical desire for a promise of salvation mediated through a non-sexual, virgin/goddess/muse figure. Eliot himself moved away from the form, and many of the themes, of *The Waste Land* towards a more meditative and religious poetry. But his 1922 poem became, in the work of the poets and critics who followed and for the rest of Eliot's lifetime, what Pound claimed it to be, the culminating statement of modernist poetry, and the modernist poem to take account of beyond any other.

## Bibliography

T. S. Eliot, *The Waste Land: A Facsimile and Transcript of the Original Drafts Including the Annotations of Ezra Pound*, ed. Valerie Eliot (San Diego, 1971).
—— *The Waste Land*, ed. Michael North (New York, 2001).

Calvin Bedient, *He Do the Police in Different Voices: The Waste Land and its Protagonist* (Chicago, 1986).
Jewel Spears Brooker and Joseph Bentley, *Reading The Waste Land: Modernism and the Limits of Interpretation* (Amherst, 1990).
Michael Grant, ed., *T. S. Eliot: The Critical Heritage* (London, 1982).

# Claude McKay, *Harlem Shadows*

## New York: Harcourt Brace, 1922

Claude McKay's 1922 *Harlem Shadows* was a pioneer volume of the 1920s Harlem Renaissance, appearing before the first books by Jean Toomer, Countee Cullen, Langston Hughes, and Sterling Brown. When he appeared prominently in Alain Locke's important anthology *The New Negro* in 1925, McKay was a good deal older than most of the other poets represented. And yet the 1922 volume is a curious one to hold such a position in the vanguard. McKay's patrons back in his native Jamaica, where he published his first two volumes of verse, and in New York, were white, and *Harlem Shadows* was published by a white publisher. McKay had spent much of the two years prior to its publication in London, and he left the United States within months of its appearance and did not return for 12 years. He published no further books of poetry, his interests turning to prose fiction, essays, and autobiography. *Harlem Shadows* is not formally innovative, as the work of Toomer and Hughes is, and relatively few of its poems are about Harlem. However, in this volume McKay treated racial themes with a militancy that would rarely be matched until the 1960s, writing on such subjects as interracial love, racial injustice, prejudice, and lynching. The themes are modern: alienation, anger, and rebellion. The impact of the volume, coupled with McKay's editorial position on the radical journal *The Liberator*, made him for a period an influential figure in the developing movements around Harlem. The volume marked an important advance from the dialect poetry of Paul Dunbar. But, as Melvin Tolson pointed out in reviewing McKay's posthumously published *Selected Poems* in 1954, the impact was in the poems' content, not their largely conventional form.

The 74 poems in *Harlem Shadows* represent those McKay considered his best since his arrival in the United States in 1912. The book contains almost all of the poems from his 1920 volume *Spring in New Hampshire*. *Harlem Shadows* opens with two introductions. The first is by Max Eastman, editor of *The Liberator*, where McKay served in 1922 as an associate editor. Eastman finds in McKay's poetry "the first significant expression of [the black] race in poetry." Eastman's introduction assaults racial prejudice and the scientific pretensions of its adherents, although his own rhetoric reflects some of the patronizing primitivism of the decade. McKay's years growing up in Jamaica are "the happy tropic life of play and affection" before they become shadowed by the oppression of the British colonial power, an oppression that McKay also found when he came to the United States. Eastman's own taste in poetry emerges as a preference for conventional lyrics, and by this standard he finds "occasional lapses of quality" and "one or two . . . rhythms I confess I am not able to apprehend at all" in the volume. McKay's "Author's Word" defends his use of formal verse, arguing that, although the speech of his "childhood and early youth was the Jamaica Negro dialect," the language that he was taught to read and write was "England's English." McKay's first two books had included dialect, but in *Harlem Shadows* he argues that within what in effect are the conventions of Victorian verse, and with the liberal use of archaic diction, his "instinct" and "moods" can achieve "directness, truthfulness and naturalness of expression instead of an enameled originality." The result can sometimes be curious, as in "One Year After," where a poem extolling passionate freedom, "gales of tropic fury," "no rigid road," and a "zest of life" that "exceeds the bound of laws," is written in verse with only a minimally varied rhyme scheme. The subject matter of this poem, however, interracial love and the poet's ambivalent guilt about the betrayal of his blackness, points to the importance of the volume as a bold expression of subjects previously treated rarely if at all by black poets.

The poems in *Harlem Shadows* fall into four broad categories: nostalgia for Jamaica and a consequent ambivalence about the United States, racial themes, poems on working-class life, and – in the volume's final 20 pages or so – love poems. Most of the poems that made the greatest impact, and which are most admired today, fall into the first two categories. An early example of one of the significant poems in the volume is the sonnet "America," showing McKay's fascination and disgust with "this cultured hell," and ending with a vision of its "granite wonders . . . / sinking in the sand." "The Tropics in New York" is a poem of exile in the vein of Yeats's "The Lake Isle of Innisfree." The title poem sees Harlem prostitutes as representing "my fallen race," but a more frequently anthologized poem, "The Harlem Dancer," is a less generalized portrait and captures the ambivalence of the narrator's own involvement with the dancer's oppression.

The poems on black working-class routine, some of them describing jobs that McKay himself held, include "Alfonso, Dressing to Wait at Table," "On the Road," and "Dawn in New York." In the first-named poem the carefree singing of the title character is soon to be stopped "by clamouring / Of hungry and importunate palefaces." The railcar waiters of "On the Road" finish the journey "weary, listless, glum" and find relief in spending "their tips on harlots, cards, and rum." The narrator of "The Tired Worker" greets the dawn with exhausted dread for its pulling him out of the brief escape offered by sleep.

McKay's angriest poems are explicitly about racial violence and oppression. "The White City" takes a different tone towards the city than does "America," expressing a "life-long hate" of the "white world's hell" to which he finds himself tied by both fascination and need. The sonnet "Enslaved" again describes its driving emotion as "hate," and calls upon "the avenging angel to consume / The white man's world of wonders utterly." "Outcast," again a sonnet, paints the picture of a double exile, separated from "the dim regions whence my fathers came," and "a thing apart" in a world dominated by "the white man's menace." That "menace" finds full expression in "The Lynching," which ends with "little lads" dancing with glee around the burned, swaying body, "lynchers that were to be" in a future offering no hope of change. "Exhortation: Summer, 1919" is a demand for "Africa" to "awake!" and force a change, while "If We Must Die" – for many years McKay's best-known poem – calls for "fighting back!" even in the face of impossible odds.

Recent scholarship has shown a resurgence of interest in McKay's poetry as well as his prose work. Such attention has helped the importance of his transitional role within the Harlem movements of the early 1920s to be acknowledged, while at the same time recognizing the achievement of his best work on its own terms.

## Bibliography

Claude McKay, *The Passion of Claude McKay: Selected Poetry and Prose, 1912–1948*, ed. Wayne F. Cooper (New York, 1973).

Houston A. Baker, *Modernism and the Harlem Renaissance* (Chicago, 1987).

Heather Hathaway, *Caribbean Waves: Relocating Claude McKay and Paule Marshall* (Bloomington, IN, 1999).

A. L. McLeod, ed., *Claude McKay: Centennial Studies* (New Delhi, India, 1992).

# Wallace Stevens, *Harmonium*

## New York: Alfred A. Knopf, 1923

Wallace Stevens was 44 when he published his first book of poems, *Harmonium*, in 1923, and following its appearance he wrote little poetry for the next few years. His next book, *Ideas of Order*, was published in 1935 – although an expanded edition of *Harmonium* appeared in 1931 adding fourteen poems to the 1923 edition (including some poems written since 1927) and removing three. After 1935 Stevens would publish five additional volumes with Knopf, the publisher of *Harmonium*, before the appearance of his *Collected Poems* in 1954 a year before his death. These later books contain many of the important meditative and philosophical poems that firmly established Stevens's reputation, but no later volume contains the wit and variety of his first book, or illustrates more clearly the development of the poet from his 1890s sensibility to the emerging major figure of twentieth-century poetry.

At Harvard as an undergraduate Stevens came under the influence of the "aesthetic movement," which saw language as decoration and a dandified persona as a way of engaging the world with imagination and humor. Such an attitude permitted effects of irony and incongruity, and for such writers signaled a separation from the confident seriousness of the Romantic poets. Important influences upon the Harvard group were the late nineteenth-century French poets Baudelaire and Laforgue. Although Stevens went on to develop this attitude in ways that are distinctly modernist, it appears in *Harmonium* in a number of comic figures, and in the precious, playfully self-conscious language of many of the poems. Three of the titles are in French, "Cy Est Pourtraicte, Madame Ste Ursule, et Les Unze Mille Vierges," "Homunculus et La Belle Étoile," and "Le Monocle de Mon Oncle." In the last named the narrator is himself a dandified figure, his playful language exploring a range of emotions about facing the onset of middle age. The short early poem "Tea" finishes with an image of "umbrellas in Java," while "The Silver Plough-Boy," also early (silver a favorite color of the aesthetes) provides ironic distance in a poem about death. Another example of playful extravagance in the volume is the lush landscape of Florida – where Stevens sometimes traveled on insurance business, and sometimes took vacations – an extravagance set against the comparative austerity of the seasons and landscape of Connecticut, Stevens's home state.

Although Stevens's foreign travel included Cuba and Mexico, he never visited Europe. But his career-long interest in European – particularly French – culture led to his purchasing many paintings and artifacts from France through his New York dealer. And despite his early association with the *Others* group, which included William Carlos Williams, Marianne Moore, and Alfred Kreymborg, with its determination to free – as its writers saw it – American poetry from the rules of English tradition, Stevens retained far more of the formal elements of that tradition in his verse than other writers in the group. He exploits such devices as alliteration in verse that celebrates the frankly lyrical, and he showed himself in this volume, as he would in later books, to be a master of the use of blank verse. In this way, as Helen Vendler has suggested, Stevens is "in one sense, a very European poet" while at the same time "in both theme and style," a poet "conspicuously and even outrageously American."

In *Harmonium* Stevens explores, from multiple perspectives, the role that language and imagination play in our perception and understanding of the world beyond ourselves. The poetry is the poetry of meditation, dramatizing the play of a mind working. In this way he interrogates in poem after poem the Romantic assumptions of harmony, although his questions remain within the Romantic frame of reference, dealing, for example, with such topics as nature, song, and religion. Sometimes the multiple perspectives are contained within a single poem, as in the well-known "Thirteen Ways of Looking at a Blackbird." Sometimes two poems in *Harmonium* taken together suggest two opposite approaches to the question of what the human imagination supplies to our understanding and articulation of the physical world. "The Emperor of Ice-Cream" declares the ordinariness of death, that mortality is integral to the pleasures of life. Death rituals should not dwell on the coldness of the body, but the celebrants should instead enjoy the coldness of ice-cream in a world where "The only emperor is the emperor of ice-cream." In the funeral described in "Cortège for Rosenbloom," however, the exotic clothes, special rituals, and mourning remove the dead figure and its mourners from the world of the earth into "a place in the sky," and thus remove him from the lyric poetry that celebrates the everyday:

> To a jangle of doom
> And a jumble of words
> Of the intense poem
> Of the strictest prose
> Of Rosenbloom.
>
> And they bury him there,
> Body and soul,
> In a place in the sky.
> The lamentable tread!
> Rosenbloom is dead.

"The Snow Man" explores the consequences of removing what is humanly imposed upon the outside world, in order to see "nothing that is not there." But the result reveals "the nothing that is," for we humanize the blankness of snow in order to understand it, as in making a snowman, and the mind without this active imagination is not human but only a figure made from snow. On the other hand, the world of Hoon in "Tea at the Palaz of Hoon" is entirely of his own making: "I was the world in which I walked, and what I saw / Or heard or felt came not but from myself."

For Stevens, systems of religious belief were similarly human frameworks constructed in various cultures at various times as a way of trying to comprehend the basic mysteries of human existence. In his later books Stevens sought to explore what such a "supreme fiction" for our own times might be, and for some readers these are Stevens's major volumes. But in *Harmonium* he explores more the context out of which his later search arises. "Ploughing on Sunday" extols the pleasures of working on the Christian sabbath. But the central poem on religious belief in the book is "Sunday Morning." A woman hears the sounds of a church service coming through her window, and thoughts of Christ's sacrifice take her back "to silent Palestine." But the poem then enacts a dialogue, either that the women has with herself or that the poet has with her, in which she yearns for both a divinity of present sensation – rather than one that has to "give her bounty to the dead" – and also the assurance of permanence. In its final lines the poem asserts that the earthly "grave of Jesus" is free of "spirits lingering," and celebrates, in lines that echo Keats's ode "To Autumn," the permanence of cycles of change. Similarly in "Peter Quince at the Clavier," where the mechanical from Shakespeare's *A Midsummer Night's Dream* produces delicate music from his earthy lusts, the beauty of the long-dead Susanna lives on in the cycles of renewal that characterize the physical world, its desires, its beauty, and its art.

Two of the later poems from the volume help explain, for some critics, Stevens's decade of near-silence following *Harmonium*'s publication. "The Comedian as the Letter C" can certainly be read as Stevens's account of his own progress as a poet. The poem's protagonist, Crispin, leaves France for North America, as Stevens began with his late nineteenth-century French interests. Sojourns in Yucatan and the Carolinas fail to satisfy Crispin's desire to be a poet of the contemporary. He moves from one formula to another, from "man is the intelligence of his soil" to "his soil is man's intelligence," and finds satisfaction in neither. He cannot be a poet merely of the local, but he cannot be a poet merely of the fanciful either. He needs to find a way to transcend his comic role and combine the two, using the language that at present traps him, via his name, in the poem's recurring range of "C" sounds. The poem's final section, titled "And Daughters With Curls," leaves Crispin with duties of a familial and a "social nature" and "no room upon his cloudy knee, / Prophetic joint, for its diviner young." Stevens intimated to a number of correspondents that his producing few poems over the next ten years was because of his need to concentrate upon his family – daughter Holly had just been born – and his career at the Hartford Accident and Indemnity Company, where he would eventually become a vice-president. One indirect result of such comments on the study of Stevens's work until recently has been to see his two careers of poet and business executive as quite separate.

But the limited, if astonishingly inventive, aesthetic concerns of the *Harmonium* poems are – for more than one critic – an inevitable dead end, and reason enough for Stevens to need time before moving on with his poetry. The way that fellow poet John Gould Fletcher put it in a 1923 review was that Stevens needed to "either expand his range to take in more of human experience, or give up writing altogether." For Fletcher, *Harmonium* "does not permit of a sequel." For some critics the poems of *Harmonium* reach a kind of sterile dead end in the inventiveness of the volume's "Sea Surface Full of Clouds." The poem is a tour de force of variety within constraints, but one in which the physical earth is represented only by the constantly shifting and reflecting surfaces of the sea and clouds, and the imagination by the series of self-conscious, impressionistic, and finally circular stanzas that describe those surfaces. Other commentators have suggested that *Harmonium*'s dandified personae – figures like the "fops of fancy" described in "Le Monocle de Mon Oncle" – prove to be inadequate vehicles for Stevens's interests, and also betray a discomfort with taking the role of poet seriously that Stevens needed time to overcome. When the major philosophical poems of the 1940s volumes emerge, for all the comedy that is still sometimes present, there is no question of the importance that the poet attaches to the issues or to the poems that address them.

## Bibliography

*The Collected Poems of Wallace Stevens* (New York, 1954).

Milton J. Bates, *Wallace Stevens: A Mythology of Self* (Berkeley, 1985).

Robert Buttel, *Wallace Stevens: The Making of Harmonium* (Princeton, 1967).

A. Walton Litz, *Introspective Voyager: The Poetic Development of Wallace Stevens* (New York, 1972).

Glen MacLeod, *Wallace Stevens and Company: The Harmonium Years, 1913–1923* (Ann Arbor, 1983).

# William Carlos Williams, *Spring and All*

## Paris: Contact Publishing Company, 1923

William Carlos Williams did not achieve wide recognition until the late 1940s with the publication of the first volumes of his long poem *Paterson*. By then he was in his sixties and close to retiring from his medical practice. He continued to publish for another dozen years, his final volume, *Pictures from Brueghel*, winning him a posthumous Pulitzer Prize in 1963. In the 1950s, and for some years following, Williams's later work was seen as his finest achievement, the culmination of a career that had begun in 1909. An alternate view that gradually gained supporters was that *Paterson*, especially the first four books, published between 1946 and 1951, showed Williams's work at its best. Both the late poetry and *Paterson* have certainly influenced subsequent poets, but in the past 25 years *Spring and All*, little noticed when it first appeared in the fall of 1923, and not available complete with the 27 poems and accompanying prose of the original volume for almost another 50 years, has received more and more attention and is, for many poets and critics, Williams's major achievement.

Although Williams's work appeared regularly in the leading avant-garde poetry magazines in New York, Chicago, London, and Paris after 1913, he had to publish his early poetry volumes wherever he could, and usually had to subsidize the cost. Before *Spring and All* he had published a small locally printed volume in 1909, *The Tempers* in 1913 in London through the help of Ezra Pound, and two volumes of poems and a book of prose improvisations with Edmund Brown's Four Seas Company in Boston. The books had barely sold at all, but in the early 1920s Williams had opportunities to publish in France thanks to the thriving expatriate community. Williams had very mixed feelings about the expatriates' migration, bitter that such artists had reneged, as he saw it, on the opportunity to develop the American art of international standard that New York in the years of the First World War seemed to promise. But, on the other hand, he was tempted in darker moments to escape the frustration and neglect that Ezra Pound warned him would continue to be his lot if he remained in New Jersey, and to join the exodus.

This tension between a nativist aesthetic and the opportunities provided by Europe, along with the challenge offered by European modernist achievement, is built in to the argument and the circumstances of publication of *Spring and All*. A volume arguing for a new beginning in American poetry, it was published in Paris in a limited edition of 300 copies. The publisher was Robert McAlmon, just a couple of years earlier Williams's collaborator on a poetry journal that they had co-founded to promote American writing before McAlmon joined the exodus to Paris. The journal's title, *Contact*, signified their commitment to the cause of US writing in the US, and gave the name to McAlmon's Paris publishing company.

Williams begins the book acknowledging that he is likely to have few readers: "If anything of moment results – so much the better. And so much the more likely will it be that no one will want to see it." Few did see it. When Ezra Pound, always an enthusiastic supporter of Williams's work, wanted to write an essay on his poetry a few years later, he had to ask his friend for a copy of the book: he had not seen it. Years later McAlmon lamented in his autobiography that many Contact books were impounded at US Customs and received very little circulation in the US or Europe.

Williams's opening sentence also indicates the book's interest in the visual and the visual arts ("no one will want to see it"), and in the immediacy ("anything of moment") that, for Williams, captured the nature of the poet's encounter with the object world before abstractions and intellectual constructs falsify the experience and compromise the moment. The book is dedicated to the American modernist painter Charles Demuth, whom Williams had met when in college, and the second poem in the book is based upon a Demuth painting that Williams owned. The book discusses a number of painters, most importantly American modernist Marsden Hartley, and the Spanish synthetic cubist Juan Gris, while many of the poems describe the act of perception, or are organized visually, moving, for example, from the sky downward to a fertile earth.

Part of Williams's strategy to make his readers see anew – for Williams this meant actually seeing the New World as new and not seeing it through a European, especially English, frame – involved the disruption of habit and expectation. He had experimented with techniques of disruption in the prose of *Kora in Hell: Improvisations* (1920), where sentences are unfinished, syntax takes off in unexpected directions, and the relationships between the improvisations and the supposed commentaries upon them are more open-ended than definitive. Williams's poetry operates in a similar way after about 1920. He rejected formal verse forms, and experimented with enjambment, rhythm, syntax, and stanza form to make the poem capture the immediacy and freshness of the landscape experienced without what Williams argued were the lazy preconceptions of history or adherence to the oppressive authority of Europe.

In *Spring and All* Williams brought these prose and poetry strategies together. In one of the prose sections of the volume he writes:

> The virtue of the improvisations is their placement in a world of new values –
> their fault is their dislocation of sense, often complete.
> But it is the best I could do under the circumstances. It was the best I could do
> and retain any value to experience at all.
>
> Now I have come to a different condition. I find that the values there
> discovered can be extended.

More than in any of Williams's earlier books, the poems in *Spring and All* fragment syntax, and their images and language take unexpected directions. Poem VIII begins:

> The sunlight in a
> yellow plaque upon the
> varnished floor
>
> is full of a song
> inflated to
> fifty pounds pressure
>
> at the faucet of
> June that rings
> the triangle of the air

The poems deal with such central modernist material as cities, jazz, advertising, vaudeville, and sport. They can be read as a loosely defined sequence, although on the other hand some critics have argued that they are purposefully random. Expectations of continuity are disrupted early in the prose by various chapter headings out of sequence, with either roman or arabic numerals, and spurious references to other parts of the text. Meanwhile the poems are numbered consecutively (although the seventh has no number), but they do not have the titles which might give the reader a clue to their theme or content (Williams added titles when he published the poems separately from the prose).

In the prose, sentences sometimes break off in the middle of a thought, or, like the poems, midway take an unexpected direction in syntax, content, or often both. Thus the prose moves through a series of discussions and assertions about, in addition to modern painting, such topics as the relationship of poetry to prose, the relationship of nature to art, the role of what Williams called the "imagination," and the writing of Shakespeare and Marianne Moore. Sometimes the prose bears a direct relationship to a nearby poem, but usually the relationship is a more tangential one. The prose opens with an apocalyptic vision that either signifies where American culture and poetry are headed or has arrived, or clears the way for the new beginning, the new "spring" signified by the first poem's capturing of the moment when the first barely noticeable energies of the new season enter the landscape.

A number of times in the book Williams associates the disjunctions of the poems and prose with the idea of spontaneity and immediacy, and as far as the visual arts are concerned with the iconoclasm of Dada and the multiple perspectives of cubism. But his most extended discussion of a particular painting is of Juan Gris's synthetic cubist *The Open Window*. Williams praises Gris's ability to take "familiar, simple things," to "detach them from ordinary experience to the imagination," and yet keep them "recognizable as the things touched by the hands during the day." Thus in the first poem of the book, the landscape is that of recognizable New Jersey, the road that the poet is taking "to the contagious hospital" that is part of his routine as a doctor. The returning energies of spring that the poem celebrates are part of the region's regular change of seasons. But within this familiar scene the poem describes an entry into a "new world." The "new world" is on one level the poem itself, "rooted" like the marshland plants in its final stanza, in the neglected landscape that the poem celebrates.

This particular modernist version of the traditional opening celebrating spring offers a stark contrast to the resisted fertility that opens Eliot's *Waste Land*, which had appeared at the end of the previous year. This contrast, and such ironic comments in the prose as "If I could say what is in my mind in Sanscrit or even Latin I would do so. But I cannot," have led some commentators to see the book as in part a response to the success of Eliot's poem and the triumph of international modernism that it represented – a success that Williams argued in subsequent years had set back the advance of American poetry by decades. A large part of Williams's late success in the 1950s, and of the subsequent attention given to this book, was that his work represented for many younger poets an alternative to the formalism that they associated with Eliot's dominance.

Many of Williams's best-known poems appear among the 27 in this book, and many focus on "recognizable" subjects. To cite the titles he added later, "The Red Wheelbarrow" concerns a neighbor's garden, "To Elsie" is about the Williams's retarded household maid, and "The Rose" seeks to remove from the familiar flower the symbolic baggage of countless love poems in order to look at it both as an actual flower and as a design. Unfortunately, these poems are usually printed as separate poems when anthologized, without any notice of their original context. The subsequent printing history of the book is in part to blame. Williams published some of the poems in a 1924 pamphlet, included a dozen in his mistitled 1934 *Collected Poems 1921–1931*, and 28 (adding a poem first included in the 1924 pamphlet) in his collected volumes of 1938 and 1951. But none of these volumes reprinted the prose. Williams regretted more than once that the full text was not in print.

The prose of *Spring and All* reappeared in print, in part, when J. Hillis Miller edited *William Carlos Williams: A Collection of Critical Essays* in 1966. Hillis Miller's selection was a response to the increasing interest in the original volume, and itself furthered that interest. In 1970 Webster Schott edited *Imaginations*, a collection of Williams's earlier works and essays that had long been hard to find, and brought together for the first time since 1923 the poems and prose of *Spring and All*. In the same year James Breslin's influential study of Williams, *William Carlos Williams: An American Artist*, made the case for the 1923 volume as Williams's work at its best, an opinion that has increasingly found supporters.

## Bibliography

William Carlos Williams, *Imaginations*, ed. Webster Schott (New York, 1970).

James Breslin, *William Carlos Williams: An American Artist* (New York, 1970).
Bram Dijkstra, *The Hieroglyphics of a New Speech: Cubism, Stieglitz, and the Early Poetry of William Carlos Williams* (Princeton, 1969).
Peter Schmidt, *William Carlos Williams, the Arts, and Literary Tradition* (Baton Rouge, 1988).
Lisa M. Steinman, "William Carlos Williams' *Spring and All*," in Neil Roberts, ed., *A Companion to Twentieth-Century Poetry* (Oxford, 2001), 403–13.

# Marianne Moore, *Observations*

## New York: The Dial Press, 1924

*Observations* was Marianne Moore's second volume of poetry, and the first over which she exercised control. The collection stands midway between her first volume, *Poems*, published in 1921 in London, and her *Selected Poems* of 1935, which carried an introduction by T. S. Eliot, and which was the volume that solidified her reputation as a major figure of American letters. *Observations* not only stands chronologically between the two other books, its poems form the heart of them. The 1921 *Poems* was published by the Egoist Press apparently without Moore's knowledge or participation, and she wrote to her brother on July 10 that she was startled to receive the book from London. Its 24 poems included three that Moore did not include in *Observations*. Moore wrote in a number of letters that she felt that the publication of *Poems* did not come at the right time, and also that there were poems that she wished had been included, or that she had had an opportunity to revise.

The opportunity to publish a volume under her own control came through her increasingly close association with the important modernist journal *The Dial*, which was published in New York. Moore progressed from being a frequent contributor to becoming acting editor in 1925, and editor in 1926 until the journal folded in 1929. This influential editorial position, along with the award of the prestigious Dial Prize for 1924, the publication of *Observations*, and a number of essays praising her work, brought Moore significant recognition. However, her editorial duties led to her publishing no verse of her own from 1925 to 1929. When the *Selected Poems* appeared in 1935, her reputation remained largely that established by *Observations*. T. S. Eliot – in his role as editor at Faber & Faber, the London publisher of *Selected Poems* – suggested using the word "Selected" in the title to imply the more substantial corpus that her reputation deserved, even though she had only published two volumes, and one of them had been substantially reprinted in the second. The 1935 volume reprinted forty of the poems from

*Observations* and added nine written subsequently. There were in both *Observations* and *Selected Poems* revisions of previously published poems, a practice that Moore undertook throughout her career.

*Observations* opens with the modest claim that the volume is "with additions . . . a reprint of 'Poems' . . . that collection being made and arranged by H.D. and Mr. and Mrs. McAlmon." (In later years Moore clarified that H.D. and her companion Bryher had arranged the 1921 volume, and that Robert McAlmon, briefly married to Bryher, had not been involved.) The volume contains many of what were to become Moore's best-known poems. Many are written in her characteristic syllabic verse, the poem patterned around lines reflecting a precise syllable count, with rhyme, when it is used, often de-emphasized by its placement within a line. Many poems follow the process of setting out a proposition, carefully describing details – often of an animal or natural scene – shifting to a unifying perspective that takes in Moore's call for an attitude recognizing the coexistence of the spiritual and the material worlds, and ending with a clipped summary comment. As Moore says of significant painting in "When I Buy Pictures": "it must be 'lit with piercing glances into the life of things'; it must acknowledge the spiritual forces which have made it."

The voice of a Moore poem in this volume and in her subsequent work is conversational, but the careful, detailed description in many of the poems, and the accompanying wide-ranging vocabulary, distance the voice from that of a speaker in a more conventional lyric. That distance is reinforced by Moore's habit of quotation. In *Observations* the sources of these quotations form 14 pages of notes which follow the poems, and which are then followed by a ten-page index that ends the book. The word often used by critics to describe this distanced quality – and by Moore herself, for example in discussing the work of Henry James, or the quiet, determined resolution of an animal, is "restraint." She uses the word of James in "An Octopus." The starting point of the poem is a mountain "Of ice. Deceptively reserved and flat." Through a series of logical, thematic, and descriptive connections, the poem arrives at the "fossil flower":

> concise without a shiver,
> intact when it is cut,
> damned for its sacrosanct remoteness –
> like Henry James "damned by the public for decorum";
> not decorum, but restraint;
> it was the love of doing hard things
> that rebuffed and wore them out – a public out of sympathy
>     with neatness.

Moore is unapologetic about the "restraint" of her own poetry, or its difficulty.

The argument of "The Fish" takes the poem through a description of the organic processes of the sea and the creatures within it, but concludes with praise of a cliff, a "defiant edifice" suggesting an eternal presence that, despite erosion from the sea and human activity, lasts longer than either, living "on what cannot revive / its youth." Human actions and values are also put into a larger context in "A Grave," where the sea defies human attempts to minimize its power and danger. Such human constructs as lighthouses, bell-buoys, and fishing boats merely touch the surface of its power, part of the arrogant human presumption that man can "stand in the middle of a thing." Such arrogance is the opposite of "restraint."

Two poems in *Observations* that discuss writing that does not display "restraint" are "Bowls" and the poem that follows in the volume, "Novices." In the former, discipline and discrimination are replaced by such pointless queries as "why I like winter better than I like summer," while in "Novices" quotations provide examples of empty verbiage, and the poem ends in a welter of tired, meaningless clichés illustrating the very qualities of bad writing that the poem describes.

"Restraint" also translates into social values and good manners, as described in the well-known "Silence" – Moore's poem on how to be a model visitor: "The deepest feeling always shows itself in silence; / not in silence, but restraint." The social and personal tensions that need to be balanced be-tween man and wife form the subject of "Marriage," the longest poem in *Observations* (the poem had been published separately the year before as a chapbook). The poem explores the compromises and understanding necessary for this "institution, / perhaps one should say enterprise" to work. These begin with the tensions between "public promises" and "private obligation," and are colored by what has been said and written of marriage through the centuries. The poem explores the demands that can be made of a husband or wife to achieve an apparently successful union. The poem's final image is of the public stance of "an archaic Daniel Webster" uttering familiar, well-intentioned rhetoric of "Liberty and union" – but behind which lies the dissecting and revealing language of this poem.

In "Poetry," reduced by Moore from the more than 30 lines of the original to three lines by the final edition of her *Collected Poems*, she makes a modest claim for the usefulness of poetry: that it contains within its imaginative frame "the genuine." Her famous formulation for such poetry in this poem is "imaginary gardens with real toads in them."

William Carlos Williams did not agree publicly with T. S. Eliot on many matters concerning the direction of modernist poetry, arguing as he did against the kind of international modernism represented by *The Waste Land*, but both poets wrote important essays on Moore at this time that contributed to the impact of *Observations* on her stature. Williams, who had offered at one point to write an introduction to the volume when Robert McAlmon's Contact Press had proposed bringing it out, praised Moore for her renovation of the language of poetry – for putting words into a context that was fresh and exact. Eliot's essay, which appeared in *The Dial* a few months before *Observations* appeared, praised Moore's language for its range of feeling and reference, as well as praising the rhythms of her verse. When Eliot wrote the introduction to Moore's *Selected Poems* in 1935, he felt that he had no reason to change his opinion:

> My conviction, for what it is worth, has remained unchanged for the last fourteen years: that Miss Moore's poems form part of the small body of durable poetry written in our time . . . in which an original sensibility and alert intelligence and deep feeling have been engaged in maintaining the life of the English language.

Eliot's 1935 introduction also summarized and anticipated some of the charges that have been levelled against Moore's work by some critics since her death. These include most centrally a response to her poetry that finds its careful descriptive and technical qualities over-fastidious and unemotional – "something that the majority will call frigid." But for Eliot in the 1920s and 1930s, and for many readers of Moore then and since, "restraint" does not preclude emotion, and the poems at their best reflect the kind of balance, determination, and grace that so many of the poems praise in individual animals, and often find lacking in human values and taste.

## Bibliography

*The Complete Poems of Marianne Moore* (New York, 1967).

Celeste Goodridge, *Hints and Disguises: Marianne Moore and her Contemporaries* (Iowa City, 1989).

Taffy Martin, *Marianne Moore: Subversive Modernist* (Austin, 1986).

Robin Schulze, *Becoming Marianne Moore: The Early Poems, 1907–1924* (Berkeley, 2002).

Elizabeth Wilson, "Marianne Moore: *Observations*," in Neil Roberts, ed., *A Companion to Twentieth-Century Poetry* (Oxford, 2001), 427–36.

# Hart Crane, *The Bridge*

## New York: Horace Liveright, 1930

Horace Liveright published Crane's *The Bridge*, the poet's second book, a month after the limited edition was published in Paris by the Black Sun Press. The critical response was mixed, and Crane was especially disappointed by the reservations of some critics whom he considered friends, such as Allen Tate. But most reviewers, whatever their final assessment of Crane's achievement in the poem, acknowledged the ambitious scope of its lyric and thematic intent, and treated Crane as an important inheritor of a Romantic and visionary tradition that set itself to answer the T. S. Eliot of *The Waste Land*. Crane's poem has important modernist features, but its forebears in the claims it makes for poetry, its language of incantation, and its theme of spatial and spiritual quest are Christopher Marlowe and the English Eliza-bethan poets, as well as Blake, Shelley, Emily Dickinson, and a poet directly addressed in the poem – Walt Whitman.

Crane began working on *The Bridge* in 1923, and, working in fits and starts, had composed most of its sections by 1927, although he was still completing the poem in 1929. Critics have usually considered the sections composed later to be the weakest parts of the poem, "Cape Hatteras," "Quaker Hill," and, especially, "Indiana." By the late 1920s Crane's life had entered the self-destructive cycle of alcoholism and self-doubt that would lead to his suicide by drowning at sea in 1932, three months before his thirty-third birthday. He was returning from Mexico to help settle his father's estate, his trip and residence in Mexico having been made possible by a Guggenheim award in 1931 that Crane saw as a vindication of his achievement in *The Bridge*.

Crane described his ambitious theme in a 1923 letter. The poem would concern:

> a mystical synthesis of "America." History and fact, location, etc. all have to be transfigured into abstract form that would almost function independently of its

subject matter. The initial impulse of our people will have to be gathered up toward the climax of the bridge, symbol of our constructive future, our unique identity, in which is included also our scientific hopes and achievements of the future.

As the poem is usually read, its eight sections break into two halves – these sections following the opening prologue poem, "To Brooklyn Bridge," that sets up the famous New York City landmark as a symbol for the potential synthesis of time, space, spirit, and language:

> O Sleepless as the river under thee,
> Vaulting the sea, the prairies' dreaming sod,
> Unto us lowliest sometime sweep, descend
> And of the curveship lend a myth to God.

The first of the two halves covers the sections "Ave Maria," "Powhatan's Daughter," and "Cutty Sark," and in this half the poem reaches across history to the earliest colonists and traces the passing of the land from its Native American inhabitants to the pioneer generation. The second half of the poem, encompassing "Cape Hatteras," "Three Songs," "Quaker Hill," "The Tunnel," and "Atlantis," brings the poem into the modern, machine world, and seeks a way for the early promise of the continent to be recovered and celebrated within the contemporary world. The power of language and lyric ("some Word that will not die," as the poem puts it) has a large part to play, for Crane, in such a recovery, and to that end *The Bridge* uses symbol, archaic diction, song, and rapid transitions and transformations that short-circuit reason and the rational, to articulate the search for the synthesizing myth. The word "curveship" in the last line of the opening poem, quoted above, begins the poem's reiteration of ideas of sweep, curve, and connection – the qualities that Crane saw embodied in John Roebling's design for Brooklyn Bridge, and that find their counterpart in Crane's visionary theme.

Different parts of the poem are spoken in different voices, some historical and some contemporary, although a common theme is that of quest. This spirit of exploration and discovery – spatial, physical and imaginative – is a vital part of the vision that Crane wants to restore to the modern nation. The first historical voice recovered, in "Ave Maria," is that of Columbus looking for new frontiers. His arrival is signaled by "The Harbor Dawn," which begins the next, "Powhatan's Daughter," section. The narrative of two lovers incorporates the story and spirit of Pocahontas, the daughter of the title, although it is set more than 400 years after Columbus's voyage. Next "Van Winkle" invokes the hero of Irving's story as an example of the bridging of past and present that the juxtaposition of Columbus and the contemporary lovers had suggested. The poem sets Crane's childhood memories alongside the experience of the figure who vaulted time with his famous long sleep. "The River" of the section's next poem is the Mississippi, the long journey south along its banks imagined as a train journey on the "Twentieth Century Limited." Some tramps gathered alongside the tracks also represent explorers, free spirits whose experience wandering from town to town the poem incorporates through their dialogue. The river itself functions as a traditional symbol of time in this section, as well as of space.

The voice of a tribal chief, Maquokeeta, speaks the next poem" The Dance," invoking the spirit of the now dead Pocahontas, who "rose with maize – to die." In "Indiana" – the last poem of the "Powhatan's Daughter" section – a pioneer mother pleads with her son, who is about to abandon the family farm, and her monologue covers a life of searching, love, and hardship as she speaks to the son about to begin his own life of discovery at sea. This part of the poem has sometimes been criticized for descending to the sentimental. The first half of *The Bridge* ends with "Cutty Sark," and a drunken sailor's half-remembered, fragmentary reminiscences of his adventures and travels.

The second half of *The Bridge* takes up the discontinuities between the American past and present, and seeks ways to rediscover and reaffirm a unity. Walt Whitman is quoted in the epigram to the first section, "Cape Hatteras," and is subsequently directly addressed. Whitman's transcendental vision and his affirmation of the power of the poem and poet to help achieve it make the earlier poet a central figure behind *The Bridge*. For Crane, the power of imagination represented by the poet must transform technological achievements – here symbolized by the Wright Brothers' discovery of flight in Kitty Hawk – into a force for progress rather than destruction.

The "Three Songs" that follow have been seen by some critics as having little thematic justification for their place in the poem, but the three women, a prostitute, a striptease dancer, and a secretary fighting off the advances of her employer, have also been read as degraded, and infertile, versions of Pocahontas in the modern world. The central theme of "Quaker Hill," which follows the "Three Songs," is announced in the quotation from dancer Isadora Duncan – whose performances Crane greatly admired – that serves as one of this section's two epigrams: *"I see only the ideal. But no ideals have ever been fully successful on this earth."* While acknowledging this split between the actual and the ideal, the poem seeks to bring them together through its visionary reach.

The last two sections of the poem, "The Tunnel" and "Atlantis," have generally been much admired. "The Tunnel" functions as a narrative of spiritual purgation, a journey through "the Gates of Wrath" of the Blake quotation that functions as an epigram. The poet travels beneath New York's East River on the city's subway. Among the voices he hears and faces, he sees – "Below the toothpaste and the dandruff ads" – that of another visionary poet, Edgar Allen Poe, whom the poet questions about his last desperate hours.

An epigram from Plato begins the last section. The poem's searching reaches a vision of Atlantis, the heavenly city. In this section, written early in the poem's composition, in 1925, Brooklyn Bridge becomes a kind of harp, a musical instrument of the ideal – "Upward, veering with light, the flight of strings." The bridge, directly addressed in this section, incorporates the spatial, spiritual, and temporal distances that the poem has explored, and the sequence ends with continuing movement and song: "Whispers antiphonal in azure swing."

This dense and complex poem has been read many ways, and many have commented upon the unevenness resulting from its composition history and Crane's physical deterioration from chronic alcoholism. Discussion also centers upon the form as well as the meaning of the poem, whether, within its swift transitions and transformations and the multiple levels of its symbols, and despite there being no clear narrative line and no consistent hero, its various sections cohere, and in what way. Some readers note that the final stanzas of the poem's two halves introduce questions, questions which may be qualifications of the poem's final visionary celebration. The poem has also been read, somewhat reductively, as a paean to the machine age represented by the bridge. But seeing the bridge as a testament to man's attempt to turn the machine world to his own larger imaginative purposes, and as a symbol of his drive to unify on all levels what is otherwise separated, takes much fuller account of the large ambition of Crane's poem.

## Bibliography

*Complete Poems of Hart Crane*, ed. Marc Simon (New York, 2000).

Edward Brunner, *Splendid Failure: Hart Crane and the Making of The Bridge* (Urbana, IL, 1985).
Paul Giles, *Hart Crane: The Contexts of The Bridge* (Cambridge, 1986).
Richard P. Sugg, *Hart Crane's The Bridge: A Description of its Life* (University, AL, 1976).

# Elizabeth Bishop, *North & South*

## Boston: Houghton Mifflin, 1946

Writing poems was always a slow process for Elizabeth Bishop. Although she had published prose and poetry in college magazines at Vassar, which she attended from 1930 to 1934, her first book of poems, *North & South*, did not appear until 1946. She worried about the thinness of the volume – it contained only 32 poems – and kept promising the publishers additional poems, which in the event were not completed in time. She also worried about the poems appearing to take no account of the recently ended world war. At her insistence the volume carried a note that "Most of these poems were written, or partly-written, before 1942." The volume appeared as a result of a prize offered by Houghton Mifflin for a poetry fellowship, the $1,000 award to be supplemented by publication of the manuscript. The publicity of the prize ensured wide reviews of the book, some by influential figures, and Bishop's literary career was established.

The title is the first of a series of volume titles that would reflect the poet's many travels and geographically dispersed residences over her lifetime. Such movement began in childhood, when she was taken care of at different times by maternal grandparents in Nova Scotia, and paternal grandparents in New England. At various times she lived in Nova Scotia, Boston, New York, Key West, and Brazil. But for some critics, the title *North & South* reflects the two geographical poles – New England and Nova Scotia – of the orphaned child's early dislocation.

The first poem in the book, "The Map," is as much about art, printing, and language as about interpreting the signs and codes of a map and the "excitement" that imaginative engagement with its promises and mysteries can bring. "The Map" is generally viewed as Bishop's first mature poem. It had appeared in an anthology titled *Trial Balances* in 1935, with an introductory note by Marianne Moore, with whom Bishop carried on a long correspondence for many years, and who was an important early influence and supporter. Learning from Moore's practice, in this poem Bishop begins her characteristic strategy of focusing carefully upon one object, using a close examination of its characteristics as the starting point of a larger exploration of its imaginative potential.

Later volumes of Bishop's work would contain poems that presented more concrete detail, and for some readers such poems represent her major achievement. In this volume "Florida" is the poem that comes closest to the later mode. In *North & South* a more characteristic vein is a dream state, in which the physical detail remains more distant, transformed by the half-waking, half-sleeping condition in which events and places are described. By one critic's count, a third of the poems begin or end with the speaker or speakers in bed. The perspective of physical dislocation is suggested most fully by the titles of the two companion poems "Sleeping on the Ceiling" and "Sleeping Standing Up."

Bishop's biography provides an important context for her poems, but its presence is muted in the poems themselves, especially in this volume, with none of the overt statement of the later 'confessional' poets. Although there are a number of poems about the importance of love, for example, Bishop was very guarded about her own lesbianism and personal relationships. Love is an anxious emotion in the poems of *North & South*, and the narrator is usually genderless or a generalized "we." One first-person poem is "Chemin de Fer," but the narrator remains an observer of a hermit living in a cabin, whose cry of "Love should be put into action!" results in his firing a shotgun. Even more ambivalent is the allegory of "The Weed." The dream upon "a grave, or bed," is of a thickly growing plant splitting the heart, almost being swept away by the results of its growth, then returning "but to divide your heart again."

A group of poems concerning Paris at the center of the book came out of a trip to Europe that Bishop took with Louise Crane, where they encountered Vassar friend Margaret Miller. An automobile accident led to the amputation of part of Miller's arm – she had been an aspiring painter. But the overt remembrance of Miller's presence in Paris recognized by the dedication of "Quai d'Orléans" to Miller was only added years later. Another later dedication is of the final poem of the volume, "Anaphora," to Marjorie Carr Stevens. As *North & South* was in final preparation Bishop's life with Stevens in Key West was coming to an end. The dedication was only added after Stevens's death in 1959.

The geographical dislocations of Bishop's life are mirrored in a number of poems about houses, places for creativity that are both shelters and at the same time threatened. The hermit's cabin in "Chemin de Fer" is one example. The closing lines of "The Monument" offer a statement of the theme:

It may be solid, may be hollow.
The bones of the artist-prince may be inside
or far away on even drier soil.
But roughly but adequately it can shelter
what is within (which after all
cannot have been intended to be seen).
It is the beginning of a painting,
a piece of sculpture, or poem, or monument,
and all of wood. Watch it closely.

Another place associated with art is the harbor scene of "Large Bad Picture," painted by Bishop's Great-Uncle Hutchinson, a one-time portrait painter and the first illustrator of Stevenson's *Treasure Island*. In this poem, whether the ships reach their destination through "commerce or contemplation" is a question raised, but left open, like the motive for the painting itself.

*North & South* was widely reviewed, and received important notices from Seldon Rodman, Marianne Moore, Randall Jarrell, and Robert Lowell. The volume was in the running for the 1946 Pulitzer Prize, although it was beaten by Lowell's book, *Lord Weary's Castle*. Bishop took nine years to publish her next volume of poems. Such was the publisher's concern about the relatively few poems in this next book that it was issued along with the poems in the 1946 volume as *Poems: North & South – A Cold Spring*. This time, however, Bishop won her Pulitzer.

## Bibliography

Elizabeth Bishop, *The Complete Poems, 1927–1979* (New York, 1983).

Harold Bloom, ed., *Elizabeth Bishop: Modern Critical Views* (New York, 1985).

Jonathan Ellis, "Elizabeth Bishop: *North & South*," in Neil Roberts, ed., *A Companion to Twentieth-Century Poetry* (Oxford, 2001), 457–68.

David Kalstone, *Becoming a Poet: Elizabeth Bishop with Marianne Moore and Robert Lowell* (New York, 1989).

John Palattella, "'That Sense of Constant Re-Adjustment': The Great Depression and the Provisional Politics of Elizabeth Bishop's *North & South*," *Contemporary Literature*, 34 (1993), 18–43.

# Ezra Pound, *The Pisan Cantos*

## New York: New Directions, 1948

The title *The Pisan Cantos* was conferred by New Directions' publisher James Laughlin on the eleven cantos, numbers LXXIV–LXXXIV, that Pound composed while a prisoner of the US army in the detention training camp north of Pisa, Italy, in 1945. Pound agreed to Laughlin's suggestion, but the poet had originally wanted to title the collection with the opening and closing canto numbers, as he had with previous volumes of his long poem as they were issued.

Pound had begun *The Cantos* during the First World War, while he was still based in London. Individual cantos appeared separately, and sometimes Pound revised them, and in 1925 he published *A Draft of XVI Cantos* with William Bird's Three Mountains Press. *A Draft of XXX Cantos* appeared in 1930, and various additions appeared up to 1940. The sequence would continue until *Drafts & Fragments of Cantos CX–CXVII* in 1968, four years before Pound's death. Following an opening canto based upon book XI of Homer's *Odyssey*, the sweep of this challenging epic takes in the social, political, economic, and cultural history of East and West, across three continents, in multiple languages, and is structured around particulars and allusions that are juxtaposed, recur, and connect – sometimes across widely separated cantos.

The central theme of the poem is the search for a just society. The China of Confucius and the United States of John Adams are two examples in the poem of what for Pound were societies that held such potential. The just society, for Pound, would be one in which art and artists could flourish, and where economic values were not distorted by charging interest – what the poem calls "usury" – and upon which a good deal of Pound's anti-Semitism in this poem and elsewhere is focused. The poem is also the story of Pound's own history, as he wrote and published the stages of his epic, and as his particular interests shifted. In *The Pisan Cantos* Pound himself enters the cantos more fully than anywhere else in the poem, and the memories, allusions, observed particulars, and lyrical heights are anchored in the present experience and recollections of a 60-year-old man held in sometimes harsh conditions, in danger of possible execution as a traitor, and coming to terms with the implications of the end of what for him was another potential just society – Mussolini's Italy.

Pound's view that the practices of American banks violated the US Constitution, and his faith in the values of Italy's fascist government – he had lived in Italy since 1924 – led him to make a series of radio broadcasts during the war in support of the Axis powers and against the allies. With the fall of Italy he was arrested on charges of treason and was incarcerated, initially in an open-air cage, in the camp just outside Pisa. He was held there from May 24 to November 16, before being flown on an hour's notice to Washington for trial. The commander of the camp, Colonel Steele, allowed the poet the use of the typewriter in the camp's dispensary in the evenings, and upon this machine he composed the cantos between July and October, although he had earlier begun writing them in longhand on toilet paper. His personal library consisted of an edition of the Confucian classics and a small Chinese dictionary, both of which he had brought with him when arrested, a Roman Catholic missal, and an anthology of English poetry that he found in one of the camp latrines. He also had access to a copy of the Bible, and, after a few weeks, to the camp's American news magazines and a few Italian newspapers. When his daughter Mary was allowed to visit him in October, he gave her the rough typescripts of the poem to take away and prepare for publication.

Canto LXXIV, the longest in the sequence, begins with the executions of Benito Mussolini and his mistress Clara Petacci, which had occurred on April 28, 1945, and the public display of their bodies, hanging from a scaffold, in Milan:

> The enormous tragedy of the dream in the peasant's bent shoulders
> Manes! Manes was tanned and stuffed,
> Thus Ben and la Clara *a Milano*
> by the heels at Milano

Manes, the third-century Persian sage and founder of the Manichaeans, was crucified and his body stuffed with hay. The thematic and historical levels that come from the association of the two events continues the structural principles of the earlier cantos and is the governing principle of this canto and those to come. The emphasis is upon particulars, not generalizations, and the particulars for Pound are to cohere in the multiple themes and levels of the poem as phrases and events are visited and revisited, alluded to later in a fragmentary way, or expanded.

The major themes of government and economics in the *Pisan Cantos* are taken up from earlier parts of the sequence, but in these cantos they are in the context of a fuller emphasis upon the world of nature (often what Pound sees from his cage) and upon memory, loss, and the attempt to reassert in this desperate time the poem's vision of paradise, by reaffirming what is indestructible.

Nature in the poem is sometimes the mountain Pound could see in the distance near Pisa that reminded him of Mount Taishan, a sacred mountain in China. Or it is the ants or wasps building, creating, around him, the fragility of their existence reminding the poet of the fragility of his own. In Canto LXXXIII:

> And now the ants seem to stagger
> > as the dawn sun has trapped their shadows,
>
> . . . . . . . .
>
> When the mind swings by a grass-blade
> > an ant's forefoot shall save you
> > the clover leaf smells and tastes as its flower

Canto LXXV consists almost entirely of a musical piece, a transcription with a heritage going back to the sixteenth century. This "Song of the Birds" combines for Pound the mutual support that song and music, art and nature, artists across the centuries, and lovers – it was a favorite piece of violinist Olga Rudge, Pound's companion, in the concerts held in Rapallo – could bring to one another.

With few books beside him when he was writing these cantos, memory became a key resource for Pound in the poem. The eleven cantos build up in a mosaic-like form the story of the poet's writing career: boyhood memories, memories of his arrival in Venice in 1908, his London years, quotations from the now dead Yeats and Ford Madox Ford and others, Paris where he knew Joyce and Hemingway, and then his 20 years in Italy. These personal memories all mingle with the other themes of the poem and with other historical periods, while the poet's present straits are never far from the poem – whether it is "old Ez" folding his blanket, or the conversation or kindnesses of his guards, or the movements or cries of his fellow prisoners – soldiers, some of them scheduled for execution.

The best-known lines in *The Pisan Cantos*, and probably in the *Cantos* as a whole, close Canto LXXXI and are often anthologized as a separate lyric. The lines begin: "What thou lovest well remains, / the rest is dross / What thou lov'st well shall not be reft from thee / What thou lov'st well is thy true heritage," and they go on to equate usury with "vanity" and with decadent art throughout history. In contrast is "true artistry," which is linked here to humility and self-discipline. Also important is nature, surrounding the poet from whom so much has been "reft." He asserts: "Learn of the green world what can be thy place," and a little earlier, "The ant's a centaur in his dragon world."

Pound was a controversial figure when he was flown to Washington for his trial, and some influential people protested the judicial finding that he was unfit to stand trial because of insanity, although many important writers came to his aid too. Pound had begun his thirteen and a half years in St. Elizabeths Hospital and the controversy was dying down a little when in 1949 a committee associated with the Library of Congress, and including Robert Lowell, T. S. Eliot, W. H. Auden, and Robert Penn Warren, awarded *The Pisan Cantos* the first Bollingen Prize for Poetry. The volume had been published on July 20 the previous year. Despite protests and pressure, and questions in Congress, the committee defended its choice and stuck to it, arguing that the poet's political beliefs, the anti-Semitic material in parts of the poem, and the poet being in effect a prisoner of the government did not detract from its achievement as the outstanding poem among those judged. Pound received a much-needed $1,000, but the prize was removed from the jurisdiction of the Library of Congress and subsequently administered by Yale University. The prize began the restoration of Pound's reputation and respectability as a writer, rescuing him from the position of being seen as a figure of largely historical interest whose finest work had appeared in the earliest years of modernism. This renewed interest and status would bring many of the new generation of poets and scholars on a pilgrimage to St. Elizabeths over the next decade.

## Bibliography

*The Cantos of Ezra Pound* (New York, 1998).

George Kearns, *Ezra Pound: The Cantos* (Cambridge, 1989).

Lawrence Rainey, ed., *A Poem Containing History: Textual Studies in the Cantos* (Ann Arbor, 1997).

Leon Surette, *A Light from Eleusis: A Study of Ezra Pound's Cantos* (Oxford, 1979).

Carroll F. Terrell, *A Companion to the Cantos of Ezra Pound* (Berkeley, 1980).

# Theodore Roethke, *The Lost Son and Other Poems*

## Garden City, NY: Doubleday & Co., 1948

*The Lost Son and Other Poems*, Theodore Roethke's second book, was published seven years after his first, *Open House*. In this 1948 volume Roethke developed a poetic style that moved away from the more formal lyrical mode of his earlier work, finding a way to express interior monologues both intense and descriptive. Assessments differ over whether the book marks Roethke's finest achievement in the form, or whether the book serves as precursor to the important work to follow.

The years around the publication of the volume brought some major changes in Roethke's life. In 1948 he left the east coast, where he had taught for many years, and took a position at the University of Washington. He received a Guggenheim Foundation award in 1945, was hospitalized at the end of the year for a recurrence of the mental illness that had afflicted him ten years earlier, and the following year spent a summer at the Yaddo writer's colony – where he wrote a number of the poems that appeared in the volume. The publication of *The Lost Son* led to another Guggenheim Fellowship in 1950, and marked his transition from a minor poet with a solid reputation to a major national and international figure.

In 1945 Roethke wrote to his friend, critic Kenneth Burke, of the poems he was writing: "I am trying to loosen up, to write poems of greater intensity and symbolical depth," and to others he wrote that he was trying to delve deeper into the memories and workings of his own psyche, to write poems that got closer to the lived and felt mental processes that they recorded. These experiences, as the book's title suggests, involved to a large extent Roethke's childhood memories, and especially his relationship with his father Otto. Otto Roethke, like his German immigrant father, had run the family horticultural business, with extensive greenhouses and nurseries in Saginaw,

Michigan, until his death from cancer a month before Roethke's fifteenth birthday.

*The Lost Son* is divided into four parts, and most discussion has centered upon the first and last sections. The 14 poems in the first section have, since their publication, been known as the "Greenhouse Poems." In these poems the process of birth from the soil, the nurturing and struggle to stay alive and grow, the skill and instincts of those who tend the plants, describe both the life processes of nature and the struggles and growth of the child/poet who recalls them. Roethke's comments on his poems are often quoted, and are frequently very helpful. He has written of the greenhouses, "they were to me, I realize now, both heaven and hell, a kind of tropics created in the savage climate of Michigan, where austere German Americans turned their love of order and their terrifying efficiency into something truly beautiful."

The opening two poems of the greenhouse sequence describe birth and renewal, and mark the close identification of the poetic voice with the life-cycles that the poems describe. In "Cuttings": "The small cells bulge // One nub of growth / Nudges a sand-crumb loose," and in "Cuttings (*later*)" "I quail, lean to beginnings, sheath-wet." The poems that follow describe growth emerging from the darkness, their concrete detail capturing in particular the smell of the earth with hands and face close to the plants. As many critics have pointed out, and as Roethke's comments quoted above make clear, the experience is as frightening and threatening as it is beautiful. Many of the images of enclosure suggest the grave as well as birth. In "Weed Puller" the "me" of the poem is "Alive, in a slippery grave." The orchids in "Orchids" have "Lips neither dead nor alive, / Loose ghostly mouths / Breathing." In "Moss Gathering" the child feels as if he were "pulling off flesh from the living planet," while in "Flower Dump" one tulip, not limp like everything else, is described as "One swaggering head / Over the dying, the newly dead." "Big Wind" describes the all-night battle to save the greenhouses when a fierce storm has cut off the crucial water supply. "Carnations," while celebrating growth, beauty, and the blooming flowers, suggests change within its evocation of timelessness – "that clear autumnal weather of eternity / The windless perpetual morning above a September cloud."

The middle two sections of *The Lost Son* contain poems on themes similar to those in the rest of the volume, but in the more formal, lyric style that is closer to the poems in Roethke's first book. They include the often antholo-gized "My Papa's Waltz," which opens section II. But the breakthrough for Roethke came with the poems of the fourth section. In his broadcast "An American Poet Introduces Himself and his Poems" Roethke described his move from the opening poems to the longer poems of section IV:

In those first poems I had begun, like the child, with small things and had tried to make plain words do the trick. Somewhat later, in 1945, I began a series of longer pieces which try, in their rhythms, to catch the movement of the mind itself, to trace the spiritual history of a protagonist (not "I" personally but of all haunted and harried men); to make this sequence a true and not arbitrary order which would permit many ranges of feeling, including humor.

All these states of mind were to be rendered dramatically, without comment, without allusion, the action often implied or indicated in the interior monologue or dialogue between the self and its mentor, or conscience, or, sometimes, another person.

The literary "ancestors" of these poems, Roethke wrote in his essay "Open Letter," are "German and English folk literature, particularly Mother Goose; Elizabethan and Jacobean drama, especially the songs and rants; the Bible; Blake and Traherne; Dürer."

In *The Lost Son* the four poems of section IV are the title poem – itself divided into five sections – "The Long Alley," "A Field of Light," and "The Shape of the Fire." These four poems subsequently became part of the second half of a 14-poem sequence that formed Roethke's third book, *Praise to the End!*, in 1951.

The first of the title poem's five sections opens at a cemetery, with "At Woodlawn I heard the dead cry," which begins the theme of alienation from his father, and from the Christian Father, which runs through these four poems as well as the later, longer sequence. The language in this and the following poems moves in and out of rational order, the images going through sudden shifts, as Roethke tries to get close to the fear and desperation of the experience, suggesting subconscious as well as conscious expression. Each poem, Roethke wrote, is "in a sense . . . a stage in a kind of struggle out of the slime; part of a slow spiritual progress; an effort to be born, and later, to become something more." The poems also follow a loose trajectory of moving back into this primordial "slime," as a kind of retreat, before moving forward. In this first section of "The Lost Son" the narrator runs from the "cry," and in an empty house, with childlike puzzlement – "in the kingdom of bang and blab" – tries to understand and give a name to his surroundings. The next section, "The Pit," takes him to "where . . . the roots go," and "the slime of a wet nest." The section titled "The Gibber" Roethke has described as ranging from "a frenetic activity" to "a crooning serenity," from "balked sexual experience" to "'rant,' almost in the manner of the Elizabethans." "The Return" section recalls a childhood experience of the greenhouse, viewing the morning light and awaiting the promise of the father's return, as well as discovering his own individual identity. Light is a major motif in this and the companion poems in the sequence, and the final, untitled, section questions the nature of a light seen traveling "over the wide field," – and this final part of "The Lost Son" ends with the exhortation, "It will come again. / Be still. / Wait."

The following poem, "The Long Alley," is centered around river imagery, and makes even clearer that the search is for a spiritual as well as an earthly father, the move from the earth to light encompassing the search for and possible presence of both. The last two poems of *The Lost Son* end with images of light. In "A Field of Light" the poet enters the "wide field" of the final section of the title poem, ending: "And I walked, I walked through the light air; / I moved with the morning." In "The Shape of the Fire," light fills and nurtures the flower, providing a containment that is an alternative to that of the grave, "a quick pouring / Fills and trembles at the edge yet does not flow over, / Still holding and feeding the stem of the contained flower."

The final poem of the sequence that Roethke later published in *Praise to the End!* that incorporates these four poems from *The Lost Son* emphasizes this opening out, and the potential reward of a search at once physical, psychological, and spiritual. "O, Thou Opening, O," ends:

> Going is knowing.
> I see; I seek;
> I'm near.
> Be true.
> Skin.

That Roethke began the following volume, *The Waking* (1953), with this poem reinforces the continuity between the poems in *The Lost Son and Other Poems* and the subsequent two books, and makes clear that the search that the 1948 volume records was for Roethke, both as son and poet, a productive one.

## Bibliography

*The Collected Poems of Theodore Roethke* (Garden City, NY, 1966).
—— *On Poetry & Craft* (Port Townsend, WA, 2001).

Peter Balakian, *Theodore Roethke's Far Fields: The Evolution of his Poetry* (Baton Rouge, 1989).
Jenijoy La Belle, "Theodore Roethke's 'The Lost Son': From Archetypes to Literary History," *Modern Language Quarterly*, 37 (1976), 179–95.
John Wheatcroft, "Naughty Child: Poet on Top of a Greenhouse," *North Dakota Quarterly*, 66 (1999), 60–8.

# Allen Ginsberg, *Howl and Other Poems*

## San Francisco: City Lights Books, 1956

City Lights Books developed as a project of the City Lights bookstore. The store had opened in June 1953 at the beginning of what would become known as the San Francisco Poetry Renaissance. Run by poet Lawrence Ferlinghetti, City Lights was the first bookstore in America devoted to selling quality paperbacks, and once Ferlinghetti had bought out his original partner, Peter Martin, he began publishing a paperback series titled The Pocket Poets. Allen Ginsberg's *Howl and other Poems* was the fourth book in the series.

A native of Paterson, New Jersey, Ginsberg had arrived in California in 1954, and originally tried to interest Ferlinghetti in the manuscript of a collection he called "Empty Mirror." These were poems written in the style of William Carlos Williams, with whom Ginsberg had begun a correspondence in March 1950 (part of which Williams included in book IV of his poem *Paterson*. Ferlinghetti was lukewarm to these poems, but expressed great interest in a poem Ginsberg had begun in early August 1955 in which he adapted Williams's three-step line to the long lines of Whitman, the interest in Whitman being a return for Ginsberg to his style of the late 1940s. Added now, along with the interest in Williams's ideas on measure, was Ginsberg's reading of the surrealists.

What Ferlinghetti saw was the first of the four sections of "Howl." The work-in-progress brought Ginsberg local fame, and even more interest from the publisher, at a legendary reading at the Six Gallery (a converted auto-repair shop) on October 7, 1955. This was Ginsberg's first public reading, and the poem's chanting rhythms, iconoclastic language, and accumulating energy had the audience weeping and cheering. The other three sections of the poem were finished within a year. When *Howl and other Poems* was published Ginsberg was serving on a merchant ship off of the coast of Alaska. The book was favorably reviewed on the west coast, and when he returned to New York in 1957 Ginsberg worked tirelessly and mostly with success to get reviews from the New York literary establishment. He was helped in this task through an important article by Richard Eberhart that had appeared in September 1956 in *The New York Times*, identifying Ginsberg as the major talent of the emerging group of west coast poets. But what propelled the book and its author to national fame was the decision of US Customs in March 1957 to impound 520 copies of the second printing (the book was typeset in England) and to prosecute the book for obscenity. Even before the subsequent not guilty verdict the book had gone on sale in an edition typeset in the United States, and the *Evergreen Review* had reprinted "Howl." By the time the trial had ended, a book about which Ginsberg had wondered upon its publication whether it would sell a thousand copies had ten thousand copies in print, and became in effect a handbook of the Beat generation. Ferlinghetti later wrote: "It would have taken years for critics to accomplish what the good [Customs] collector did in a day, merely by calling the book obscene."

The volume is dedicated to Ginsberg's closest writer friends, William Burroughs, Neal Cassady, and the then unpublished Jack Kerouac. The dedication originally also included New York friend Lucien Carr, but was removed at Carr's request to be able to have "a certain anonymity in life." Carl Solomon, to whom the title poem is dedicated and addressed, later regretted some of the public notice that the poem brought him, concerned as it is with his period in a mental hospital.

The 64-page booklet carried a two-page introduction by Williams, to whom Ginsberg had sent "Howl" and some of his other recent work in 1956 (Williams included parts of Ginsberg's accompanying letter in *Paterson V* in 1958). In the introduction, Williams's stroke-impaired memory confuses the first and second world wars when he writes of his own correspondence with the poet, but he praises "Howl" as "a howl of defeat. Not defeat at all for he has gone through defeat as if it were an ordinary experience, a trivial experience." For Williams, "Howl" is the triumph of an affirmation of love coming out of defeat, the theme, he might have said, of his own long poem of the mid-1950s, "Asphodel, that Greeny Flower."

Part of Ginsberg's intention in these poems is to be true to actual events, and to bring an immediacy to the record of the authentic experience through the apparent spontaneity of the speaking voice, and the extremity of the passion behind the reciting of events. There is nevertheless a range of intensity, sometimes urgent, sometimes quiet, within the poems. Ginsberg also wants to short-circuit the usual processes of logic and categorization, which for him are the weapons of a dehumanizing culture that represses the sexual and creative potential of the individual. The erasing of such boundaries through – for example, the long lists, particularly in "Howl," that refuse to use the grammar of subordination – is to be followed by a lifting of the reading consciousness into a realm of greater physical, imaginative, and spiritual freedom. Such a condition was signified for Ginsberg particularly in the poetry of William Blake. Thus the first section of "Howl" is one long, chanted sentence, its almost 80 verse paragraphs of varying lengths set off from one another by their arrangement on the page, and by commas – as in the famous opening lines:

> I saw the best minds of my generation destroyed by madness, starving
> hysterical naked,
> dragging themselves through the negro streets at dawn looking for an
> angry fix,
> angelheaded hipsters burning for the ancient heavenly connection to the
> starry dynamo in the machinery of night,

The "I saw" is key to the poem's claim to authority – the events cataloged are a recital of the adventures and tragedies of Ginsberg, his family, friends, and acquaintances in the years leading up to the poem. This first section towards its end identifies with Carl Solomon, 3,000 miles away on the east coast in the mental hospital that the poem later identifies as Rockland (although Solomon was actually institutionalized in another hospital): "ah, Carl, while you are not safe I am not safe." The mystical state of mind that the poem wants to induce means breaking free from the imprisonment of material values and the oppressive mores of convention. These latter are among the qualities of section II's "Moloch," the force threatening insanity by its demands for standardization. Breaking free of Moloch allows the crossing of physical boundaries so that at the end of section III the narrator can address Carl Solomon:

> I'm with you in Rockland
>     in my dreams you walk dripping from a sea-journey on the
>     highway across America in tears to the door of my cottage
>     in the Western night

The short section that follows is a "Footnote to Howl" rather than a 'section IV,' Ginsberg has explained, because in its assertion of what is "Holy" it is a counter to section II's refrain of "Moloch" rather than an additional section of the poem. For some critics, however, this is the weakest part of "Howl."

The booklet contains five additional poems from the same period as "Howl." "A Supermarket in California" describes a vision of Walt Whitman in the "neon fruit supermarket." The two poets to walk together, each solitary, "never passing the cashier," and the contemporary poet addresses and finds reassurance – sexual and creative – from the older master. "Transcription of Organ Music," "Sunflower Sutra," and (included at Ferlinghetti's behest) "In the Baggage Room at Greyhound" make explicit the mystical visions that conclude the processes they describe, seeing, as the first of these three puts it, "the feeling in the heart of things." The last of the five poems, "America," displays the inventive, sardonic wit that is also an important part of "Howl" and like that poem is more of a direct assault upon the reader. The poem acknowledges the poet's own inevitable complicity in the "Time Magazine" version of America, but this complicity is ironically accepted in order to challenge such falsity from within.

Four "earlier poems" complete the book, and to various degrees they are pastiches of Williams's style. "An Asphodel," uses a central image that Williams himself developed in "Asphodel, that Greeny Flower." "Song" is reminiscent of Williams's poetry around 1920, "Wild Orphan" takes its argument from Williams's well-known "To Elsie," and "In back of the real" is a dress-rehearsal for "Sunflower Sutra" but in the Williams vein. The poems are instructive of Ginsberg's journey towards the innovative line of "Howl," and illustrate what he gained by returning to the long catalogs of Whitman, while retaining the particular immediacy and directness that he had found in Williams.

The reviews of the book generally acknowledged the excitement generated by the poems and the importance of this new voice, and it has gone on to become the quintessential poetic text of the 1950s counterculture. There were some dissenting voices. John Hollander in *Partisan Review* accused the book of "sponging on one's toleration for pages and pages," and proclaiming "in a hopped-up and improvised tone, that nothing seems to be worth saying save in a hopped-up and improvised tone." Hollander later modified his view, but Ginsberg's poetry had its detractors throughout his career, some of whom see *Howl and other Poems* more important as a cultural event than as poetry, while others point to what they see as the lack of any significant poetic development in Ginsberg's subsequent work.

In 1986 Harper & Row published an edition of "Howl" annotated by the author. Many accompanying period photographs and reprinted contemporary documents provide a very useful history of the poem, its composition, and reception. Among the "model texts" that Ginsberg reprints as "precursors" to "Howl" in this edition are poems by Christopher Smart, Shelley, Hart Crane, and Williams. In 1994 Rhino Records issued an early, 1956, recording of Ginsberg reading "Howl" in San Francisco, which adds a dimension to the poem not to be missed.

## Bibliography

Allen Ginsberg, *Howl*, ed. Barry Miles (New York, 1986).

James E. B. Breslin, *From Modern to Contemporary: American Poetry, 1945–1965* (Chicago, 1984).

Ann Charters, "Beat Poetry and the San Francisco Poetry Renaissance," in Jay Parini, ed., *The Columbia History of American Poetry* (New York, 1993), 581–604.

Michael Davidson, *The San Francisco Renaissance: Poetics and Community at Mid-Century* (Cambridge, 1989).

# Robert Lowell, *Life Studies*

## New York: Farrar, Straus & Cudahy, 1959

Robert Lowell had a distinguished reputation from his three earlier volumes of poetry before *Life Studies* as the master of the kinds of qualities praised by the then dominant New Critics – poetry that was dense, allusive, impersonal, and difficult. The third of these volumes had been published in 1951, *The Mills of the Kavanaughs*. But in *Life Studies* Lowell wrote in a verse form freer than any he had previously allowed himself, and in a barely disguised autobiographical vein that exposed many of the personal, family, and marital crises of his own life. The four parts of the book are in some ways a record of the journey his poetry took from the 1951 volume to the poems of *Life Studies*, from the studied, still distanced poems of Part One, through the autobiographical prose of Part Two, written after a breakdown and hospitalization in the mid-1950s, to the looser poems begun in the summer and fall of 1957 after a reading tour of the west coast that sometimes included sharing a platform with Allen Ginsberg. Lowell had also begun a warm correspondence with William Carlos Williams. Writing to and meeting Williams, and listening to Ginsberg's powerful readings, were among the factors that encouraged Lowell to be more direct in his work, looser in the structure of his poems, and more openly personal in his subject matter. This direction was further reinforced by the move by a number of poets in the middle and late 1950s towards a more personal "confessional" poetry. For a number of reviewers of *Life Studies*, and even for Lowell himself, there remained an uncertainty about where his new style would take him, and what its possibilities, if any, might be.

The poems and prose of *Life Studies* set up multiple connections through recurring themes and motifs. These interweaving connections provide a counterpoint to the more linear narratives, such as the shift in the book's poetics, the family histories, and the poet's move away from the community of beliefs offered by the Catholic Church (one subject of the first poem

"Beyond the Alps") to the ironic observation of courage and commitment in the actions of a mother skunk and her family in the final poem, "Skunk Hour." Additional themes include the role of failed fathers and leaders, "killer kings" as "Beyond the Alps" terms them (the Pope, Mussolini, the exiled writers of Part Three of *Life Studies*, the Harvard graduates institutionalized in a mental hospital in "Waking in the Blue," and most importantly Lowell's own father); oppressive and powerful women, Marie de Medici of the second poem "The Banker's Daughter," deposed by her son – and Lowell's own mother, "still her Father's daughter," dominating her weak husband in "Commander Lowell," and dying in Italy in "Sailing Home from Rapallo"; and the oppression of the Lowell name, added to by his mother's Winslow heritage, both among the first names of New England, and associated with a history of leadership and achievement now diminished in a century in which identity and a role had to be discovered rather than merely inherited. As part of this latter theme there is a strain of nostalgic envy in *Life Studies*, introduced in the first poem, for the

> conspicuous
> waste of our grandparents on their grand tours –
> long-haired Victorian sages [who] accepted the universe,
> while breezing on their trust funds through the world.

This nostalgia becomes, in "Skunk Hour," "the actions of "Nautilus Island's hermit / heiress" who, "Thirsting for / the hierarchic privacy / of Queen Victoria's century / . . . buys up all / the eyesores facing her shore, / and lets them fall." But *Life Studies* is the story of a figure who can no longer so easily accept the universe, including the academic and literary world that had bestowed praise and prizes on his earlier work, and who is no longer able or content to purchase shelter with inherited wealth, or to – as he came to feel he had been doing – hide the real subjects of his verse behind the dense, complex, allusive style of his first three books.

Lowell had converted to Catholicism in 1940, itself an act of rebellion against his family's long association with the Calvinism of Boston history. "Beyond the Alps" describes a train journey from Rome to Paris, in effect leaving the Church behind, as well as the idealism represented by the mountains. In 1950, the date of this poem, "Everest was still / unscaled." This and the other three poems of Part One are representative of Lowell's earlier style. "Inauguration Day: January 1953" describes the beginning of the Eisenhower presidency, and what "Memories of West Street and Lepke" in Part Four terms "the tranquillized *Fifties*" (Lowell's own prescription medicines are included in the phrase).

Part Two consists of the autobiographical prose "91 Revere Street" – missing from the first edition of *Life Studies*, which was published in Britain, because of the haste required to have the book eligible for a literary prize that in the event it did not win. This account of Lowell's childhood from 1925 to 1928 is both a record of the self-examination he underwent as a result of his breakdowns in the 1950s and a repository of the major themes of the book. Within the prose are accounts of relatives living out the last rituals of the old Boston Brahmin heritage, the child's fascination with a history and heritage which in the poems becomes both redundant and oppressive, and descriptions of Lowell's parents, the tensions of their marriage, and the father's slide into failure once he gives up his naval career – the last place where hierarchy still served as a central principle of order. The tensions between parents are echoed in the son's own marriage in the Part Four poem "Man and Wife," where the couple "lie on Mother's bed."

The four poems on writers that make up Part Three are also earlier poems. Thematically they present the risks of breaking away from the safety of the familiar. In various ways all four die in exile, and represent the scant value that the diminished contemporary world gives to its writers. All four were also important figures to Lowell personally. Lowell knew Ford Madox Ford at the end of the older writer's life through their mutual association with the group of southern poets and critics that included such figures as Allen Tate, John Crowe Ransom, and Robert Penn Warren. Poet and philosopher George Santayana, the subject of another poem, spent much of his life fighting against entrenched New England values. Delmore Schwartz, the subject of a third, Lowell knew from his time at Kenyon College. Schwartz burst upon the literary scene as a poet of great promise, but suffered a series of personal crises that would eventuate in his lonely death in New York City in 1966. Finally "Words for Hart Crane" pays tribute to a poet who was an important stylistic influence on Lowell's work. Crane's suicide is a final reminder of the hostility facing all four writers, who have in common with the Lowell of *Life Studies* a refusal to take the easy route of conformity.

The final part of the book, actually subtitled "Life Studies," displays the newer, looser style that Lowell had developed after his west coast trip, and is in two sections. In the first of the poems, "My Last Afternoon with Uncle Devereux Winslow," Lowell recalls being "five and a half" and his own yearning to "stay with Grandpa!" and the solid comforts that his home and garden represented, rather than returning with his parents. Meanwhile, the figures peopling that afternoon are beginning to disappear, "My Uncle was dying at twenty-nine," or like Great Aunt Sarah are going through the rituals of madness. In another of the book's motifs that accumulate meaning as the sequence progresses, the young Lowell "picked with a clean finger nail at the blue anchor / on my sailor blouse washed white as a spinnaker." The action among other things associates the boy with his father's naval career, abandoned at the insistence of his wife, and the loss of the "anchor" of generational stability represented by the apparent solidity of the grandfather's house. The "décor" in this house "Like my Grandfather . . . / was manly, comfortable, / overbearing, disproportioned" as the weight of this past will come to seem to the mature poet.

The rest of this first section records the deaths of family members – Lowell's father died in 1950 and his mother in 1954 – as well as the poet's own mental instability and institutionalization. In "Waking in the Blue," he is, like the other inmates of the hospital, one of the "old-timers" and he struts "in my turtle-necked French sailor's jersey" through the wards populated by "Mayflower / screwballs" whose movements are monitored by "Roman Catholic attendants."

In the last of the poems in this first half of Part Four, "Home After Three Months Away," the poet returns home after electric shock treatment, his cure, a temporary one, coming at the price of displacement: "I keep no rank nor station. / Cured, I am frizzled, stale and small." The lines prepare for the ironic comparison of Lowell's condition with that of mass murderer Lepke in the poem that follows and begins the final section of Part Four, "Memories of West Street and Lepke." Lepke, an inmate of the "West Street Jail" where Lowell was held for his conscientious objection to the Second World War, faces the electric chair, and like the aristocratic Lowells of the past has special privileges that set him apart from "the common man." Lepke's segregation is juxtaposed to the isolation of the poet who looks back from the 1950s on the memory and on his idealistic pacifism – a pacifism which he now sees as naive. But Lowell's isolation is not only from his "nine months' daughter"; he also, like Lepke, has in the 1950s a special privilege – a comfortable teaching job, "Only teaching on Tuesdays." Like the lobotomized Lepke, the poet's world is one of "lost connections," but unlike Lepke's "sheepish calm" the loss and its consequences still haunt him and the pages of this book.

The depth of the isolation is reinforced in the two poems that follow, both on marriage. But the final poem, "Skunk Hour," offers a possible way to continue, through the determined survival instincts of the skunk. The poet's distance from the skunk family, which significantly has no father present, is emphasized just as much as any comfort that the mother skunk's courageous actions may offer to him as example. Earlier in the poem the possibility of such renewal through family is problematized by the narrator's voyeuristic prowling, and his discovery of mechanistic lovemaking in "love-cars" that "lay together, hull to hull, / where the graveyard shelves on the town." But the narrator acknowledges directly "'My mind's not right. //

. . . I myself am hell." There are no more evasions. In addition, the poem is dedicated to Lowell's friend and fellow poet Elizabeth Bishop, whose "The Armadillo" (which is dedicated to Lowell) he acknowledged as an important poem in showing him the way towards his new style. There is thus, through the dedication, at least this community of two poets, which, along with the frankness of the self-examination, could begin to counter the poem's forlorn "nobody's here – // only skunks . . ."

The reviews of *Life Studies* ranged from the mostly somewhat tepid notices in Britain to some enthusiastic reviews in the United States. Some reviewers regretted Lowell's abandonment of the grand style for one they considered little more than anecdotal, but it was recognized that for a major poet to change his style so drastically was itself an important event. The book went on to win Lowell a National Book Award. He continued further with what he called in a letter to Randall Jarrell the "opening" provided by *Life Studies* in 1964's *For the Union Dead*, the reviews of which spoke of him as the major poet of his generation, completing the canonization inaugurated by the earlier volume.

## Bibliography

Robert Lowell, *Life Studies and For the Union Dead* (New York, 1964).

Steven Gould Axelrod, ed., *The Critical Response to Robert Lowell* (Westport, CT, 1999).

Stephen Matterson, "Robert Lowell: *Life Studies*," in Neil Roberts, ed., *A Companion to Twentieth-Century Poetry* (Oxford, 2001), 481–90.

Katherine Wallingford, *Robert Lowell's Language of the Self* (Chapel Hill, NC, 1988).

Terri Witek, *Robert Lowell and Life Studies: Revising the Self* (Columbia, MO, 1993).

# Donald Allen, ed., *The New American Poetry*

New York: Grove Press, 1960

Donald Allen's 1960 anthology had a far-reaching impact upon the careers of some of the poets that it included, upon later anthologies, and upon the categories in which the poets were often subsequently discussed. Among the poets whose work gained greater recognition and status through this volume were Charles Olson, Robert Creeley, Allen Ginsberg, Robert Duncan, John Ashbery, Denise Levertov, and Gary Snyder, while the poetry of the "New York school", the Beat poets, and the Black Mountain College poets were all introduced to a wider audience through Allen's selection.

Allen became an editor at Grove Press, in New York, in the mid-1950s. In 1957 he edited an issue of the journal published by the press, *The Evergreen Review*, devoted to the San Francisco Renaissance, which included a reprinting of Allen Ginsberg's "Howl" then being charged with indecency by the US Customs Service. He began work on *The New American Poetry* in 1958, motivated in part by the anthology *New Poets of England and America* which had appeared in 1957 edited by Donald Hall, Robert Pack, and Louis Simpson. The 1957 volume, carrying an introduction by Robert Frost, only included poets under 40, but foregrounded formalist poetry. The inclusion of English as well as American poets acknowledged a common heritage within contemporary work that Allen's anthology implicitly denied. The appearance of *The New American Poetry* in 1960 inaugurated what came to be called the "anthology wars," both collections being supplemented by further editions containing the work of additional poets. In the first editions of the two anthologies no poet appeared in both volumes, although in Hall and Pack's "Second Selection" in 1962 Denise Levertov made an appearance.

Allen's original plan was to illustrate the historical antecedents of the contemporary poets with selections of recent work from such modernist writers as William Carlos Williams, Wallace Stevens, Ezra Pound, and Marianne Moore, followed by a few poems from "second-generation" poets

Kenneth Rexroth, Kenneth Patchen, and Louis Zukofsky, before a larger selection from 24 "new" poets. But Charles Olson convinced Allen that the new poets had their "own character," and that their work represented a "change of discourse" whose qualities and characteristics could be misinterpreted if historical precedents were included. Olson's own poetics endorsed immediacy and an active presentation of history, and he was an important advisor to Allen in the final selection (in 1997 Allen co-edited Olson's *Collected Prose*). In the event, Allen found room for 44 poets, the selection leading off with Olson's "The Kingfishers."

In his introduction Allen claimed that the first generation of modernists had produced some of its "finest achievements" since 1945, a judgment that allowed him to present Pound, Williams, H.D., Moore, Stevens, and Cummings as relatively contemporary figures, and by implication to argue for a literary history that foregrounded the achievement of these poets at the expense of the New Critical formalists.

Allen divided his selections into five groups, corresponding, as he saw it, to the major movements in contemporary poetry, although his introduction recognized some inevitable overlap. For Allen, the poets had "shown one common characteristic: a total rejection of all those qualities typical of academic verse." The first section included poets associated with Black Mountain College, its journal *Black Mountain Review*, and Cid Corman's journal *Origin*. This group included Olson, Robert Duncan, Robert Creeley, and Denise Levertov. The San Francisco Renaissance poets formed the second group. Allen separated this group, which included Lawrence Ferlinghetti and Jack Spicer, from the Beat poets, who were originally associated with New York, even though the four representative figures of the Beat group, Allen Ginsberg, Jack Kerouac, Gregory Corso, and Peter Orlovsky, came to prominence through public readings in San Francisco. Allen's fourth group comprised the "New York poets," centered around the trio of Harvard-educated John Ashbery, Kenneth Koch, and Frank O'Hara, a group closely associated with the city's abstract expressionist painters. The fifth group was a catch-all for poets "who have evolved their own original styles and new conceptions of poetry," and who included Gary Snyder on the west coast and LeRoi Jones (Amiri Baraka) on the east.

The biographical notes at the end of the volume offered the poets what for many of them was their first opportunity for a national hearing. Ashbery, Creeley, Olson, and O'Hara dutifully recorded their education and writing careers. Some biographical entries were short and cryptic, while others noted the poets who had most influenced the particular writer. Gregory Corso, in two pages, told the harrowing tale of his childhood in foster homes and prisons, and of the impact of his subsequently meeting Allen Ginsberg. In four pages Robert Duncan carefully laid out his developing sense of poetry and the important figures who helped him to shape it. Jack Spicer recorded the year and place of his birth, observed that he "does not like his life written down," and gave an address to write to for anyone curious for more information. Such diverse entries were themselves a challenge to the standard practices usually governing such biographical notes.

As "aids to a more exact understanding of literary history," as Allen's introduction puts it, 15 of the poets are represented in a "Statements on Poetics" section just before the biographical notes. The section leads off with Olson's essay "Projective Verse," and, in keeping with Olson's insistence upon open form and lack of closure, Allen presents these statements as "interim reports by the poets." A final section provides a short bibliography of books, anthologies, recordings, periodicals, "mimeographs and irregular" publications, and a listing of the addresses of the small presses where readers might be able to obtain the materials listed. A measure of the volume's prescience, and the subsequent careers of many of the poets included, is the necessarily limited bibliography in the 1999 reissue of the book (carrying an Afterword by Allen), cataloging the selected and collected volumes of 32 of the poets.

In large part the response to Allen's volume divided along the lines represented by this and the Hall/Pack/Simpson anthologies. William Carlos Williams wrote to congratulate Allen. But X. J. Kennedy, who would appear in Hall and Pack's second selection in 1962, in a review in *Poetry* (July 1961) noted the impact of Allen's book, grudgingly conceded the value of the New York poets, but lamented "the stodginess of most of the rest of the book – so much of it in a language like instant mashed potatoes." In much discussion since, Allen's book has served as a useful touchstone for literary historians of mid-twentieth-century poetry. Allen's five categories provided labels within which the poets are often discussed, sometimes to the irritation of the poets themselves. For some critics, too, the groupings are restrictive, going against the resistance to categorization that is the spirit behind much of the poetry – although Allen in his introduction recognized their fluidity.

Allen originally planned to issue updated selections every two or three years, an idea that he abandoned, but in 1982 he edited with George F. Butterick *The Postmoderns: The New American Poetry Revised*. Allen and Butterick argue in their introduction that "our purpose was to consolidate the gains of the previous anthology and confirm its predictions." The five categories were dropped, on the grounds that the poets had moved beyond these starting points, and they are all grouped under the term "postmodern." The poets appear in chronological order, with Olson still the first poet. Fifteen of the poets from the original volume are omitted as not having "endured" (including more than half of the original 13 in the San Francisco Renaissance group), but still in the selection are six of the volume's poets who had died since 1960, including three of the best-known figures: Frank O'Hara, Jack Kerouac, and Olson. Nine poets were added, including Jackson Mac Low, Jerome Rothenberg, and Anne Waldman. Quite aside from their historical importance, both volumes still provide a useful introduction to the early work of the poets who fill their pages.

## Bibliography

Donald Allen, ed., *The New American Poetry: 1945–1960*, with a new Afterword (Berkeley, 1999).

Alan Golding, "*The New American Poetry* Revisited, Again," *Contemporary Literature*, 39 (Summer, 1998), 180–211.

Jed Rasula, *The American Poetry Wax Museum: Reality Effects, 1940–1990* (Urbana, IL, 1996).

# Sylvia Plath, *Ariel*

## London: Faber & Faber, 1965

Sylvia Plath took her own life on February 11, 1963, just three weeks after her novel *The Bell Jar* had been published in London, and having published one volume of poetry, *The Colossus* (London, 1960; New York, 1962). She had been preparing a volume of poems from those she had written in 1961 and 1962 to be titled *Ariel*, many of which have as background the break-up of her marriage with poet Ted Hughes, who had left her and the couple's two children for another woman. The couple had married in June 1956, when Plath, a native of Boston, was at Cambridge University on a Fulbright scholarship.

Plath arranged the "Ariel" poems in a black spring binder towards the end of 1962, including in the selection many of the poems she had written in a furious spurt of creativity following the couple's separation in October, when she wrote a poem almost every day for more than two months. But the published version of *Ariel*, when it appeared in 1965, edited by Hughes, differed in what some readers argue are important ways from Plath's 1962 ordering. Hughes removed 11 poems from Plath's arrangement, characterizing them in his introduction to Plath's *Collected Poems* (1981) as "some of the more personally aggressive poems," and added nine others – most of them written in January and February 1963 in the last weeks of Plath's life. The effect of these substitutions, some have argued, is to turn the book from a sequence about a betrayed spouse who finds a way to face the future without the adulterous partner to one illustrating an impassioned woman whose mental illness accelerates into self-destructive madness. Most of the poems missing from Plath's arrangement appeared subsequently in *Winter Trees* and *Crossing the Water*, both published in 1971.

The volume as it was published established Plath's posthumous reputation as a major figure of mid-twentieth-century poetry. Its major themes are the tensions and losses of a marriage; maternity, often with ambivalence about childbirth (in January 1962 Plath's second child, Nicholas, was born); an awareness – sometimes accompanied by violence – of the body as object; the rituals of writing; domesticity, hospitals, and beekeeping (the last an interest of Plath's father); oppressive male figures; the pain that love can bring; escape, and death. Although the subjects and even the attitudes of many of the poems can be tied to the persons, places, and events of Plath's private life in the period in which she wrote *Ariel*, her placement within the mode of Confessional poet has sometimes obscured the ways in which the poems project a self or series of selves that are not necessarily the individual poet, but rather a more wide-ranging self facing the oppression of history, particularly that of the Second World War, in addition to private losses and betrayals. In particular, some of Plath's imagery of the Holocaust and of male oppression as historically associated with fascism, which has come in for some criticism as self-indulgent, insensitive, or excessive, could be seen instead in the light of the volume's appropriation of recent European history. One example is her poem "Getting There," while one of the volume's best-known poems, "Daddy," contains the lines:

> I never could talk to you.
> The tongue stuck in my jaw.
>
> It stuck in a barbed wire snare.
> Ich, ich, ich, ich,
> I could hardly speak.
> I thought every German was you.
> And the language obscene
>
> An engine, an engine
> Chuffing me off like a Jew.
> A Jew to Dachau, Auschwitz, Belsen.
> I began to talk like a Jew.
> I think I may well be a Jew.

Here the lines could be describing a wider victimization rather than that only of the poet. In her own comments on the poem Plath spoke of it as an "allegory," and of the speaker's father as "a Nazi," which Otto Plath certainly was not.

Other well-known poems in the volume include "Lady Lazarus," a poem about surviving suicide, the wild horse ride of the title poem "Ariel," and "Fever 103°" where the speaker swings from hell to paradise. Part of the power of these poems comes from the intensity of the emotions described – disgust, despair, fury – and the startling juxtapositions of imagery that illustrate them. Two characteristics of the poems that further contribute are repetition of a single word to take up a single line, as in the quotation above, as if the speaker becomes trapped momentarily in the language of her own poem, or is positing a private crescendo of meaning associated with the repetition; and the surprise of a sudden matter-of-fact voice that undercuts the intensity produced by the heightened language, though that intensity immediately resumes. One example of many occurs in "A Birthday Present": "Is this the one for the annunciation? / My god, what a laugh!"

The last poems of the published volume are sparer than the earlier ones. The final 12 were added by Hughes to Plath's original arrangement, and, as noted above, most of them date from 1963. The last four poems concern isolation, refusing kindnesses, a shutting down of "the heart" ("Contusion"), of maternal care ("Edge"), and a fatalistic giving up of individual will "From the bottom of the pool, fixed stars / Govern a life" ("Words").

Plath's original ordering of the *Ariel* poems is recorded in the notes to her *Collected Poems* (1981). In the latter volume the poems are printed in chronological order of composition, and here the interested reader can find the 13 poems that the published version of *Ariel* omits: "The Rabbit Catcher," "Thalidomide," "Barren Woman," "A Secret," "The Jailor," "Magi," "Lesbos," "The Other," "Stopped Dead," "The Courage of Shutting-Up," "Purdah," "Amnesiac," and "The Swarm" (although the last-named appeared in the first New York edition in 1966, but not in the 1965 London edition). Many of these poems concern stark responses to maternity, and the body, and many concern the tensions of a marriage. "The Rabbit Catcher" is also the title of a poem in Hughes's 1998 volume *Birthday Letters*, which centers upon his life with Plath.

"The Swarm," is one of a sequence of five poems centered upon beekeeping that Plath intended to close the book. It concerns a procedure that allows the keeper to control a swarm of bees, moving them into a new hive. Plath's ordering of the poems invites us to read the last lines of "Fever 103°" – "(My selves dissolving, old whore petticoats) – / To Paradise" – as a prelude to the bee poems that immediately follow, and the determination to face isolation and adversity without the male figures, father and husband, who have peopled many of the earlier poems. In taking on the role of beekeeper, being initiated into beekeeping rituals, the poet takes on one of her father's major interests (he had written a book on the subject), and in "The Swarm" learns the secrets of male control. Most significantly, for this reading of Plath's ordering, her intended final poem, "Wintering," ends with her own bees, her own store of "honey," and a period of waiting through the winter – "The bees are all women . . . // Winter is for women" – that addresses the question of survival, and appears to affirm its possibility:

> Will the hive survive, will the gladiolas
> Succeed in banking their fires
> To enter another year?
> What will they taste of, the Christmas roses?
> The bees are flying. They taste the spring.

This poem is dated October 9, 1962, early in the almost daily series of poems that she would write through October and November. In December Plath moved with her children to London, leaving the house in rural Devon that she and her husband had purchased in 1961. She then wrote the final poems of January and February 1963, which close the volume as it appeared in print. The poet who wrote those verses, verses which Plath evidently thought of as belonging to a new and subsequent book, would not "taste the spring" of that year.

## Bibliography

Sylvia Plath, *The Collected Poems*, ed. Ted Hughes (New York, 1981).

Susan R. Van Dyne, *Revising Life: Sylvia Plath's Ariel Poems* (Chapel Hill, NC, 1993).
Marjorie Perloff, "The Two *Ariels*: The (Re)Making of the Sylvia Plath Canon," in *Poetic Licence: Essays on Modernist and Postmodernist Lyric* (Evanston, IL, 1990).
Sue Vice, "Sylvia Plath: *Ariel*," in Neil Roberts, ed., *A Companion to Twentieth-Century Poetry* (Oxford, 2001), 500–12.

# John Berryman, *The Dream Songs*

## New York: Farrar, Straus & Giroux, 1969

Before their 1969 publication *The Dream Songs* appeared separately in book form as *77 Dream Songs* in 1964, and *His Toy, His Dream, His Rest* in 1968, although some songs published separately did not appear in any of the three volumes. Berryman's achievement was recognized by the first volume being awarded the Pulitzer Prize, and the second the National Book Award. The whole sequence is divided into seven books, of which the first three appeared in the 1964 volume. There is some critical debate about the organizing and unifying principles behind the 385 songs. The events they describe are not arranged chronologically, and the central speaker, "Henry," as Berryman pointed out in an introductory note, "talks about himself sometimes in the first person, sometimes in the third, sometimes even in the second." But the character of Henry gives a coherence to the sequence while not confining it, just as the events of Berryman's life and many of Berryman's attitudes and concerns are versions to a greater or lesser degree of Henry's.

Berryman's introductory note characterizes the poem's speaker as "an imaginary character (not the poet, not me) named Henry, a white American in early middle age, sometimes in blackface, who has suffered an irreversible loss." Berryman's distance from Henry allows him to extend the range of the poem's social and political opinions beyond those Berryman held at any particular time; nevertheless the issues that Henry returns to again and again, including his ambivalence about the United States and about fame, his criticism of academia, his fascination with and fear of death, his uncertain religious belief, his isolation amidst friends and family, his failed marriages and sometimes nostalgic recall of sexual adventures, his journeys – which correspond to the travels Berryman took on fellowships and speaking tours – and a sense of "an irreversible loss" are all part of Berryman's own life and are feelings and opinions also expressed in his non-*Dream Songs* poems.

With only nine exceptions, each song consists of three six-line stanzas, variously rhymed. Within this form Berryman constructs a poem whose language veers from the formal to slang, from despairing to comic, and incorporates not only the speech of Henry but also his friend, "never named," as Berryman points out, "who addresses him as Mr. Bones and variants thereof." The name "Mr. Bones" and some of the repartee between Henry and his friend is based upon two characters from nineteenth-century minstrel shows, "Tambo" and "Bones," played by white men in black face. The second song is dedicated to "Daddy" Rice, who originated the format in the 1820s.

The *Dream Songs* are all the more powerful for their inclusion of a broad sociopolitical context as well as their concern with the obsessions and struggles of their central speaker. The poem expresses contempt for President Eisenhower and ambivalence about President Kennedy, and is critical of the war in Vietnam. The lack of progress in achieving racial equality is condemned, and the poem scorns the country's smug sense of superiority and self-satisfaction. Henry's sojourn in Ireland, corresponding to Berryman's 1967 sabbatical leave from the University of Minnesota which he spent in that country and where he wrote many of the final songs, allows him a distanced perspective upon the United States as well as a culture against which to contrast it.

Henry is critical of what he sees as the petty politics, pedantry, and unoriginality of academia and of much scholarship, although Berryman himself began a career in 1939 as a scholar, critic, and teacher that continued until his death. From 1955 he was based at the University of Minnesota, and he published a number of scholarly articles and books on a range of topics. Songs 35–8 begin at the annual meeting of the Modern Language Association. Henry calls on professors of all ranks to "forget your footnotes" on the dying Robert Frost, and their various moral arguments, and to "dance around Mary," a professor's wife, the name Mary a reminder that the convention always takes place just after Christmas. In Song 373, one of a number in which Henry imagines his death (and is deeply concerned about the difficult situation it would put his family in), he wonders about being a source for academic promotions – "will assistant professors become associates / by working on his works?"

Death is a central theme in *The Dream Songs*. The whole of book IV, Songs 78–91, is imagined by Henry as a series of posthumous lyrics written after his death, and elsewhere Henry thinks about suicide, and envies those who have died. He is surrounded by death through the loss of fellow poets, some of whom were close friends, while others shared more generally Henry's serious interest in writing, but all through their deaths contribute further to Henry's sense of isolation and exile. Among the many writers whose deaths he recalls are Ernest Hemingway, Sylvia Plath, William Carlos Williams, Theodore Roethke, and R. P. Blackmur – Hemingway and Plath being suicides. But among writers the greatest losses for Henry are the deaths of Randall Jarrell and Delmore Schwartz – particularly the latter. Berryman's friendship with Schwartz began in 1938–9 and lasted until Schwartz's lonely death in a run-down New York City hotel in July 1966. In Songs 146–58 Henry records his sorrow at the evaporation of Schwartz's early promising talent, and at the paranoia that drove Schwartz to lose so many friends, as well as his guilt at not being on hand when Schwartz suffered his fatal heart attack. One of the two dedications of *His Toy, His Dream, His Rest* is "to the sacred memory of Delmore Schwartz." The death of Schwartz haunts Henry in later songs too, as does the death of poet and critic Jarrell in 1965, a suspected suicide, who unlike Schwartz died, Song 121 asserts, at the peak of his powers: "His last book was his best." These deaths, Song 153 laments, along with those of Roethke, Blackmur, and Plath, have "wrecked this generation," making a "first rate haul" for a god who has "left alive / fools I could number like a kitchen knife." More than once in these songs Henry wonders why he does not join these figures in death.

The greatest loss for Henry in *The Dream Songs*, as it was for Berryman himself, is the suicide of his father. Berryman's father had shot himself when the boy was 11, having earlier threatened to swim out to sea to drown both himself and his child. In the penultimate song of *77 Dream Songs* Henry tells his friend: "in a modesty of death I join my father / who dared so long agone leave me," and, as noted above, *His Toy, His Dream, His Rest* opens with a series of songs supposedly written following Henry's own death. Henry's ambivalent feelings about the suicide end book V (Song 145):

> Also I love him: me he's done no wrong
> for going on forty years – forgiveness time –
> I touch now his despair . . .
>
>                                                    I'm
> trying to forgive
> whose frantic passage, when he could not live
> an instant longer, in the summer dawn
> left Henry to live on.

The penultimate song (384) of *His Toy, His Dream, His Rest*, like the penultimate song (76) of *77 Dream Songs*, concerns Henry's father. At his father's grave in Song 384, Henry's actions suggest not only the fruitless grappling with loss, fighting with a dead man, but also the way that his fury will lead him to the same fate, even to the same grave – his own death directly related to his battle with his father:

> I'd like to scrabble till I got right down
> away down under the grass
>
> and ax the casket open ha to see
> just how he's taking it, which he sought so hard
> we'll tear apart
> the mouldering grave clothes ha and then Henry
> will heft the ax once more, his final card,
> and fell it on the start.

Henry's anticipated suicide is not carried out in *The Dream Songs*, although his creator ended his own life on January 7, 1972, at the age of 57 by jumping from a bridge in Minneapolis onto a frozen river bank of the Mississippi.

## Bibliography

John Berryman, *The Dream Songs* (New York, 1969).

John Haffenden, *John Berryman: A Critical Commentary* (New York, 1980).

Richard J. Kelly and Alan K. Lathrop, eds., *Recovering Berryman: Essays on a Poet* (Ann Arbor, 1993).

Thomas Travisano, *Midcentury Quartet: Bishop, Lowell, Jarrell, Berryman, and the Making of a Postmodern Aesthetic* (Charlottesville, VA, 1999).

# Amiri Baraka, *Black Magic: Sabotage, Target Study, Black Art; Collected Poetry, 1961–1967*

## Indianapolis: Bobbs-Merrill, 1969

Amiri Baraka's poems from the late 1950s and early 1960s came out of his association with the multi-racial, bohemian avant-garde centered upon New York's Greenwich Village. But in a change that Baraka has identified as culminating with the assassination of black leader Malcolm X in 1965, he moved to Harlem, in uptown Manhattan, and subsequently to his hometown of Newark. With this move his writing focused upon his desire to separate himself from what he came to see as a bohemian culture that was self-indulgent and apolitical, to root his writing in his own black experience and the suffering of the black community, and to advocate radical measures to alleviate that suffering. This move towards Black Nationalism, which led in 1967 to his discarding the name LeRoi Jones and taking up his Muslim name, is traced in *Black Magic*, his third book of poems. These poems, from a figure who had become well known in 1964 for his Obie Award-winning play *Dutchman*, made Baraka a major influence upon a future generation of black writers in the 1960s, pointing the way to a writing rooted in ethnic experience – an influence that has been compared to the impact 40 years earlier of the Harlem Renaissance. The poems are characterized by anger at white oppression and hypocrisy, a call to action – often to violence – and a demand for pride in the beauty and the potential of a free black America. While not denying the influence of these poems, some, mostly white, critics echoed Kenneth Rexroth's complaint that a promising poet had succumbed to a rhetoric that had become increasingly undisciplined.

The volume opens with Baraka's short prose essay, "An Explanation of the Work," in which he explains his division of the book into three parts: Sabotage, Target Study, and Black Art. In the first, he wants to see fall "the superstructure of filth Americans call their way of life." The second is more specific study, "less passive," and more "like bomber crews do [to] the soon to be destroyed cities" (the "targets" include President Johnson and the Vietnam War). The third section is "the crucial seeing, the decisions, the actual move." His subsequent work, the poet explains, writing this "Explanation" in 1968, has gone on to be more "spiritual."

Baraka's study of black music, and his claim in the 1960s that in music the American negro had made his only original contribution to art, is reflected in the longer line that he uses in this book than in his earlier poems, and in the multiple rhythms, and chant-like phrases which build one upon one another. The stanzas fill the space on the page in various and unpredictable patterns and directions. These musical parallels reinforce his sense of the poem as part of a sacred ritual, bringing the community together in a set of shared beliefs, for that community's mutual understanding and protection. "Sacred Chant for the Return of Black Spirit and Power" is one example of these features. In a number of other poems in the volume this sense of the sacred is contrasted with what the poems denounce as the oppressive white religions of Christianity and Judaism. Akin to these white religions is the oppressive power of white popular culture. A number of poems condemn the role models offered by Hollywood and by national television shows, and the denial of physical fact as well as cultural heritage by blacks who see the figures of white popular culture as figures to copy. (An example is "Poem for HalfWhite College Students").

In this book Amiri Baraka is thus putting white culture behind him, as well as the identity of LeRoi Jones. A number of poems bear titles echoing well-known texts by white writers, the poems appropriating the titles for their own purposes. Examples are "Babylon Revisited," "Return of the Native," and "David Copperhead," while "Citizen Cain" extends the practice to film. More generally, the legacy of Byron, Kipling, and Eliot is disowned in "The Bronze Buckaroo," the poem that ends section I. But the most important transformation recorded in the volume is that of the poet himself. He wants to serve the future by changing his legacy. The poem "leroy" asserts:

> When I die, the consciousness I carry I will to
> black people. May they pick me apart and take the
> useful parts, the sweet meat of my feelings. And leave
> the bitter bullshit rotten white parts
> alone.

In the prose paragraphs of "Gatsby's Theory of Aesthetics," he affirms that he writes "to invest the world with a clearer understanding of it self, but only by virtue of my having brought some clearer understanding of my self into it."

Despite the criticism that the white bohemian avant-garde receives in the volume, the style of many of the poems is a more vigorous and angry, and obscene, version of the line developed most famously by Allen Ginsberg in "Howl." Ginsberg is singled out in particular in "Western Front," as representative of the apolitical, self-indulgent bohemianism that Baraka wants to separate himself from. The long line, cataloguing through apparently spontaneous random examples the characteristics of a culture, its contradictions and hypocrisies, was as well suited to the oral directness, multiple shifts of tone and rhythm, and breaking of established poetic conventions of Baraka as of the poet of "Howl." But where Ginsberg's poems call for a change in consciousness, Baraka's call not only for this but also for the violence that he feels is the only way to achieve it. Thus a poem early in the volume, "A POEM SOME PEOPLE WILL HAVE TO UNDERSTAND" ends with the call, "Will the machinegunners please step forward?" The "Black Art" section begins with "SOS," a poem which makes the urgency explicit, while the volume ends with "Black People!" a post-1966 poem that Baraka says he added "cause I felt like it." This poem identifies the necessary communal act for the "we" who are addressed to be the killing of the "white man" and the remaking of a world fit for the future of black children:

> We must make our own
> World, man, our own world, and we can not do this unless the white man
> is dead. Let's get together and killhim my man, let's get to gather the fruit
> of the sun, let's make a world we want black children to grow and learn in
> do not let your children when they grow look in your face and curse you by
> pitying your tomish ways.

In 1974, five years after the publication of this volume, Baraka came to regard his Black Nationalist position as itself unproductively racist, and taking up a Marxist perspective his concerns broadened to treat economic and political oppression outside of exclusively racial terms. But, as he noted in a "Preface to the Reader" for the 1991 *LeRoi Jones/Amiri Baraka Reader*, commenting upon his comparative lack of visibility after the 1960s, "it was easier to be heard from with hate whitey than hate imperialism!" (p. xiii).

## Bibliography

Amiri Baraka, *The Autobiography of LeRoi Jones/Amiri Baraka* (New York, 1984).
—— *The LeRoi Jones/Amiri Baraka Reader*, 2nd edn., ed. William J. Harris (New York, 2000).

William J. Harris, *The Poetry and Poetics of Amiri Baraka: The Jazz Aesthetic* (Columbia, MO, 1985).
Theodore R. Hudson, *From LeRoi Jones to Amiri Baraka: the Literary Works* (Durham, NC, 1973).

# Galway Kinnell, *The Book of Nightmares*

## Boston: Houghton Mifflin, 1971

Galway Kinnell wrote *The Book of Nightmares* over a period of four years.
The book is dedicated to his two children, Maud and Fergus, whose births
are described in the opening and closing poems, "Under the Maud Moon,"
and "Lastness." Maud had been born in 1966 and Fergus two years later, and
a central theme of the book is their place in a legacy of inevitable mortality,
the poems exploring ways in which to face it and even in part conquer it.
The themes of cruelty, mortality, and love, articulated in a style that is
carefully detailed while also giving that detail symbolic meaning, characterizes
Kinnell's earlier work too, but in this book such elements are most fully
integrated. Each of its ten sections has seven strophes, and the sequence
enacts a journey between the two births into a world of horror and inhu-
manity, violence and darkness, that the poet finds a way to face, and to
articulate for the children when they, too, have to enact that inevitable
journey. For some critics the structure of the book is overloaded, and some
have seen little that is particularly new in its philosophy, but the book is
almost universally praised for the power of its language, its evocation of the
spirit that insists on fighting despair, on passing on as honestly as possible an
account of and understanding of what has been experienced, and what can
be hoped for in a century of diminished faith..

The book opens on a woodland scene. The poet lights "a small fire in the
rain" and then after a while resumes walking. A nearby bear senses the man
and "trudges away." A similar landscape begins poems IX and X, and the
book has been read as a dream that takes place in this physical setting,
within which the poet journeys. But the journey is more than a physical
one, involving the discoveries and decisions that the poet must make within
the mental and emotional landscape of memory, fear, and hope that is the
setting of most of the book. Poem II introduces one of the motifs that
integrate the ten poems, the killing and eating of a hen – necessary killing

for survival, but an act which, as the poet looks "by corpse-light" at the eggs inside the body in various stages of formation, affects the future birth and growth of life beyond the present moment and generation. Characteristic of the book's movement is its move out within a few lines from this carefully examined detail of the hen's carcass to cosmic questions, the possibility of an afterlife, and of the truth of promised Christian salvation.

Poems III, IV, and V enact scenes of isolation, degradation, loss, and fear. The motifs in III and V center around hotels where desperate lives end in lingering smells, a few clothes, and an empty space in a sagging, tired bed. In poem IV letters from "Virginia" to "Galway" reveal her fear of losing identity to a "demon lover" in a world in which for her "God is my enemy."

In poem VI (all of the poems have titles, this one is "The Dead shall be Raised Incorruptible") the poem broadens out to condemn acts of cruelty and dishonor in American history, in particular the treatment of Native Americans, and the current war in Vietnam. A voice in the second section admits to the thrill of firing a gun, of shredding a pilot's body "down to catgut." The nightmare here is the nightmare of the whole century. But in poem X the earlier reference to "catgut" is echoed in "the sliced intestine / of cat" that makes a violin string, and thus produces the music at a Bach concert. The beauty of the music, the echo suggests, is one way we can express sorrow and set aside for a while the thought of mortality. Beauty comes out of death.

In the much-admired poem VII, "Little Sleep's Head Sprouting Hair in the Moonlight," the poet comforts baby Maud after she screams, "waking from a nightmare." Against this pre-vision of mortality by the child the poet offers love and the wish that death were not the fate of every generation. At the center of the poem are three scenes, one a disarming exclamation by the baby in a restaurant, the second an imagination by the poet of Maud as a young woman with a future love, in which he hopes that his daughter will fully enjoy the moment and not allow the recognition that *"one day all this will only be memory"* to spoil her happiness. The third incident is a memory of the last moments of the poet's father, the dying light in his eyes paralleled by the present moonlight reflected in Maud's eyes.

The book's theme of limitation, and the power of love to make it both bearable and potentially unbearable at the same time, is turned in poem VIII upon the poet's marriage. Lying next to his pregnant wife, "two mismatched halfnesses lying side by side in the darkness," he recalls meeting for a few hours the "lost other" who could complete him, but whom "necessity" and loyalty made him leave. (The poem reminds us that the idea of half-persons is "nightmared" by Aristophanes – in Plato's *Symposium*.) The poet calls his action of leaving the other lover "cowardice," and the conflict between fate and will that is raised throughout this book is once again focused here; was leaving her an exercise of free will against the fates dominating human lives in this book, or a failure to exercise that will? What, in the suffering we could bring to those we love, would be the cost of trying to lead something more than a "half life" if the opportunity were offered?

Poem IX more directly returns to the physical landscape that opened the book, and enacts in little the descent and ascent trajectory of the whole sequence, the poet stepping down into a mineshaft and then ascending, finding, as the poem's title puts it, "The Path Among the Stones." In the final and tenth poem Fergus is born, and "one / and zero / walk off together" the ten poems making up both the fate of the individual one against the zero of death, but also the "song" of the ten sections born of memory, experience, and hope that can be company and a legacy for each of the children, as well as for the individual poet himself. The legacy, as poem I puts it, of "this book, even if it is the book of nightmares."

## Bibliography

Galway Kinnell, *The Book of Nightmares* (Boston, 1971).
—— *Walking Down the Stairs: Selections from Interviews* (Ann Arbor, 1978).

Howard Nelson, ed., *On the Poetry of Galway Kinnell: The Wages of Dying* (Ann Arbor, 1987).
Nancy L. Tuten, ed., *Critical Essays on Galway Kinnell* (New York, 1996).

# Anne Sexton, *Transformations*

## Boston: Houghton Mifflin, 1971

In *Transformations* Anne Sexton retells some of the fairy tales of the Brothers Grimm, making them "very contemporary" as she said in a letter, adding prologues at the beginning and interpolated comments throughout by "a middle-aged witch, me – ." "I take the fairy tale," she wrote in another letter, "and transform it into a poem of my own, following the story line, exceeding the story line and adding my own pzazz. They are very wry and cruel and sadistic and funny." Although with their fairy-tale narratives and mordant commentaries these poems differ from the intimate, confessional poems of Sexton's earlier four published volumes, the poems finally center around themes similar to those in the earlier poetry: uneasy relations between parents and children, ambivalence over women's roles, and anxiety over the awakening of sexual desire. In his introduction to the volume Kurt Vonnegut writes that Sexton's work "domesticates my terror," but in these poems such domestication offers no solutions. Brides are oppressed by their savior princes, sudden riches are an empty reward, daughters take on the sins of their mothers, and children might be abandoned.

Sexton wrote the 17 long poems of *Transformations* between the winter of 1969/70, and November 1970. The book is dedicated to her daughter Linda, born in 1953, whose interest in the tales had sparked that of her mother. The bitterness of the poems made Houghton Mifflin hesitant to publish the book, and earlier, when it came to magazine publication, Sexton could not place the poems in the mainstream outlets that were usually eager to publish her work. The volume received wide critical acclaim upon its appearance, and went on to have the highest hardcover sales of any Sexton volume.

The poems begin with the voice of the "middle-aged witch" narrator gathering her – adult, not child – audience around her. The witch persona is one Sexton sometimes adopted in other volumes. The familiar tale of "Snow White and the Seven Dwarfs" follows next, and its treatment sets the pattern for the tales that follow. In the opening prologue to the poem the witch emphasizes Snow White's virginity, her passive and decorous sexual attractiveness "rolling her china-blue doll eyes," eyes that say "Good Day Mama" but which are closed, for the moment, to "the thrust of the unicorn." The evil stepmother hears of Snow White's beauty in a mirror whose pronouncements are "something like the weather forecast." This method of bringing contemporary, day-to-day, references into the fairy tale – the traditional appeal of which is its narrative distance, and possibilities not tied to earthly limitations – is a frequent one in the witch's narration. In other poems, Coca-Cola, Joe DiMaggio, Linus (from the Peanuts comic strip), Al Jolson, Johnny Carson, and Brooklyn all find their way into the narrative, and there are many more examples. Similarly, contemporary diction exists side by side with the more archaic terms usually associated with the tales. This is one way in which Sexton emphasizes the psychological and social realities behind the escapism of the stories. By bringing them back to the contemporary world, the poems can puncture the escapist fantasies of castle weddings, sudden riches, miracle cures, and triumphs over death. The poems emphasize that such escapes can only occur in fantasy, in a childlike imagination or lifestyle removed from the challenges posed by sexual initiation or the expected female duties of domesticity. Cinderella, a "doll" like Snow White, finds her happiness in a marriage that is both child-like and fictional:

> Cinderella and the prince
> lived, they say, happily ever after,
> like two dolls in a museum case
> never bothered by diapers or dust,
> never arguing over the timing of an egg,
> never telling the same story twice,
> never getting a middle-aged spread,
> their darling smiles pasted on for eternity.
> Regular Bobbsey Twins.
> That story.

Such an escape, for Sexton, as the repeated "never" makes clear, does not happen in the real world of domestic life, only perhaps in a "Never-Never Land" like that of J. M. Barrie's story of perpetual childhood, *Peter Pan*.

For Snow White's stepmother, age and its anxieties, and sexual competition, override any sense of parental responsibility; thus she orders the violent death of the young girl. Sexton emphasizes, as the Grimm tale does not, the sexual threats in Snow White's journey to the dwarfs' cottage, once she is spared by the hunter. The "wildwood" contains many a "hungry wolf / his tongue lolling out like a worm." Birds call out "lewdly," and snakes hang from the trees. Not surprisingly, the dwarfs' cottage is "as droll as a honey-moon cottage."

The queen's temptations, once she finds her stepdaughter, are all symbols of sexual growth: a "bodice," a "comb," and an apple. Snow White, the narrator comments, is a "dumb bunny" for opening the door a third time. But within the context of the volume's themes, she is also a victim of parental force and manipulation (as are Hansel and Gretel in a later poem). The parent's role as guide to the mysteries of sexual awakening is caught up with the desire to destroy the child who is a reminder of aging and death – an aging and death to which marriage and childbearing make major contribu-tions, outside of fairy tales. An additional feature of Snow White's behavior that the narrator's comment points up is the girl's failure to heed the advice of her dwarf protectors. In *Transformations* deformity is presented as both fascinating (hence its frequent appearance in the fairy tales) and disturbing. The deformed characters can be miraculously healed, as in "The Maiden Without Hands" – whose hands were cut off by her father – or "Iron Hans," who is cured without the need of a medical plan or "electroshock." In "Rumplestiltskin" the dwarf is part of a duality of self, but can be identified and defeated (in a fantasy) in order to find happiness (in this case with a mercenary king). Sexual and material ambition drive Cinderella's stepsisters to deform themselves in attempting to make the identifying slipper fit. The two-eyed girl achieves marriage to the prince in "One-Eye, Two-Eyes, Three Eyes," and years later takes in her sisters to "become her children." In the poems, when some deformed characters are not healed, their sexual needs can drive them to a violent physical death, while other deformed characters might remain physical children with adult drives. This latter is the case with the dwarfs in "Snow White." They are "little hot dogs," as the narrator describes them, but Snow White the "dumb bunny" does not take seriously their warnings of the sexual trap that her stepmother – and her own body and vanity – are setting. Of course, the central recurring deformed figure in the book is the narrator herself, the witch. For Sexton's own despair and suicidal drives there were no miracle cures.

Snow White's beauty and sexual attractiveness, once she has swallowed the poisoned apple, turn her literally into desirable coin, asleep she "lay as still as a gold piece." Her body in the glass coffin becomes the prince's property, given up by the dwarfs, and awakened and married she "held court, / rolling her china-blue doll eyes open and shut."

The queen stepmother dies of excess passion, dancing to her death in "red-hot iron shoes," but has merely been replaced by the no longer virgin Snow White, who has now begun the aging process, and who "sometimes [refers] to her mirror / as women do."

The stepmother's actions in "Snow White and the Seven Dwarfs" reveal her to be a sexual predator and rival to her stepdaughter, but in "Rapunzel" the mother gives away the child because of the attractions of "a witch's garden / more beautiful than Eve's." The witch then becomes not a protector but a lover – this perhaps the alternative to a garden containing a male partner, Adam. With the daughter imprisoned in her room, "thus they played mother-me-do." Returned to the world of heterosexual love, again by a prince, Rapunzel joins the world "made up of couples" where "a rose must have a stem." The witch, Mother Gothel, is reduced to loneliness and a world of memories, the punishment that the conventional world imposes upon those who don't follow the path of its supposed "cure-alls" of domestic bliss and romantic love.

In the final poem of the volume, "Briar Rose (Sleeping Beauty)," her father's possessive love for Sleeping Beauty, another "little doll child," is revealed to be close to sexual possession, the prince/husband merely a replacement, as her fearful dreams reveal:

> my father
> drunkenly bent over my bed,
> circling the abyss like a shark,
> my father thick upon me
> like some sleeping jellyfish.

Again there is no escape from the trap, and threat, of family or of growing up, and sleep only brings nightmares that reinforce that truth.

As she wrote the poems of *Transformations*, Sexton also began preparing what would be two of her final books, *The Book of Folly* and *The Death Notebooks*. Three years after the publication of *Transformations* she committed suicide. Death is to the fore in the more intimate poems of the last two books, but it is no less a central theme in *Transformations*, where escape is fantasy, sexual maturity is threatening, married and domestic life is oppressive, and parents can be betrayers. The last word of the final poem of *Transformations* is "death."

## Bibliography

Anne Sexton, *The Complete Poems* (Boston, 1981).

Carol King Barnard, "*Transformations*: A Magic Mirror," in Frances Bixler, ed., *Original Essays on the Poetry of Anne Sexton* (Conway, AR, 1988), 107–29.

Steven E. Colburn, ed., *Anne Sexton: Telling the Tale* (Ann Arbor, 1988).

Carol Leventen, "*Transformations*' Silencings," in Linda Wagner-Martin, ed., *Critical Essays on Anne Sexton* (Boston, 1989), 136–49.

# John Ashbery, *Self-Portrait in a Convex Mirror*

## New York: Viking, 1975

*Self-Portrait in a Convex Mirror* won the three major poetry awards of 1976, the Pulitzer Prize, the National Book Award, and the National Book Critics Circle Award. Its appearance established John Ashbery as a central figure of late twentieth-century poetry, and the major poet to emerge from the New York school of the 1950s, which also included Frank O'Hara and Kenneth Koch. The book contains what are for many readers Ashbery's most accessible poems, his work before and after this volume often being noted for its "difficulty." But following *Self-Portrait in a Convex Mirror* there was no question that Ashbery's work had earned the right to demand the attention that it required.

Ashbery's poems follow in the path of Wallace Stevens, Marianne Moore, and W. H. Auden in being poems of meditation that can take unexpected directions as part of their account of the mind thinking. In the case of Ashbery's poetry, this is part of his exploration of the nuances of ordinary experience, the origins of a poem that records it, and the interruptions and diversions that the act of recording encounters. The poems are organized around what the poem "Tenth Symphony" calls "connexion," either as noticed by the poet or as imposed upon the narrative by the circumstance of their happening. No great claim is usually made for the experience examined beyond the implicit one that it is of interest, and that poetry is an appropriate medium in which to address it. Some poems offer in their titles apparent claims to significance, as with "The One Thing That Can Save America," and "Poem in Three Parts [Love, Courage, and I Love the Sea]," only to deflate such claims in their content. In the poems of this volume, as elsewhere in Ashbery's work, poetic diction bumps against everyday language and slang; the poem's narration can be interrupted by a speech by another, unnamed character; or a poem's conclusion may be an anti-climax, almost a dismissal of what has gone before, at any rate once its moment has past.

"Grand Galop" ends: "But now we are at Cape Fear and the overland trail / Is impassable, and a dense curtain of mist hangs over the sea." Or a final line can offer almost a parody of an aphorism: "No one has the last laugh" ("Farm"); "And the man who made the same mistake twice is exonerated" ("Scheherazade"); "And the past slips through your fingers, wishing you were there" ("A Man of Words"). Such rhetoric challenges the idea of finality, and the self-containment of the poem. Ashbery is unwilling, as David Kalstone has observed, "to take permanent shelter in his work."

In the title poem of the collection, which has become Ashbery's best-known poem, the circumstances of a work of art, the impossibility of its separation from the world around it, and the process of creation are central themes. Thus in the first of the poem's six sections Ashbery quotes the biographer Vasari on the circumstances behind sixteenth-century painter Parmigianino undertaking his famous painting in Rome, and later the history of the poet's own relationship to the painting: "Vienna where the painting is today, where / I saw it with Pierre in the summer of 1959; New York / Where I am now. . . ." The fact of seeing the painting with another, and of thinking about the painting in New York, have equal status with the fact of seeing the painting itself. The painting provides a starting point for the poet's own self-portrait, a self, as always in Ashbery's work, that is an accumulation of ongoing experiences, and a self-portrait that moves beyond what the poem argues is the restrictive aesthetic of Parmigianino's painting. In addition, the poem's account of its own genesis and development parallels the conceit of Parmigianino's painting, where the painter's arm looms in the foreground in the act of painting the picture, offering a further level of perspective against the receding and distorted mirror image behind it, the rendition of which is a tour de force of painterly conventions depicting space. "As Parmigianino did it," the poem begins; but the self-portraits of painter and poet become themselves mirror images, and the poet's direct address to the painter in the poem is a reminder of the two separate worlds that can be brought together through the alchemy of the artistic process.

In Parmigianino's painting Ashbery found a perfect subject for his themes, and the success of the title poem has overshadowed in critical discussion the achievement of the many other fine poems in the volume, and even threatened to overshadow Ashbery's subsequent work. For a poet interested in the "recurring wave / Of arrival" as the poem puts it, the poem's status threatened to compromise the poet's insistence upon the relevance of present experience, and readerly interest in his ongoing work. It has been the ongoing quality and innovation of Ashbery's subsequent poetry that has largely stopped this from happening, not the attempts he has sometimes made to disparage his most famous poem.

## Bibliography

John Ashbery, *Self-Portrait in a Convex Mirror; Houseboat Days* (New York, 1977).

Lee Edelman, "The Pose of Imposture: Ashbery's 'Self-Portrait in a Convex Mirror,'" *Twentieth Century Literature*, 32 (1986), 95–114.

David Herd, "John Ashbery: *Self-Portrait in a Convex Mirror*," in Neil Roberts, ed., *A Companion to Twentieth-Century Poetry* (Oxford, 2001), 536–46.

David Kalstone, *Five Temperaments: Elizabeth Bishop, Robert Lowell, James Merrill, Adrienne Rich, John Ashbery* (New York, 1977).

# Adrienne Rich, *The Dream of a Common Language: Poems 1974–1977*

## New York: Norton, 1978

The questioning of patriarchal assumptions, the need for change, courage, and the power of the will, are themes in Adrienne Rich's poetry before *The Dream of a Common Language*, but in this volume for the first time they are fully focused upon the relationships between women, and the language that could express those relationships in poetry. Rich seeks a space for the voice of women free from the patriarchal tradition that the poetry claims has named things, defined form, and imposed an identity and definition upon women, thus limiting their actions and self-expression. Rich's poems in *The Dream of a Common Language* explore this space and search for this new language in a number of ways; most of the poems are in the personal voice of the poet speaking out, describing, exercising the courage and freedom that the poems insist is essential. Many of the poems describe experiences only available to women: lesbian love, childbirth, motherhood, sisterhood. Some use a frank, intimate voice to describe physical love between women as a way to subvert the conventions of male love poetry addressed to women, especially the traditions of romance that objectify women as love objects. Sometimes the language is radically minimalized, to strip it as much as possible of patriarchal associations, while another strategy advocates tenderness alongside courage, as a contrast to the conventions of aggressive male heroism. Some poems give voice to heroic or defeated figures from the past, bringing language to women formerly silenced, in the spirit of the work of H.D., whose lines from *The Flowering of the Rod* serve as the volume's epigram:

> I go where I love and where I am loved,
> into the snow;
>
> I go to the things I love
> with no thought of duty or pity

Rich's volume is divided into three parts, titled "Power," "Twenty-One Love Poems," and "Not Somewhere Else, But Here." In the book's first two poems, courageous women pay with their lives for their determination to take on what has formerly been inscribed as male territory. The isolated Madame Curie dies from "wounds [that] came from the same source as her power." In "Phantasia for Elvira Shatayev" – the leader of a climbing team, all of whom perished in a storm while climbing Lenin Peak – Shatayev's voice comes to speak for all of the women in her team. The courage to strive for their goal, and to face the suffering, comes from an inner strength discovered through the communal drive. The real "danger" is "separateness," *"but till now / we had not touched our strength."*

Speaking for her group, Shatayev says that realizing such communal strength had always been something "dreamed," and the idea of "dream" here, in the volume's title, and in other poems in the book acknowledges the ideal nature of the search, as well as the dangers of its confronting and challenging both the physical world and the time-bound conventions that have insisted upon shaping our understanding of that world. The next poem, "Origins and History of Consciousness," which provides the volume's title, terms this search "The drive / to connect. The dream of a common language." Its history includes the "photographs of dead heroines" such as those of the first two poems.

What binds the communal effort in these poems is love, either sexual and individual, as in the next poem "Splittings," or in a shared sense of purpose and fearlessness in the freedom of newly asserted identity, as with the mountain climbers. "Until we find each other, we are alone," ends the poem "Hunger," which describes the suffering of mothers for their children in the Third World within a system of inequality that economically and politically keeps women in both rich and poor countries from being free.

At the center of *The Dream of a Common Language* are the "Twenty-One Love Poems" of the second section. These free-form sonnets had earlier been published in a limited, hand-printed edition of 1,000 copies in 1976. The love for the loved woman brings an understanding to the poet in poem V of the "centuries of books unwritten" piled behind the shelves of books by male authors, some of those authors scorning women and homosexual love. The result is a "civilization" that is a "half-world." The poems are a meditation upon the pain, joy, and necessary courage of lesbian love, the need for "tenderness" (poem X) and avoiding evasion. Following poem XIV is "(THE FLOATING POEM, UNNUMBERED)" which is the most frank in its physical description of intimacy, as if to take its praise of the physical joy of one woman's body for another beyond this particular relationship to the realm of possibility for all women. What is important, the final poem in this sequence asserts, is to choose how to love, not merely to be passively acted upon.

The final section of the book contains instances of promise thwarted, courage failed, but the need to learn from such experience and continue the journey. "Paula Becker to Clara Westhoff," as its accompanying note glosses, imagines a letter between two woman artists whose careers, and in the case of Becker her life, are subordinated to the careers of their artist husbands (Westhoff was married to Rainer Maria Rilke). The marriages also separate the mutual support that each woman brought to the other. "Sibling Mysteries," as part of the book's articulation of experiences open only to women, explores the connection of daughters to their mothers, a bond, the poem argues, early made "taboo" as women are made to conform to a world of patriarchal values. "Let me hold and tell you" the poet's voice tells her sibling in the final line; the "common language" as often in this book is linked to physical action, to the associated language of performance. Such telling did not happen between the childhood friends described in "A Woman Dead in her Forties," as the regret expressed by the surviving friend recounts.

Refusing to be a victim, escaping the past, having the courage to try to survive, these themes continue in the volume's final poems. As the last poem, "Transcendental Etude," dedicated to Michelle Cliff – with whom Rich began sharing her life in 1976 – puts it:

> No one who survives to speak
> new language, has avoided this:
> the cutting-away of an old force that held her
> rooted to an old ground

And no one has avoided what follows – isolation, self doubt and fear. The common language that these poems seek is an attempt to mitigate that isolation, to open up feminist choices for love, action, and community, and for the poetry that describes and records it.

## Bibliography

Adrienne Rich, *The Dream of a Common Language: Poems 1974–1977* (New York, 1978).
—— *On Lies, Secrets, and Silence: Selected Prose, 1966–1978* (New York, 1979).

Joanne Feit Diehl, "'Cartographies of Silence': Rich's *Common Language* and the Woman Poet," in Jane Roberta Cooper, ed., *Reading Adrienne Rich: Reviews and Revisions, 1951–81* (Ann Arbor, 1984).
Alice Templeton, *The Dream and the Dialogue: Adrienne Rich's Feminist Poetics* (Knoxville, TN, 1994).

# Carolyn Forché, *The Country Between Us*

## New York: Harper & Row, 1981

*The Country Between Us* was Carolyn Forché's second book, following her *Gathering the Tribes* published in the Yale Younger Poets series in 1976. The earlier book is composed of personal, often sensual, lyrics, but the second marked a political direction in Forché's poetry that has characterized all of her work since. The book, which was awarded the Lamont Poetry Prize of the Academy of American Poets, is divided into three parts: "In Salvador, 1978–80," "Reunion," and "Ourselves or Nothing" – the third section consisting of a single poem. The book renewed some of the debates about political poetry, and about whether a poet's reporting such events as Forché's poetry describes depends too much upon the melodrama of the narratives themselves, using horrific events in merely voyeuristic ways. For Forché, however, all language is politically charged, and to argue otherwise is an evasion.

The poems in the first section, centering upon the poet's extended visits to El Salvador between January 1978 and March 1980, have received the most comment. Forché became particularly interested in the civil war in El Salvador through her friendship with Nicaraguan poet Claribel Alegría (whose poetry Forché translated in *Flowers from the Volcano* in 1982). The poems in this first section describe a number of Forché's experiences during her visits – which included undertaking work for Amnesty International. Her aim is to bring to the fore in these poems the violence and torture being committed in the country, and the consequences of the United States' role in the continuing turmoil. The section is dedicated to the "memory of Monsignor Oscar Romero," the archbishop who was murdered by a right-wing death squad while conducting mass at a hospital for the terminally ill on March 24, 1980. Forché's 1981 prose essay, "El Salvador: An Aide Memoire," explains a number of the references in the poems.

An early poem in the sequence, "The Island," is an account of a dialogue with Claribel Alegría, and makes clear the importance, but difficulty, of achieving the strength that community can bring. "Carolina," the voice of Alegría asks in the poem's two final lines, "do you know how long it takes / any one voice to reach another?" This need for community points up the ambiguity of the volume's title, that "between" can refer to that which separates as well as that which is shared. The short poem "The Visitor" captures the hope and despair of a man in one of El Salvador's notorious prisons. In "The Colonel" the highly placed officer who gives the poem its title lives in what amounts to a defended fortress. Broken glass is embedded in the walls, and the windows are grated "like those in liquor stores." Within the ordinariness of family life inside the house – the television on, the pet dogs, a daughter filing her nails – there is a reminder of violence, "a pistol on the / cushion" beside the dog. The poem builds up from further images of order – dinner, a gold bell for calling the maid, "good wine," and conversation on politics – to a moment when the colonel suddenly gets up from the meal to return with a bag, spilling "many human ears on the table." Both his action and the bravado of his accompanying vulgar comments are a challenge to the poet and those from the United States who would criticize the methods of those holding power. The hope of the poem is that listening readers will bring justice to the ears that the colonel sweeps from the table. Some of the severed ears are imagined as hearing the colonel's voice, while others have their ears to the ground as if listening for the first sounds of those coming to provide such justice.

"Return" is another poem built around a dialogue, this time with the poem's dedicatee, Josephine Crum, a long-time resident in Latin America. While the poet examines her own responses now upon returning to the US after what she has seen and experienced, and her sense of powerlessness against the forces dictating events, Crum comments on the relative superficiality of the poet's experience, an experience, she points out, seen from the perspective of a visitor and not of one who has lived with and seen the horrors for years. "You have not returned to your country," the friend accuses, "but to a life you never left."

The final poem in this first sequence is dedicated to José Rudolfo Viera, a government minister who was assassinated when he tried to expose the corrupt diversion of aid funds designated for agrarian reform. He was killed alongside two American consultants on agrarian reform, and the title, "Because One is Always Forgotten," refers to some of the news reports in the US mentioning only the consultants and not Viera. It is a central purpose of the poetry in this section, and Forché's subsequent work, not to allow such events or figures to be forgotten.

Displacement and disruption of lives, against a broader historical backdrop of pogroms, communist oppression in eastern Europe, and the American involvement in Vietnam form the subjects of the central section of the book. A figure who appears in a number of poems, and had appeared earlier in *Gathering the Tribes* (in "Burning the Tomato Worms") is Forché's paternal grandmother, Anna Bassar Sidlosky. She escaped from her Slovak village in the Second World War and came to the United States knowing little English. Her accounts of her earlier life, and comments upon her adopted country, offer a perspective upon Forché's own narrative voice and upon contemporary events in a number of poems.

Forché's first husband was a veteran of the Vietnam War, and two poems, "Joseph" (a line from which provides the volume's title) and "Selective Service," describe lives ruined by the experience of the war. A "bundle of army letters / . . . sent from Southeast Asia" are among the catalog of items that make up a "Photograph of My Room," along with – amongst other things – a quilt that once belonged to Anna, stitches now coming loose since her death. Soldiers going to the "Far East" are among the many passing lovers of Victoria in "As Children Together," a poem about a childhood friend of the poet's, and a reminder of her working-class background (Forché was the first of her family to attend college). This poem calls for an end to the separation between the former friends brought about by time and distance, asking "If you read this poem, write to me."

The final poem, "Ourselves or Nothing," is dedicated to Holocaust historian Terrence Des Pres. The poem's theme is "the mass graves of the century's dead," and the poem lists many of the names of places by which the horrors and exterminations have become part of the century's history. Included is the story of Russian poet Anna Akhmatova asserting "*I can*" when asked if she can describe Soviet prison conditions, as she then did in her "Requiem." Forché is also determined to find the necessary words for what she has witnessed, and the poem and book end with the recognition that Americans live with "a cyclone fence between / ourselves and the slaughter," hovering behind it in a "protected world." But this is a poetry that demands taking notice of what is beyond that fence, and of choosing, "ourselves or nothing" – where to choose "ourselves" is to become an engaged part of the country and countries beyond that protective fence.

## Bibliography

Carolyn Forché, *The Country Between Us* (New York, 1981).

Imogen Forster, "Constructing Central America," *Red Letters: A Journal of Cultural Politics*, 16 (1984), 48–55.

Michael Greer, "Politicizing the Modern: Carolyn Forché in El Salvador and America," *Centennial Review*, 30 (1986), 160–80.

Paul Rea, "The Poet as Witness: Carolyn Forché's Powerful Pleas from El Salvador," *Confluencia*, 2 (1987), 93–9.

# James Merrill, *The Changing Light at Sandover*

## New York: Atheneum, 1982

With *The Changing Light at Sandover* James Merrill found his own way to write an epic sacred poem in the second half of the twentieth century. The poem describes a world in which DNA, atoms, the history and future of mankind, nature, the angels, and God all find a place – and vital to the design is the role of culture, and particularly poetry. In an impressive variety of poetic forms and styles, and with considerable verbal wit, the narrative of the poem describes the experiences over 20 years that Merrill and his male partner David Jackson had with a Ouija board, and is organized, on one level, around Dante's triad of Hell, Purgatory, and Paradise, and on another around the structure of the board itself, its letters, numbers, and its YES, NO, and ampersand. The voices from the spirit world are transcribed in small upper-case letters, while the rest of the poem involves scene-setting, and commentary, questions and discussion by the two mortals. The details of Merrill's cosmology have been variously identified as borrowed from Plato, Dante, and Tolkien, but the impressive part of the achievement is its wide-reaching synthesis. Through the three books of the poem, and the coda, emerges a vision of man's fate both predetermined and dependent upon his actions, and a poem both the poet's own and one for which – whether from his subconscious or from the worlds claimed by the spirit characters – he is a vehicle of transmission. In fact the poem raises questions generally of what constitutes individual identity and what the relationship of the individual is to a creative work (*The Waste Land* and the *Odyssey*, Merrill and Jackson are told, were dictated by the spirit world). These are central questions of this extraordinary poem – raised by the ideas of reincarnation, the presence of spiritual guides and patrons, the actions of dark and white angels, the multiple transformations, and the importance of love, friendship, and self-knowledge that are at the center of the poem's record of Merrill and Jackson's sessions.

Merrill's volume *Divine Comedies* (1976) – which was awarded the Pulitzer Prize – contains a number of autobiographical poems leading up to the 90-page "Book of Ephraim" that was to be the first book of the trilogy. Ephraim's mortal life was as a Greek Jew in the first century. He was killed by the Roman guard on the orders of Emperor Tiberius for having been the lover of the emperor's nephew, Caligula. Ephraim first contacts Merrill and Jackson (JM and DJ in the poem) in 1955, and over a period of years describes a system of reincarnation containing nine stages, and the roles of patrons and representatives within these cycles. This section of the poem is divided into the letters of the alphabet on the Ouija board. The sessions begin in Merrill's house in Stonington, Connecticut, but over the course of the trilogy follow the couple's travels, particularly to Greece and Italy. Also incorporated into the poem are the deaths that occur within the couple's family and friends, some of whom go on to make appearances, important or minimal, as spirits, and to a lesser extent the poem incorporates more global events too. These larger events are also linked to the knowledge being imparted to JM and DJ: examples include a hurricane, Queen Elizabeth II's Silver Jubilee, and the deaths of two popes. At various times in the poem well-known literary figures from the past appear, such as Yeats, Wallace Stevens, and Vladimir Nabokov.

An important part of the poem's narrative is that knowledge is accumulated, and sometimes corrected, as the poem moves towards its final stages. Ephraim is a lower spirit and not – in that identity – privy to the higher knowledge revealed later. Sometimes the higher powers intervene to regulate what is being imparted. Two important spirits who learn along with JM and DJ are the poet W. H. Auden – who becomes a kind of father and mentor to JM – and Maria Mitsotaki, a friend of the couple's who died in 1974, and who serves as an earth mother figure. Both join many of the sessions and offer commentaries and supply visual details that the mortals cannot see (which allows Merrill to include those details in the poem).

A more reliable, but still limited, medium, is Mirabell of *Mirabell: Books of Number*, the second volume, which appeared in 1978, and won the National Book Award the following year. JM and DJ provide the name, from a character in Congreve's *The Way of the World*, to supplement his number, 741. Number is the governing frame of this section, which contains more transcription, and thus exposition of the book's vision, than the first book.

While Ephraim's focus was on culture, Mirabell's is more on science – thus the "objectivity" of number. In this book JM and DJ learn that God's angels have created two previous civilizations, each of which has ended in catastrophe. The third, mankind, may suffer the same fate. Nature's attempts to help mankind are being thwarted by some of the advances of science. Medical knowledge is leading to overpopulation (and thus some animal souls are having to be circulated, with possibly dangerous results), and mankind's splitting of the atom is coming too close to usurping Nature's own power. An important purpose of the lessons that form the third book, they are told, will be to allow the poem to sound a warning from the angels. JM and DJ also learn that there are five periodically reincarnated souls who figure importantly in Western history in various guises (for example Plato and Einstein) to try to keep mankind from self-destruction.

Mirabell promises to introduce the poet to the angels, and Michael appears at the end of this second book to foreshadow the central role that he, Emmanuel, Raphael, and Gabriel will play in this third book. Of the four, Gabriel is most inclined to give up on mankind's potential for reform. In the third book, *Scripts for the Pageant* (1980), JM and DJ, with the help of Auden and Maria, argue for mankind to be allowed a chance to progress, pointing out that creativity, determination, and will are qualities to admire, as well as being qualities which have led to the serious problems that humankind has caused.

Three important new characters help the mortals in this book, two of them recently deceased – the scientist George Cotzias (who joins Auden, Maria, JM, and DJ in the sessions) and the musician Robert Morse, both friends of JM's (Morse appears in the second book while still alive as a reader of the poem-in-progress). They are joined by a unicorn spirit from one of the two previous earthly civilizations, Unice. This third book is the poem's *Paradiso*, and throughout the imagery is suffused with light as part of its emphasis upon the visionary. The balance upon which mankind's fate depends is represented by the book's being organized around the Ouija board's three stations YES, &, NO. The central encounters are presented as dramas, the "pageants" of the title.

The poem's coda, titled "The Higher Keys," appeared when the three books were collected under the title *The Changing Light at Sandover*. In this section mankind appears to have some hope of avoiding the fate of the previous two civilizations. Robert Morse is reborn and given the gift of the five senses through visits from the various angels – the process is watched in its various stages by the mortals. Maria, who has been reincarnated in India, is a childhood prodigy, and holds the promise of being a future guide for mankind. Maria turns out to have been in part the manifestation of Nature, while Ephraim is discovered to have been the vehicle through whom the angel Michael spoke to JM and DJ. The poem's conclusion returns upon itself, and to Merrill's own childhood. Twenty-six assembled spirits and angels gather to hear the poem that Merrill has fashioned from the 20 years of transcriptions. The audience comprises figures upon whom – like the hope of the poem itself – rests the progress of civilization, and thus the constructive rather than destructive future of mankind. The setting turns into the ballroom at Sandover, a reminder of the poet's childhood, and thus of his parents' divorce and the broken home that had been a recurring theme in his earlier poems. As the poet begins to read to the audience, the last word of the poem is also its first – "Admittedly."

## Bibliography

James Merrill, *The Changing Light at Sandover* (New York, 1992).

Alison Lurie, *Familiar Spirits: A Memoir of James Merrill and David Jackson* (New York, 2001).
Timothy Materer, *James Merrill's Apocalypse* (Ithaca, NY, 2000).
Robert Polito, *A Reader's Guide to James Merrill's The Changing Light at Sandover* (Ann Arbor, 1994).

# Rita Dove, *Thomas and Beulah*

## Pittsburgh: Carnegie–Mellon University Press, 1986

Dove's sequence of poems based upon the lives of her maternal grandparents won her the Pulitzer Prize for Poetry in 1987, and was only her third book. In direct but evocative concrete detail, the poems tell the story of the courage amidst the hardship and racial injustice of two of the many blacks among those who traveled from the south to the industrial north for work in the early and mid-century, in this case to the tire city of Akron, Ohio. Dove has said that one concern was to show the complexity of the inner lives of the poor. In the final pages of the book a chronology sets out the main events of the lives of Thomas and Beulah alongside a chronology of the major public events of the time – events as localized as an airship accident at the Goodyear tire factory, and as national as the 1963 Civil Rights march on Washington. The Civil Rights movement promised to radically change the opportunities for Beulah's children and grandchildren, but it leaves the by then widowed Beulah feeling that such changes have little to do with her sense of her self, a self composed of her memories and those of her dead husband – memories that, as passed on to the poet's mother, make for the foundation narrative, and the telling detail of the individual poems.

*Thomas and Beulah* is divided into two sections, devoted respectively to the point of view of the husband and the wife. The book is dedicated to Dove's mother, Elvira Elizabeth. The dedication page details the structure of the book: "These poems tell two sides of a story and are meant to be read in sequence." The first section, "Mandolin," tells the story of Thomas, from his journey with best friend Lem up the Mississippi river to look for work in the north, to Thomas's death from a stroke. The first poem, "The Event," recounts Lem's death by drowning on the riverboat trip north, when Thomas dares him to swim across to an island in the river to gather chestnuts. The two were childhood friends, as later poems that recount Thomas's memories of his earlier life make clear, and throughout "Mandolin" he is haunted by the guilt of his role in his friend's death. The two were song-and-dance men on the riverboats, and the mandolin that titles the first part of the sequence follows Thomas like the guilt, a recurring motif in a number of the poems. Dove has said that this story of Lem's death, never told to her by her grandfather, was the starting point of the book – as she tried to understand how her grandfather could live with such guilt, and what the relationship could be between the young man traveling the riverboats and the older, kindly figure she came to know in her childhood.

Thomas arrived in Akron, the chronology tells us, in 1921. A number of poems describe his continuing pain, his determination, and poverty – in one poem, "Straw Hat," sharing a bed in shifts with two other men – and his vague romantic hopes. "Courtship" pictures his wooing of an initially distant Beulah, as he gives her his yellow scarf (her perspective appears later in "Courtship, Diligence") and a gnat flies into his eye and she thinks he is crying and is thus softened towards him. Such are the small chance events that change lives, Dove has said. In many poems in the book, the individual voices play an important role in the narrative and characterizations. Even though the speech is often in stock phrases, the phrases are spoken with passion and given an individuality by the context supplied in the poem: *"Fine evening may I have / the pleasure . . ."* is how "Courtship" begins. Other poems give glimpses of Beulah's voice (*"Nothing nastier than a white person!"* thinks a frustrated Beulah in "The Great Palaces of Versailles"), and other voices include Lem's, those of the later grandchildren, and even Death's. Sometimes the voices are more general – songs and rhymes remembered from childhood that punctuate the experience of the present. Recurring habits play a similar role in piecing together the picture of shared lives – Thomas's love of fishing, and a routine of moviegoing being two examples.

Later poems in "Mandolin" record the milestones of a marriage, tinged with the ever-present memories of Lem's death, one reminder being the musical instrument hanging on the wall; the birth of a child, purchasing a car, the impact of the Depression. The 1929 disaster of the airship *Akron* is a backdrop to poems from both parts of the sequence, Thomas's and Beulah's. Later in the marriage Beulah's canary comes to signify a distance Thomas feels from her emotionally, and the bird provides the title of her own sequence. With the coming of war employment in the aircraft industry is plentiful, one of the couple's daughters marries a soldier, and – in an event that then figures in a later poem – Thomas purchases in a "basement rummage sale" 24 volumes of a 25-volume *Werner's Encyclopedia*. Entries missing because the missing volume is the last one are characteristic of the historical gaps that a sequence like *Thomas and Beulah* seeks to fill: "no zebras" (one of nature's harmonious patterns of parallel black and white), "no Virginia," with its central role in slavery, and "no wars." In "Roast Possum" Thomas describes trapping and eating the animal to his enthralled grandchildren, but at one point:

> He could have gone on to tell them
> that the Werner admitted Negro children
> to be intelligent, though briskness
> clouded over at puberty, bringing
> indirection and laziness.

Instead he continues his story.

In the first of the final three poems of "Mandolin" Thomas has his first stroke (with "Lem's knuckles tapping his chest in passing"). Then, forced to be less active and thrown back further on memory he recalls his cleaning job during the Depression. Thomas's final stroke, while driving his car to fill a prescription, is imagined in telling detail, but is simultaneously his actual death "at the wheel," and, with the rain outside, a death that parallels Lem's in the river. "Thomas at the Wheel" begins:

> This, then, the river he had to swim.
> Through the wipers the drugstore
> shouted, lit up like a casino,
> neon script leering from the shuddering asphalt.
>
> Then the glass doors flew apart
> and a man walked out to the curb
> to light a cigarette. Thomas thought
> the sky was emptying itself as fast
> as his chest was filling with water.

"Canary in Bloom" is the title of Beulah's sequence. The 21 poems begin with her childhood, her mother taking in washing and her father coming home drunk and threateningly violent. The second poem, "Magic," establishes a recurring dream of Beulah's that is never realized, to go to Paris, and it gives particular resonance to the later "The Great Palaces of Versailles." In her job in a dress shop ironing alterations, she is forced to stay in the back because of her color, and the ironing process releases the stale odor of "Evening of Paris" perfume from the clothes. As she irons Beulah imagines the finery of the eighteenth-century French royal court. Another later poem, from the time of Thomas's post-stroke convalescence, reveals that "Years ago he had promised to take her to Chicago" – another dream apparently unfulfilled.

Courtship, marriage, memories of earlier romantic hopes fill out earlier poems in her sequence. In the Depression she sometimes helps feed those passing through looking for work, or just trying to survive. The wonder of pregnancy and motherhood, her ballooning body paralleled to the Goodyear airship, are the subject of "Weathering Out" and "Motherhood." But this family life is no more sentimentalized than any other part of the narrative in the book. The canary comes to play a central part in bringing beauty and pleasure into Beulah's life. And in "Daystar" she relishes at night the hour of afternoon quiet she found while her youngest child slept:

> Later
> that night when Thomas rolled over and
> lurched into her, she would open her eyes
> and think of the place that was hers
> for an hour – where
> she was nothing,
> pure nothing, in the middle of the day.

Private dreams and memories increasingly make up the texture of Beulah's life in the poems that follow, although she runs the house, takes care of her ailing husband, and sees her children off on their own lives with little complaint. Invited to an Independence Day picnic in 1964 by her daughters, she thinks of the now dead Thomas, of her own and Thomas's childhoods, and is "scared" when told by daughter Joanna *"Mother, we're Afro-Americans now!"* anxiously wondering "What did she know about Africa?" The previous August she had watched the march on Washington on television with similar fear. In the first of the last two poems she remembers the dead Thomas, and in the final poem – one of the finest in the sequence – Beulah, now bedridden and with glaucoma – hears and sees the transformations of a twirling ballerina on a music box, her world now much more limited, but her imaginative response to experience still richly detailed in the poem.

## Bibliography

Rita Dove, *Thomas and Beulah* (Pittsburgh, 1986).

Charles Berger, "The Granddaughter's Archive: Rita Dove's *Thomas and Beulah*," *Western Humanities Review*, 50–1 (Winter 1996–Spring 1997), 359–63.

Joe Pellegrino, "Moving Through Color: Rita Dove's *Thomas and Beulah*," *Kentucky Philological Review*, 14 (Mar. 1999), 27–31.

Therese Steffen, *Crossing Color: Transcultural Space and Place in Rita Dove's Poetry, Fiction, and Drama* (Oxford, 2001).

# Topics

# Twentieth-Century American Poetry and Other Arts

The interaction of various arts with one another is often difficult to discuss without appearing to make reductive claims of influence or of mutual support. An additional issue concerns terminology, whether a term such as "color" when applied to one art can be usefully applied to another when a comparison or contrast is being discussed. Even if similar terms might cover the signs, codes, and patterning of different arts, claims of similarity may ignore differences that it is crucial to keep to the fore. The different arts move in conjunction with the cultural, economic, political, and other major influences of their time, some possibly taking different directions than others for reasons connected to fashion, major creative figures, or technological shifts. Nevertheless, fruitful relationships can be charted between the arts, sometimes supported explicitly by the statements and careers of particular artists, sometimes by direct quotation within a piece of writing or work of art. In the case of American poetry, its history in the twentieth century is arguably intimately tied at various periods to other arts, particularly the avant-garde visual arts. Some poets, in their attempts to move away from various kinds of conventions, saw in other arts some similar aims that might provide fruitful parallels.

Ezra Pound noted in his manifestos in London between 1912 and 1914 that poetry was behind the novel, painting, and music, in finding a contemporary form for the new century. There were some exceptions to Pound's claim, but they indicated what modern poetry could gain from looking at developments in other arts. As far as the novel was concerned, the directness of prose had already had an impact upon the poetry of Stephen Crane, while the psychological explorations of novelists such as Henry James and Edith Wharton showed poets Edwin Arlington Robinson and Robert Frost some ways in which to enrich narrative poetry with psychological depth, to move landscape beyond the merely decorative, and to use the power of understatement.

At the time that Pound wrote, the visual arts were beginning to have an impact upon American poetry in New York. Around the photography and patronage of Alfred Stieglitz developed a group of photographers determined to take photography out into the streets and away from the set pieces and foggy negatives of late Victorian work. The photographers also took pictures that emphasized the qualities that made up the composition of a photograph – light, shape, texture, and pattern. Such work, and that of the painters, invited poetry to similarly foreground its own expressive materials – language and space – an invitation taken up most radically in the work of Gertrude Stein, whose Paris apartment was famous for its collection of modern painting.

Stieglitz's journals *Camera Work* and *291* were forerunners of a number of journals that appeared around the years of the First World War and which emphasized the mix of the arts, with reproductions of paintings, photographs, and drawings alongside essays, stories, and poems. Sometimes photographs of machines were included in the mix, as in *The Soil*, which included in its pages photographs of steam engines, suggesting that such engineering feats, like the poems and prose it published, were all modern products of American skill and imagination. Alfred Kreymborg (1883–1966), little remembered for his poetry now, was an important bridge between the arts in New York. He knew many visual artists, started a journal promoting modern music, and was the contact for Ezra Pound to send over a sheaf of imagist poems from London for publication. Kreymborg's impressionistic autobiography, *Troubadour* (1925), is a valuable record of the iconoclastic atmosphere and creative ferment of the time. An even more varied mix of genres appeared in the pages of *The Dial* in the 1920s. Along with its modernist poetry and prose it published reproductions of modern art, and reviews of boxing matches and vaudeville shows. Articles in *The Dial* praised the quality of the writing in advertisements, pointing out that their directness and economy displayed virtues lacking in much conventional literature. Advertisements were better models for modernist writers, the argument ran, than the products of most contemporary American authors.

When Pound complained that poetry was behind the other arts in modernizing itself, that it was still too often seen as a "pastime" through which an amateur might pleasantly express his or her feelings, he was fighting a battle Henry James had had to wage for the novel at the end of the previous century. Pound cited the novels of James as an example for modern poets, along with the painting of Kandinsky, and the music of Claude Debussy. He published a study of the sculpture of his friend Henri Gaudier-Brzeska after Brzeska was killed in the trenches of France in 1915. Pound praised the sculptor's hard-edged surfaces and multiple planes, and many commentators have noticed the parallels to the multiple planes of *The Cantos*.

This influential pictorial dimension in Pound's work was reinforced by his study of classical Chinese poetic forms, Chinese ideograms, for Pound, representing a language more directly visual than the abstract signs of Western language. Radical painters and poets came together in London for the short-lived but energetic vorticist publication *Blast* (1914–15), which Pound, again at the center of things, saw as a way to give the image energy and movement. Pound was also interested in music, wrote music criticism, and explored research into early musical instruments.

One of the experimental forms to come out of the modernist visual arts that had a major impact upon the long poem was collage. Collage often formed its patterns from "found objects" juxtaposed by the artist to suggest multi-directional relationships. The collage form found sophisticated expression in the poetry of Marianne Moore, whose poetry incorporated quotations from classical writers, business documents, textbooks, and many other sources. Collage was also one of the influences behind William Carlos Williams's *Paterson* (1946–58). The five books of Williams's long poem contain poetry interspersed with prose material that Williams took from newspapers, letters, histories, economic tracts, and the creative prose of other writers. Charles Olson also used a collage-like structure for his *Maximus* poem in the 1950s, and there are many other examples.

The art of display is a more tangential branch of the visual arts, but a number of recent studies have argued for the role of museum display as a source for modernist poems and the organization of modernist texts. Moore, again, is a central example. Her notebooks and letters reveal the hours she spent in New York's Museum of Natural History carefully studying the dioramas in which animals and birds are displayed in reproductions of their natural surroundings. The typography and layout of a poem upon the page is the subject of a number of recent studies that argue that the visual dimension of the presentation is an important part of the language of the poem.

Although both Pound and Kreymborg recognized that innovations in music provided possible models, if only in radical spirit, for the direction of modern verse, Langston Hughes, a central figure of the Harlem Renaissance, integrated musical form much more fully into his poetry. Hughes incorporated forms from the legacy of black music. His adaptation of the blues form, for example, supplied an innovative lyric form, diction, and rhythm, an emotional tone, and a narrative – the temporary relief of suffering through self-expression and communal experience. Sometimes such a poem was itself about hearing the blues performed, as in the well-known "The Weary Blues." In this poem both musician and listener derive a degree of comfort from the performance. Hughes similarly adapted jazz rhythms in his poetry, and sometimes he published a musical score alongside the words of the poem.

In contrast to poems that had a visual dimension on the page, these were poems to hear, and to see performed. Hughes's late long poem, *Montage of a Dream Deferred* (1951), seeks the variety, the author wrote in a prefatory note, of be-bop jazz. Hughes himself was in high demand as a performer of his own work, as a few years later was Allen Ginsberg, another poet who sometimes published music along with his poems. In both cases the music contributed not only to the breaking of conventional rhythms, but also to the change in consciousness that the poems sought to achieve, music being recruited for its power to affect mood in a way more direct than through language alone. More recently, Amiri Baraka has written on jazz and performed his poetry with jazz musicians, and Yusef Komunyakaa has published two books on the relationship of jazz to poetry. In the case of the black writers, jazz is one part of a heritage that their poetry seeks to articulate, but jazz techniques also feature in the work of some white poets, who value its characteristics of spontaneity, improvisation, and innovation, as well as its status as an original American form. On the other hand, when ragtime appears in T. S. Eliot's *The Waste Land*, it is to suggest decadence, superficial values, and another instance in the poem of the merely mechanical.

Among poets who wrote opera librettos with varying degrees of public success were William Carlos Williams and W. H. Auden. Louis Zukofsky included a Handel musical score in the 240-page masque that forms one section of his book-length poem *"A"*, and in his work as a whole Zukofsky was very interested in musical analogues to poetic forms. T. S. Eliot's *Four Quartets* is also constructed around verbal and structural parallels to musical leitmotifs. Allen Ginsberg usually accompanied his readings with music from various instruments, and in 1968 Anne Sexton formed a rock group, Anne Sexton and Her Kind, to accompany her poetry readings.

Cinema is treated as merely mechanical in Ezra Pound's *Hugh Selwyn Mauberley*, as part of the culture's taste for mass-produced and shoddily manufactured artifacts. William Carlos Williams refers to film similarly in his 1920s work, but by the 1940s he was an admirer of Russian pioneer director Sergei Eisenstein, and by the 1950s was interested in cinema's ability to break temporal sequence into a series of momentary images. For Hart Crane, the films of Charlie Chaplin combined technology and creativity in a way that he celebrated in "Chaplinesque." This short poem was a forerunner to *The Bridge*, his celebration of similar qualities in the architecture of Brooklyn Bridge a few years later. H.D. wrote poems and film criticism for the British avant-garde film journal *Close-Up*, and appeared in the early Paul Robeson film *Borderline* (1930) as Helga Doorn. *Borderline* is an experimental film, and is an instance of H.D.'s connections with the Harlem Renaissance.

Mainstream Hollywood cinema comes in for scorn in Gwendolyn Brooks's more recent poem "To Those of My Sisters Who Kept Their Naturals," which praises black women not driven to copy the look of white movie stars. Black Mountain College poet Ed Dorn borrows another cinema stereotype, from the Western, for his long poem *Gunslinger* (1968–72). The rise of performance poetry has resulted in some performances being an important part of a film, one of the most controversial examples being Marion Rigg's *Tongues Untied* (1994), featuring performances from the gay black poets Assotto Saint (1957– ) and Essex Hemphill (1957–95).

While some of the modernists denigrated the reproducible and mass-market qualities of cinema, live performance arts were treated with more respect. The iconoclasm of vaudeville humor was welcomed by reviewers in *The Dial*, who delighted in the Marx Brothers' performances on Broadway. The innovative choreography and dancing of Diaghilev's Ballets Russes was praised in *The Dial* and elsewhere, and even formed the subject of some poems, its anti-lyrical patterning offering a parallel to the jagged lines and shifting rhythms of modernist verse. A number of the New York modernist poets, including Stevens, Williams, and Kreymborg, wrote plays that eschewed conventional characterization, narrative, and themes. There were poets associated with the Provincetown Players, home of the early experimental dramas of Eugene O'Neill. Williams went on to write a number of plays, and in the 1950s had an off-Broadway hit with his *Many Loves*. Most famously, T. S. Eliot, following *Four Quartets*, devoted much of his energies to writing verse dramas for the London stage, seeking to bring, initially to historical, and then to contemporary scenes the force of Elizabethan drama, with its combination of foregrounded rhetoric, ritualistic staging, and characters acting within a larger cosmos that bears down upon and shapes their lives. The success of Amiri Baraka's play *Dutchman* (1964) brought national attention to his poetry. Baraka's move to Harlem shortly after the play was produced, and his work in the Black Arts movement, where he continued to produce drama as well as poetry, marked his rejection of the kind of white-world seduction represented by the flirtatious but deadly apple-carrying blonde in his play. Robert Lowell also wrote plays in the mid-1960s, and his *Benito Cereno*, based on Herman Melville's short story about slavery, had a successful run in New York. This interest in drama is manifested in some contemporary performance poetry, where in recent years Latino poets have joined African American poets in being particularly drawn to the genre because of its affinities with their vernacular traditions.

The return of the personal lyric to a degree of popularity with some post-Second World War poets made playwriting an attractive alternative for some to what they saw as the problematic genre of the long poem. Drama also offered an opportunity to reach a larger audience than that typically reached by poetry. That there was an audience for drama that accepted heightened language in a semi-realistic setting was demonstrated by the renewed success of the plays of Eugene O'Neill, and the associated style of Tennessee Williams.

The fruitful relationship between painting and American poetry that was firmly established with imagism and the little magazines of the 1910s and 1920s continued through the century. When the European surrealists came to the United States to escape the Nazis and the war, a number of American poets responded to their interest in dreams, myths, and transformations, which the surrealists saw as a way to express the self more directly and imaginatively. The "greenhouse" poetry of Theodore Roethke was one response, and the poetry of Galway Kinnell a little later was another, as was the poetry of such Deep Image poets as James Wright. Williams was interested enough to translate some of the poems of surrealist critic Nicholas Calas in the 1940s, although other poets, such as Wallace Stevens, remained undecided about the movement's usefulness. Photography has also remained an interest of some poets, either supplying subject matter or contributing to the visual context of particular poems or books. To cite two examples: the poems in Thom Gunn's *Positives* (1966) are accompanied on facing pages by photographs by his brother Ander Gunn; Chicano poet Rudolfo Gonzales uses photographs and reproductions of Mexican and Mexican American art to accompany the poems in his *I Am Joaquin/Yo Soy Joaquin: An Epic Poem* (1967).

An indigenous American movement that developed in the late 1940s and 1950s from some of the tenets of surrealism, abstract expressionism, influenced the "New York" poets Frank O'Hara, John Ashbery, Kenneth Koch, and James Schuyler. A particular interest was the way that abstract expressionist painting drew attention to its own materials – the largeness of the canvas, and the dripping paint that made up its patterns. Also of interest to these poets, some of whom worked at *Artnews* and published art criticism, was the way that the paintings emphasized the moment-by-moment passing of time through the linear streams of paint that recorded the application of color; they also responded to the open-endedness of such painting, there being no definitive starting and finishing places for the seeking eye. But what is probably the most admired poem written by these poets, Ashbery's *Self-Portrait in a Convex Mirror* (1975) does not explicitly take abstract expressionism as its starting point, but sixteenth-century Italian mannerist painter Parmigianino's painting of that name. The poem articulates a number of the critical issues surrounding the relationship between poetry and painting, and more broadly between any two related arts. The degree to which such a poem depends upon knowledge of the painting and its background is just one of its questions. The poem is finally concerned with such issues as the coherence of individual identity, the arbitrariness of the measures of time, and the nature – personal, artistic, historical – of the differences and connections between painting and poem, painter and poet.

# Continuities and Nationality in Twentieth-Century American Poetry

A recurring theme in discussion of American literature generally, and including American poetry, has been to ask what common characteristics might mark a text as belonging to a literary tradition or history that could be called "American." This question has particular resonance within a culture that has been a colony, and a literary history in which the power of the former colonizer continued as a major force for many years after independence. Eighteenth-century American poets followed the maxims of neoclassical poetry for some decades after its decline in English poetry, while Romantic poetry also exercised a continuing hold on American poetry, into the twentieth century in some cases. The attraction of the Romantic tradition was its lyrical uplift – which appealed to a strain of American idealism – and its concern with nature to a continent offering untamed scenery wilder and grander than anything in the Lake District. This problem of literary colonialism was compounded by American writers being faced with using the language of the culture that they sought independence from, which has led to sometimes strident claims by various poets that "American" is a different language than "English." As far as many nineteenth-century English writers and critics were concerned, American literature, if such a thing existed, was merely a provincial offshoot of English literature.

The modernist American poets of the 1910s and 1920s mark one of the periodic declarations of independence from English tradition in American literary history, but this time the rebels had the examples of Whitman and Emily Dickinson to draw upon, and the undeniable importance of what had become the world's most powerful industrial economy. Whitman's verse had broken the rules of conventional poetics, was celebratory, inclusive (for its time), and looked to the future. Dickinson's verse offered, in addition to its formal experiments, the complexities of New England religious rhetoric and doubt, heightened passion beneath a surface attempting emotional control, and the appeal of the self-made poet. But alongside the claims for independence being made by some American modernists, Americans Ezra Pound, T. S. Eliot, and H.D., based in London, were writing poetry founded upon their reading of European writers and the classical tradition. They made little mention of the United States, and if they did it was rarely posit-ive. The difference between the two kinds of American modernist echoed a long debate from the nineteenth century about where and when an Amer-ican tradition began. For some nineteenth-century commentators, Shake-speare could be claimed as part of an American literary heritage, since the two countries were not at that time separate.

The poets, critics, and novelists who rejected the international modernism represented by the work of Pound, Eliot, and H.D., writers mainly based in New York, offered definitions of an American tradition that were sometimes carefully argued and sometimes aggressively mystical. The critics included Waldo Frank, Van Wyck Brooks, and Paul Rosenfeld. Conversely Eliot's influential essays argued for a broader view of tradition, as did Pound's, although Pound emphasized the importance of "the new" more than did the conservative Eliot. Pound had found it necessary to reject American literature almost entirely as he formed his earliest style, but in "A Pact" (1913) he acknowledged a poetic and national kinship with Whitman, and the later *Cantos* have a good deal to say about American history and politics. Pound's only prolonged stay in the United States after the 1910s was a forced one, when he was confined to St. Elizabeths Hospital in Washington DC after being arrested for treason following Italy's fall in the Second World War. H.D. and Eliot remained in Europe. Eliot became a British citizen, and has found his place in the canon of British literature, at least in the syllabuses of many English departments, although the work of Pound, H.D., and even Henry James – who also became a British citizen – remains classified as "American" when such distinctions are made.

What these cases of writers who lived abroad foreground is the problem of literary nationality, one that goes beyond the papers of citizenship that a particular writer holds, and involves the tradition in which the writer feels that he or she is writing – or the tradition in which the judgment of history categorizes the particular writer. For some critics Eliot's "Americanness" is demonstrated by his work's innovation, its search for physical and spiritual roots, and a moral earnestness associated with sexual disgust. Spiritual autobiography, one category in which Eliot's work could be placed, was an established genre in seventeenth-century New England. Eliot's concern with tradition, some would say, is a response to a cultural inheritance that emphasizes its differences from the past, a culture notorious for having little sense of history, even of its own.

Such issues of nationality and tradition are complicated by the case of W. H. Auden, who came to the United States in 1939 and became a citizen a few years later, but whose urbane poetry arguably remained largely unchanged by the move. Attempts to characterize "the American Auden" mainly come down to historical accounts of his sojourn in the United States, and he seems to have been motivated to cross the Atlantic by a wish to create some distance between himself and the pressures of a political generation – or at any rate to enjoy the freedom of being an outsider. Denise Levertov, from a subsequent generation, consciously changed her poetry from that in her first book, published in her native London, becoming interested particularly in the Black Mountain College poets. From the 1960s she became increasingly disaffected with mainstream American politics and values, and used her position as outsider to protest the direction of her adopted country (she became a citizen in 1955) as well as that of Britain. A poet represented in almost all anthologies of twentieth-century American poetry, and relatively little known in Britain, at the end of her life Levertov was working within a literary and Christian tradition as European as Auden's, but alongside a strong interest in Native American poetry that for her represented the particular American tradition and America with which she wished to be associated. The poetry of Thom Gunn (b. 1929) similarly defies national category. Rejecting, like Levertov, the English neo-Romantic movement, but also the modernist revolution of Eliot and Pound, Gunn has lived since the mid-1950s on the west coast of the United States writing poems in both metered and free-verse forms.

Poets whose subject matter is regional would appear to be easiest to categorize as "American," but in the case of the major regionalist of twentieth-century American poetry, Robert Frost, his poetry is more usefully seen alongside the Georgian poets writing in London in the years just before the First World War. Hart Crane's definitively American subject of Brooklyn Bridge and American history in "The Bridge" is the center of a poem that comes in many ways out of the English visionary tradition as much as anything American. Robert Lowell's early affinities with the Southern Fugitives and New Critical norms root his verse in an Anglo-American movement, one he never quite forsook.

Much of Elizabeth Bishop's poetry was written abroad, although one could argue that its rootlessness and sense of the contingency of "home" is itself an American quality with some affinities to the cause of Eliot and Pound's consuming interest in tradition and history. Wallace Stevens's retention of many formal qualities of lyric verse, and his interest in a modernist examination of Romantic issues, can allow a critic like Harold Bloom to relate his poetry to Wordsworth as much as to Emerson. The issue of "which tradition" was actively debated among the Harlem Renaissance poets, with Claude McKay and Countee Cullen seeing themselves as poets first, writing in a tradition with roots in English verse, who happened to be black men writing on racial subjects (a split that had developed as far back as nineteenth-century anthologies of Negro poetry). Marianne Moore's innovative poetry of quiet Christianity appealed to formalist Auden, and Eliot in his London editorial office – although neither knew quite what to make of Williams.

Such diversity and diverse origins would appear to bear out W. H. Auden's comment, writing in mid-century on "American Poetry," that "the first thing that strikes a reader about the best American poets is how utterly unlike each other they are." But in this essay, reprinted in his collection *The Dyer's Hand*, Auden nevertheless attempts to discover some common characteristics, offering via a concluding quotation from de Tocqueville that American poetry is quintessentially "modern" in its concern with "the destinies of mankind, man himself taken aloof from his country and his age." Two influential studies from the 1960s sought to discuss possible continuities within four centuries of American poetry. In the first of them, Roy Harvey Pearce's *The Continuity of American Poetry* (1961), Pearce echoed the view that American poetry was concerned with "the dignity of man," but found its major continuities to be a refusal to accept the status quo, and at the same time "the reconciliation of the impulse to freedom with the impulse to community." Hyatt Waggoner's *American Poets: From the Puritans to the Present* (1968) claimed to eschew the "thesis" method of Pearce, but argued for the centrality of Emerson to throwing "more light on the question of what's *American* about American poetry than any other approach could have." Other critics have also argued this position for Emerson. Other frameworks that have been suggested are discrete periods, for example Bernard Duffey's Age of Bryant, Age of Whitman, and Age of Pound, in his *Poetry in America* (1978), and Mutlu Konuk Blasing's four distinct lines stemming from Emerson, Poe, Whitman, and Dickinson, in *American Poetry: The Rhetoric of its Forms* (1987).

Pearce gives little attention to African American poetry in his study, and Waggoner gives none, and this points up the issue that attempts at defining "Americanness" run the risk of being reductive as well as of assuming closed systems, the borders of which are too readily defined by the author's thesis. From one perspective, much American poetry since the 1960s can be seen as an argument demanding to be included in what it is to be "American," whether the demand is from poets whose perspective is largely political, racial, ethnic, or gender-based. The polarities against which American poetry defined itself in the last decades of the century are no longer England – or even Europe – and a new continent. They are instead any one, or a mix, of an array of cultures – both internal and those that are the result of broader, especially Latin American and Asian, immigration – that define themselves against a mainstream culture, and make a claim to be part of the nation. For such poets the definition of the nation should include the multiplicity of such voices, and respect for the multiple continuities that are part of their heritage.

Discussions of continuity are further complicated by a number of other issues. One concerns the shift from modernism to post-modernism, usually dated around 1950, and the degree to which there is any major change in the poetry beyond that of emphasis. Attempts to define the qualities of post-modernism are met with claims by others that these are merely different terms for the principles of modernism. Another complication comes from variations of the "anxiety of influence" argument most associated with critic Harold Bloom. One version of this argument, offered by James Breslin in his *From Modern to Contemporary: American Poetry 1945–1965*, argues that there is in effect a missing generation in American poetry following the modernist writers. The argument runs that, because the major modernist figures Pound, Eliot, Williams, Stevens, Moore, H.D., and Hughes continued to produce major work into the 1950s, American poets of the 1930s and 1940s were faced with either returning to the tired traditions that had preceded modernism or accepting the modernist revolution and competing with the established masters of that mode. The consequence is a series of false starts and truncated careers in poets such as Hart Crane, Delmore Schwartz, Louis Zukofsky, and Charles Olson, with Robert Lowell saving himself from a similar fate with the breakthrough of *Life Studies* in 1959, which includes tributes to Crane and Schwartz as part of its record of loss. Whatever degree of assent one wants to give to such a view, it provides a context for such issues as Crane's determination to answer *The Waste Land*, and Olson's ambivalent attitude to Pound and Williams. Olson thought Pound's *Cantos* too ego-centered, and Williams's *Paterson* too sentimental. Yet Olson's *Maximus* poems are indebted on almost every page to the two earlier long poems.

An important set of voices to emerge that do not come from recent generations of immigration are those of Native American poets, voices previously written out of histories of American poetry as effectively as the Native Americans themselves were driven from their own lands. In writing down and printing their poetry, and in writing in English, Native American poets are already separating themselves from the past oral, communal, and performance traditions associated with parallel forms in Native American history. This act of adopting an alien form of expression is itself the subject of some poems, and more generally the relationship of the present to a lost or threatened past is a frequent theme. That sense of loss can be through a silenced or diminished voice (the poetry of Joy Harjo and Wendy Rose), a divided self (Louise Erdrich) or through changes in the landscape that threaten to obliterate the mythical associations and presences associated with place (Ray Young Bear). The act of writing is often associated with an act of recovery, or a way to keep alive stories connected with individual or communal identity. The emergence of voices such as those mentioned above, and of such poets as Leslie Marmon Silko and Simon Ortiz, offer further challenges to the traditional attempts to define an American canon. They broaden our concepts about what is "American" in important ways, and challenge the received history of that term. They also challenge readers and academies to find a way to incorporate their work into anthologies and course syllabuses, to move beyond merely reading such work as exotic, or allowing interest in it to be at the whim of passing fashion.

# American Poetry and a Century of Wars

Many essays on twentieth-century poetry and war are likely not to mention any examples of American poetry. Nevertheless, American poets have fought in and responded to many of the major conflicts of the century, and a case can be made that war, and the subject of war poetry, has been a significant concern for a number of American poets.

The United States entered the First World War late, in 1917, and did not have such poets as Wilfred Owen, Siegfried Sassoon, and Isaac Rosenberg on the front lines sending back to a naively patriotic public reports of the actual horrors of the war. The English war poets came out of the Georgian tradition, and its Romantic praise for the beauties of nature was capable of powerful effects when inverted to describe the nightmarish landscape of the trenches. The American poets associated with the First World War are not united by a common style. The foremost were Alan Seeger, John Peale Bishop, Archibald MacLeish, and E. E. Cummings, while writing in New York, Wallace Stevens responded to the war in his poem "Lettres d'Un Soldat." Seeger was the only one of these figures killed in the war, and nothing that these poets produced on the conflict equaled the achievement in prose of Hemingway's *A Farewell to Arms* or Cummings's *The Enormous Room*.

Ezra Pound, H.D., and T. S. Eliot, writing in London, present a different case. Pound saw a number of the artists that he regarded as essential to the modern movement going off to fight, some of them subsequently to be killed. The greatest loss, for Pound, was the sculptor Henri Gaudier-Brzeska, killed in France in 1915. Some of Pound's Chinese translations in his *Cathay* (1915) concern war themes and echo contemporary events, but sections IV and V of his *Hugh Selwyn Mauberley* contain his most overt denunciation of a war that he regarded as evidence of a degenerate culture – on both sides. For the modernists generally the war was not what it was for the English war poets, a terrible aberration that needed to be stopped; it was instead one further stage in a culture's broader cycle of self-destruction. H.D.'s "Fragment Sixty-Eight," about a loved one leaving for the war, evokes a larger context though its allusion to Sappho. The most famous poem of the modernist movement, *The Waste Land*, also puts its post-war landscape and contemporary allusions into a larger context of history and tradition. The degree to which these poems of Pound, H.D., and Eliot can be considered "war poetry" depends finally on the definitions applied, but they are among the most powerful responses to the war produced in the language.

As far as the Spanish Civil War (1936–9) is concerned, W. H. Auden wrote in support of the Republican cause in the early years of the war, before his move to the United States in 1939 and the famous declaration in his poem "In Memory of W. B. Yeats" that "poetry makes nothing happen." *And Spain Sings* (1937), edited by Rolfe Humphries, was a significant book of translations of Spanish poets intended to raise funds for the Republican cause and including translations by Elizabeth Bishop, Muriel Rukeyser, and William Carlos Williams. But the most prominent literary work to come out of the war by an American was a prose work, Ernest Hemingway's *For Whom the Bell Tolls*.

In the case of the Second World War, a conflict in which 400,000 Americans died, most of the poetry associated with the war is formalist in structure, reflecting the New Critical dicta of the time, the prominence of Auden, and perhaps a felt need to order what would otherwise seem a world of chaos. The style went out of favor to some extent in the decade that followed, but a case has recently been made for a re-examination of the poetry by Harvey Shapiro in his collection *Poets of World War II* (2003) published by the popular Library of America. Shapiro's anthology includes 62 poets, 40 of whom served in the army, navy, air force or merchant marine. For Shapiro, American poems coming out of the war are irreverent about military hierarchy, "often bawdy, bitchy," not glorying in brotherhood or patriotism. Shapiro's purpose, he argues in his introduction, is "to demonstrate that the American poets of this war produced a body of work that has not yet been recognized for its clean and powerful eloquence." Shapiro discovers a mythologizing perspective in many of the poems, alongside the documentary details. The last stanza of Karl Shapiro's "Troop Train" serves as a representative example:

> Trains lead to ships and ships to death or trains,
> And trains to death or trucks, and trucks to death,
> Or trucks lead to the march, the march to death,
> Or that survival which is all our hope;
> And death leads back to trucks and trains and ships,

But life leads to the march, O flag! at last
The place of life found after trains and death –
Nightfall of nations brilliant after war.

The best-known poem to come out of the war is Randall Jarrell's five-line "The Death of the Ball Turret Gunner," although Jarrell himself spent the war in the United States as a training instructor for the air force. Gwendolyn Brooks writes of the ironies of racial segregation in the armed forces in her "Negro Hero" (1945). Robert Lowell's retrospective "Memories of West Street and Lepke" from his 1959 volume *Life Studies* describes his confinement as a conscientious objector in West Street jail, where a fellow inmate was the notorious murderer Louis "Lepke" Buchalter. Lepke was jailed for killing and Lowell for refusing to kill, as Lowell pointed out later.

Ezra Pound's *The Pisan Cantos* (1948) represent the most sustained achievement by an American poet to come out of this war. This section of Pound's long poem, controversially awarded the Bollingen Prize for Poetry, was written while he was in a military prison on a charge of making treasonous broadcasts in Italy against the allies.

Wallace Stevens, for many years viewed as a poet whose work made little reference to contemporary events, has been seen more recently as a much more engaged writer, and this has led to his wartime volume, *Parts of a World* (1942) – formerly often read as merely a transitional volume on the way to the achievement of his *Notes Toward a Supreme Fiction*, written in the same year – as centrally informed by the war. In particular the book examines the idea of heroism and the possible role for poetry in a time of war. In a prose statement that concludes the book he argues that, "In the presence of the violent reality of war, consciousness takes the place of imagination. And consciousness of an immense war is a consciousness of fact." For Stevens, the poetry written during a war could not but reflect that war, and, he continues, the poetic imagination faces a particular challenge when writing of war because its power as fact can overpower the poem as an act of the imagination. Stevens's point raises the question of the degree to which war poetry can or should avoid becoming polemical. Later poetry upon such catastrophes can at any rate offer the perspective of time, as in the case of Caroline Forché's work on the Holocaust, and of Marc Kaminsky in his *The Road from Hiroshima* (1984), based upon the recollections of survivors of the Hiroshima and Nagasaki bombings.

The second half of the century saw wars directly involving US forces in Asia, the Middle East, and Latin America, and all have been the subject of poetry. For some readers these poems illustrate the issue raised by Stevens. Poetry that overtly takes sides can for some readers sacrifice too much of what poetry does so well, bringing a sensitive and nuanced response to events and surroundings, and using language to suggest levels, ambiguity, and a complex mood.

The Vietnam War produced the most protest. Many American poets were opposed to the war early on and an important early anthology of this opposition is *Where Is Vietnam? American Poets Respond* (1967). A later anthology, *Carrying the Darkness: The Poetry of the Vietnam War*, edited by W. D. Ehrhart (1985), also carries poems by veterans of the war. Its omission of representative women veterans is corrected in *Visions of War, Dreams of Peace: Writings of Women in the Vietnam War* (1991), edited by Lynda Van Devanter and Joan A. Furey. Among prominent poets, Denise Levertov and Muriel Rukeyser were particularly to the fore in their protests, and both visited North Vietnam. Levertov's "What Were They Like?" decries the destruction of an ancient peasant culture by those oblivious to it, and her "Advent 1966" compares a Christian vision of the burning Christ-child to images of napalmed Vietnamese children. Muriel Rukeyser's earlier poetry, as noted above, had included work supporting the loyalist side in the Spanish Civil War. Both poets lost many readers as a result of their anti-war commitment in the 1960s.

Robert Lowell protested the war, usually more through political activism than through his poetry. However his *Notebook 1967–68* records his activities that year in the anti-war movement. In his well-known "Waking Early Sunday Morning," the war is put into the larger context of the decline of civilized values and the anonymous, dehumanizing forces of destruction – rather as he treats the Second World War in his "For the Union Dead." Deep Image poets such as Galway Kinnell also protested the war, and its presence is at the center of his *The Book of Nightmares* (1971). Opposition to the war is also a feature of Robert Duncan's work, for example *Tribunals* (1970), where it appears in the more visionary context that is characteristic of his poetry. In his *From Sand Creek* (1981) Native American poet Simon J. Ortiz uses a speaker who is a hospitalized Vietnam veteran to explore the wider subject of the history of violence between whites and Native Americans and its relationship to the Vietnam War.

Yusef Komunyakaa's *Dien Cai Dau* (1988) is considered by many to be the finest book of American poetry to emerge from the war. Portions of the volume were reprinted in *Neon Vernacular* (1993), which was awarded the Pulitzer Prize in 1994. Komunyakaa spent 1969–70 as a war correspondent and editor for a US army newspaper, and was awarded a Bronze Star. He has said that it took him 14 years to be able to approach the topic of the war in his poetry. His Vietnam War poems record in detail the routine and pain of conflict which he saw when accompanying patrols: rape, death, burning, the fascination with and fear of an enemy glimpsed, troop shows, the city brothels, shadowy lines of prisoners emerging from helicopters, lucky escapes, the boat people, and enemy propaganda aimed at the black soldiers following the assassination of Martin Luther King. In "Facing It" the ghosts of lost companions mix with the living in the bright Washington morning when the poet visits the Vietnam Memorial.

The civil war in El Salvador is the subject of a major section of Carolyn Forché's *The Country Between Us* (1982), and in subsequent volumes she has written of the war in Yugoslavia. While the poems on El Salvador come out of Forché's own experience, the poems in *The Angel of History* (1994) cross a broad span of time to speak with the voice of a quasi-religious collective memory. Public and private details make up the texture of the poems. Forché has also edited *Against Forgetting: Twentieth-Century Poetry of Witness* (1993), a volume which, along with her own poetry, is determined to make sure that the personal experiences behind a century of wars remain part of the record alongside the dates and names of more public, official histories.

# The Twentieth-Century American Long Poem

The long poem in twentieth-century American poetry has taken a variety of forms and raised a number of critical issues, including the question of exactly how a long poem might be defined, and what principles of coherence it could and should have. These questions became more difficult to answer as the century progressed. Certainly, however, the long poem retained for many poets its traditional status as "important" for a poet for write, although the New Critical poets of the 1940s and 1950s are an exception, generally favoring well-crafted, shorter lyrics.

Before the collages of such modernist long poems as Ezra Pound's *Cantos* (1916–69), T. S. Eliot's *The Waste Land* (1922), and William Carlos Williams's *Paterson* (1946–58) appeared, Edwin Arlington Robinson and Robert Frost both wrote long poems that borrowed from drama and the novel, poems that use narrative to explore the uncertainties of a world that had lost some of its earlier comfortable beliefs. Frost's early "marriage poems," such as "The Death of the Hired Man," "The Witch of Coös," and "Home Burial," remain among his best longer poems, dramatizing and revealing through dialogue and action, rather than stating explicitly, the tensions within the marriages at their center. Some of Frost's later treatments of the theme, such as "West-Running Brook," are rather over-structured and somewhat too neatly resolved by comparison. Robinson's longer poems have found less favor with modern audiences, but in a poem such as "The Man Against the Sky" he claimed the long poem as a suitable and serious vehicle for the examination of some central philosophical issues. In this work Robinson presents a dramatic backdrop that serves as a vivid counterpoint to the poem's more abstract speculations, although for the modern reader his later long poems, centered upon Arthurian England, do so less successfully.

This use of the long poem for philosophical speculation was taken up by Wallace Stevens in the late 1930s and for the next 15 years he produced a number of complex, sophisticated long poems. An earlier long poem by Stevens, "The Comedian as the Letter C," had been framed around a narrative of settlement, although as always with Stevens the poem was centrally about the poet's relationship to the world in which he found himself, and to the language with which he could express it. The letter C, and its associated sounds, are to the fore of the poem's witty narrative. This poem appeared in Stevens's playful first volume *Harmonium* (1923). But with such long poems as "The Man With the Blue Guitar" (1937), "Examination of the Hero in a Time of War" (1942), "Notes Toward a Supreme Fiction" (1947), and "An Ordinary Evening in New Haven" (1950) Stevens claimed for the long poem the seriousness that Robinson had claimed, and these poems are often seen as Stevens's finest achievement. The long poem particularly lends itself to poetry of meditation. In the case of "The Man Against the Sky," the poem explores multiple possibilities that all finally have equal status, while Stevens foregrounds process, the action of the mind constructing meaning piece by piece, always conscious that such meaning has no absolute status, is always a necessary fiction. By contrast, the searching in Eliot's poem of meditation, *Four Quartets*, is founded upon the certainty of the poet's Anglican faith. As Eliot's title suggests, musical parallels are an important unifying device in the poem.

Eliot also published, 20 years earlier, the most famous of the collage poems, *The Waste Land*. Pound's editing of the poem, as the manuscripts demonstrate, made it more fragmented than it originally was, dissolving continuities and allowing juxtaposition to suggest open-ended thematic possibilities. But in this and many collage poems in which fragmentation is a central feature, there remains the issue of what status to give to the poem's continuities – its motifs, symbols, myths, recurring figures and voices. Are they ironic echoes of a form that can no longer bring coherence? Or do they reflect a foundational potential that has some possibility of recovery – a reading in the case of *The Waste Land* possibly invited by Eliot's later poetry.

Ezra Pound's *Cantos* came out of the same post-war London avant-garde milieu as *The Waste Land*, although Pound's poem is open-ended both in conception and in its eventual accumulated record of 50 years of its author's ongoing interests and experiences. As more material from history, economics, literature, various cultures, and Pound's own life enter the poem as new cantos appeared over the years, thematic significances shift as the new material impacts upon the existing poem. While there is a self-contained – although multiple and complex – set of associations in *The Waste Land*, in Pound's poem these associations are never complete, in fact the poem itself is unfinished. Critical debate differs over whether the parts of the poem "cohere" – to use Pound's own term – and Pound himself late in life felt that he had failed in this task. But the demand for such coherence is itself arguably an arbitrary imposition upon a poem concerned with process and open-ended possibilities. Nevertheless for many readers the most successful section of *The Cantos* is the "Pisan Cantos," numbers LXXIV–LXXXIV, written while Pound was held prisoner by the allies facing charges of treason for his broadcasts over Italian radio in support of Mussolini. In these cantos, more than elsewhere in the poem, the poet himself enters as a unifying focus for the memories, observations, regrets, and spirit of determination that make up this section of the poem. The detail is alongside, more than elsewhere in the poem, a recognizable voice with a recognizable – and often moving – range of emotions.

*Paterson* came late in William Carlos Williams's career, after he had spent 30 years exploring the implications of imagism in shorter lyrics. But Williams is an example of a writer attracted to the challenge, even the necessity, of writing a long poem, and his five-book *Paterson* is in many ways conceived as his "local" answer to Eliot and Pound's longer poems. There is critical debate over the nature of his achievement. Marjorie Perloff, for example, sees the poem as a late, derivative work following but not contributing to Pound and Eliot's innovations. But for other critics, for example Paul Mariani, Williams's biographer, the poem is Williams's major work. The poem represents his particular solution to the problem of how to write a long poem that is still rooted in the imagist principle of immediacy. Although, like the *Cantos*, it is in its way a poem about history, *Paterson* foregrounds the process of composition and reception much more than does Pound's poem. "Dr. Paterson," the protagonist, is engaged in a quest to write the poem, and a search for an adequate language in which in can be written. The letters, historical extracts, and other prose documents that accompany the poetry are part of the poem's examination of language itself, historically and in terms of immediate need. The poem emphasizes open form in theme and structure, although there are a number of what appear to be attempts at formal closure, or at any rate summation, at the end of book IV and again in book V. Michael Bernstein has suggested that these multiple attempts at closure cancel each other out, and finally reinforce the poem's open-endedness, almost despite Williams's formal gestures. At any rate, like the other collage poems, *Paterson* is an example of a poem where a first-time reader would never notice if ten or twenty pages were missing. This is part of the challenge that such poems present to what they regard as restrictive conventions.

Charles Olson's *Maximus* poems (1960–75) also use the collage form, and, like the modernist writers, Olson wanted to move the long poem away from the inwardness of the Romantic poets and return it to social relevance. Olson felt that Williams's account of Paterson contained too little of the reality of the city, while he felt that Pound's *Cantos* centered too much upon the poet himself. Using the Dr. Paterson-type figure of Maximus of Tyre, and the locale of Gloucester, Massachusetts, Olson set out to write a poem avoiding what he felt were these two faults. In later books of the poem Olson became less interested in Gloucester and more in myth. Whether the result represents an advance upon his two models or is finally derivative of them has been a matter of critical debate.

Two poets who returned to more traditional devices in their long poems were Hart Crane and W. H. Auden. Crane saw the affirmations of *The Bridge* (1930) as an answer to *The Waste Land*, and sought to move beyond the denotative functions of language through symbols, most centrally the evocative power of the Brooklyn Bridge itself; the sweep of the poem, like that of the bridge, was to transcend its individual parts. Crane's poem is intended as itself a bridge, taking in American history and looking to the nation's future. Crane's achievement was hindered by his having to write the poem over a number of years, and by a decline in his health towards the end. Readers differ on the degree to which the poem's consequent unevenness compromises its unity. In another alternative to the fragmentary collages of the modernists, Auden used the resources of various literary genres in a number of long poems written after he took up residence in the United States in 1939, for example "New Year Letter" (1940) and the dramatic form of *The Age of Anxiety* (1944–6), which he subtitled "A Baroque Eclogue."

In the 1950s long poems that resembled frank, open-ended personal epics were one reaction against the well-wrought short lyric of New Criticism. Whitman's long lines provided a model, used famously by Allen Ginsberg in "Howl" (1956). A major difference is that, whereas Whitman's catalogs cohere through his affirmations of inclusiveness, in Ginsberg's poem the experiences that the poem's long lines recount cohere only as representative examples of a generation destroying itself fighting a culture that would repress its sexual and imaginative energies. When the poem reaches out to a reader, as Whitman reached out to his readers, Ginsberg's particular reader, Carl Solomon, is in a mental hospital. In Ginsberg's later *Kaddish* (1961) his mother's tortured days find an end in death, and a comforter in the poet's recitation of the funeral rites that she did not receive when she was buried.

Ginsberg's affirmations, even with the ironies that surround them, leave more of a sense of the speaker's ability to function in the hostile world outside of the poem than is the case with the personal epics of some other poets. In the long sequences of Theodore Roethke, in John Berryman's *Homage to Mistress Bradstreet* (1956) and *The Dream Songs* (1969), and Robert Lowell's

*Life Studies* (1959), the character behind the personal voice is more unstable, the outcome less predictable. With such personal poems, the poet becomes a public figure, although one who cannot always function in public. The self-destructive public and private behavior of Berryman, and to a lesser extent Lowell, almost seem an extension of their poems.

Open form and the personal narrative found another kind of expression in the "notebook" poems of the 1960s, examples of which appear in the work of Lowell, *Notebooks, 1967–1968* (1969) and Denise Levertov, *Relearning the Alphabet* (1970). Such work emphasizes the immediacy of the poet's engagement with the issues described – in Levertov's case her opposition to the Vietnam War – and the open form suggests resistance to or ambivalence about convention, an aesthetic committed to the nuances of the moment, and unpredictable results. For some critics the notebook poem degenerated into a fashion, or an excuse for some unfinished and weak writing, and perhaps more than some other examples of the long poem looks dated from the perspective of the twenty-first century.

The long poem in the century's African American writing has been used most effectively to integrate history and folk traditions even while – as in Langston Hughes's *Montage of a Dream Deferred* (1951) – it embraces fragmentation, distortion, and broken rhythms. For Hughes this is the musical and oral heritage of an oppressed but vital black culture. Melvin B. Tolson's *Libretto for the Republic of Liberia* (1953) and his posthumously published *A Gallery of Harlem Portraits* (1979) also integrate much African and African American history and culture into the poems, although their dense and complex allusions give them affinities – especially the *Libretto* – with the work of Eliot and Pound more than with that of Hughes. More recently Rita Dove's history of her family, *Thomas and Beulah* (1986), is an example of a sequence that gives voice to a more personal past, although one that is representative of the millions of quiet lives lived by America's black population that have until recently found little voice in American poetry.

Affirmation of cultural and/or sexual identity is the subject of a number of recent extended poems by poets writing on ethnic or gender issues. Adrienne Rich's "Twenty-One Love Poems" in her *The Dream of a Common Language* (1978) is a prominent example of the latter. This sonnet sequence frankly celebrating lesbian love reclaims what had formerly been, at any rate in literary history, a form for male writers. Rich's volume begins with an epigram from one of H.D.'s late long poems. Feminist poets and critics have helped return attention to these poems of H.D., a contemporary of Pound, Eliot, and Williams, who was formerly studied more for her imagist poems of the 1910s and 1920s than for the 1940s wartime trilogy *The Walls Do Not Fall*, *Tribute to the Angels*, and *The Flowering of the Rod*, or the early

1950s *Helen in Egypt*, all of which are concerned with the rediscovery of feminine creativity.

James Merrill and John Ashbery have both made signal contributions to the long poem form. Merrill's *The Changing Light at Sandover* (1982) finds a way to bring epic scope back into the long poem with the account of his and David Jackson's experiences with a Ouija board over a number of years. The long poem form here allows for multiple voices and a cast of protagonists whose characters develop and are even radically transformed over the length of the poem. The narrative concerns nothing less than the fate of the human race and what might be done to avert its doom. Time is a constant presence in Merrill's poem, as a marker for important spiritual events, and as a reminder of the short span of earthly life (some of Merrill's friends featured in the poem die during the years of the poem's composition). Time functions in a different way in Ashbery's long poems, where it is sometimes the only constant in a poem's shifts of direction and language reflecting the poet's ongoing experience of the world. Ashbery has said that he finds the long poem more useful than shorter lyrics for recording his central interest in the engagement of consciousness with reality.

The flux of time in Ashbery's poems parallels the flux of language in long poems by poets associated with Language poetry such as Ron Silliman, Lyn Hejinian, and Susan Howe. Such poems call attention to how language constructs a version of reality that pretends to referentiality, although the poems insistently call the reader back to the process of construction. In such poetry the long poem is being deconstructed at the same time as it is being constructed. Such avant-garde poetry is sometimes associated with the gender and ethnic poetry discussed earlier – the parallel concern being how systems can impose meaning and value in a way that can be oppressive or marginalizing to certain groups. Notable examples are Silliman's *Tjanting* (1981), Hejinian's *My Life* (1980 and 1987) and Howe's *Pierce-Arrow* (1999).

The different forms taken by the twentieth-century American long poem, whether the emphasis is upon personal or social narrative, fragmentation, flux, a dispersed history, or an identity that the poem seeks to integrate, kept it a vital and innovative form throughout the century. But such diversity has sometimes made difficult the identification of what *is* a long poem. Contemporary volumes of poetry are often carefully arranged by the authors in thematic groupings – unlike the days when a publisher threw together the gatherings of the poet's most recent few years of work – and such thematic categories sometimes extend to the whole volume. When should a group of related lyrics be regarded as a long poem? Such a sequence certainly exhibits some of the characteristics of the modern long poem in its disjunctions, recurring motifs and themes, and sometimes disparate forms and languages. Many readers would want to define as "long poems" the collections of lyrics in Galway Kinnell's *The Book of Nightmares* (1971), Dove's *Thomas and Beulah*, Lowell's *Life Studies* (1959), and perhaps Sylvia Plath's *Ariel* (1965) – which she planned the arrangement of carefully, although that arrangement was not followed in the posthumous publication. The problem extends back to modernist sequences too. The 27 poems of William Carlos Williams's *Spring and All* were published with interspersed prose as a book in 1923, the poems numbered successively with Roman numerals, poem I arguably a "beginning" and poem XXVII a "summary." But in later volumes Williams dispensed with the prose, published separate groups of the poems, and when he did publish all 27 added a twenty-eighth poem. Such transformations led Donald Davie to conclude that even Williams himself did not know what kind of book *Spring and All* was. Meanwhile classroom anthologies print poems from this book and from the related lyric sequences of other twentieth-century poets, usually with no notice of the context of the poem, as if the poems were individual lyrics. In effect, an editor is thus making his or her own decision as to the status of the work from which the poem is drawn. Of course, the reason that this is an issue at all is the challenges that American twentieth-century long poems have made to received ideas of form. In the process of making such challenges they have enriched the possibilities of the long poem in ways that have kept the form innovative, contemporary, and relevant.

# Anthologies: Polemical and Historical

Anthologies have always served a valuable purpose in bringing back into print poems that have appeared in the more ephemeral media of newspapers, magazines, or journals, putting the poems between hard – or, later in the century, soft – covers, at least as a bridging operation until the poet published the poem in his or her next collection. Such was the value, for example, of the annual *Anthology of Magazine Verse and Year Book of American Poetry* edited by William Stanley Braithwaite from 1913 to 1939. Such anthologies usually claim to be reprinting "the best" of the period covered, although of course such a claim inevitably involves often unstated premises. A contemporary series that claims to reprint "the best" is *The Best American Poetry*, published each year by Simon & Schuster and initiated in 1988 by David Lehman. This series is edited and introduced by a different leading contemporary poet each year, and while the magazines from which the poems are selected rarely include very radical, experimental publications, the series serves as a useful introduction to at any rate the mainstream poetry being published in the journals that it covers. Here the reader will find famous and emerging names, selected by editors who in recent years have included Louise Glück, A. R. Ammons, Adrienne Rich, Robert Creeley, Robert Bly, and Rita Dove.

As Alan Golding has pointed out in his discussion of the role of anthologies in canon formation, American poetry anthologies have always had an ideological purpose of one kind or another, ever since the earliest in 1793. This purpose is usually some mixture of political nation-building, literary nationalism, moral and/or aesthetic assumptions, or a broader claim for historical or contemporary assessment.

Thus when, early in the modernist period, poets and editors began using anthologies to promote modernist poetry, it was part of a long tradition. Emerson, Whittier, and Bryant had all published anthologies of American poetry in the 1870s that emphasized their own New England mode (and that did not include Whitman or Melville, and ranked Poe as a minor poet). *Des Imagistes* (1914), published in London and New York, allowed Ezra Pound to introduce the poets working around the principles articulated in the earlier imagist manifestos, as well as some poets that he considered suitably "modern." This enterprise was followed up – not with Pound's endorsement – by Amy Lowell in *Some Imagist Poets* (1915, 1916, 1917). Alfred Kreymborg, who found a publisher for the New York *Des Imagistes*, was also associated with the little magazine *Others*, an avant-garde journal that appeared erratically, and whose pages included poems by William Carlos Williams, Wallace Stevens, and Marianne Moore, and which issued annual anthologies in 1916, 1917, and 1919. Pound continued to edit polemical anthologies throughout his career, not always focusing exclusively on contemporary work, since part of his concern was to place modernist poetry within a reshaped historical canon.

Harriet Monroe, the founder of *Poetry* in Chicago, along with co-editor Alice Corbin Henderson, published an anthology that included a generous selection from the modernist poets in 1917, and the editors revised and expanded the selection in various editions into the 1930s. Other anthologizers sympathetic to some degree to modernist work in the first half of the century were Conrad Aikin and Louis Untermeyer. By contrast, Bliss Carman's edition of the *Oxford Book of American Verse* in 1927 included no work by Eliot, Williams, Moore, Stevens, Hart Crane, or E. E. Cummings, only one poem by Pound, and no black poets except Paul Laurence Dunbar. F. O. Matthiessen corrected many of these omissions in his 1950 revision for the second edition, in which he drastically pruned the selection from the nineteenth-century poets, but Matthiessen removed Dunbar and included no poems by black American writers. As late as the mid-1960s two classroom anthologies, Karl Shapiro's *American Poetry* (1960) and Gay Wilson Allen, Walter Rideout, and James Robinson's *American Poetry* (1965) included no black poets.

Another prominent volume from 1950, John Ciardi's *Mid-Century American Poetry*, allowed the poets to introduce their own work in the form of answers to a questionnaire. Ciardi's selection and introduction is, like Matthiessen's, based on New Critical criteria, but his influential selection marked the first anthology appearances of Elizabeth Bishop, Richard Eberhart, Theodore Roethke, Muriel Rukeyser, and Richard Wilbur. Three other poets of the 15 that he included were first anthologized here and concurrently in Matthiessen's volume. No other anthology could count so many new poets being introduced until the famous "anthology wars" of 1957 and 1960, between Donald Hall, Robert Pack, and Louis Simpson's *The New Poets of England and America* and Donald Allen's *The New American Poetry*. Jed Rasula, in an extensive study of the impact that anthology appearance has had upon the careers of poets in the second half of the century, *The American Poetry Wax Museum* (1996), argues that these two anthologies, together with Ciardi's, exerted a major influence upon the formation of the canon of writers most extensively read and taught in the years following the anthologies' appearance. Rasula's study contains a series of very suggestive statistical appendices that list such things as the major anthologies published, the poets first introduced in them, the winners of literary prizes, and the most anthologized poets (at the time of the book's publication, Richard Wilbur topped the list).

The Hall/Pack/Simpson anthology and Allen's three years later revealed a split in conceptions of the most significant new American poetry, between the more formal poets of the 1957 volume and the more radical poets of Allen's collection. An introduction by Robert Frost set the tone for the 1957 volume, while Charles Olson was a major advisor to Allen. Allen's volume printed in its back pages statements by the poets on their work, while the 1957 collection adhered more to the new critical position of letting a poem stand on its own. Allen's division of his poets into the Beats, the San Francisco poets, the Black Mountain College poets, the New York school, and a miscellaneous group served as a convenient if schematic guide, and influenced anthologies, classrooms, and scholarly discussion for many years subsequently. The categories were abandoned in Allen's revised collection, *The Postmoderns* (1982) edited with George Butterick, where the poets are organized chronologically by birthdate.

The 1957 volume has come in for a good deal of criticism from those who insist that the social, cultural, and political context of a poet's work should be recognized in some way in an anthology, and also for failing to recognize and include the open form and Beat poets who were challenging New Critical formalism in the mid-1950s. In defense, one might say – as one of the editors has – that it was easier to see the importance of these movements in 1960 than in 1957. Anthologies take time to prepare, and Ginsberg's *Howl and other Poems* appeared in 1956 when the earlier anthology was being put together. Nevertheless, Charles Olson had published his theory of "Projective Verse" in 1950, and William Carlos Williams had given it an endorsement and some publicity in 1951 in his *Autobiography* – published by mainstream publisher Random House.

The rhetoric surrounding the "anthology wars" gained much of its heat from another aim underlying the act of anthologizing contemporary poetry, the motive behind the Pound and Monroe volumes – the implicit or explicit claim that this is the major poetry of the moment and for the future, and that these are the poets who will write it. This division between the historical and predictive functions of an anthology – the difference between the aims of the Braithwaite and Pound volumes – has become more complex with the development of the higher education market for twentieth-century and contemporary poetry anthologies which took off in the early 1960s. Hayden Carruth's *The Voice That Is Great Within Us* (1970) attempted to be broadly comprehensive, but consequently was able to give only two or three pages to many of the poets – although Carruth initiated Cid Corman and Lorine Niedecker into anthology publication. A more mainstream classroom text, Richard Ellmann's *Norton Anthology of Modern Poetry* (which collects British and American poets) initiated only one poet into anthology status in its first edition of 1973, although a measure of the pace of change in the canon and in poets newly emerging was that in the second edition (1988), of the 180 poets, 61 were new to the collection. Ellmann's selection (made with Robert O'Clair for the 1988 edition) attempted historical comprehensiveness, but such was its widespread use in colleges that it also helped to shape future reputations. Like all histories, it inevitably reflected the judgments of the moment, and the selection was increasingly seen to have inadequacies – for example in the selection of H.D.'s poetry and that of African American poets, and in such details as Louis MacNeice receiving more space than Charles Olson. The recent third edition (2003), newly edited by Jahan Ramazani, attempts to bring the text into the new century. Tellingly, while it includes only 16 more poems than the second edition, half of the selection has been changed. Some attention is given to the problem of anthologies representing long poems only with extracts, and at the end of each of its two volumes appear statements by a number of the poets on their work and its aims – in the spirit of the earlier Ciardi and Allen selections. The second of the two new Norton volumes (they are now titled separately *Modern* and *Contemporary Poetry*) begins, like Allen's, with Olson.

In another prominent text intended for classroom use, Cary Nelson's *Anthology of Modern American Poetry* (2000), a section draws attention to the graphic design of some of the original printings of the poems. Some recent critics, such as George Bornstein, Jerome McGann, and Nelson himself, have argued that graphic design should be considered as part of a text's overall meaning, the visual language sometimes suggesting a context within which a poem is intended to be read. Nelson's is the first anthology to reprint in full one of William Carlos Williams's books of poetry and interspersed prose, his experimental *The Descent of Winter* (1928), thus contributing to a more accurate presentation of a poet particularly poorly represented in the usual anthology selections. This anthology, like the third edition of the Norton, generally does fuller justice to the century's longer poems. But again an attempt at comprehensiveness (Nelson's anthology also includes a generous selection of Native American poets) means that space is constricted, most evident in the somewhat perfunctory introductions to the individual poets. Formalist principles can still sometimes guide an anthology primarily intended for classroom use, as in Helen Vendler's *The Harvard Book of Contemporary American Poetry* (1985), which, controversially, even omits a poet as established as Robert Creeley. On the other hand, an ambitious anthology dedicated to the work of the Language poets, for whom Creeley would be a seminal figure, is Ron Silliman's *In the American Tree* (1986), which in addition to providing a rich selection of the group's work, raises challenging questions about the assumptions behind genre categories.

In general, the changes in most classroom-oriented anthologies of contemporary poetry since the 1980s have been in the direction of trying to represent the range of multi-cultural writing in contemporary American poetry, in a general broadening and questioning of received canons that has been part of an ongoing debate in the academy. This change reflects, too, the impact of the discipline of American Studies upon more traditional Eurocentric conceptions of American literature. For some commentators, however, such a criterion of selection has become almost a quota system that threatens to exclude from attention poets who are making innovative contributions not based exclusively on content. A further charge is that the most favored poems on ethnic subjects are those that affirm the poet's culture without offering serious challenges to white readers. Along with such complaints is the claim that academic programs such as the Master of Fine Arts degrees offered by many graduate schools foster an "official" kind of poem, a personal lyric that lends itself particularly to the detailed description of ethnic background; that in turn such poems find favor in academically oriented journals, and such poets find favor with hiring committees looking for new writing teachers. *The American Poetry Review* is a leading journal that is generally seen as associated with the work of MFA programs. An anthology representative of work from the journal, which was founded in 1972, is *The Body Electric*, edited by Stephen Berg, David Bonanno, and Arthur Vogelsang (2000). The volume's affinities with the Romantic tradition are signaled by its being introduced not by its editors but by Harold Bloom, whose scholarly work is associated with the transmission of the Romantic writers. For new formalist poets, advocating a return to more traditional rhyme and meter, such "official" poems tend towards the self-indulgent and undisciplined. Timothy Steele and Dana Gioia are two of the leading theorists of new formalism, and *Rebel Angels: 25 Poets of the New Formalism* (1996), edited by Mark Jarman and David Mason, is a useful introduction to poets connected to the movement.

Time has brought together many of the poets separated by the Allen and Hall/Pack/Simpson anthologies, and they began to appear together in anthologies that historicize post-war poetry and those that publish contemporary verse. In particular, a number of the poets from the 1957 volume began to experiment with more open forms, for example Robert Lowell and Adrienne Rich. But divisions among more contemporary poets remain, according to the editors of a number of recent anthologies. For Marjorie Perloff, such claims amount only to a wish for the radical moment of Allen's 1960 anthology. For Perloff, most anthologies of the last decades of the century are retrospective and not particularly radical.

Some of the most useful discussion of the role and contents of recent anthologies has come from Perloff, along with Golding and Rasula. Perloff's suggested alternative to anthologies that belatedly claim to be countering a "mainstream" official culture is a "yearbook" format that could be much more fluid in its contents, experimental in its juxtapositions, and less definitive in its claims. Golding is interested in the role that anthologies play in perpetuating or challenging canons, and while this is also a central concern of Rasula's, and he also sees the "nostalgia" identified by Perloff, he is interested in particular in the representation in recent anthologies of the Language poets – as a measure of how comprehensive the selection actually is.

Rasula singles out for particular rebuke A. Poulin Jr. and Michael Waters's editions of *Contemporary American Poetry*, primarily a classroom text, published by Houghton Mifflin, which up to its seventh edition (Spring 2000) did not include any Language poets, and *The Vintage Book of Contemporary American Poetry* (1990) edited by J. D. McClatchy, which is even more conservative. Whereas the January 2000 preface to the Poulin/Waters volume by the surviving editor Waters admits that the selection reflects "Poulin's biases," McClatchy's volume, although much more restricted in its range than the Poulin/Waters volume, claims not to be choosing sides. Its opening poets are Elizabeth Bishop and Robert Lowell.

The trade series *New American Poets of the 80s* and *New American Poets of the 90s*, edited by Jack Myers and Roger Weingarten, claim implicitly to be forecasting the future of the decade in their titles, since the volumes were issued early in the decades to which they refer. The foreword to the 1990s volume claims to offer "a representative array of some of the best and most exciting poetry being written today by young to mid-career poets whose work, the editors feel, is provocative, timely, important and accessible." Again Language poetry, which its adherents would claim is provocative but would agree is not conventional (if that is what "accessible" means here) is not included.

Three volumes that have received a good deal of discussion as part of reviews of how contemporary American poetry has been anthologized in the 1990s are Paul Hoover's *Postmodern American Poetry* (1994), Eliot Weinberger's *American Poetry Since 1950: Innovators & Outsiders* (1993), and Douglas Messerli's *From the Other Side of the Century: A New American Poetry* (1994).

Hoover's volume generally gains admiration for its inclusiveness, but the price paid, once again, is in the lack of space to represent the range of a poet's work: 411 poems by 103 poets averages out to four poems a poet. Hoover's anthology is published by Norton, giving it the visibility and importance of being put out by the leading textbook publisher, and this has produced some grudging praise of Norton's willingness to commission it, from critics otherwise harsh on the publisher's American anthologies. Hoover's selection places itself consciously in the line of Allen's anthology, beginning the poetry selections with Charles Olson, quoting him in the first line of the volume's introduction, and printing after the poetry selections, as Allen had, statements by the poets themselves – beginning with Olson's "Projective Verse." For commentators who see Louis Zukofsky's work as an essential link to modernist poetry, Hoover's following Allen in not including the poet is a crucial omission. And a number of reviewers have pointed out that Hoover's introduction uses the slippery term "post-modern" both historically – meaning post-Second World War – and ideologically, to suggest an "avant-garde poetry" that resists "mainstream ideology." This, for Perloff and Rasula, is an example of "belatedness" and "nostalgia."

Eliot Weinberger's anthology sets a date of 1950 for its earliest selection, but since many of the modernists associated with later open form movements were still publishing into that decade, Weinberger is able to include selections from Williams, Pound, H.D., and Langston Hughes in his volume, as well as a subsequent generation represented by Charles Reznikoff, Lorine Niedecker, Louis Zukofsky, Kenneth Rexroth, and George Oppen, before – after 116 pages – getting to Charles Olson. For sympathetic reviewers, Weinberger is putting his contemporary poets into a context, a historical lineage back to Pound and Williams that bypasses the now marginalized era of the New Critical poets. Less sympathetically, for Perloff this is "buttressing," another example of re-fighting Allen's fight of the 1960s, as is his "A Note on the Selection," which once again sets up a "ruling party" against which the "Innovators and Outsiders" rebel. However, in addition to the canonized modernists, the later Olson, Duncan, Levertov, Creeley, Ginsberg, O'Hara, Ashbery, Snyder, and Baraka are all represented in most classroom antho-logies. All but Baraka are even in McClatchy's collection. These figures may not be "outsiders," but Weinberger's limited number of poets, 35, allows him to give a much more representative space to each poet than does Hoover. He also includes a handful of Language poets – fewer than one might have thought, given the literary history that the opening selections set up. Another feature of Weinberger's volume deserves mention. It was originally published in translation to introduce Spanish readers to these poets. For this reason, no doubt, the poems have a thematic unity rare in anthologies, often concerned with other countries or cultures, beginning with the first selection, Williams's "The Desert Music" set on the US–Mexico border. A particular criticism of Weinberger's selection has been its lack of representation of women and black writers. Given this volume's claims to be setting out a history, and its emphasis upon other cultures, this amounts, for some reviewers, to writing women and blacks out of history, and celebrating white male poets' "exoticizing view of the *Other*."

Messerli's volume cites Weinberger's collection in its introduction as an example of the well-intentioned collections since Allen's that either fail to present "a significant enough selection of their poets to help readers contextualize the work," or which are "too often . . . based on personal agendas." Messerli offers an Allen-like set of categories in this introduction, but plays down its claims for definitiveness: first, poets concerned with cultural issues, myth, politics, history, place, and religion; secondly, poets concerned with these things but also "issues of self, social group, urban and suburban landscape . . . and visual art"; thirdly, poets emphasizing "issues of language, reader and writing communities"; and finally poets "who focus on issues of performance, voice, genre, dialogue, and personae." Messerli's historical foundation starts later than Weinberger's, with Reznikoff, followed by Niedecker, Rakosi, Zukofsky, and Oppen, before coming to Olson and Duncan. Messerli does not give more space to individual poets than Weinberger – in fact he usually gives less – but there are far more poets (over 80) and far more pages (1,135), and the poetry included is often more radical. But the collection has been criticized for its lack of critical selection. Messerli himself comments that the book turned out to be twice the size that he had intended because of "unwillingness to exclude any more poets than I have." Messerli had edited an earlier anthology of Language poets, and the general orientation of this anthology, while being more broadly conceived, also points in that direction.

Perloff and Weinberger are among the prominent figures on the "Advisors" list of the ambitious two-volume *Poems for the Millennium: The University of California Book of Modern & Postmodern Poetry*, edited by Jerome Rothenberg and Pierre Joris (1995 and 1998). This anthology is not devoted only to American poetry but is global in its scope, and includes many kinds of texts beyond those normally considered verbal. The volumes are arranged in a broadly historical way, but around movements and "galleries" rather than in any strict chronology. The intention is the open-ended effect of collage, of multiple relationships suggested through juxtaposition, but not defined, systematized, or prioritized in any way. The editors want to emphasize, as far as poetry is concerned, "an overall sense that what has characterized the century's poetry has been an exploration of new forms of language, consciousness, and social/biological relationships . . ." In American poetry, for the editors, this amounts to the objectivist–Olson line of history: Pound, Williams, H.D., before a selection from the objectivists themselves, then Olson, Duncan, and the Language poets. But this lineage is presented as less phallocentric than is often the case, with selections from the work of Gertrude Stein, Marianne Moore, Mina Loy, and Laura Riding. Included too are T. S. Eliot (*The Waste Land* is acknowledged but not reprinted), Hart Crane, and Wallace Stevens. All of the established contemporary poets that Hoover shares with McClatchy are included, but only seven of the 26 poets listed by Rasula as the most anthologized in anthologies of contemporary poetry. Not included are such figures as Wilbur, Lowell, Bishop, Berryman, and Plath – writers of personal lyrics, often in more or less formal verse; the seven included from Rasula's list are Ginsberg, Levertov, Snyder, Creeley, Ashbery, Sexton, and Rich. However one wants to judge the selection in this anthology (even for Perloff "Volume 2 has a lot of third-rate poetry in it" – as do, for this critic, the Messerli and Hoover volumes), it presents a context for twentieth-century American poetry of avant-garde poetry, prose, and visual culture – and works that defy categorization – that goes beyond the ambition of most anthologies. In the spirit of the Rothenberg and Joris volumes, which they acknowledge as a model, Jed Rasula and Steve McCaffery's *Imagining Language: An Anthology* (1998) goes even further in its historical scope and its conception of contexts for twentieth-century American poetry.

This discussion of anthologies has focused in the main on anthologies that either claim a broad inclusiveness, or claim to correct omissions in such anthologies. But there are many useful anthologies appearing every year that specifically limit their scope – anthologies devoted to work by feminist poets, gay poets, black poets, minority poets, etc. In many ways, the editors of such anthologies have an easier task than the editors of classroom anthologies (at any rate those who do more than merely copy others' selections), or than the editors of collections that claim to be broadly representative. One criterion of selection has already been established, and the "establishment" against which the poets are aligned is easily identified. Golding has suggested that it may be impossible, at the beginning of the twenty-first century, to compile a genuinely representative anthology of the twentieth century's American poetry, or even of the full contemporary poetry scene. And the Rothenberg/Joris, Rasula/McCaffery, and even the

Ramazani/Norton collections raise the issue of whether "American" poetry can be separated out as a category in a way that genuinely represents its context. And then why exclude poetry written in English in other countries and continents? Borders become somewhat arbitrary in an age of global travel, the internet, and the international reach of academic institutions. If Rasula is right about the condition of nostalgia affecting many anthology editors, one can have sympathy for the possible reason. Both the polemical and historical/classroom anthologist may well pine for the Golden Age of 1950–60, when, as Perloff puts it, "there really was an East Coast establishment" against which the polemicist could do battle, and only half as much – actually even less – poetry for the historian to have to represent.

# Guide to Further Reading

## Thematic and Historical Studies Ranging across Periods

Mutlu Konuk Blasing, *American Poetry: The Rhetoric of its Forms* (New Haven, 1987). Takes issue with the notion of Emerson as the main precursor of modern American poetry, seeing Poe, Emerson, Whitman, and Dickinson as each serving an important role.

David Bromwich, *Skeptical Music: Essays on Modern Poetry* (Chicago, 2001). Perceptive essays ranging from Frost and Stevens to Rich and Ashbery.

Juliana Chang, ed., *Quiet Fire: A Historical Anthology of Asian American Poetry, 1892–1970* (New York, 1996). Representative poems from important figures and helpful essays make this volume a valuable survey.

Robert Crawford, *The Modern Poet: Poetry, Academia, and Knowledge since the 1750s* (Oxford, 2001). Argues that the course of modern poetry and the development of modern academia are closely entwined.

Stephen Cushman, *Fictions of Form in American Poetry* (Princeton, 1993). Argues for the relationship of ideas about America to the forms of its poetry, treating Dickinson, Pound, Bishop, and Ammons.

Margaret Dickie and Thomas Travisano, eds., *Gendered Modernisms: American Women Poets and their Readers* (Philadelphia, 1996). Essays re-examine the work of eight poets, including H.D., Moore, Bishop, Rukeyser, and Brooks.

Denis Donoghue, *Connoisseurs of Chaos: Ideas of Order in Modern American Poetry* (New York, 1984). This second edition of an important book adds a chapter on Bishop.

Betsy Erkkila, *The Wicked Sisters: Women Poets, Literary History and Discord* (Oxford, 1992). Examines the lives and works of Dickinson, Moore, Bishop, Rich, and Brooks.

Roger Gilbert, *Walks in the World: Representation and Experience in Modern American Poetry* (Princeton, 1991). A well-argued study of the genre of the "walk poem" as a way of representing immediate experience, covers a number of major figures.

Ian Hamilton, ed., *The Oxford Companion to Twentieth-Century Poetry in English* (Oxford, 1994). A very useful reference guide.

Kenneth Lincoln, *Sing with the Heart of a Bear: Fusions of Native and American Poetry, 1890–1999* (Berkeley, 2000). A well-written account that integrates Native American voices with mainstream Anglo-American poetry.

Robert K. Martin, *The Homosexual Tradition in American Poetry* (1979; expanded edn. Iowa City, 1998). Argues for a homosexual tradition in American poetry. Begins with Whitman; later poets discussed include Crane, Ginsberg, Duncan, Merrill, and Gunn.

James E. Miller, *The American Quest for a Supreme Fiction* (Chicago, 1979). Takes Whitman as the starting point for a discussion of a number of major long poems.

Aldon Lynn Nielsen, ed., *Reading Race in American Poetry: "An Area of Act"* (Urbana, IL, 2000). Essays by a number of scholars, some on often overlooked figures.

Roy Harvey Pearce, *The Continuity of American Poetry* (Princeton, 1961). An early and still useful attempt to place modern American poetry into a history going back to the Puritans.

David Perkins, *A History of Modern Poetry*, 2 vols. (Cambridge, MA, 1976, 1987). Although now somewhat dated, a well-integrated overview of the major currents in British and American poetry.

Marjorie Perloff, *The Poetics of Indeterminacy: Rimbaud to Cage* (Princeton, 1981). Argues for the importance of modern and contemporary poets writing outside of the Romantic/symbolist tradition.

Neil Roberts, ed., *A Companion to Twentieth-Century Poetry* (Oxford, 2001). Essays on British, American, and Colonial poetry, organized by topics, movements, and texts.

M. L. Rosenthal and Sally M. Gall, *The Modern Poetic Sequence: The Genius of Modern Poetry* (New York, 1983). A broad-ranging study of British and American long poems and poetic sequences.

Jerome Rothenberg and Pierre Joris, *Poems for the Millennium: The University of California Book of Modern and Postmodern Poetry*, 2 vols. (Berkeley, 1995, 1998). An ambitious attempt to document the cultural history of modern, not just US, poetry.

Louis D. Rubin, *The Wary Fugitives: Four Poets and the South* (Baton Rouge, 1978). Examines the careers of Ransom, Tate, Davidson, and Warren.

Mark Royden Winchell, *Cleanth Brooks and the Rise of Modern Criticism* (Charlottesville, 1996). The first extended biography of Brooks, a leading New Critic. Documents the impact of New Criticism upon twentieth-century American poetry, and Brooks's association with such figures as Warren, Tate, and Ransom.

Gregory Woods, *Articulate Flesh: Male Homo-Eroticism and Modern Poetry* (New Haven, 1987). Looks at homo-erotic themes in the work of D. H. Lawrence, Crane, Auden, Ginsberg, and Gunn.

## Studies Focused upon Modernism and Other Movements, 1900 to the Second World War

Charles Altieri, *Painterly Abstraction in Modernist American Poetry* (Cambridge, 1989). A difficult but important study of modernist poetry and the visual arts.

Houston A. Baker, *Modernism and the Harlem Renaissance* (Chicago, 1987). A groundbreaking discussion looking at the Harlem Renaissance on its own terms.

Michael Bernstein, *The Tale of the Tribe: Ezra Pound and the Modern Verse Epic* (Princeton, 1980). Stimulating study of the modernist collage poem, focusing on Pound, Williams, and Olson.

Rachel Blau DuPlessis, *Genders, Races, and Religious Cultures in Modern American Poetry, 1908–1934* (Cambridge, 2001). Looks at the work of a number of figures from the point of view of such social issues as suffrage, sexuality, and racial and ethnic identity.

—— and Peter Quartermain, eds., *The Objectivist Nexus* (Tuscaloosa, 1999). Essays by leading scholars on such objectivist poets as Oppen, Niedecker, Reznikoff, and Zukofsky.

John Gage, *In the Arresting Eye: The Rhetoric of Imagism* (Baton Rouge, 1981). Argues that for all of its stance against rhetoric, imagist poetry developed a distinctive rhetoric of its own.

Mary E. Galvin, *Queer Poetics: Five Modernist Women Writers* (Westport, CT, 1999). The poets discussed include Amy Lowell, Mina Loy, and H.D.

Albert Gelpi, *A Coherent Splendor: The American Poetic Renaissance, 1910–1950* (Cambridge, 1987). Traces two strains, symbolism and imagism, as central to the poetry, and stemming from the response to Romanticism.

J. B. Harmer, *Victory in Limbo: Imagism, 1908–1917* (London, 1975). Very useful study of this influential movement.

George Hutchinson, *The Harlem Renaissance in Black and White* (Cambridge, MA, 1995). Explores the interracial aspects of the movement.

Hugh Kenner, *The Pound Era* (Berkeley, 1971). An influential book that argues the case for its title.

—— *A Homemade World* (New York, 1975). Treats the American context of Moore, Williams, and Stevens.

Michael Levenson, ed., *The Cambridge Companion to Modernism* (Cambridge, 1999). Useful essays by a number of leading scholars.

David Levering Lewis, *When Harlem Was In Vogue* (New York, 1981). An important and wide-ranging study of the Harlem Renaissance.

Alain Locke, *The New Negro* (repr. New York, 1997). A seminal text of the Harlem Renaissance, first published in 1925. Includes poems by Hughes, Cullen, Toomer, and McKay; this reprint has a useful introduction by Arnold Rampersad.

James Longenbach, *Modernist Poetics of History: Pound, Eliot, and the Sense of the Past* (Princeton, 1987). Puts Eliot's view of tradition and Pound's of history into valuable context.

—— *Stone Cottage: Pound, Yeats and Modernism* (New York, 1988). Treats the important relationship between these two poets, and the broader literary context.

Cary Nelson, *Repression and Recovery: Modern American Poetry and the Politics of Cultural Memory, 1910–1945* (Madison, WI, 1989). An important study which raises issues of canon formation and the writing of literary history, and argues for the reassessment of a number of neglected writers.

—— *Revolutionary Memory: Recovering the Poetry of the American Left* (New York, 2001). An argument for the importance of poetry concerned with political themes, especially of the 1930s.

Michael North, *The Dialect of Modernism: Race, Language and Twentieth-Century Literature* (New York, 1994). Examines the complexities of the use of dialect among white and black modernist writers, especially Pound, Eliot, Williams, McKay, and Toomer.

Catherine Paul, *Poetry in the Museums of Modernism: Yeats, Pound, Moore, Stein* (Ann Arbor, 2002). Well-researched study argues for the influence of museum iconography and display innovations upon these poets' response to culture and audience.

Marjorie Perloff, *The Dance of the Intellect: Studies in the Poetry of the Pound Tradition* (Cambridge, 1985). Essays ranging from Pound and Williams to the Language poets by a distinguished critic.

—— *The Futurist Movement: Avant-Garde, Avant Guerre, and the Language of Rupture* (Chicago, 1986). Treats an important early avant-garde movement in the visual and verbal arts.

—— *21st-Century Modernism: The "New" Poetics* (Malden, MA, 2002). A well-made argument for the contemporary relevance of modernism.

Lawrence Rainey, *Institutions of Modernism: Literary Elites and Public Culture* (New Haven, 1998). A study of publishing history and patronage that includes discussion of Pound, Eliot, and H.D.

Sanford Schwartz, *The Matrix of Modernism: Pound, Eliot, and Early Twentieth-Century Thought* (Princeton, 1985). Puts the early work of Pound and Eliot into the context of developments in philosophy, science, and the arts.

Michael Thurston, *Making Something Happen: American Political Poetry Between the World Wars* (Chapel Hill, 2001). Looks at the political poetry of Edwin Rolfe, Pound, Hughes, and Rukeyser.

Jeffrey Walker, *Bardic Ethos and the American Epic Poem: Whitman, Pound, Crane, Williams, Olson* (Baton Rouge, 1989). This discussion of the modernist long poem is particularly useful on Williams.

Cheryl A. Wall, *Women of the Harlem Renaissance* (Bloomington, IN, 1995). The main focus is on novelists, but discusses some often ignored poets associated with the movement.

## Studies Focused upon Post-Second World War Poets and Poetry

Charles Altieri, *Self and Sensibility in Contemporary American Poetry* (Cambridge, 1984). Particularly helpful on the work of Creeley, Ashbery, and Rich.

Lee Bartlett, *The Sun is But a Morning Star: Studies in West Coast Poetry and Poetics* (Albuquerque, 1989). Includes essays on Rexroth, Everson, Duncan, and Snyder.

Christopher Beach, ed., *Artifice & Indeterminacy: An Anthology of the New Poetics* (Tuscaloosa, 1998). Helpful introduction to the work of the Language poets.

Stephen Berg, David Bonanno, and Arthur Vogelsang, eds., *The Body Electric: America's Best Poetry from the American Poetry Review* (New York, 2000). Selections from an important mainstream contemporary journal.

James E. B. Breslin, *From Modern to Contemporary: American Poetry, 1945–1965* (Chicago, 1984). Excellent study of five representative poets: Ginsberg, Lowell, Levertov, James Wright, and O'Hara.

Paul Breslin, *The Psycho-Political Muse: American Poetry Since the Fifties* (Chicago, 1987). A discussion of Confessional, Deep Image, and Projectivist work, with particular attention to Lowell, Plath, Merwin, and Wright.

Cordelia Candelaria, *Chicano Poetry: A Critical Introduction* (Westport, CT, 1986). Begins with the 1960s and provides a valuable introduction to the poetry, includes discussion of Alberto Ríos and Gary Soto.

Michael Davidson, *The San Francisco Renaissance: Poetics and Community at Mid-Century* (Cambridge, 1989). A well-researched discussion of the various groups active in the city; includes chapters on Ginsberg, Duncan, and Snyder.

Annie Finch, *After New Formalism: Poets on Form, Narrative, and Tradition* (Ashland, OR, 1999). Essays by a number of leading figures associated with new formalism.

Thomas Gardner, *Regions of Unlikeness: Explaining Contemporary Poetry* (Lincoln, 1999). The main focus is upon the poetry of Jorie Graham, Robert Hass, and Michael Palmer.

Alan Golding, *From Outlaw to Classic: Canons in American Poetry* (Madison, WI, 1995). An important study of post-war canon formation.

Sam Hamill, ed., *Poets Against the War* (New York, 2003). Poems from the 1990s and later by poets protesting the 2003 war against Iraq.

Paul Hoover, ed., *Postmodern American Poetry* (New York, 1994). A good selection of poems by many figures from the 1950s to the 1990s.

David Lehman, *The Last Avant-Garde: The Making of the New York School of Poets* (New York, 1998). Covers 1948–66, a highly readable account of the lives and work of Koch, Schuyler, O'Hara, and Ashbery, including their association with the abstract expressionist painters.

James Longenbach, *Modern Poetry after Modernism* (New York, 1997). Argues for a nuanced relationship to modernism in the work of a number of poets, including Bishop, Jarrell, Wilbur, and Jorie Graham.

Jeffrey Meyers, *Manic Power: Robert Lowell and his Circle* (New York, 1987). Examines the relationship of creativity to such personal crises as alcoholism, breakdown, and suicide in the work of Lowell, Jarrell, Berryman, Roethke, and Plath.

Larry Neal, *Visions of a Liberated Future: Black Arts Movement Writings* (New York, 1989). Essays by a scholar who was a central figure in the Black Arts movement.

Cary Nelson, *Our Last First Poets: Vision and History in Contemporary American Poetry* (Urbana, IL, 1981). Perceptive readings of Roethke, Kinnell, Duncan, Rich, and Merwin, as well as a useful general essay on the poetry of the Vietnam War.

Sherman Paul, *Olson's Push: Origin, Black Mountain, and Recent American Poetry* (Baton Rouge, 1978). Excellent study of Olson and the poets associated with Black Mountain College.

Marjorie Perloff, *Radical Artifice: Writing Poetry in the Age of Media* (Chicago, 1991). Looks especially at the work of the Language poets in relation to the visual language of such mass media as network television, advertising, and the computer.

Robert Pinsky, *The Situation of Poetry: Contemporary Poetry and its Traditions* (Princeton, 1976). Highly readable comments by a former Poet Laureate.

Jed Rasula, *The American Poetry Wax Museum: Reality Effects, 1940–1990* (Urbana, IL, 1996). Well-documented, polemical account of the role of anthologies, the literary establishment, and the avant-garde in the formation of the post-war canon.

Linda Reinfeld, *Language Poetry: Writing as Rescue* (Baton Rouge, 1992). Useful study includes discussion of Charles Bernstein, Michael Palmer, and Susan Howe.

Harvey Shapiro, ed., *Poets of World War II* (New York, 2003). An anthology on an often overlooked theme.

Eileen Tabios, *Black Lightning: Poetry-in-Progress* (New York, 1998). Fourteen leading Asian American poets discuss their successive drafts of a poem in progress. A good introduction to their work.

Helen Vendler, *Part of Nature, Part of Us: Modern American Poets* (Cambridge, MA, 1980). Essays by one of the most prominent commentators on modern poetry.

—— *The Music of What Happens: Poems, Poets, Critics* (Cambridge, MA, 1988). A further collection of essays by Vendler, mostly on contemporary poets.

Robert von Hallberg, *American Poetry and Culture, 1945–1980* (Cambridge, MA, 1985). Very useful study, includes discussion of Creeley, Merrill, Lowell, and Dorn.

Norma Wilson, *The Nature of Native American Poetry* (Albuquerque, 2001). Discusses eight major Native American poets, including Scott Momaday, Ortiz, and Harjo, and has a valuable bibliography.

# Index

works: "Among School Children,"
91; "The Lake Isle of Innisfree,"
10, 188
*Yugen,* 152

Zukofsky, Louis, 82–4
 anthologized, 229
 influence, 5, 126, 300
 influences on, 280

music, 272
objectivist movement, 20, 48, 87
works: "A," 82, 83–4, 272; *Anew:
Poems,* 84; *Bottom: On Shakespeare,*
84; "Ferry," 84; *55 Poems,* 84;
"Mantis," 84; "Program:
'Objectivists' 1931," 83; "Sincerity
and Objectification," 83; *A Test of
Poetry,* 84; "To My Washstand," 84